T0226190

Lecture Notes of the Institute for Computer Sciences, Social Informatics and Telecommunications Engineering 224

More information about this series at http://www.springer.com/series/8197

Rashid Mehmood · Budhendra Bhaduri
Iyad Katib · Imrich Chlamtac (Eds.)

Smart Societies, Infrastructure, Technologies and Applications

First International Conference, SCITA 2017
Jeddah, Saudi Arabia, November 27–29, 2017
Proceedings

 Springer

Editors
Rashid Mehmood
King Abdulaziz University
Jeddah
Saudi Arabia

Budhendra Bhaduri
Geographic Information Science
  and Technology
Oak Ridge National Laboratory
Oak Ridge, TN
USA

Iyad Katib
King Abdulaziz University
Jeddah
Saudi Arabia

Imrich Chlamtac
European Alliance for Innovation
Bratislava
Slovakia

ISSN 1867-8211   ISSN 1867-822X (electronic)
Lecture Notes of the Institute for Computer Sciences, Social Informatics
and Telecommunications Engineering
ISBN 978-3-319-94179-0   ISBN 978-3-319-94180-6 (eBook)
https://doi.org/10.1007/978-3-319-94180-6

Library of Congress Control Number: 2018947428

This Springer imprint is published by the registered company Springer Nature Switzerland AG
The registered company address is: Gewerbestrasse 11, 6330 Cham, Switzerland

Preface

Rapidly increasing capacities, decreasing costs, and improvements in computational power, storage, and communication technologies have led to the development of a multitude of applications carrying an increasingly large amount of traffic (i.e., big data) on the global networking infrastructure. What we have seen is a rapid evolution: An infrastructure looking for networked applications has evolved into an infrastructure struggling to meet the social, technological, and business challenges posed by a multitude of bandwidth-hungry emerging applications. Smart city applications are at the forefront of these developments.

Smart cities provide the state-of-the-art approaches for urbanization, having evolved from the developments carried out under the umbrella of the knowledge-based economy, and subsequently under the notion of digital economy and intelligent economy. Smart cities encompass all aspects of modern-day life, transportation, health care, entertainment, work, businesses, social interactions, and governance. Smart cities exploit physical and digital infrastructure, as well as the intellectual and social capital, for urban and social development. Technically, smart cities are complex systems of systems that rely on converged and ubiquitous infrastructures. The smart city phenomenon is driven by several interdependent trends including a pressing need for environmental sustainability, and peoples' increasing demands for personalization, mobility, and higher quality of life.

The notion of smart cities can be extended to smart societies; i.e., digitally enabled, knowledge-based societies, aware of and working towards social, environmental, and economic sustainability. Since knowledge and human and social capital are at the heart of smart city and smart society developments, the role of education should extend beyond the mainstream "education for employment" scope. It should extend to the notion of social and collaborative governance where society collaborates to train each other in maintaining its knowledge, moral fiber, operations, good practice, resilience, competitiveness, and for bringing innovation and becoming a knowledge-based economy. The key to such efforts would be the creation of an ecosystem of digital infrastructures that are able to work together and enable dynamic real-time interactions between various smart city subsystems.

We are delighted to introduce the proceedings of the First EAI (European Alliance for Innovation) Conference on Smart Societies, Infrastructure, Technologies and Applications (SCITA) held at King Abdulaziz University (KAU), Jeddah, Saudi Arabia, during November 27–29, 2017. This event, SCITA 2017, brought together decision-makers, top researchers, industry executives, and government officials to discuss directions of smarter societies research and development. We named this summit SCITA, meaning "the sum of all the political, economic, technological, scientific, military, geographical, and psychological knowledge of the masses and of their representatives."

The SCITA 2017 conference was organized to cover topics related to five broad themes: smarter society applications (e.g., health care, mobility); smart infrastructure (distributed systems, HPC, big data, etc.), social capital development and eGovernance, innovation and entrepreneurship, and cross-cutting themes. SCITA 2017 provided a rich agenda comprising over 50 talks including three keynote speeches, eight invited talks, one workshop, and six tutorials. It received a total of 62 submissions from around the world, 35 of these were accepted. The proceedings are organized into four sections: Infrastructure, E-Governance and Transportation, Health Care, and Applications. The Applications section comprises general smart society applications that do not fall within health care, eGovernance, or transportation applications. A poster session was also organized comprising 25 posters selected from 40 posters. Three best poster and three best paper awards were given.

The three keynotes were: "Superclouds – Scalable High-Performance Nonstop Infrastructure for AI and Smart Societies" by Prof. Bill McColl, CTO, Parallel Computing, Huawei Research & Professor, University of Oxford, UK; "Challenges and Opportunities in the Analysis for Future Urban Transport Systems" by Prof. John Polak, Professor of Transport Demand, Head of the Centre for Transport Studies, Imperial College London, UK; and "Toward the Genomic-Information Society" by Prof. Takashi Gojobori, Distinguished Professor, CBRC (Computational Bioscience Research Center), King Abdullah University of Science and Technology (KAUST), Saudi Arabia. The invited talks include "Big Urban Data, Geospatial Computing, and My 2 Cents in an Open Data Economy" by Dr. Budhendra Bhaduri, Director, Urban Dynamics Institute, Oak Ridge National Laboratory (ORNL), USA; "AI Computing for Smart Cities" by Prof. Simon See, Director and Chief Solution Architect, Nvidia AI Technology Center, Chief Scientific Computing Officer and Professor, Shanghai Jiao Tong University, Prof (Adjunct) KMUTT and NTU (Singapore); "The Korean IFEZ Smart-City and Its Cloud Data Center for the Local Government" by Sangho Lee, Director, IFEZ Smart-City Integrated Operation Center, Korea, Incheon U-City Corporation, Korea; "What Makes Things Smart" by Stefan Weidner, Director, SAP University Competence Center Magdeburg (SAP UCC) & SAP Big Data Innovation Center, Magdeburg, Germany; "Lightweight Crypto Solutions for Cyber Physical Systems and Mobile Cloud Computing Environment" by Dr. Lo'ai Tawalbeh, Umm Al-Qura University, KSA; and "A Smarter Jeddah" by Prof. Arwa Al-Aama of King Abdulaziz University & CIO, Jeddah Municipality. Fujitsu and IBM also delivered talks on "Infrastructure for Smarter Societies" and "Smarter Cities: The Next Generation," respectively.

The third day of SCITA 2017 was devoted to multiple parallel training workshops and tutorials. A full-day workshop "How Things Are Made Smart(er)" was delivered by Stefan Weidner of SAP UCC Magdeburg. The tutorials included "Big Data Analytics Using Apache Spark with Smart City Applications," "How to Run Applications on the Aziz Supercomputer," "Location Privacy and the Emerging Smart Cities," "Programming Deep Learning in TensorFlow with Smart City Applications," "Programming for Smart Cities with NVIDIA CUDA," and "Parallel Computing with MPI."

We would like to acknowledge the support from members of various committees, which was critical to the success of SCITA 2017. These include Steering Committee members Dr. Robert Eades, IBM, and Dr. Jeff Nichols, Oak Ridge National Laboratory (ORNL), USA. The organizational support from King Abdulaziz Staff in various capacities was also important: these include Dr. Naif Aljohani, Dr. Maysoon AbuAlkahir, Dr. Manar Salamah, Dr. Fatmah Assiri, Dr. Aiiad Albeshri, Dr. Raed Saeed, Dr. Nasser Albagami, and Dr. Abdullah Algarni. The publicity chairs, Dr. Saleh Altowaijri, Northern Border University, Saudi Arabia, and Dr. Ali Algarwi, King Khalid University, Saudi Arabia, also played an important role in disseminating the call. Many thanks to all the authors who submitted the papers to the conference and the TPC committee who reviewed the papers to enable excellent author presentations during the conference. Thank you very much also to the conference manager, Dominika Belisová, European Alliance for Innovation, and other EAI staff who worked in the background on many aspects of the conference and these proceedings.

Our special thanks go to Prof. Yusuf A. Al-Turki, Vice President Research, King Abdulaziz University, and the honorary chair, Prof. Amin Noaman, Vice President of Development, King Abdulaziz University, whose support enabled us to get the financial aid and logistics to organize SCITA 2017. We would also like to acknowledge the financial support of our Diamond Sponsor Fujitsu.

The SCITA 2017 conference attracted immense interest from people and organizations. A total of 1,374 people registered for the conference; around 500 of them attended the conference. SCITA is a very timely conference, as Saudi Arabia announced its plans to build a smart city called NEOM supported by $500 billion from the Saudi government. We believe the future of SCITA conference series has just begun.

June 2018

Rashid Mehmood
Budhendra Bhaduri
Iyad Katib
Imrich Chlamtac

Conference Organization

Honorary Chair

Amin Noaman   King Abdulaziz University

Steering Committee

Imrich Chlamtac   European Alliance for Innovation, Slovakia
Robert Eades   IBM Middle East and Africa, Qatar
Iyad Katib   King Abdulaziz University, Saudi Arabia
Bill McColl   Huawei Research and Oxford University, UK
Rashid Mehmood   King Abdul Aziz University, Saudi Arabia
Jeff Nichols   Oak Ridge National Laboratory (ORNL), USA

Organizing Committee

General Chairs

Rashid Mehmood   King Abdul Aziz University, Saudi Arabia
Budhendra Bhaduri   Urban Dynamics Institute, Oak Ridge National
                           Laboratory (ORNL), USA

Local Organization Chairs

Iyad Katib   King Abdulaziz University, Saudi Arabia
Naif Aljohani   King Abdulaziz University, Saudi Arabia

Web Chairs

Aiiad Albeshri   King Abdulaziz University, Saudi Arabia
Raed Saeed   King Abdulaziz University, Saudi Arabia

Government Relations Chair

Nasser Albagami   King Abdulaziz University, Saudi Arabia

Publicity Chairs

Saleh Altowaijri   Northern Border University, Saudi Arabia
Ali Algarwi   King Khalid University, Saudi Arabia

Poster Track Chair

Abdullah Algarni   King Abdulaziz University, Saudi Arabia

Conference Manager

Dominika Belisová   European Alliance for Innovation, Slovakia

Technical Program Committee

Aasia Khanum	FC College, Lahore, Pakistan
Aiiad Albeshri	King Abdulaziz University, Saudi Arabia
Budhendra Bhaduri	Urban Dynamics Institute, Oak Ridge National Laboratory (ORNL), USA
Angel Garcia Olaya	Universidad Carlos III de Madrid, Spain
Atif Alvi	FC College, Lahore, Pakistan
Imrich Chlamtac	European Alliance for Innovation, Slovakia
Cecilia Gomes	New University of Lisbon, Portugal
Didem Unat	Koç University, Turkey
Eduardo Cerqueira	Federal University of Pará (UFPA), Brazil
Florin Nemtanu	Polytechnic University of Bucharest, Romania
Iyad Katib	King Abdul Aziz University, Saudi Arabia
Jacek Malasek	Instytut Badawczy Dróg i Mostów, Poland
Lee McCluskey	University of Huddersfield, UK
Rene Meier	Lucerne University of Applied Sciences and Arts, Switzerland
Toni Janevski	Ss. Cyril and Methodius University, Republic of Macedonia
Robert Eades	IBM Middle East and Africa, Qatar
Bill McColl	Huawei Research and Oxford University, UK
Rashid Mehmood	King Abdul Aziz University, Saudi Arabia
Jeff Nichols	Oak Ridge National Laboratory (ORNL), USA
Saber Feki	KAUST, Saudi Arabia
Saleh Altowaijri	Northern Border University, Saudi Arabia
Ali Algarwi	King Khalid University, Saudi Arabia
Takashi Gojobori	KAUST, Saudi Arabia
Wadee Alhalabi	King Abdul Aziz University, Saudi Arabia
Aalaa Mujahid	King Abdul Aziz University, Saudi Arabia
Reem Alotaibi	King Abdul Aziz University, Saudi Arabia
Mostafa Saleh	King Abdul Aziz University, Saudi Arabia
Abdullah Algarni	King Abdulaziz University, Saudi Arabia
Maysoon AbuAlkahir	King Abdulaziz University, Saudi Arabia
Manar Salamah	King Abdulaziz University, Saudi Arabia
Fatmah Assiri	King Abdulaziz University, Saudi Arabia

Contents

Applications

Infrastructure

Superclouds: Scalable High Performance Nonstop Infrastructure for AI and Smart Societies

Bill McColl[(⊠)]

Huawei Research, Paris, France
bill.mccoll@huawei.com

Abstract. We describe a new approach to building high performance nonstop infrastructure for scalable AI and cloud computing. With AI as the technological driving force behind future smart cities and smart societies, we will need powerful new nonstop AI infrastructures at both the cloud level and at the edge.

Keywords: AI · Smart cities · HPC Big Data

1 Introduction

Future smart cities and smart societies will require powerful new nonstop AI infrastructures at both the cloud level and at the edge. Unfortunately, today's cloud computing architectures are not capable of delivering what is required, as they lack support for high performance general purpose parallel computing with fault tolerance and tail tolerance.

2 The Problem – Fault Tolerance and Tail Tolerance

In many scenarios in large-scale parallel computing, it is not possible to simply run the computation again, or to use simple methods such as checkpointing, to handle faults or long latencies (tails). For example, with petaflop and exaflop computations it will be very costly to "just run again or use checkpointing". Another example is where we are running infinite continuous nonstop computations. In such a case, "just run again or use checkpointing" is impossible, as it is in the case where we are running realtime computations.

Many modern large-scale parallel computing applications are both highly iterative and communication-intensive. For example, Big Data Analytics, Graph Computing, Machine Learning, Deep Learning, Artificial Intelligence, HPC, Modelling, Genomics, Network Optimization, Simulation.

Large-scale parallel computing in the cloud requires new software architectures that:

- Can be used to efficiently run any parallel computation, at any scale
- Can be used on cost-effective commodity architectures
- Can be used to efficiently run computations continuously, without interruptions
- Offers high performance

© ICST Institute for Computer Sciences, Social Informatics and Telecommunications Engineering 2018
R. Mehmood et al. (Eds.): SCITA 2017, LNICST 224, pp. 3–5, 2018.
https://doi.org/10.1007/978-3-319-94180-6_1

- Offers high availability, with automatic fault tolerance and tail tolerance, self-healing and self-optimizing

Cloud computing offers parallelism, scale and cost-effectiveness, but clouds are very unpredictable. Maximum latency is often more than 100 times greater than average latency for identical tasks. In some cases the multiple can even be 1000 times or more. These long tails are a major problem, and quite different from the related problem of handling faults.

However, with modern software container technology, containers can be relaunched very quickly – in seconds rather than the minutes normally required to relaunch a virtual machine or physical server. So containers provide a means of restarting computations quickly, but there remains the challenge of deciding when to restart.

In this new era of large-scale cloud computing with frequent long tails, traditional checkpointing-based approaches to recovery are inadequate for a variety of simple reasons:

- The latency of writing to, and reading from, resilient storage is very high
- We need to choose frequent checkpointing or long recovery times - both are very bad, and there is no good tradeoff
- We need to choose frequent recovery or long tail limits - both are very bad
- With checkpointing, nonstop performance or continuous realtime performance are both impossible, due to stopping and restarting.

Are there alternatives to checkpointing for parallel computing with fault tolerance and tail tolerance?

3   General Purpose Parallel Computing - Computing in Rounds

Most large-scale parallel algorithms "compute in rounds", irrespective of whether the actual software they are written in is MPI, BSP, MapReduce, Spark, Pregel, Giraph, Petuum, or other parallel programming models and systems. This style of parallel computing in rounds is normally referred to as Bulk Synchronous Parallel (BSP) computing. With BSP style parallel algorithms and software, the basic computational model is:

1. Compute on data in local memory
2. Globally communicate across the network
3. Synchronize
4. Repeat

Simple parallel models such as MapReduce provide an adequate framework for parallel computations that involve only a small number of rounds. Other models such as Spark provide an adequate framework for parallel computations of limited scale, where the low performance obtained by automatic management of communications is acceptable. For general purpose parallel computing at large scale, BSP style parallelism, either using MPI or BSP message passing software, has proven to be capable of delivering the highest levels of performance in all kinds of applications, including: Dense Linear

Algebra; Sparse Linear Algebra; Spectral Methods, e.g. FFT; N-Body Methods; Structured Grids; Unstructured Grids; Monte Carlo; Graph Computing; Dynamic Programming; Combinatorial Search, e.g. Branch-and-Bound; Machine Learning; Discrete Event Simulation.

So BSP, or "computing in rounds" is a proven method for general purpose parallel computing that can handle any type of large-scale parallel application. Moreover, many of the most important modern large-scale commercial parallel applications such as machine learning, deep learning, AI, network optimization, and graph analytics, are highly iterative, involving thousands of rounds, and can be very naturally and easily expressed as BSP computations.

4 Superclouds

In this talk I will show that BSP provides not only a foundation for the development of algorithms and software for HPC, Big Data Analytics, Graph Computing, and Machine Learning, but that is can also be adapted to provide a foundation for the design of next-generation nonstop "superclouds" for AI, that offer not only high performance, but also fault tolerance and tail tolerance.

Artificial Intelligence Computing for a Smart City

Simon See[(⊠)]

Nvidia AI Technology Center, Singapore, Singapore
ssee@nvidia.com

Abstract. Recently, AI has progressed and continues to progress rapidly. AI technology and ideas are not new but the rapid rise is due to the facts that we have exponential growth in both data and computing power. In this talk, the author is giving trends on AI, computing technology and how it is being applied in Smart Cities.

Keywords: AI · Smart Cities

1 AI Computing for a Smart City

With the ability of new IOT devices and technology, governments can now gather real time data. Together with new with the capabilities of artificial Intelligence, cities are realizing interesting new ways to run more efficiently, effectively and hopefully more friendly.

The world's population grows and our species becomes rapidly more urbanized. There were just 14% of people on earth lived in cities in beginning of the 20th century. In the short 100 years, half the world's population lived in urban areas, and the rate continues to grow.

Between 2016 and 2030, the population in all city size classes is projected to increase, while the rural population is projected to decline slightly. While rural areas were home to more than 45% of the world's population in 2016, that proportion is expected to fall to 40% by 2030. A minority of people reside in megacities—500 million, representing 6.8% of the global population in 2016. But, as these cities increase in both size and number, they will become home to a growing share of the population. By 2030, a projected 730 million people will live in cities with at least 10 million inhabitants, representing 8.7% of people globally.

There were just 83 cities on earth in 1950. In 2016 there were 512 cities with more than one million residents compare to 83 of such in 1950. China's tier 1 cities (e.g. Beijing and Shanghai) has more than 25 million residents and growing. This put tremendous pressure on local government to improving the living standards and safety of the residents.

R. Mehmood et al. (Eds.): SCITA 2017, LNICST 224, pp. 6–8, 2018.
https://doi.org/10.1007/978-3-319-94180-6_2

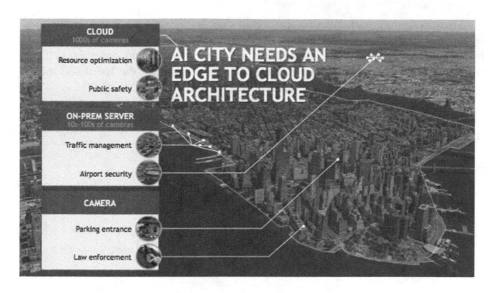

Modern cities have wealth of possible data sources, such as retail and shoppers movement data, traffic sensors, ticket sales on mass transit, police reports, and local weather stations. One huge source of raw data that AI pattern recognition technology is making significantly more manageable is video and photos. It is predicted that by 2020 there will be more than 1 billion cameras deployed on government property, infrastructure, and on commercial buildings.

China continues its huge expansion in monitoring technology. Recently Beijing police have ordered supermarkets and shopping malls to install high-definition security cameras. The country has added millions of surveillance cameras over the last five years, part of a broader increase in domestic security spending. In the city of Changsha, the Furong district alone reportedly has 40,000 – one for every 10 inhabitants.

There are cameras on streets and in stores, in university classrooms and outside the doors of dissidents.

DAHUA "DEEP SENSE" SMART VIDEO STRUCTURE SERVER

- Moving target detection and recognition

- Human, Non-motor vehicle, vehicle classification

- Human and vehicle features extraction and storage

- 24 channels 1080P streams simultaneously analyzed by each NVIDIA Tesla P4 card

There is far too much raw data than could ever be viewed, processed, or analyzed by humans. This is reason only a small fraction of cameras are ever actively monitored by human. With artificial intelligence, one can count vehicles and pedestrians. It can process or read license plates and recognize faces. It can track the speed and movements of millions of vehicles to establish patterns.

This is only a small fraction on where AI can be applied to smart city.

In this talk, we shall how we can use AI right now in cities. We also look some of the new interesting development of AI.

Cities Are Getting Smarter Than Ever Before

Sangho Lee[1,2](✉)

[1] IFEZ Smart-City Integrated Operation Center, Incheon, Korea
[2] Incheon U-City Corporation, Incheon, Korea
sangho.lee@incheonucity.com

Abstract. Technology enables National or City governments around the globe to improve various aspects of daily life. Smart-City is currently the next urban model for most of countries in the world. For the developing countries, Smart-City can be the most effective tool model to solve urban problems because of the uncontrolled fast urban population growth and for the developed countries, Smart-City can be the model for next economic growth and energy efficient.

Keywords: Smart Cities

1 Smarter Cities

Smart City has three main elements: (1) Infrastructure, (2) Service, and (3) Platform. The infrastructure and services are linked to each other in the Smart City Platform.

The Smart-City platform is a solution that collects data and information from all around city and provides these data and information in the form of proper services or solutions to citizens at the right time. (1) how to collect a lot of different data and information; (2) how to store and manage data and information, and how to convert data and information into services; (3) How to provide citizens services. Cloud, IoT, Big Data and other cutting-edge technologies are important for better service. IFEZ, Korea's famous smart city, embeds innovative technologies to build an intelligent and connected community.

IFEZ Smart City Software Platform is the core software of city control service, and we have completed the integrated software framework that provides various smart services by combining ESB, Big-Data, CCTV video system and GIS technologies. It collects data based on standardized interface definitions for all on-site facilities in the city (CCTV, traffic equipment, sensors, etc.) and monitor equipment status. It uses data gathered through linkage with external organizations to provide information to citizens.

IFEZ Smart City Hardware Platform adopted Cloud datacenter technologies and design concept to Smart City' infra environment configuration and operation system.

The IFEZ cloud data center has standardized system units for all the elements that make up the data center: data center facilities, center network infrastructure equipment, and center system infrastructure equipment. In addition, the cloud data center has been configured to expand step by step to respond to the follow-up business of IFEZ Smart City. It is also designed to integrate the available resources of existing businesses into one, and utilize infrastructure resources flexibly as needed.

© ICST Institute for Computer Sciences, Social Informatics and Telecommunications Engineering 2018
R. Mehmood et al. (Eds.): SCITA 2017, LNICST 224, pp. 9–10, 2018.
https://doi.org/10.1007/978-3-319-94180-6_3

From now on, IFEZ Smart City will continue to develop services to create a future city by combining with new service technology of the 4th revolution and will expand services based on IFEZ Smart City H/W and S/W platform. The IFEZ Smart City business area will continue to grow by expanding smart city services to the whole city rather than being limited to specific areas.

Big Data and HPC Convergence:
The Cutting Edge and Outlook

Sardar Usman[1(✉)], Rashid Mehmood[2], and Iyad Katib[1]

[1] Department of Computer Science, FCIT, King Abdulaziz University,
Jeddah 21589, Saudi Arabia
usmansardar@hotmail.com, iakatib@kau.edu.sa
[2] High Performance Computing Center, King Abdulaziz University,
Jeddah 21589, Saudi Arabia
RMehmood@kau.edu.sa

Abstract. The data growth over the last couple of decades increases on a massive scale. As the volume of the data increases so are the challenges associated with big data. The issues related to avalanche of data being produced are immense and cover variety of challenges that needs a careful consideration. The use of (High Performance Data Analytics) HPDA is increasing at brisk speed in many industries resulted in expansion of HPC market in these new territories. HPC and Big data are different systems, not only at the technical level, but also have different ecosystems. The world of workload is diverse enough and performance sensitivity is high enough that, we cannot have globally optimal and locally high sub-optimal solutions to all the issues related to convergence of big data and HPC. As we are heading towards exascale systems, the necessary integration of big data and HPC is a current hot topic of research but still at very infant stages. Both systems have different architecture and their integration brings many challenges. The main aim of this paper is to identify the driving forces, challenges, current and future trends associated with the integration of HPC and big data. We also propose architecture of big data and HPC convergence using design patterns.

Keywords: HPC · Big data · Hadoop · HPDA · Design patterns
IoT · Smart cities · Cognitive computing

1 Introduction

Over the years, HPC has contributed a lot in scientific discoveries, improved engineering designs, enhanced manufacturing, fraud detection, health care, and national security, thus played crucial role towards quality of human life. The world has seen exponential data growth due to social media, mobility, E-commerce and other factors. Major chunk of data has been generated in the last few years alone and is even growing at more rapid rate [1]. To deal with ever growing volume of data, researchers have been involved in developing algorithms to accelerate the extraction of key information from massive data. Big data is a buzzword, which catches lots of attention in the recent years. It means massive amount of structured, semi structured and unstructured data

© ICST Institute for Computer Sciences, Social Informatics and Telecommunications Engineering 2018
R. Mehmood et al. (Eds.): SCITA 2017, LNICST 224, pp. 11–26, 2018.
https://doi.org/10.1007/978-3-319-94180-6_4

collected from different resources and is not possible to store and process this data by traditional databases and software techniques.

Historically only the largest companies, government research organizations and academic computing centers have had an access to the computing power necessary to get to valuable conclusions in a reasonable amount of time. All that is rapidly changing with vast improvement in the price, performance, availability and density of compute power beyond the human imagination.

The categorization of data vs. computing affected by solution urgency i.e. real time solution, and also depends on what we trying to achieve. As the volume of data is growing bigger, it brings more challenges to process that data in real time. As projected, in 2018 over 4.3 Exabyte of data will be created on daily basis [2]. Over the years HPC community have not been deprived of huge volume of data i.e. climate modeling, design and manufacturing, financial services etc. that resulted in high fidelity models and interdisciplinary analysis to explore data for deeper insights. The use of High Performance Data Analytics HPDA is increasing at brisk speed in many industries resulted in expansion of HPC market in these new territories.

Powerful analytics is a key to extract a value from data by confronting budget and marketing challenges and plays huge roles in making plans, predicting business trends and understanding customer demands. Choosing a right solution depends on the size of data, urgency of results, prediction about the needs of more processing power as the size of data increases, fault tolerance for applications in case of hardware failure, data rate and scalability etc. A real time application with high response time especially when dealing with huge volume of data, is still a challenging task and is one of the driving forces towards the convergence of big data and HPC.

Both HPC and Big data are different system not only at the technical level but also have the different ecosystem. Both have different programming model, resource manager, file system and hardware. HPC are mainly developed for computational intensive applications but recently data intensive applications are also among the major workload in HPC environment. Due to recent advancements of data intensive applications, number of software frameworks has been developed for distributed systems, cluster resource management, parallel programming models and machine learning frameworks. High performance computing have very well established standard programming model e.g. Open MP/MPI. Big data analytics have been grown up in different perspective and have different population of developers that uses java and other high level languages with primary focus on simplicity of use, so that problem domain can be solved without a detailed knowledge of HPC. These difference in the infrastructure, resource manager, file system and hardware makes the system integration a challenging task.

As the data is getting bigger and bigger in volume so is the need of high computing. HPC community has been dealing with massive amount of data and big data analytics for years. The solutions evolved over the years to deal with large volume of data, should be useful for big data analytics [3]. The main aim of this paper is to identify motivation and driving forces towards the integration of HPC and big data. Also highlighting the current trends, challenges, benefits and future aspects of unified integrated system. We also present architecture for the convergence of HPC and Big data using design patterns.

The rest of the paper is organized as follows. The next section examines the difference between HPC and Hadoop framework with respect to hardware, resource management, fault tolerance and programming model. Literature survey is presented in Sect. 3 and Convergence challenges are discussed in Sect. 4 followed by the future directions in Sect. 5. The architecture using design pattern for the convergence of HPC and big data is presented in Sect. 6 and paper is concluded in the final section.

2 HPC and Big Data Frameworks and Their Differences

Different solutions emerged over the years to deal with big data issues and are successfully implemented. But never the less, all these solutions do not satisfy the ever-growing needs of big data. The issues related to big data are immense and cover variety of challenges that needs a careful consideration, for example data representation, data reduction/compression, data confidentiality, energy management, high dimensionality, scalability, real and distributed computation, non-structured processing, analytical mechanism and computational complexity etc. The exponential outburst of data and rapidly increasing demands for real time analytical solutions urges the need for the convergence of high-end commercial analytics and HPC. Business intelligence/analytical solutions today lack the support for predictive analytics, lack of data granularity, lack of software flexibility to manipulate data, lack of intuitive user interface, relevant information is not aggregated in a required manner and slow system performance [4].

HPC community have been dealing with complex data and compute intensive applications, and solutions have been evolved over the years. As the volume of data is increasing at brisk speed so are the associated challenges i.e. data analysis, minimizing data movement, data storage, data locality and efficient searching. As we are heading towards exascale era, the increase in system concurrency introduced a massive challenge for system software to manage applications to perform at extreme level of parallelism. Large-scale applications use most widely deployed message-passing programming model MPI along with traditional sequential languages, but with the introduction of architectural changes (many core chip) and high demand in parallelism make this programming model less productive for exascale systems. Billion-fold parallelism is required to exploit the performance of extreme scale machines and locality is critical in terms of energy consumption. As the complexity and scale of software requirements is on a rise, simple execution model is a critical requirement, which ultimately reduce the application programming complexity required to achieve the goals of achieving extreme scale parallelism. A current trend in HPC market includes use of advanced interconnects and RDMA protocols (Infinity Band, 10–40 Gigabits Ethernet/iWARP, RDMA over converged Enhanced Ethernet), enhanced redesign of HPC middleware (MPI, PGAS), SSDs, NVRAM and Burst buffer etc. Scalable parallelism, synchronization, minimizing communication, task scheduling, memory wall, heterogeneous architecture, fault tolerance, software sustainability, memory latencies, simple execution environment and dynamic memory access for data intensive application are some of the core areas that requires considerable time and efforts to address Exascale challenges [5]. The difference between Hadoop and HPC framework is highlighted in the following section.

2.1 Hardware

Most of the modern HPC and Hadoop clusters are commodity hardware. In HPC environment, Compute nodes are separated from data nodes. There are two types of data storage, temporal file system on local nodes and persistent global shared parallel file system on data nodes. The existing HPC clusters have limited amount of storage on each compute node. LUSTRE is most widely used parallel file system in HPC and almost 60% of the top 500 supercomputers use LUSTRE as their persistent storage. Data needs to be transferred from data nodes to the local file system on each compute node for processing. Data sharing is easy with distinct data and compute nodes but spatial locality of data is an issue [6, 7].

Hadoop cluster uses local disk space as a primary storage. The same node serves as a data node and compute node. The computational task is scheduled on same machine where data is resided resulting in enhanced data locality. Hadoop is write-once and read-many framework. I/O thorough put of Hadoop is much higher, due to co-locating of data and compute node on the same machine [7].

2.2 Resource Management

Another major difference between Hadoop and HPC cluster is resource management. Hadoop's Name node has Job tracker daemon. Job tracker supervised all map-reduce tasks and communicates with the task trackers on the data node. Compared to Hadoop's integrated job scheduler, HPC scheduling is done with the help of specialized tools like Grid engine, Load leveler etc., [8] with controlled resources (memory, time) provided to the user.

2.3 Fault Tolerance

HPC resource scheduler use checkpoint mechanism for fault tolerance. In case of node failure, it reschedule job from the last stored checkpoint. It needs to restart the whole process if the checkpoint mechanism is not used. On the other hand, Hadoop uses job tracker for fault tolerance. As data and computation are co-located on same machine, job tracker can detect a node failure on run time by re-assigning a task on a node where duplicate copy of data is resided [8, 9].

2.4 Programming Model

Hadoop uses map-reduce programming model, which makes life easier for the programmers as they just need to define map step and reduce step, when compared to the programming efforts needed for HPC applications. In HPC environment, programmer needs to take fine-grained responsibilities of managing communication, I/O, debugging, synchronization and checkpoint mechanism. All these tasks needs considerable amount of efforts and time for effective and efficient implementation. Hadoop does provide a low level interface to write and run map-reduce applications written in any language, although Hadoop is written in Java. Following Table 1 summarizes the difference between HPC and Hadoop framework [7].

Table 1. HPC vs. Hadoop eco system

	Big Data	HPC
Programming model	Java applications, SparQL	Fortran, C, C++
High level programming	Pig, Hive, Drill	Domain specific language
Parallel run time	Map-reduce	MPI, Open MP, OpenCL
Data management	HBase, MySQL	iRODS
Scheduling (Resource management)	YARN	SLRUM (Simple LINUX utility for resource management)
File system	HDFS, SPARK (Local storage)	LUSTRE (Remote storage)
Storage	Local shared nothing architecture	Remote shared parallel storage
Hardware for storage	HDDS	SSD
Interconnect	Switch ethernet	Switch Fiber
Infrastructure	Cloud	Supercomputer

Both Hadoop and Spark are big data frameworks and do perform the same tasks, are not mutually exclusive and able to work together. Spark is mostly used on the top of Hadoop and advance analytics of spark are used on data stored in Hadoop's distributed file system (HDFS). Spark has the ability to run as Hadoop's module through YARN and as a standalone solution [10] and can be seen as an alternative to map-reduce rather than a replacement to Hadoop framework. Spark is much faster compared to Hadoop because it handles in memory operations by copying data from distributed file systems in to faster logical RAM. Map-reduce writes all data back to distributed storage system after each iteration to ensure full recovery whereas Spark arranges data in resilient distributed datasets that are capable of full recovery in case of failure. Spark capability of handling advance data analytics in real time stream processing and machine learning is a much more advance that gives Spark edge over Hadoop. The choice of selecting either of the data processing tool depends on the needs of an organizations e.g. Dealing with big structured data can be done efficiently with map-reduce and there is no need to installed a separate layer of Spark over Hadoop [11]. Spark on demand allows users to use Apache Spark for in situ data analysis of big data on HPC resources [12]. With this setup, there is no longer to move petabytes of data for advance data analytics.

3   Research Related to HPC and Big Data Convergence

The integration of HPC and Big data started at different levels of their Eco systems and these integrated solutions are still at very infant stages. The convergence of both these technologies is the hottest topic for the researcher over the last few years. In [6] Krishnan et al. proposed a myHadoop framework using standard batch scheduling system for configuring Hadoop on-demand on traditional HPC resources. The overhead in this setup includes site-specific configuration, keeping input data into HDFS and then staging results back to persistent storage. HDFS is heavily criticized for its I/O bottleneck. Availability of limited storage is big challenge to integrate Hadoop with HPC clusters. Islam et al. [13] proposed a hybrid design (Triple-H) to reduce I/O bottleneck in HDFS and efficient resource utilization for different analytics system performance and cluster efficiency with overall low system cost.

Data intensive applications have been intensively used in HPC infrastructure with multicore systems using Map-reduce programming model [14]. With increase in parallelism, the overall throughput increases resulted in high-energy efficiency as the task is completed in shorter span of time. When Hadoop runs on HPC cluster with multiple cores and each node is capable of running many map/reduce tasks using these cores. This ultimately decreases the data movement cost and increase throughput but due to high disk and network accesses of Map-reduce tasks, the energy consumption and through put cannot be predicted. High degree of parallelism may or may not affect energy efficiency and high performance.

Tiwari et al. [15] studied the Hadoop's energy efficiency on HPC cluster. Their study shows that energy efficiency of map-reduce job on HPC cluster changes with increase in parallelism and network bandwidth. They determine the degree of parallelism on a node for improving the energy efficiency and also benefits of increasing the network bandwidth on energy efficiency by selecting configuration parameters on different types of workloads i.e. CPU intensive and moderate I/O intensive, CPU and I/O intensive workloads, also energy and performance characteristics of a disk and network I/O intensive jobs. When the number of map slots reached beyond 40, number of killed map tasks almost doubled. Thus increasing the parallelism to certain extent has positive impact on energy efficiency.

Scientific data sets are stored in back end storage servers in HPC environment and these data sets can be analyzed by YARN map-reduce program on compute nodes. As both compute and storage servers are separated in HPC environment, the cost of moving these large data sets is very high. The High-end computation machine and analysis clusters are connected with high-speed parallel file system. To overcome the shortcomings of offline data analysis, "in situ" data analysis can be performed on output data before it is written to parallel file system. The use high-end computation node for data analysis results in slowing down simulation job by the interference of the analysis task and inefficient use of computation resources for data analysis tasks. Spark on demand allows users to use Apache Spark for in situ data analysis of big data on HPC resources [12]. With this setup, there is no longer to move petabytes of data for advance data analytics.

According to Woodie [16], the use of InfiniBand for large clusters is most cost effective then standard Ethernet. The performance of HPC oriented Map-reduce solutions (Mellanox UDA, RDMA-Hadoop, DataMPI etc.) depends on the degree of change in Hadoop framework as more deep modification means an optimal adaption to HPC systems. Hadoop with IPoIB (IP over InfiniBand) and Mellanox UDA requires minimal or no changes in Hadoop implementation and only requires minor changes in Hadoop configuration. RDMA-Hadoop and HMOR are the HPC oriented solutions to take advantage of high speed interconnects by modifying some of the subsystems of Hadoop. DataMPI is a framework that developed from the scratch, which exploits the overlapping of map, shuffle and merge phases of map-reduce framework and increases data locality during the reduce phase. DataMPI provides the best performance and an average energy efficiency [17]. The use of InfiniBand improved the network bandwidth, as InfiniBand being widely used in HPC environment. Communication support in Hadoop relies on TCP/IP protocol through Java sockets [17]. So it is difficult to use high performance interconnects in an optimal way so different HPC oriented map-reduce solutions came that addresses the problem of leveraging high performance interconnects RDMA –Hadoop, DataMPI etc. Wang et al. [18] compared the performance of 10 GigaBit Ethernet and InfiniBand on Hadoop. With small intermediate data sizes the use of high speed interconnect, increased the performance by efficiently accelerating jobs but doesn't shows the same performance with large intermediate data size. The use of InfiniBand on Hadoop provides better scalability and removes the disk bottleneck issues. As the Hadoop cluster is getting bigger, organizations feel the need of specialized gear like solid-state drives (SSDs) and the use of InfiniBand instead of standard Ethernet. The use of infiniBand with RDMA (remote direct memory access) allows 40 Gigabits/s raw capacity out of Quad Data Rate (QDR) infiniBand port which is four times as much bandwidth as 10 GigaBit Ethernet port can deliver [16].

The use of infiniBand allows maximum scalability and performance while overcoming the bottlenecks in the I/O. Islam et al. [19] proposes an alternative parallel replication scheme compared to pipelined fashioned replication scheme by analyzing the challenges and compared its performance with existing pipelined replication in HDFS over Ethernet, IPoIB, 10 GigE and RDMA and showed performance enhancement with parallel model for large data sizes and high performance interconnects.

4   Challenges of Convergence

The world of workload is diverse enough and performance sensitivity is high enough that, we cannot have globally optimal and local high sub-optimal solution to all the issues related to convergence of HPC and big data. HPC and Hadoop (big data) architectures are different and have different eco system. The cross fertilization of HPC and Big data is the hottest topic for the researchers over the last few years. Most of the research related to the convergence of HPC and big data started at distinct levels of eco system but do not address the problem of moving data especially in HPC environment. The integration of data intensive applications in HPC environment will bring many challenges. In Exasacle environment cost of moving big data will be more then cost of floating point operations. There is a need for high energy efficient and cost effective interconnects for high bandwidth data exchange among thousands of processors. We also need a data locality aware mechanism especially when dealing with big data in HPC shared memory architecture. The cost of moving big data for processing also brings another challenge of high power consumption. With massively parallel architecture with hundreds of thousands of processing nodes, the cost of moving data will be very high. According to Moore et al. [20], and energy efficiency of 20 pJ (Pico Joules) per floating point operation is required for exascale system where as current state of art multicore CPUs have 1700 pJ and GPUs have 225 pJ per floating point operation.

Minimizing the data movements means the innovation in memory technologies with enhanced capacity and bandwidth. To deal with 3Vs (volume, velocity, veracity) of big data, efficient data management techniques need to be investigated included data mining and data co-ordination [13] as most of the HPC platforms are compute centric, as opposed to the demands of big data (continuous processing, efficient movement of data between storage devices and network connections etc.). To deal with massive parallel architecture and heterogeneous nature of big data, innovation needed at the programming model to deal with the next generation of parallel systems. Thus reducing the burden of parallelism and data locality for application developer as MPI leave it to the programmer to handle issues related to parallelism. Hadoop being widely used as a big data framework, achieve fault tolerance by the replication of data on multiple nodes and job tracker assign job to other node in case of node failure. Fault tolerance in HPC is by means of checkpoint mechanism, which is heavily criticized and not suitable for exascale environment. In exascale systems hardware failure will be a rule not an exception. The MTBF (mean time between failures) window in current Peta-scale system is in days and for exascale systems it will be in minutes or may be few seconds. So there is need for a comprehensive resilience at the different levels of exascale eco system. Exascale systems will be constrained by power consumption, memory per core, data movement cost and fault tolerance. The integration between HPC and big data must address the issues of scalability, fault resilience, energy efficiency, scientific productivity programmability and performance [21].

Resilience, power consumption and performance are inter-related to each other. High degree of resilience or fault tolerance is achieved but on the expense of high power consumption. As we are heading towards exascale era, convergence of both HPC and big data will make energy efficiency a core issue to handle. Severs and data-centers are facing the same problem of power consumption including companies like Google, Amazon and Facebook etc. According to an estimate the actual cost of exascale system will be less then cost of power consumption for maintaining and running exascale system for one year [22].

The energy efficiency techniques in big data can be broadly categorized as software/hardware based energy efficient techniques, energy efficient algorithms and architectures. As set of commodity hardware is used in both HPC and Big data platforms for processing of data. The integrated hardware solution for data intensive applications and computational intensive applications wouldn't work for exascale systems as hardware solution helps to achieve fault tolerance but on the expense of high energy consumption. The current Peta scale high performance computing with checkpoint mechanism to achieve fault tolerance and energy efficiency does not suit well for the integrated solution of HPC (Exascale) and big data. Soft, hard and silent errors in exascale environment will be rule not an exception. Thus collaborative efforts are needed at system level or application level resilience to deal with fault tolerance and energy efficiency for the integrated solution.

As we have seen that both HPC and Hadoop (big data) architectures are different and have different eco system. Both have different programming model, resource manager, file system and hardware. These difference in the infrastructure, resource manager, file system and hardware makes the system integration a challenging task. As the data is getting bigger and bigger in volume so is the need of high computing. One of the biggest challenges, that both big data and HPC community facing is energy efficiency. Exascale Parallel computing system will have thousands of nodes with hundreds of cores each and is projected to have billions of threads of execution. The frame of Main Time between Failures MTBF in super computers is in days and weeks. But for Exascale computing with million times more components, the perception of MTBF is in hours or minutes or may be in seconds. Each layer of Exascale Eco system must be able to cope with the errors [23].

Real time data analysis is also a driving force behind the urgency of the need for the necessary convergence of the analytics, big data, and HPC when dealing with computation, storage and analysis of massive, complex data sets in high scalable environment. Scalability issues addressed by the HPC community by capitalizing the advancements in network technologies (low latency network), efficient and large memory should also address the scalability issues of the data analytics [24].

5 Driving Forces and Future Aspects

High performance data analytics HPDA includes tasks involving massive amount of structured, semi-structured and unstructured data volumes and highly complex algorithms that ultimately demands the needs of HPC resources. Companies now have the computing power they need to actually analyze and act upon their data. This translates into numerous benefits for the company, environment and society over all. In the energy sector companies are now able to more accurately drill for oil. Automobiles and airlines are much safer due to rapid modeling of operational data design optimization and aerodynamics analysis, allowing them to deliver more cost effective products that operate safer and are more fuel-efficient. In the financial sector banks and card issuers can do fraud detection in real time. Stock investors can quickly track trends in the market to better serve their investing customers. Retailers and advertisers can now review historic purchasing data to better deliver the right products and advertisement to their customers and whether researchers can study thousands of years of weather data in hours or days instead of weeks or months, improving the quality of predictions and safety of people worldwide. HPC industry has been dealing with data intensive simulations and high performance analytics solutions also evolved over the years urges the commercial organizations to adopt HPC technology for competitive advantage to deal with time critical and highly variable complex problems. The chasm between data and compute power is becoming smaller all the time. The global HPDA market is growing rapidly and according to forecast HPDA global market size was US 25.2 billion and with the growth of nearly 18%, it is projected to be around US 82 billion in 2022 [25] (Fig. 1).

Fault tolerance, high power consumption, data centric processing, limitations of I/O and memory performance are few of the driving forces that are reshaping the HPC platforms to achieve Exascale computing [26]. Data intensive simulations, complex and time critical data analytics requires high performance data analytics solutions for example Intelligence community, data driven science/engineering, machine learning, deep learning and knowledge discovery etc. These competitive forces have pushed relatively new commercial companies (Small and Medium scale Enterprises SMEs) into HPC competency space. Fraud/anomaly detection, affinity marketing, business intelligence and precision medicine are some of the perusable new commercial HPC

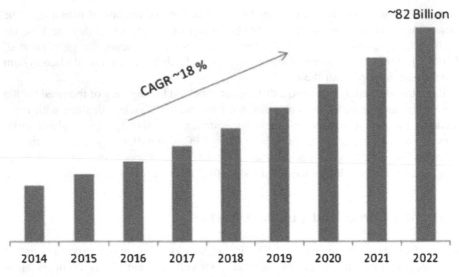

Fig. 1. HPDA market forecast [25]

market segments that require high performance data analytics. The use of HPDA will increase with time in future demanding convergence of HPC and big data. HPDA is becoming an integral part of future business investments plans of enterprises, to enhance customer experience, anomaly detection marketing, business intelligence, security breaches etc. and discovery of new revenue opportunities.

5.1   The Internet of Things IoT and Smart Cities

IoT links physical devices (computers, sensors, electronics,) equipped with sensors to the Internet and network connectivity enabling them to communicate. The common IoT platform brings heterogeneous information together and facilitates communication by providing common language. According to Gartner [27] IoT units installed base will reach 20.8 billion by 2020 resulted in massive amount of data which will further highlight the security, customer privacy, storage management and data centric networks challenges. Smart city demands better and more inventive services to run whole city smoothly and improve people's life through the innovative use of data.

Smart cities and IoT are some of the emerging HPDA application areas. HPC has been involved in managing power grids and transport for the upstream design of vehicles and urban traffic management in smart cities for quite some time and its use over time will increase in the markets of cognitive computing/AI, driverless vehicles and healthcare organizations. Baz [28] investigated the connection between IoT and HPC by highlighting some of the challenges in smart world applications (smart building management, smart logistics and smart manufacturing) and possible opportunities with HPC enable solutions. China's HPC-IoT plan 2030 is based on the use of HPC in IoT network wellness management and security [29].

5.2 Cognitive Technology

Cognitive systems are capable of understanding complex language constructs, correlate the association and help to rationalize information and discover insights. The key in cognitive systems is learning, adaptability and how the system is evolving, helps in decision-making process, discovery of new ventures, improved production and operation systems, optimizing resources, proactive identification of faults ahead of failure etc. The motive of cognitive computing is to handle complex problems without no or little human intervention. According to IBM estimate 80% of data is unstructured and is of no use for the machines and not fully exploited. The cognitive computing can be seen as a potential candidate for the exploration of unstructured data to get more useful information insights and efficient decision-making. The rapid growth of data from multidisciplinary domains requires powerful analytics but lacks human expertise to tackle the diverse and complicated problems. The cognitive computing allows people with less experience to interact with machine thanks to the advancement in natural language processing and Artificial intelligence technologies e.g. Google DeepMind and Qualcomm's Zeroth Platform. The advancement in cognitive technology with the integration of AI and machine learning for big data tools and platforms will increase the quality of information, dealing with the complex data analytics with lesser human intervention but requires rapid data access (low latency), faster time to insights, hardware acceleration for complex analytics [2]. Extracting information from vast amount of data requires innovation in compute and storage technologies, which should provide cost effective storage, improved performance in a desired time frame. The infrastructure required cognitive storage with learning ability for computers to store only relevant and important data. The computing requires efficient processing which demands high memory bandwidth and extreme scale parallelism for efficient resource utilization within energy efficiency constraints. Open power foundation [2] is an initiative towards partnering technology solutions with diverse companies coming together to provide technology solutions to a variety of problems. With data centric computing, time to solution will be dramatically reduced. Cognitive computing though still at its infancy stages but in future will be a key technology for the success of modern businesses, to get insights of the vast amount of unstructured data by leveraging computing technology to work better with the way humans want to work and smoothing the natural relationship between human and the computer.

6 Design Patterns

The need for HPDA demands innovative ways, to accelerate data and predictive analysis to target above-mentioned complex challenges by revolutionary and evolutionary changes in programming models, computer architecture and runtime systems to accommodate potential interoperability and scaling convergence of HPC and Big data eco systems [2]. There is growing need for the efficient exploration of novel techniques to allow HPC and Big data applications to exploit billion-fold parallelism (Exascale systems), improved data locality, unified storage systems, synchronization and ultimately the single system architecture to overcomes the cost and complexity of moving data which also improves the total cost of ownership and brings in flexibility to manage workflows and maximize system utilization. Design patterns and skeletons are the potential candidates to address above-mentioned challenges to design scalable, robust software development and applicable proved solutions in both HPC and big data community.

The parallel programing problem has been an active area of research for decades focusing primarily on programming models and their supporting environments. As we move towards Exascale (millions of components, billions of cores) programming parallel processors and handling billion-way parallelism is one of the major challenge that research community is facing. Software architecture and design plays a vital role in designing robust and scalable software. Common set of design elements (derived from domain expert's solutions), are captured in a design pattern of that particular domain to assist the software designer to engineer robust and scalable parallel software. These patterns define the building blocks of all software engineering and are fundamental to architect parallel software. The design problem at different level of software development is addressed by developing layered hierarchy of patterns by arranging patterns at different levels. These design patterns have been developed to assist software engineers to architect and implement parallel software efficiently. Our Pattern Language OPL is one of prominent source of cataloguing and categorizing the parallel patterns [30]. A design pattern provides a clean mechanism to cater common design problems using generic guidelines.

Big Data design patterns provide the concrete representation of analysis and technology centric patterns of most common occurring problems in BigData environment [31]. These design patterns provides the building blocks for the efficient design of big data architecture. The standardization and integration of design patterns can be seen as the potential candidates for the efficient and effective convergence of HPC and big data. Figure 2 shows the logical architecture of different layers and design patterns (HPC & BigData) can then be applied at distinct levels to address the issues related to big data and HPC convergence. One of the challenges associated with data visualization and interactive management is huge volume, variety and velocity of data and is often hard to evaluate and reapply the design solution. The visualization and management layer involves applying patterns for distributed and parallel visualization, interactive data exploration, rendering data visualization, real time monitoring for live analysis and recommendations.

The analytics/processing layer includes patterns for analytics and depending on the problem domain includes in-situ, in-transit, real time or batch processing. Advanced analytics requires predictions, advance algorithms, simulations and real time decisions that require high performance computing for processing and managing massive volume of data [32].

There is a trade-off between Performance, resilience and power consumption. Trade-off patterns needs to identify and accommodate these trade-offs in best possible way by indulging the best practices from both HPC and Big data communities. The processing pattern includes analytics patterns for unstructured and structured data, algorithms for conversion of unstructured to structured data, large-scale batch and graph based processing patterns and also parallel design patterns. The access/storage layer includes design patterns for the effective and efficient retrieval and storage mechanism for parallel

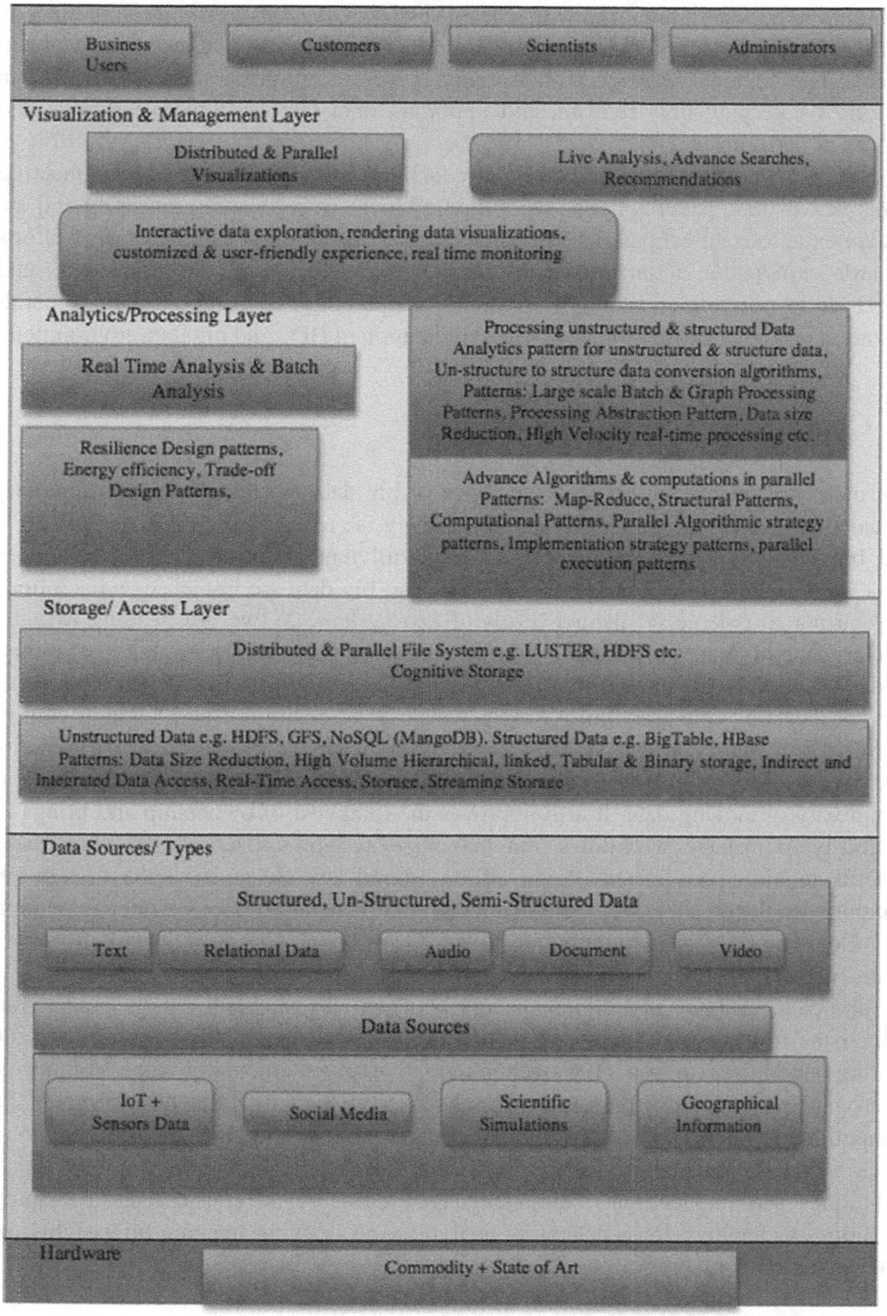

| Business Users | Customers | Scientists | Administrators |

Visualization & Management Layer

Distributed & Parallel Visualizations

Live Analysis, Advance Searches, Recommendations

Interactive data exploration, rendering data visualizations, customized & user-friendly experience, real time monitoring

Analytics/Processing Layer

Real Time Analysis & Batch Analysis

Processing unstructured & structured Data Analytics pattern for unstructured & structure data, Un-structure to structure data conversion algorithms, Patterns: Large scale Batch & Graph Processing Patterns, Processing Abstraction Pattern, Data size Reduction, High Velocity real-time processing etc.

Resilience Design patterns, Energy efficiency, Trade-off Design Patterns,

Advance Algorithms & computations in parallel Patterns: Map-Reduce, Structural Patterns, Computational Patterns, Parallel Algorithmic strategy patterns, Implementation strategy patterns, parallel execution patterns

Storage/ Access Layer

Distributed & Parallel File System e.g. LUSTER, HDFS etc. Cognitive Storage

Unstructured Data e.g. HDFS, GFS, NoSQL (MangoDB). Structured Data e.g. BigTable, HBase Patterns: Data Size Reduction, High Volume Hierarchical, linked, Tabular & Binary storage, Indirect and Integrated Data Access, Real-Time Access, Storage, Streaming Storage

Data Sources/ Types

Structured, Un-Structured, Semi-Structured Data

| Text | Relational Data | Audio | Document | Video |

Data Sources

| IoT + Sensors Data | Social Media | Scientific Simulations | Geographical Information |

Hardware

Commodity + State of Art

Fig. 2. Logical layered architecture of design patterns

and distributed file systems. This includes data size reduction for high volume hierarchical, linked, tabular and binary cognitive storage for real time in-direct and integrated access. The cognitive storage with learning ability to automate the process of data purging by keeping only relevant and important data for cost effective storage and improved performance.

HPC software development community lack the expertise of software engineering principles as these patterns define the building blocks of software engineering and are fundamental to architect parallel software. There is a need to invest the research efforts towards exploration of innovative approaches to make use of design patterns and skeletons to overcome scalability, elasticity, adaptability, robustness, storage, parallelization and other processing challenges of the unified HPC and big data environment.

7 Conclusion

The increased processing power, emergence of big data resources and real time analytical solutions are the prime drivers that pushing the realm of big data. As both HPC and big data systems are different and have different architecture. The challenges associated with inevitable integration of HPC and big data are immense and solutions are starting to emerge at distinct levels of eco system. As we are heading towards convergence of both, we will have to deal with modality, complexity and vast amount of data. Currently we have distinct and perhaps overlapping set of design choices at various levels of infrastructure. A single system architecture but with enough configurability in it that you can actually serve different design points between compute intensive and design intensive. The single system architecture overcomes the cost and complexity of moving data. It also improves the total cost of ownership and brings in flexibility to manage workflows and maximize system utilization. Realizing these benefits requires coordinated design efforts around key elements of the system i.e. compute (multicore, FPGA), interconnect (next generation fabric), memory (Non Volatile memory, storage burst buffer, Luster file system). This coordinated effort may result in useable, effective and scalable software infrastructure.

The connected and ubiquitous synergy between HPC and Big data is expected to deliver the results which cannot be achieved by either alone. There is a need for the leading enterprises to use HPC technology to explore efficiently huge volume of heterogeneous data to surpass static searches into dynamic pattern discovery for the competitive advantage. The integration of computing power in HPC and demands for a quick and real time analytics for big data with cognitive technology (computer vision techniques, Machine learning, natural language processing) are considered as reshaping the future technology for accelerating analytics and deriving meaningful insights for efficient decision-making.

Acknowledgments. The authors acknowledge with thanks, the technical and financial support from the Deanship of Scientific Research (DSR) at the King Abdul-Aziz University (KAU), Jeddah, Saudi Arabia, under the grant number G-661-611-38. The work carried out in this paper is supported by the HPC Center at the King Abdul-Aziz University.

References

1. Singh, K., Kaur, R.: Hadoop: addressing challenges of big data. In: 2014 IEEE International Advance Computing Conference (IACC), pp. 686–689. IEEE (2014)
2. Charl, S.: IBM - HPC and HPDA for the Cognitive Journey with OpenPOWER. https://www-03.ibm.com/systems/power/solutions/bigdata-analytics/smartpaper/high-value-insights.html
3. Keable, C.: The convergence of High Performance Computing and Big Data – Ascent. https://ascent.atos.net/convergence-high-performance-computing-big-data/
4. Joseph, E., Sorensen, B.: IDC Update on How Big Data Is Redefining High Performance Computing. https://www.tacc.utexas.edu/documents/1084364/1136739/IDC+HPDA+Briefing+slides+10.21.2014_2.pdf
5. Geist, A., Lucas, R.: Whitepaper on the Major Computer Science Challenges at Exascale (2009)
6. Krishnan, S., Tatineni, M., Baru, C.: myHadoop-Hadoop-on-Demand on Traditional HPC Resources (2011)
7. Xuan, P., Denton, J., Ge, R., Srimani, P.K., Luo, F.: Big data analytics on traditional HPC infrastructure using two-level storage (2015)
8. Is Hadoop the New HPC. http://www.admin-magazine.com/HPC/Articles/Is-Hadoop-the-New-HPC
9. Katal, A., Wazid, M., Goudar, R.H.: Big data: issues, challenges, tools and good practices. In: 2013 Sixth International Conference on Contemporary Computing (IC3), pp. 404–409. IEEE (2013)
10. Hess, K.: Hadoop vs. Spark: The New Age of Big Data. http://www.datamation.com/data-center/hadoop-vs.-spark-the-new-age-of-big-data.html
11. Muhammad, J.: Is Apache Spark going to replace Hadoop? http://aptuz.com/blog/is-apache-spark-going-to-replace-hadoop/
12. OLCF Staff Writer: OLCF Group to Offer Spark On-Demand Data Analysis. https://www.olcf.ornl.gov/2016/03/29/olcf-group-to-offer-spark-on-demand-data-analysis/
13. Islam, N.S., Lu, X., Wasi-ur-Rahman, M., Shankar, D., Panda, D.K.: Triple-H: a hybrid approach to accelerate HDFS on HPC clusters with heterogeneous storage architecture. In: 2015 15th IEEE/ACM International Symposium on Cluster, Cloud and Grid Computing, pp. 101–110. IEEE (2015)
14. Ranger, C., Raghuraman, R., Penmetsa, A., Bradski, G., Kozyrakis, C.: Evaluating MapReduce for multi-core and multiprocessor systems. In: 2007 IEEE 13th International Symposium on High Performance Computer Architecture, pp. 13–24. IEEE (2007)
15. Tiwari, N., Sarkar, S., Bellur, U., Indrawan, M.: An empirical study of Hadoop's energy efficiency on a HPC cluster. Procedia Comput. Sci. 29, 62–72 (2014)
16. Woodie, A.: Does InfiniBand Have a Future on Hadoop? http://www.datanami.com/2015/08/04/does-infiniband-have-a-future-on-hadoop/
17. Veiga, J., Exp, R.R., Taboada, G.L., Touri, J.: Analysis and Evaluation of Big Data Computing Solutions in an HPC Environment (2015)
18. Wang, Y., et al.: Assessing the performance impact of high-speed interconnects on MapReduce. In: Rabl, T., Poess, M., Baru, C., Jacobsen, H.-A. (eds.) WBDB-2012. LNCS, vol. 8163, pp. 148–163. Springer, Heidelberg (2014). https://doi.org/10.1007/978-3-642-53974-9_13
19. Islam, N.S., Lu, X., Wasi-ur-Rahman, M., Panda, D.K.: Can parallel replication benefit Hadoop distributed file system for high performance interconnects? In: 2013 IEEE 21st Annual Symposium on High-Performance Interconnects, pp. 75–78. IEEE (2013)

20. Moore, J., Chase, J., Ranganathan, P., Sharma, R.: Making scheduling cool: temperature-aware workload placement in data centers (2005)
21. Reed, D.A., Dongarra, J.: Exascale computing and big data. Commun. ACM **58**, 56–68 (2015)
22. Rajovic, N., Puzovic, N., Vilanova, L., Villavieja, C., Ramirez, A.: The low-power architecture approach towards exascale computing. In: Proceedings of the Second Workshop on Scalable Algorithms for Large-Scale Systems - ScalA 2011, p. 1. ACM Press, New York (2011)
23. Cappello, F.: Fault tolerance in petascale/exascale systems: current knowledge, challenges and research opportunities. Int. J. High Perform. Comput. Appl. **23**, 212–226 (2009)
24. Gutierrez, D.: The Convergence of Big Data and HPC – insideBIGDATA. https://insidebigdata.com/2016/10/25/the-convergence-of-big-data-and-hpc/
25. High Performance Data Analytics (HPDA) Market-Forecast 2022. https://www.marketresearchfuture.com/reports/high-performance-data-analytics-hpda-market
26. Willard, C.G., Snell, A., Segervall, L., Feldman, M.: Top Six Predictions for HPC in 2015 (2015)
27. Egham: Gartner Says 8.4 Billion Connected "Things"; Will Be in Use in 2017, Up 31 Percent From 2016. http://www.gartner.com/newsroom/id/3598917
28. El Baz, D.: IoT and the need for high performance computing. In: 2014 International Conference on Identification, Information and Knowledge in the Internet of Things, pp. 1–6. IEEE (2014)
29. Conway, S.: High Performance Data Analysis (HPDA): HPC - Big Data Convergence - insideHPC (2017)
30. Keutzer, K., Tim, M.: Our Pattern Language_Our Pattern Language (2016). Keutzer—EECS UC Berkeley, Tim—Intel. file:///Users/abdulmanan/Desktop/Our Pattern Language_Our Pattern Language.htm
31. Bodkin, R., Bodkin, R.: Big Data Patterns, pp. 1–23 (2017)
32. Mysore, D., Khupat, S., Jain, S.: Big data architecture and patterns, Part 1: Introduction to big data classification and architecture. https://www.ibm.com/developerworks/library/bd-archpatterns1/index.html

A Framework for Faster Porting of Scientific Applications Between Heterogeneous Clouds

Waseem Ahmed[1], Mohsin Khan[2(✉)], Adeel Ahmed Khan[2], Rashid Mehmood[3], Abdullah Algarni[1], Aiiad Albeshri[1], and Iyad Katib[1]

[1] Faculty of Computing and Information Technology, King Abdulaziz University, Jeddah, Kingdom of Saudi Arabia
`waseem.pace@gmail.com,`
`{amsalgarni,aaalbeshri,iakatib}@kau.edu.sa`
[2] Department of Computer Science and Engineering, HKBK College of Engineering, Visvesvaraya Technological University, Bangalore, India
`mohsin1510@gmail.com, khan.aak004@gmail.com`
[3] High Performance Computing Center, King Abdulaziz University, Jeddah, Kingdom of Saudi Arabia
`rmehmood@kau.edu.sa`

Abstract. The emergence of pay-as-you-use compute clouds has enabled scientists to experiment with the latest processor architectures and accelerators. However, the lack of standardization in cloud computing, more specifically in the interoperability context, makes the task of portability of applications between clouds challenging. Two main tasks that users of multi-vendor clouds will need to perform are porting cost analysis and faster source-to-source translation. Cost analysis is essential to help evaluate the feasibility and cost of portability. And any automation of the source-to-source translation step will help developers perform the translation faster while taking advantage of platform-specific features. This paper presents a framework that assists a developer in performing these two tasks. The first task is achieved using the *Maintainability Analyzer* module which generates unique funnel shaped patterns that give an insight about the maintainability of an application and its potential for porting. Different scientific applications from various domains, that were developed using different programming paradigms, were evaluated using this module. For the second task, a set of modules use a knowledge repository to perform source-to-source translations while ensuring the maintainability of the generated code. The framework has been tested with different architecture and library combinations with promising results.

Keywords: Maintainability · Code transformation
Source-to-source translation · Portability · Heterogeneous architecture

© ICST Institute for Computer Sciences, Social Informatics and Telecommunications Engineering 2018
R. Mehmood et al. (Eds.): SCITA 2017, LNICST 224, pp. 27–43, 2018.
https://doi.org/10.1007/978-3-319-94180-6_5

1 Introduction

Proliferation of the pay-as-you-use offering by compute cloud vendors has provided a new opportunity and a financially viable alternative for researchers in the high performance computing (HPC) community looking for bigger and faster computational resources. Future offerings by cloud vendors are expected to include widely heterogeneous architectures with different processor and accelerator combinations, possibly from multiple processor and accelerator vendors. Although few challenges have prevented large scale deployment of scientific applications on the cloud, the HPC-on-the-cloud community is expected to grow.

One such challenge is to enable faster portability of applications from one cloud vendor to another. While live portability of scientific applications between different cloud vendors will enable researchers to experiment with different architecture combinations, a lot of challenges will have to be overcome for this to become a practical reality. Additionally, despite the many groups working on developing comprehensive standards, the progress in the cloud interoperability context, has been slow [1]. This lack of standardization in cloud computing has made the task of switching cloud providers more challenging for the end users.

An obvious solution is to design for portability. However, portability, although a desirable characteristic in generic software applications, neither is desirable nor an aim in the design of scientific applications. In scientific applications, kernels and libraries are highly optimized for specific platforms with device-specific optimizations performed to enable them to execute most efficiently on that particular architecture. Portability, thus, is neither an important need nor objective in scientific computing. This places scientific applications in a different niche in the cloud computing world.

Portability of scientific applications in some form from one platform to another, on the other hand, is more common. The process of porting and optimizing programs and libraries is repeated whenever system architecture, tools or requirements change [2]. Considering the large lifetime of scientific applications, and the change of architectures and system tools over this period, porting and optimizations become a natural and required part of scientific application maintenance.

From the portability perspective, this poses two main challenges. Firstly, the application will have to be correctly translated to the new architecture while maximizing the utilization of the underlying computing resources. Secondly, this may need to be done more frequently to take advantage of the newer and faster computing resources that a cloud vendor may introduce; regular scaling and upgradation of their systems is important to cloud vendors to attract more customers and for market survival.

Manual translation of serial code into its correct parallel equivalent is a lengthy and complex process that involves programmer creativity, domain expertise, large solution space exploration and intricate knowledge of both the computer architecture and the programming paradigm. The last few decades have seen a lot of work in the form of experience reports, case studies and real examples on the subject of manual parallelization. Although there has been a lot of research over the past few decades on automating this task, manual parallelization continues to outperform automatic parallelization tools, in the general case. Indeed, manual parallelization continues to dominate in the GPGPU community [3]. This trend can be expected to continue as the performance gap in terms of efficiency and computing resource utilization between automatic and manual parallelization continues to widen as newer and hybrid architectures are introduced into the market [3]. Also, the varying architectural spectrum of scientific computing being witnessed in HPC will necessitate a radical change in compiler design. Traditionally, compilers have focused on homogeneous architectures; code was either compiled for the host processor(s) or a cross compiler was used to compile for a target(s) processor. As heterogeneous architectures on the HPC horizon will employ a mix of multi-vendor processors, GPUs, FPGA and other accelerators, compiling code for these heterogeneous architectures will definitely become a prerequisite for compiler development.

Until recently, porting had to be performed by researchers only when newer computer resources were made available to them. This porting process, in most cases, lasted a few months. The ratio (R_t) of *period-of-ownership* of the new platform to *time-to-translate* was sufficiently large to justify the cost of porting. But with scientific applications starting to move to the cloud, the portability process will have to be placed in a different perspective.

To address these challenges, research on developing sophisticated automatic parallelization environments and frameworks to help improve developer productivity will be needed as they will have an important role to play in inter-cloud application porting. Also, the need to focus on maintainability and modularity during scientific application development will become more essential to facilitate easier portability between different architectural platforms.

This paper aims to address a few of the aforementioned challenges. More specifically, three main contributions of this work are as follows

1. A mechanism to qualitatively evaluate the feasibility of porting scientific applications between heterogeneous platforms
2. A source-to-source transformation process based on a knowledge repository to facilitate portability between widely disparate architectures
3. Approach to improve maintainability of scientific application by kernel extraction into blocks and the use of wrappers around them. While the concept of using wrappers to address interoperability problems is not new, this is the first attempt to use it to address cloud interoperability issues in HPC

The rest of the paper is organized as follows. The next section gives a background of the porting process from the perspective of scientific application development. Section 3 formally describes the relationship of the cost with other design parameters. Section 4 describes the working of the framework followed by its evaluation in Sect. 5. Section 6 places the work presented in this paper against similar work present in literature. This is followed by conclusion and future work.

2   Background

2.1   Maintenance of Scientific Applications

Unlike conventional software, requirements of scientific applications do not exhibit drastic change over time. As these applications are developed to study specific and well defined scientific phenomena which the scientists can clearly articulate and formally express, the requirements of these applications are relatively stable even over a period of time. Main changes made to software during its evolution fall in the following categories

1. When a newer environment is available (faster processors, interconnect, accelerators, programming paradigms, etc.) or if the existing platform is scaled
2. When the new environment offers faster execution and larger memory, scientists are provided with an opportunity to study larger problems, work at a finer granularity on the same problem or obtain results with a lesser degree of error, things which were not possible on the earlier platform. This scaling of the problem to take advantage of the new environment features may necessitate changes in software
3. When a more efficient algorithm or library for the application is available.

Reference to *change* or *maintenance* in the rest of the paper refers specifically to the changes listed above unless specified otherwise.

2.2   Porting Process

Consider an application that needs to be migrated from one heterogeneous platform (P_s) on a cloud to another (P_t). Consider an application, shown in Fig. 1 (a), that has been initially developed in CUDA on a GPU and uses the cublas-Dgemm function call from the CUBLAS library. If this code were to be migrated to a platform that uses an Intel MIC (Xeon Phi) and the Intel MKL, many changes to code will be needed even for a small and a simple application like dense matrix-matrix multiplication. Direct porting of code from P_s to P_t in such cases, although possible, is very challenging and prone to errors as the two representations are very different and do not have a one-to-one mapping as shown in Fig. 1. A better option would be to introduce an additional step in the translation process, i.e. translate the application to its equivalent representation on an intermediate reference platform (P_r) and then translate it from P_r to P_t. The primary advantage in using an intermediate platform for translation is that it reduces the number of mapping combinations required from m^2 to $2m$ (derived from [4]), where m is the number of platform options available.

In general, a translation from P_s to its intermediate representation on P_r would have a lot of platform specific code clipped or removed. For example, if the source is in CUDA, CUDA specific initializations and memory allocation routines will be eliminated in the first translation as can be seen in Fig. 1(a) and (b). Likewise, the pre-processor directives in OpenMP and OpenACC will be

```
10  #include<cuda_runtime.h>          10  #include <mkl.h>
11  #include<cublas_v2.h>                 ...
12  #include<helper_cuda.h>               ...
    ...                                30  cblas_dgemm(rowmjr, ...);
20  cublasHandle_t hndl;                  ...
    ...
30  findCudaDevice(..);
40  status = cublasCreate(&hndl);
    ...
50  cudaMalloc(..);
60  cublasSetVector(n2,..);
    ...
70  cublasDgemm(hndl,rowmjr,...);
    ...
80  cublasGetVector(..);
    ...
90  cudaFree(..);
```

(a) Source platform (CUDA on a GPU)   (b) Reference platform

```
10  #include <mkl.h>
20  #include <omp.h>
    ...
30  _declspec(target(mic))
40  void gemm(char rowmjr,...)   {
60      cblas_dgemm(rowmjr,...);
70  }
    ...
80  ...//Align = 64
90  #pragma offload target(mic)
100     in(A[0:M*K]:align(Align))
110     in(B[0:K*N]:align(Align))
120     inout(C[0:M*N]:align(Align))  {
140     gemm(transa,...);
150 }
```

(c) Target platform (OpenMP on an Intel MIC Xeon Phi)

Fig. 1. Application porting between heterogeneous architectures

removed. Platform specific library calls need to be mapped to their equivalent on the reference platform.

In the second step of the translation, i.e. from P_r to P_t, code that performs platform-specific initializations and memory allocations needs to be inserted at appropriate places. Also, generic library calls will have to be mapped to their equivalent calls on the target platform. Device-specific optimizations may need to be inserted where necessary. For example, 512-bit registers for MIC requires a 64-byte alignment and should thus, be specified in the code (Fig. 1(c)). This knowledge is absent in P_s's code.

Also, in cases where P_s has specialized extensions to standard library functions and equivalent functions are not available on either P_r or P_t, intelligent decisions based on the knowledge of the platform need to be taken. Moreover, if either P_s or P_t have multiple accelerators with static load distribution, the translation process will have to be more intelligently done as will be elaborated later in Sect. 3.3. Thus, the presence of an external knowledge repository in such a framework is very essential when platform-specific decisions and platform-specific optimizations need to be taken and made, respectively.

3 Cost of Porting

Before porting an application to another platform, it is important to assess whether it is economically more feasible to migrate the application or develop it from scratch. This section describes factors that influence porting cost.

3.1 Maintainability Related Costs

The design and maintainability of an application has a direct effect on its porting cost. An application that is poorly designed will have high maintenance; porting this application to another platform will thus involve a larger effort. Qualitatively or quantitatively determining the maintainability of an application is thus, an important step.

To determine the maintainability of an application, a *Maintainability Visualizer* has been developed as part of the framework. As described later in Sect. 4.2, the tool, besides providing a graphical summary of maintenance performed on a given application over its lifetime, helps a scientist or a developer to qualitatively evaluate the design of the architecture of the system and its potential for faster portability. The output of the module is a funnel-shaped pattern described in later sections and shown in Fig. 3.

From these funnel-shaped patterns, the maintainability cost (C_{main}) can be formally described as follows

$$C_{main} \propto \sum_{i=1}^{n_f} \delta_i - w_c n_f \tag{1}$$

where δ_i gives the magnitude of the total changes performed on source file i, w_c gives the width of the channel and n_f is the number of source files in the application. The value of w_c is user-defined and is an indicator of tolerance to change desired. A higher value of w_c indicates a higher tolerance level. In the plots shown in Fig. 3, w_c has been chosen as 0.1 (10%)

Additionally, a well designed architecture should be modular with low coupling between the components. Low coupling prevents change ripples [5] spreading to other parts of the code. This also makes the code more maintainable. Thus,

$$C_{main} \propto \sum_{i,j=1}^{n_c} g(c_i \to c_j) \forall i \neq j \tag{2}$$

where $g(c_i \to c_j)$ gives the degree of coupling (uni-directional) of component c_i with c_j.

3.2 Platform Related Costs

Besides costs related to maintainability, the source-and-target platform combination greatly influences the cost of porting. The choice of a platform to use as reference and as an intermediate representation is thus, an important decision. It should be chosen such that it is be easy to produce and easy to translate from and to different platforms. In this research, a system with a single node, single socket, single core, single thread, with no accelerator and using Intel MKL where needed is used as a reference platform (P_r).

With reference to P_r, if the cost required to develop a new application from scratch for a platform, P_i is denoted as c_i, then, an upper-bound for the porting cost from P_i to another platform, P_j or vice versa can be represented by ($c_i + c_j$). Cost (c_i) is a function of the number and type of bottlenecks (kernels) present in the application, the number and type of library calls used in the application, and the maturity of the system tools and libraries available for P_i. For example, to convert a single *dgemm* call from a system with an Intel MIC using Intel MKL library to a system using an Nvidia K40 using *cublas*, CUDA code needs to be added for device-to-host and host-to-device data transfers, library initialization, device-specific memory allocation/deallocation and error checking while being placed correctly in the code and in the proper order. Also, the *dgemm* call needs to be replaced with its equivalent cublas call plus the additional parameters. For the reverse case, all corresponding CUDA code needs to be deleted. Thus,

$$C_{plat} \propto \sum_{i=1}^{m}(c_{lib})_i + \sum_{j=1}^{n}(c_b)_j \tag{3}$$

where, c_{lib} and c_b are platform-specific and relate to the cost of translation of a particular library call and bottleneck respectively. It can be seen from Eq. 3, that more bottlenecks or library calls an application uses, the higher will be is its associated porting cost.

From Eqs. 1, 2 and 3 we get

$$C_{mig} \propto \mathcal{F}(C_{main}, C_{plat}) \tag{4}$$

This implies that a system with low maintainability will have a higher cost of maintenance and hence a higher porting cost. Similarly, a platform that has a relatively more complex representation will be more costly to migrate.

The next section further explains how platform heterogeneity can have an increasing influence on C_{plat}.

3.3   Mapping to Heterogeneous platforms

A large portion of the scientific computing community has been porting code to accelerators to speed up their applications. In most of the early research using accelerators like GPUs, all parallelizable portions of serial code were offloaded and executed on the GPU. Significant speedups have been reported in these cases with code being craftily moved to utilize the GPU architecture. Many source-to-source translators that converted OpenMP code to CUDA [6] were introduced to ease the GPGPU application programmer's burden. However, the host CPU remained unutilized in most of these cases; a hybrid approach where the load was balanced between the CPU and GPU was not considered.

Recently, many researchers have attempted to manually overlap CPU and GPU computations by adopting a hybrid approach [7–9]. By attempting to utilize all the available computational units, the speedup obtained in these cases was much higher than with just utilizing the computational units on the GPU. But as expected, the effort (C_{plat}) involved in obtaining the load-balanced parallelized version was also much higher.

Consider a computation being performed on a computer with n number of processors (or general purpose cores) and m number of coprocessors. Also, consider that the code can be separated into a serial (c_{ser}) and parallel (c_{par}) portion. The total time to compute is given by the following

$$t_{tot} = t_{ser} + max(t_{proc_1}, ..., t_{proc_n}, t_{acc_1}, ...t_{acc_m}) + t_{com} \qquad (5)$$

where t_{ser} is the time taken to execute c_{ser}, t_{proc_i} and t_{acc_j} represent time taken to execute code on the processor ($proc_i$) and accelerator (acc_j) respectively, and t_{com} is the total time for data transfers between computational units.

The following also holds true for the parallel portion of the code.

$$c_{par} = c_{proc_1} + ... + c_{proc_n} + c_{acc_1} + ... + c_{acc_m} \qquad (6)$$

where c_{proc_i} and c_{acc_1} represent the portion of the parallel code executed on the host processor and accelerator respectively.

In heterogeneous computing, the objective is to minimize t_{tot} and to increase the portion of c_{par} in the provided code. For the former, while it is obvious that t_{ser} and t_{com} need to be minimized, the relationship between t_{proc} and t_{acc} and its effect on t_{tot}, and the behavior of the ratio $c_{acc}/(c_{proc} + c_{acc})$ may vary between different platforms. All these factors have an influence on C_{plat} in Eq. 3. Determining the exact relationship between these values for various platform combinations is beyond the scope of this paper.

4   Description of Framework

This section gives an overview of the framework developed for help in application portability and describes portions of the framework presented in this paper.

4.1   Overview

Figure 2 shows the block diagram of the framework. It comprises of four modules and one data repository. The *Maintainability Visualizer* analyzes the history of changes made to application code over its lifetime and summarizes this information into a graphical pattern. The *Knowledge Repo* serves as a repository that contains descriptions about (1) specific accelerators and libraries and their mappings to and from the reference platform (P_r) and (2) patterns of commonly occurring kernels (or dwarfs) in scientific applications. The *Profiler* identifies and ranks the *blocks* or segments of code that appear as bottlenecks when executed on P_r. The *Block Extractor* extracts the blocks identified by the *Profiler*

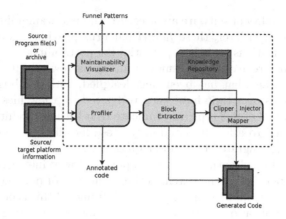

Fig. 2. Porting framework

into functions (similar to *Function extraction* in refactoring [10]) that also serves as a generic wrapper for the block. The main objective of the *Block Extractor* is to reduce the value of δ_i and $g(c_i \rightarrow c_j)$ in Eqs. 1 and 2. The *Code Transformer* consists of three complementary modules, *Clipper, Injector* and *Mapper*. The first two modules transform the application code from the source platform to its equivalent representation in P_r and from its representation in P_r to its equivalent on the target platform, respectively. The *Mapper* is responsible for code modifications on kernel patterns and library calls present in the *Knowledge Repo*.

The framework takes three inputs from the user. First is the application source which may be given as a single file, a source directory or a zipped archive. The second input provides descriptions of the existing platform - details regarding the processors, accelerators and libraries used. The third input provides similar descriptions about the target platform. The focus of this paper is on the *Maintainability Visualizer, Block Extractor* and a few functionalities of the *Code Transformer*.

4.2 Maintainability Visualizer

The primary function of this module is to provide an insight to the user about the maintainability of the application and, subsequently, aid him in taking a decision about platform porting. A higher degree of maintainability implies an easier portability. If the code base shows poor maintainability, rewriting the code for the target platform may be more cost effective.

The module uses a locally cloned Git repository for analysis. The history of each file, which includes commits, insertions, deletions, dates of commits, etc., is analyzed. Files are arranged in descending order of the number of changes made to them over their lifetime and associated with their corresponding magnitude of change. This generates an interesting funnel-shaped pattern which provides insights into the quality of software architecture and maintainability of the application. As will be seen later, these *funnel* patterns provide a good insight into the design of applications and their potential for portability.

A funnel with a relatively large mouth and a narrow rapidly tapering stem depicts an application that has been well designed, with a robust architecture where modifications over time have been restricted to a few files. For scientific applications, a funnel of this type may indicate that kernels (architecture specific code) were confined to a few files and only these files had to be changed when the application was migrated to a newer platform.

In contrast, a funnel with its mouth tapering slowly into a relatively thick stem indicates a poorly designed architecture. The cost of porting these systems to newer platforms would be more expensive. A funnel of this type would suggest rewriting of the application from scratch or a major restructuring or refactoring [10] of the application to improve its maintainability.

4.3 Knowledge Repo

The *Knowledge Repo* serves as one of the main constituents contributing to the intelligence of the framework. It is primarily used in decision making during code transformation.

Knowledge is stored in a two-level, dictionary-based scalable tree partitioned into sections. The following are a few types of knowledge that can be built in to the repository

- Mapping of standard scientific library functions from various platforms to P_r and vice versa. This includes function names, details about number, type and relative order of parameters and other specifics.
- Platform-specific device initialization calls, calls for memory allocation/deallocation and data transfers
- Platform-specific optimizations
- Patterns of commonly occurring kernels in scientific computation
- Information about platform-specific preprocessor directives

The efficiency of the framework is based on the maturity and comprehensiveness of this repository. Populating this repository with correct and pertinent knowledge about various platforms is, thus, an important pre-requisite for the efficacy of the framework.

4.4 Block Extractor

The main objective of this code is block extraction. It takes a block-annotated file from the *Profiler* as input and extracts this block into a separate function. This rearrangement of code, which has a positive influence on $g(c_i \rightarrow c_j)$ and also implicitly impacts $\sum_{i=1}^{n_f} \delta_i$, is referred to as *Function Extraction* in refactoring [10]. The block is embedded into a function with a generic signature which serves as a wrapper to facilitate easier code replacement in future by minimizing code ripples during code changes.

While the concept of using wrappers to address interoperability problems is not new [11–13], this is the first attempt of using them to address cloud interoperability issues in scientific computing.

4.5   Code Transformation

Although the basic translation of code to a newer architecture to obtain a correct functional executable is not difficult and can be performed in a reasonably short time, optimization of the ported code to take advantage of the features of the newer architecture requires a much longer time. Additionally, if the code has evolved over different architecture generations, identifying the (sometimes retained) previous platform-specific optimizations and correctly replacing them with the newer platform-specific optimizations or removing them altogether is also an intense task that requires skill. This module attempts to automate these transformation steps where possible.

Code transformation is done in three overlapping stages by the *Clipper, Injector* and *Mapper* sub-modules which constitute the *Code Transformer*.

The *Clipper* is responsible for deannotating, clipping or cleaning out platform-specific code from P_s's representation. For example, CUDA-specific calls (*cudamalloc*) or OpenMP-specific pre-processor directives (*#pragma offload*) are identified based on inputs from the *Knowledge Repo* and truncated from the source representation. For a few statements, relevant information from the statement is extracted into a temporary dictionary ($Dict_{temp}$) prior to clipping. If P_s's representation indicates the use of static load balancing between its heterogeneous computing units (described earlier in Sect. 3.3), pertinent function calls have to be intelligently identified and *fused* into a single call. Likewise with data.

The *Injector* module basically reverses the steps of the *Clipper* but the translation is from P_r's representation to the equivalent representation of P_t. Input from the *Profiler*, $Dict_{temp}$ and the *Knowledge Repo* is used to appropriately place OpenACC-specific preprocessor directives or CUDA-based calls (*cudasetvector, cudafree*), for example, where needed. Additionally, two intelligent decisions need to be taken if P_t has a heterogeneous architecture. Firstly, for every bottleneck, a decision about where to execute the kernel is to be taken; for example, some kernels may execute faster on the host itself, for some data-parallel type of kernels, it would be more profitable to execute it on the accelerator and for some, the fastest implementation might involve a combination of both. Secondly, if the choice of the first decision is a mixed implementation, the kernel (bottleneck) may need to be split into its equivalent call on each of the heterogeneous devices, if required. But only a skeleton for this set of functions can be generated as a proper load distribution between the devices will require adaptive refinement techniques on these devices to determine the best setting as described in Sect. 3.3.

The responsibility of the *Mapper* module is to search for every replaceable function or library call between the P_r and P_t representations based on data from the *Knowledge Repo*. If found, pertinent code in P_r needs to be replaced

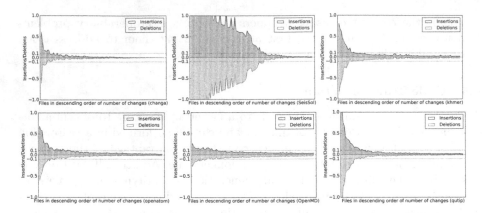

Fig. 3. *Funnels* for a few scientific applications generated by the *Maintainability Visualizer*

with its corresponding representation in P_t using information from $Dict_{temp}$, if needed. If an irreplaceable function or library call (a few iterative solvers in Intel's MKL do not have equivalent definitions in the CUDA standard libraries) is found, appropriate messages need to be provided to the user.

5 Evaluation of Framework

Development on the framework was largely done in Python 2.7 on the Linux platform.

The *Maintainability Visualizer* module was used to analyze a few popular scientific applications maintained on GitHub. The Git repository was cloned locally and provided as input to the module. Details about the applications are given in Table 1. The *Funnel* patterns generated by the module for these applications are shown in Fig. 3.

In case of ChanGA and OpenAtom, the *Funnel* has a relatively broad mouth and a very narrow tapering stem. As implied by the funnel, only a few files in these applications subsumed most changes over the years. Porting applications with such *funnels* to newer platforms should be easier. An important observation made was that these applications have been developed in Charm++, which is a machine independent parallel programming system which allows programs written using this system to run unchanged on different architectures [14]. The generated *funnel* pattern for these two applications very well substantiates this claim and our reasoning about the portability.

QuTiP, developed in Python, has a typical funnel shape with a large mouth slowly tapering into a narrow stem. OpenMD, on the other hand, has an interesting funnel with a very narrow mouth tapering into a stem. Considering its lifetime of 12 years, the funnel implies that the application has been designed with good foresight and an architecture robust to change. Porting this application to a newer platform will also be easy.

Table 1. Application details

Name	Domain	Language	Years of dev.	Last commit
ChaNGa [15]	N-body Gravity solver	Charm++	13	Nov 2015
khmer [16]	Nucleotide Sequence k-mer counting	Python	5	Nov 2015
OpenAtom [17]	Atomic and molecular system simulation based on quantum chemical principles	Charm++	10	Dec 2015
OpenMD [18]	Molecular Dynamics	C++	12	Jan 2016
QuTiP [19]	Simulation of dynamics of closed and open quantum systems	Python	5	Jan 2016
SeisSol [20]	Numerical Simulation of Seismic wave phenomenon and earth quake dynamics	C++	1	Jan 2016

SiesSol is a relatively new application in the set with development started a little more than a year back. However, the extremely large mouth of the funnel and a thick neck made it stand out among the funnels generated. On further study of the source files of the application, it was observed that many of the files were auto-generated. These appear to be code for commonly occurring kernels used in Scientific applications. Porting these kind of application to newer platforms will have a high cost as changes are not confined to a limited set of files.

The framework's applicability was studied with synthetic benchmark applications using a small set of frequently occurring kernels in scientific computing. Porting of these applications between different architecture combinations (no accelerator, single accelerator, multiple accelerators) and different implementations (textbook code, OpenBLAS, Intel's MKL BLAS and Nvidia's CUBLAS) were contrasted.

6   Related Work

The emergence of compute clouds while opening up new frontiers for the HPC community has brought with it many challenges. One main challenge is application portability. For general applications, close to live application porting is already offered by many cloud vendors. For example, for multi-cloud deployment, applications packaged as Docker images [21] can just be dropped on any of the cloud vendors supporting Docker containers regardless of the underlying architecture, operating system or libraries. Other approaches like [22] offer solutions for multiple-cloud deployment which require the adoption of their design process from the application's inception.

In case of scientific applications, this may not be currently possible or desired. For example, when porting a scientific application to a newer platform or when a cloud provider decides to upgrade to a newer architecture, the scientist will want the application to take full advantage of the underlying platform's special characteristics. If the newer platform is not offering any significant advantage over the existing platform, the portability will not be justified and thus, not needed. Also, if the cost of porting exceeds the cost of new development, porting should not be an option.

Source-to-source translators and auto-parallelizing environments play an important role in portability. There has been a lot of research in developing source-to-source compilers for scientific applications in the last few decades. A few of them have met with mixed success [23–26] and have no active development in the recent past. Among the recent ones, some [24,27,28] use standard C or annotated C (OpenMP/ OpenACC/ OpenCL) representation as input to generate an equivalent representation for a single or a very small set of parallel architectures. Others [2,14,29] have introduced a new implicitly parallel input representation paradigm, the use of which is largely confined to a small set of researchers. Also, most of the source-to-source transformers generate generic code that may not be optimized for a particular architecture; device-specific optimizations have not been not considered. For example, particular grid combinations may result in faster CUDA kernel execution on some GPUs and not in others.

[30] most closely resembles the approach presented in this paper. Like a few other approaches, it uses code in which parallel portions have already been identified using OpenMP/OpenACC syntax. Similar to [27], it identifies kernels based on pre-defined patterns. These and other library calls are then mapped to a target platform. But, like many other approaches, targets a single platform.

The main impediment in applying these and other source-to-source compilers to application porting is that they are all uni-directional; i.e. translation of code is from a reference platform to a target platform but not vice versa. For application portability it is important that the translation works both ways. Moreover, considering the increasing adoption of accelerators in the scientific community, represented by increasing heterogeneity of architectural choices available, this becomes more important.

Also, to the best of our knowledge, there is no existing work that qualitatively or quantitatively evaluates the feasibility of scientific application portability or gives an indicator to its cost.

7   Conclusion and Future Work

Porting of scientific applications typically involves a few man years of development and is a large and expensive exercise. In the past, this typically happened once or twice in the lifetime of an application when large grants were procured every few years for a faster and newer system. But the pay-as-you-use philosophy of the compute cloud is expected to dramatically alter this equation with larger and newer systems being made more frequently available by the cloud vendors. The emergence of compute clouds has provided new avenues for researchers; scientists will have an opportunity of experimenting with different accelerator and platform combinations. But for this to become a practical reality in scientific computing, a domain which is characterized by heavily optimized platform-specific kernels and libraries, two tasks need to be automated. First is portability analysis to assess the feasibility of portability and second is source-to-source translation.

This paper presented a framework that addresses these challenges. A preliminary evaluation of the proposed framework on a set of architecture and library combinations have shown encouraging results. Future work will focus on developing a comprehensive and mature *Knowledge Repo* in order to properly evaluate all the modules. A thorough qualitative analysis of the framework's efficacy and its influence on programmer productivity during application portability over a wider range of platform combinations would also be performed.

Acknowledgements. The work on this paper was supported by the HPC Center at the King Abdulaziz University, Jeddah, Saudi Arabia.

References

1. Ortiz Jr., S.: The problem with cloud-computing standardization. IEEE Comput. **7**, 13–16 (2011)
2. Ansel, J.: Autotuning programs with algorithmic choice. Ph.D. thesis, Massachusetts Institute of Technology (2014)
3. Garcia, S., Jeon, D., Louie, C., Taylor, M.B.: The Kremlin oracle for sequential code parallelization. IEEE Micro **32**, 42–53 (2012)
4. Lam, M., Sethi, R., Ullman, J., Aho, A.: Compilers: Principles, Techniques and Tools (2006)
5. Madhavji, N.H., Fernandez-Ramil, J.C., Perry, D.E.: Software Evolution and Feedback: Theory and Practice. John Wiley & Sons Ltd., New York (2006)
6. Lee, S., Min, S.-J., Eigenmann, R.: Openmp to GPGPU: a compiler framework for automatic translation and optimization. ACM Sigplan Not. **44**(4), 101–110 (2009)
7. Tomov, S., Dongarra, J., Baboulin, M.: Towards dense linear algebra for hybrid GPU accelerated manycore systems. Parallel Comput. **36**(5), 232–240 (2010)
8. Vömel, C., Tomov, S., Dongarra, J.: Divide and conquer on hybrid GPU-accelerated multicore systems. SIAM J. Sci. Comput. **34**(2), C70–C82 (2012)
9. Vetter, J.S., Glassbrook, R., Dongarra, J., Schwan, K., Loftis, B., McNally, S., Meredith, J., Rogers, J., Roth, P., Spafford, K., Yalamanchili, S.: Keeneland: bringing heterogeneous GPU computing to the computational science community. Comput. Sci. Eng. (2011)
10. Fowler, M., Beck, K., Brant, J., Opdyke, W., Roberts, D.: Refactoring: Improving the Design of Existing Programs. Addison-Wesley, Reading (1999)
11. Ahmed, W., Myers, D.: Concept-based partitioning for large multidomain multifunctional embedded systems. ACM Trans. Des. Autom. Electron. Syst. (TODAES) **15**(3), 22 (2010)
12. Braun, F., Lockwood, J., Waldvogel, M.: Protocol wrappers for layered network packet processing in reconfigurable hardware. IEEE Micro **22**, 66–74 (2002)

13. Gharsali, F., Meftali, S., Rousseau, F., Jerraya, A.A.: Automatic generation of embedded memory wrapper for multiprocessor SoC. In: Proceedings of the Design Automation Conference (DAC 2002) (2002)

14. Acun, B., Gupta, A., Jain, N., Langer, A., Menon, H., Mikida, E., Ni, X., Robson, M., Sun, Y., Totoni, E., Wesolowski, L., Kale, L.: Parallel programming with migratable objects: Charm++ in practice. In: SC (2014)

15. Jetley, P., Gioachin, F., Mendes, C., Kale, L.V., Quinn, T.: Massively parallel cosmological simulations with ChaNGa. In: IEEE International Symposium on Parallel and Distributed Processing, IPDPS 2008, pp. 1–12. IEEE (2008)

16. Crusoe, M.R., Alameldin, H.F., Awad, S., Boucher, E., Caldwell, A., Cartwright, R., Charbonneau, A., Constantinides, B., Edvenson, G., Fay, S., et al.: The khmer software package: enabling efficient nucleotide sequence analysis. F1000Res. **4** (2015)

17. Bohm, E., Bhatele, A., Kale, L.V., Tuckerman, M.E., Kumar, S., Gunnels, J.A., Martyna, G.J.: Fine-grained parallelization of the Car-parrinello ab initio molecular dynamics method on the IBM blue gene/L supercomputer. IBM J. Res. Dev. **52**(1.2), 159–175 (2008). OpenAtom

18. Meineke, M.A., Vardeman, C.F., Lin, T., Fennell, C.J., Gezelter, J.D.: Oopse: an object-oriented parallel simulation engine for molecular dynamics. J. Comput. Chem. **26**(3), 252–271 (2005). OpenMD 1

19. Johansson, J., Nation, P., Nori, F.: Qutip: an open-source python framework for the dynamics of open quantum systems. Comput. Phys. Commun. **183**(8), 1760–1772 (2012). QuTiP

20. Breuer, A., Heinecke, A., Rettenberger, S., Bader, M., Gabriel, A.-A., Pelties, C.: Sustained petascale performance of seismic simulations with SeisSol on SuperMUC. In: Kunkel, J.M., Ludwig, T., Meuer, H.W. (eds.) ISC 2014. LNCS, vol. 8488, pp. 1–18. Springer, Cham (2014). https://doi.org/10.1007/978-3-319-07518-1_1

21. Docker (2015). https://www.docker.com/. Accessed Jan 2015

22. Ardagna, D., Di Nitto, E., Casale, G., Petcu, D., Mohagheghi, P., Mosser, S., Matthews, P., Gericke, A., Ballagny, C., D'Andria, F., et al.: Modaclouds: a model-driven approach for the design and execution of applications on multiple clouds. In: Proceedings of the 4th International Workshop on Modeling in Software Engineering, pp. 50–56. IEEE Press (2012)

23. Liao, S.-W.: Suif Explorer: An Interactive and Interprocedural Parallelizer. Ph.D. thesis, Stanford (2000)

24. Dave, C., Bae, H., Min, S.-J., Lee, S., Eigenmann, R., Midkiff, S.: Cetus: a source-to-source compiler infrastructure for multicores. IEEE Comput. (2009)

25. Blume, B., Eigenmann, R., Faigin, K., Grout, J., Hoeflinger, J., Padua, D., Petersen, P., Pottenger, B., Rauchwerger, L., Tu, P., Weatherford, S.: Polaris: the next generation in parallelizing compilers (1994)

26. Wilson, R.P., French, R.S., Wilson, C.S., Amarasinghe, S.P., Anderson, J.M., Tjiang, S.W.K., Liao, S.-W., Tseng, C.-W., Hall, M.W., Lam, M.S., Hennessy, J.L.: Suif: an infrastructure for research on parallelizing and optimizing compilers (1994)

27. Nugteren, C., Corporaal, H.: Bones: an automatic skeleton-based C-to-CUDA compiler for GPUs. ACM Trans. Architect. Code Optim. (TACO) **11**(4), 35 (2014)

28. Bondhugula, U., Hartono, A., Ramanujam, J., Sadayappan, P.: Pluto: a practical and fully automatic polyhedral program optimization system. In: Proceedings of the ACM SIGPLAN 2008 Conference on Programming Language Design and Implementation (PLDI 2008), Tucson, AZ, June 2008. Citeseer (2008)

29. Ansel, J.: Petabricks: a language and compiler for algorithmic choice. Master's thesis, MIT (2009)
30. Tan, W.J., Tang, W.T., Goh, R.S.M., Turner, S., Wong, W.-F.: A code generation framework for targeting optimized library calls for multiple platforms. IEEE Trans. Parallel Distrib. Syst. **26**(7) (2015)

Efficient Execution of Smart City's Assets Through a Massive Parallel Computational Model

Muhammad Usman Ashraf[(⊠)], Fathy Alboraei Eassa,
and Aiiad Ahmad Albeshri

Department of Computer Science, Faculty of Computing and IT,
King Abdulaziz University, Jeddah, Saudi Arabia
m.usmanashraf@yahoo.com, fathy55@yahoo.com,
aaalbeshri@kau.edu.sa

Abstract. Urban areas are at the forefront for upcoming wave of emerging technologies in building smart sustainable cities. These real time fashion based smart cities will be combined with physical infrastructures and services to improve the lives of its citizens. Transformation to smart city, innovation in performance increasing, data processing, planning and management will be required for smart city's assets. In order to achieve monolithic performance and data processing, an efficient parallel computational approach can bring us closer to the desired smartness in societies. In this study, we have proposed a massive parallel computational model to deal smart city's assets and maintain real time connectivity among them. This model will be considered as initiative for emerging exascale computing system which will be used to deal the applications in intelligent smart cities.

Keywords: Parallel computing · Hybrid programming · HPC
Smart cities

1 Introduction

Since last three decades, smart cities have been established and become operational in developed countries [1]. According to united nation report (UNR) [5], more than 50% people are living in urban areas and facing a wide range challenges to bring sustainability in their lives. The vision of smart cities is to improve the quality of lives in urban areas by using advance information communication technologies (ICT) [2], information processing technologies (IPT) [3] and internet of things (IoT) [4]. There are many definitions proposed for smart cities. According to Chourabi et al. [6] "*A smart sustainable city is an innovative city that uses information and communication technologies (ICTs) and other means to improve quality of life, efficiency of urban operation and services, and competitiveness, while ensuring that it meets the needs of present and future generations with respect to economic, social and environmental aspects*". According to the definition, these facts illustrates that smart cities are not only leveraging technologies but considered as a complex ecosystem where different

© ICST Institute for Computer Sciences, Social Informatics and Telecommunications Engineering 2018
R. Mehmood et al. (Eds.): SCITA 2017, LNICST 224, pp. 44–51, 2018.
https://doi.org/10.1007/978-3-319-94180-6_6

stakeholders are tightly coupled each other. Figure 1 presents the key grouping technology aspects of a complex ecosystem for a smart society [7] where different players facilitate to others by providing solutions efficiently and maintain connectivity among them. The idea of smart cities is similar to the theory of ubiquitous computing which was proposed by 'Mark Weiser' co-founder of ubiquitous computing [24, 25].

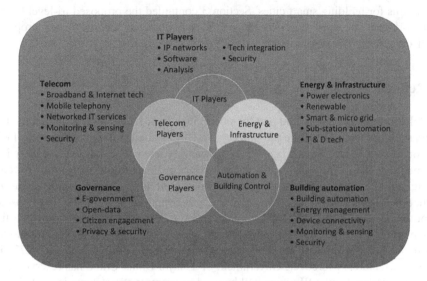

Fig. 1. Technology aspects of an ecosystem in smart city

This real-time data-driven based complex system requires a powerful computing system that can process data promptly and make the cities smarter.

In a sequel, advances in HPC play a vital role to bring smartness in urban areas [8]. Therefore, an effective usage of parallel computing can bring us closer to the desired smartness in intelligent cities [9]. For instance, usage of machine learning can discovered the solutions and make real time decisions. Similarly HPC parallel computing can be promising paradigm to deal smart city's assets.

According to HPC studies, trend is going to be changed and projected to introduce a new powerful computing system called "Exascale" which will be able to achieve ExaFlops number of calculation per second till 2020 [10, 20]. Exascale will be thousands fold increase in current Petascale system. Though Exascale is facing some tremendous challenges due to strict limitation in power consumption and increase in resources [11]. Consequently, instead of continue traditional way of increasing resources, parallel computing can be an integral part to make it possible to achieve massive performance in the system [12]. In current study, we emphasized how to achieve massive parallelism to deal digital city's assets in an efficient way. Previously, parallelism was achieved through homogenous (CPU cores) systems but now tread has been changed where data computation is performed with collaboration of CPUs and accelerated GPU devices [13, 21]. These accelerated GPU devices are very powerful that compute data in parallel using all integrated cores on it [14]. In order to program such heterogeneous computing system, a new parallel programming model is required that can achieve massive parallelism (combining coarse-grain, fine-grain and GPU computation) through inter-node and intra-node computation over a distributed cluster system [15]. Therefore we have proposed a new tri-level hybrid parallel computing model which is implementable on distributed cluster systems. Furthermore, rest of the paper is organized in such a way that, Sect. 2 describes the advances in HPC and its motivations for building smart cities. Section 3 contained the proposed tri-level hybrid framework and its work flow. Moreover, Sect. 4 depicted the impact of proposed model on smart city's assets.

2   Related Work

Parallel computing is an integral part for smart cities to provide efficient and innovative services for citizens. Therefore the pioneers in HPC started different projects to facilitate smart cities like 'Smart Japan' which was invented to catalyze its nation into sustainable growth. They planned a national strategy to promote their cities by connecting all manners of things through an intelligent ICT [31]. Keeping focus on international economics competitiveness, they are hoping to develop the first Exascale computing system in 2020 to facilitate smart cities. China also committed for their five years plan (2016–2020) to cultivating Smart Cities with smart buildings, new urbanization and smart grid initiatives. They already invested $13 billion to develop 277 city with smart features. Moreover, Government of Tianjin Binha China has reserved $2.5 billion to develop Tianhe III which will be used to promote smart societies [32, 33]. In the sequel, united state announced 160 million in 2015 for new smart cities development to deliver smart services. In september 2016, US government announced $80 million for smart societies initiative. In order to efficient processing of these smart services, they committed to deliver a powerful exascale computing system at the end of current decade which will be able to deliver 1 ExaFlops calculation per second by 20 MW power consumption [34]. Likewise, United Kingdom launched new forums for smart cities development named "Ministerial Smart Cities (MSC) and Future Cities Catapult (FCC)" [35]. The primary goal of these forums was to solve facing challenges during providing intelligent services in smart cities. Carry on promoting smart city's assets, national strategy and ICT plans in Singapore established their public & private sectors and branded as world's first smart city [36]. Singapore national strategy (SNS) planned to deliver a smart cities by addressing isolated challenges including traffic management, street lights, water management, weather forecasting, tracking and gene permutations etc. Leading to a rapid development in smart cities and efficient processing requirement, we have proposed a massive parallel computational model which will be applicable for future exascale computing systems.

3 Massive Parallel Computing Model

This section contained the proposed massive parallel computational model which is tri-level hybrid of MPI, OpenMP and CUDA. This model was developed specifically for attaining massive parallelism in heterogeneous cluster systems that can be achieved through inter-node, intra-node and accelerated GPU computation. However massive parallelism was in three levels of granularity including coarse-grain, fine-grain and finer-grain parallelism. Figure 2 depicts three levels of granularity from different computing environments.

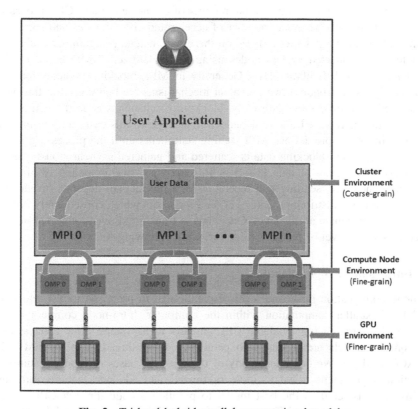

Fig. 2. Tri-level hybrid parallel computational model

In proposed massive parallel computational model, we implemented 'divide and conquer strategy algorithm' [17] that reduced 'n' problems into 'm' sub-problems and scattered over processors using different parallel programming libraries. Once processing of 'm' sub-problems was completed, the original solution for 'n' problem was obtained by gathering the solutions of 'm' sub-problems. Following this strategy, user interacts with user application through any native programming language (C/C++ or FORTRAN) where parallel computing statements are defined to be executed and broadcasted to parallel computing world. A detailed description of three parallel computing environments is given as follows:

3.1 Inter-node Computational

The first level of parallelism in our proposed model was achieved through inter-node communication. In parallel computing, our systems are not much intelligent, however programmer needs to inform the system that which statement will be executed in parallel. Once parallel computing statements are confirmed then broadcasted over all connected nodes in the system. Before scattering data over nodes, some necessary information of computer is gathered like number of connected nodes, CPU processors, available CPU threads per node, number of accelerated GPU devices and some other system configuration parameters. Based on these parameters, programmer analyze and distribute over connected system nodes using a standardized SIMD based message passing interface (MPI) library [16]. Generally in MPI, blocking (synchronous) and non-blocking (asynchronous) two prevalent mechanisms are being used to transferred and gathered from processors. Normally, blocking mechanisms is used when a strong synchronization is required due to dependency in data. In this case, the resources are reserved using some pre-defined MPI waiting statements until the processing is completed. Unlike, in non-blocking data is scattered and gathered asynchronously because there is no dependency in data [18, 19]. Resource are free immediately after data processing. Therefore, sending and receiving MPI mechanism depends on nature of data. As we are just distributing data over the processors which consequently provides coarse-grain parallelism at this level. Once data is transferred over connected nodes, it entered in second level of parallelism described in following section.

3.2 Intra-node Computational

Intra-node computation is second level of parallelism in proposed model which was thread level parallel computation within the computer. Intra-node computation was performed by parallelizing available CPU threads in a system. Now a days, many programming models are available to parallelize CPU threads like OpenMP [22], OpenACC [23] etc. We can choose any of them on the bases of model features and application requirements. Due to more optimized and advance features, ordinarily OpenMP is considered as the best model to parallelize code through CPU threads. Within outer region of OpenMP, we can define multiple OpenMP parallel sections as well as multiple directives to make fine granularity. Again, here programmer must be assured about the statements which are going to define in OpenMP parallel regions and sub sections. Once, OpenMP thread level computation is completed, we can start serial code execution at outside of OpenMP scope. According to our model, we start the third level of parallelism within the OpenMP regions and make run-time library calls.

3.3 Accelerated GPU Computational

Accelerated GPU computing is the third level of parallelism in our proposed model. Accelerated GPU devices are being used prevalently for massive parallel computation by consuming a small amount of energy. After completing second level parallelism over CPU cores, data is transferred on GPU devices to achieve finer granularity. At this stage, multiple GPU kernels are defined to which are programmed for GPU computation. Based on installed GPU structure and configuration, different parameters are defined and passed along with data through kernel call. In order to define a generic kernels, we can define 'template' class as a generic datatype, however after execution, kernel will return data with similar datatype as received. Many programming models are available now to program GPU devices including CUDA [27], OpenACC [26], OpenCL [28] and OpenMP [29] etc. Due to space limitations, we recommend kan et al. [30] for reader to find the best model for GPU programming. Based on optimization and advance features, CUDA is considered as best model for GPU programming yet. However, CUDA kernels return the results from GPU devices to Host CPU cores and complete third level of parallelism. Using divide and conquer strategy, processed data is returned to previous levels and eventually gathered by MPI master process.

4 Discussion

The urban question raised many challenges for current and emerging technologies to provide new data sources with greater spatial temporal solutions. Advances in HPC are becoming the reasons to deal such challenges to develop intelligent cities. Although, different approaches were proposed in past to deal HPC application but demand of innovative applications in smart cities imposes to rethink about introduce efficient computing technologies and models. These technologies should fulfil demand of future massive computational technology under strict constraints of energy consumption, number of cores in the system and budget as well. However, new adaptive, intelligent and energy efficient approaches are the fundamental demands of such HPC systems. In this context, we have proposed a novel massive parallel model in current study. The purpose of proposed model was to provide such platform where smart city's assets can be respond efficiently. This could be possible only through massive parallel computation in the system. This approach was tri-level hybrid of MPI, OpenMP and CUDA and provide massive parallelism through different levels. The major advantage of proposed model was that it is applicable for heterogeneous cluster systems where energy efficient accelerated GPU devices are installed in traditional CPU machines. Moreover, the proposed model was able combine all categories of parallelism including coarse-grain, fine-grain and finer-grain through inter-node, intra-node and GPU computation respectively. However, the proposed research can be an initiative HPC applications in smart cities.

5 Conclusion

Smart cities initiatives are becoming attention in marketplace to develop innovative services for the citizens through ubiquitous computing applications in urban spaces. Smart cities are required to deal a large number of citizens and intelligent devices that collect and share data in infinite ways. Such data is strictly belongs to the territory on which they are defined and perform computation through dispersed computing nodes.

In this way, parallel computing can play an integral part to compute smart city related applications. In current study, we have proposed a novel massive parallel computational model which is tri-level hybrid of MPI, OpenMP and CUDA. The proposed model is applicable for heterogamous cluster systems where a large number of nodes are connect along with accelerated GPU devices. Data computation is performed through three different parallel computing levels (coarse-grain, fine-grain and finer-grain) and complete computation efficiently. The proposed model will be considered as initiative for emerging exascale computing system. By future perspectives, tri-level hybrid model is required to implement at large level through different HPC innovative smart cities applications.

References

1. Balsamo, D., et al.: Wearable and autonomous computing for future smart cities: open challenges (2017)
2. Yaqoob, I., Hashem, I.A.T., Mehmood, Y., Gani, A., Mokhtar, S., Guizani, S.: Enabling communication technologies for smart cities. IEEE Commun. Mag. **55**(1), 112–120 (2017)
3. Lv, Z., et al.: Managing big city information based on WebVRGIS. IEEE Access **4**, 407–415 (2016)
4. Khare, P., Khare, A.: Internet of things for smart cities. In: Exploring the Convergence of Big Data and the Internet of Things, p. 96 (2017)
5. Urbanization UNFPA, 25 September 2017. http://www.unfpa.org/urbanization
6. Chourabi, H., et al.: Understanding smart cities: an integrative framework. In: Proceedings of 2012 45th Hawaii International Conference on System Science (HICSS), pp. 2289–2297. IEEE, January 2012
7. Allwinkle, S., Cruickshank, P.: Creating smart-er cities: an overview. J. Urban Technol. **18**(2), 1–16 (2011)
8. Klein, B., Koenig, R., Schmitt, G.: Managing urban resilience. Informatik-Spektrum **40**(1), 35–45 (2017)
9. Kettani, H.: Advances in high performance computing and their impact on smart cities. In: Proceedings of the 2017 International Conference on Smart Digital Environment, pp. 229–231. ACM, July 2017
10. Putman, W.M., Suarez, M.J.: GEOS Atmospheric Model: Challenges at Exascale 2017
11. Geist, A., Reed, D.A.: A survey of high-performance computing scaling challenges. Int. J. High Perform. Comput. Appl. **31**(1), 104–113 (2017)
12. Ferreira, K., et al.: Evaluating the viability of process replication reliability for exascale systems. In: Proceedings of 2011 International Conference for High Performance Computing, Networking, Storage and Analysis (SC), pp. 1–12. IEEE, November 2011
13. Mittal, S., Vetter, J.S.: A survey of CPU-GPU heterogeneous computing techniques. ACM Comput. Surv. (CSUR) **47**(4), 69 (2015)
14. Gruber, L., West, M.: GPU-accelerated Bayesian learning and forecasting in simultaneous graphical dynamic linear models. Bayesian Anal. **11**(1), 125–149 (2016)
15. Varbanescu, A.L., van Nieuwpoort, R.V., Hijma, P., Bal, H.E., Badia, R.M., Martorell, X.: Programming models for multicore and many-core computing systems. In: Programming Multi-core and Many-core Computing Systems, pp. 29–58 (2017)
16. Pajankar, A.: Message passing interface. In: Raspberry Pi Supercomputing and Scientific Programming, pp. 61–65. Apress, New York (2017)

17. Farzan, A., Nicolet, V.: Automated synthesis of divide and conquer parallelism. arXiv preprint arXiv:1701.08345 (2017)
18. Coti, C., et al.: Blocking vs. non-blocking coordinated checkpointing for large-scale fault tolerant MPI. In: Proceedings of the 2006 ACM/IEEE Conference on Supercomputing, p. 127. ACM, November 2006
19. Shi, R., et al.: Designing efficient small message transfer mechanism for inter-node MPI communication on InfiniBand GPU clusters. In: Proceedings of 2014 21st International Conference on High Performance Computing (HiPC), pp. 1–10. IEEE, December 2014
20. Ashraf, M.U., Eassa, F.E.: Hybrid model based testing tool architecture for exascale computing system. Int. J. Comput. Sci. Secur. (IJCSS) 9(5), 245 (2015)
21. Ashraf, M.U., Fouz, F., Eassa, F.A.: Empirical analysis of HPC using different programming models. Int. J. Mod. Educ. Comput. Sci. 8(6), 27 (2016)
22. Chapman, B., Jost, G., Van Der Pas, R.: Using OpenMP: Portable Shared Memory Parallel Programming, vol. 10. MIT press, Cambridge (2008)
23. Kirk, D.B., Wen-Mei, W.H.: Programming Massively Parallel Processors: A Hands-on Approach. Morgan kaufmann, San Francisco (2016)
24. Ashraf, M.U., Khan, N.A.: Software engineering challenges for ubiquitous computing in various applications. In: Proceedings of 2013 11th International Conference on Frontiers of Information Technology (FIT), pp. 78–82. IEEE, December 2013
25. Weiser, M.: Ubiquitous computing. In: ACM Conference on Computer Science, p. 418, 1994 March
26. Wienke, S., Springer, P., Terboven, C., an Mey, D.: OpenACC — First Experiences with Real-World Applications. In: Kaklamanis, C., Papatheodorou, T., Spirakis, P.G. (eds.) Euro-Par 2012. LNCS, vol. 7484, pp. 859–870. Springer, Heidelberg (2012). https://doi.org/10.1007/978-3-642-32820-6_85
27. Sanders, J., Kandrot, E.: CUDA by Example: An Introduction to General-Purpose GPU Programming, Portable Documents. Addison-Wesley Professional, Boston (2010)
28. Stone, J.E., Gohara, D., Shi, G.: OpenCL: a parallel programming standard for heterogeneous computing systems. Comput. Sci. Eng. 12(3), 66–73 (2010)
29. Li, H.F., Liang, T.Y., Lin, Y.J.: An openMP programming toolkit for hybrid CPU/GPU clusters based on software unified memory. J. Inf. Sci. Eng. 32(3), 517–539 (2016)
30. Kan, G., He, X., Ding, L., Li, J., Liang, K., Hong, Y.: A heterogeneous computing accelerated SCE-UA global optimization method using OpenMP, OpenCL, CUDA, and OpenACC. In: Water Science and Technology, p. wst2017322 (2017)
31. Obi, T., Ishmatova, D., Iwasaki, N.: Promoting ICT innovations for the ageing population in Japan. Int. J. Med. Inform. 82(4), e47–e62 (2013)
32. Smart, E.C., Cooperation, G.C.: Comparative Study of Smart Cities in Europe and China. Current Chinese Economic Report Series. Springer, Heidelberg (2014). https://doi.org/10.1007/978-3-662-46867-8
33. Dongarra, J.: Sunway TaihuLight supercomputer makes its appearance. Nat. Sci. Rev. 3(3), 265–266 (2016)
34. Simon, H.: Why we need exascale and why we won't get there by 2020. In: Optical Interconnects Conference, Santa Fe, New Mexico, May 2013
35. Moir, E., Moonen, T., Clark, G.: What Are Future Cities?: Origins, Meanings and Uses. PDF). Foresight Future of Cities Project and Future Cities Catapult (2014)
36. Nam, T., Pardo, T.A.: Conceptualizing smart city with dimensions of technology, people, and institutions. In: Proceedings of the 12th Annual International Digital Government Research Conference: Digital Government Innovation in Challenging Times, pp. 282–291. ACM, 2011 June

Power Efficiency of a SBC Based Hadoop Cluster

Basit Qureshi[1(✉)] and Anis Koubaa[1,2,3]

[1] Prince Sultan University, Riyadh, Saudi Arabia
{qureshi,akoubaa}@psu.edu.sa
[2] Gaitech Robotics, Hong kong, China
[3] CISTER, INESC-TEC, ISEP, Polytechnic Institute of Porto, Porto, Portugal

Abstract. Security, reliability and energy efficiency are key requirements in any smart cities applications. In this paper, we investigate the use of a power efficient cloud cluster composed of Single Board Computers (SBC). A Low-Cost Cloud Computing Cluster (LoC4) is designed using Raspberry Pi and Odroid Xu4 Single Board Computers. The LoC4 cluster is thoroughly tested for performance and power efficiency using TeraGen and TeraSort benchmarks that are used primarily for stress testing the Hadoop cluster. Results show that Odroid Xu4 computers consume more energy compared to RPi computers, however the overall energy consumption in the cluster for completion of a task was 91% and 72% better for Odroid Xu4 with workloads of 800 MB and 400 MB respectively.

Keywords: Hybrid cloud computing · Low cost cluster · Power efficiency

1 Introduction

In recent times, Cloud computing technology is widely being adopted by businesses and organization. A major motivation for this change is the decrease in maintenance of infrastructure, deployment and management overheads as well as overall reduced operating costs. Energy consumption in data centers is a major concern for green computing research. NRDA [1] estimated in 2013, in US alone, the data centers consumed 91 billion kilowatts hours (kWh) of energy, which accounts to 5% of total energy consumed per year. It is estimated to increase by 141 billion kWh every year until 2020, costing businesses $13 billion annually in electricity bills and emitting nearly 100 million metric tons of carbon pollution per year. Rightly so, the environmental impact of maintaining large computational infrastructure and data centers is a big concern, prompting the need for research in "greener" technologies for data centers.

Apache Hadoop framework [2] is a popular platform commonly used for analysis of data intensive operations and is widely used for research in Big Data analysis where large volumes of data cannot be analyzed using traditional technologies. Hadoop's Map/Reduce [3] has become a benchmark tool for comparing performance of various architectures for compute, network, storage and IO operations [7, 8]. Recent works have provided an opportunity for further investigating efficiency of Map/Reduce workloads in a Hadoop clusters. Authors in [4, 5] and [6] outline the need for understanding the

© ICST Institute for Computer Sciences, Social Informatics and Telecommunications Engineering 2018
R. Mehmood et al. (Eds.): SCITA 2017, LNICST 224, pp. 52–60, 2018.
https://doi.org/10.1007/978-3-319-94180-6_7

potential for energy saving in MapReduce Jobs in the context of CPU-bound, IO-bound or network-bound workloads. Tiwari et al. in [7] argue that varying MapReduce parameters have a significant impact on computation performance and energy consumption for typical MapReduce workloads.

On the other hand, deploying private cloud requires large investment in addition to costs incurred due to energy usage, maintenance and software upgrades etc. For small healthcare organizations and universities, it is cost abhorrent to establish expensive datacenters and maintain these. Recently, researchers in academia have used low cost and low power cloud clusters composed of Single Board Computers (SBC) [9, 10]. Baun [9] developed a Hadoop based cluster using 8 Raspberry Pi Model 2B Computers. Qureshi et al. in [10] utilize a Hadoop cluster composed of 20 Raspberry Pi 2B and 20 Odroid Xu-4 computers for image processing applications.

In this paper, we investigate power consumption behavior of Hadoop Map/Reduce jobs utilizing the LoC4 cluster. LoC4 is an affordable and low-cost cloud computing cluster for research in universities and academic institutions. The contributions of this work are in two folds. We first describe the design and implementation details for the LoC4 cluster as well as deployment settings and parameters. Second, we extensively test this cluster and measure power consumption for medium and heavy intensity workloads. We also study the impact of heavy workloads on the two types of SBCs used in this cluster in terms of power efficiency and, completion time of various stages of applied workloads.

The rest of the paper is organized as follows. Section 2 describes the LoC4 cluster. Section 3 presents the power efficiency results of the cluster followed by conclusions and discussion in Sect. 4.

2 LoC4: SBC Based Cluster

A single-board computer (SBC) is a complete computer built on a single circuit board [9, 10]. A SBC incorporates microprocessor(s), memory, I/O as well as host of other features required by a functional computer. In this work, we build a cluster using Raspberry Pi Model 3B [12] and Hard Kernel Odroid Xu-4 [11] SBCs.

Figure 1 shows the LoC4 cluster. The LoC4 cluster is composed of 11 SBCs of while five RPi Model 3B and six Odroid Xu-4 computers are interconnected with power supplies, network cables, Storage modules, connectors and cases. All the Raspberry Pi computers are equipped with 16 GB Class-10 SD cards for primary bootable storage. The Odroid Xu-4 devices are equipped with 32 GB eMMCv5.0 modules. The Odroid Xu-4 s are housed in a compact layout racks using M2/M3 spacers, nuts and screws. The Raspberry Pi 3B's are housed in cases and connected to the rest of the cluster. Currently each Raspberry Pi computer is individually supplied by 2.5 Amp power supply; each Odroid Xu-4 computer is supplied by a 4.0 Amp power supply that provides ample power for running each node.

Each SBC's network interface relates to a Cat6e Ethernet cable through the RJ-45 Ethernet connector. All Ethernet cables connect to a 16-port Cisco switch which in turn is connected to the university network equipment. The size of the cluster can be easily scaled by introducing a core switch that connects to the 16-port switch. Additional

Fig. 1. The LoC4 cluster with 6 Xu4 (Rack mounted) and 5 RPi 3B in cases.

nodes can be included in the network configuration scaling the size of the cluster. For Hadoop deployment, one of the Xu-4 SBC is used as the master node whereas the rest of the nodes server as slaves' nodes. We compare the performance of Xu-4 sub cluster (composed of five Xu-4 nodes) with RPi sub cluster also composed of five RPi 3B nodes. The purchase cost for all equipment for the LoC4 Cluster was as low as $1179.

Hadoop version 2.6.2 was installed due to availability of YARN daemon which improves the performance of the map-reduce jobs in the cluster. To optimize the performance of these Clusters, `yarn-site.xml` and `Mapred-site.xml` were configured with 512 MB of resource size allocation. The primary reason for this setting is the limited amount of RAM available in the RPi Model 3B. The Raspbian operating system as well as the shared GPU memory bus consume over 200 MB or RAM out of a total of 1 GB. The default container size on the Hadoop Distributed File System (HDFS) is 128 MB. Each SBC node was assigned a static IPv4 address based on the configuration and all slave nodes were registered in the Master node. For YARN Resource manager, we allocated up to 4 cores which means up to 4 containers can execute per node (one container per core). The replication factor for HDFS is 2 which means only two copies of each block would be kept on the file system.

3   Power Efficiency of LoC4

As mentioned earlier in our cluster setup, we use a single SBC to run the master node of the cluster, which executes the namenode as well as the YARN ResourceManager Hadoop applications. The slave nodes execute the datanodes as well as the YARN NodeManager tasks. In order to avoid influence of the namenode, we attach the power measurement equipment to the clusters slave nodes only and collect power consumption data. The WattsUp Pro.net[1] meter is capable of recording power consumption in terms of watts, each reading is collected every second and is logged in the meter's onboard memory. The meters are initialized 10 s before each TeraGen and TeraSort job is initiated and stops reading 10 s after the job is completed. In addition to power consumption readings, we also periodically measured (every minute) the CPU temperature (Celsius) for both RPi's as well as Odroid Xu-4 boards in the cluster. Average Power Consumption in terms of kilo watts per hour W_t, can be given by the following equation:

$$W_t = \Delta t \cdot \frac{E}{kWh} \tag{1}$$

Where is $\Delta t = t_f - t_s$ the interval time from start of the task to its completion, E is the Energy consumed in terms of Watts as recorded using the Wattsup meter.

We study the power consumption on LoC4 cluster using two types of applications widely used in benchmarking of Hadoop clusters:

- The TeraGen is light to middle weight workload benchmark that stresses CPU and IO (Network, Storage etc.) in the cluster
- TeraSort benchmark gives intensive workload stressing CPU and IO (heavy workload).

In this experimental setup, we isolate RPi devices from Xu4 devices and study the performance of the two using medium workload (TeraGen) and heavy workload (TeraSort) benchmarks with 100 MB, 200 MB, 400 MB and 800 MB datasets. The experiments are repeated 10 times for each run to obtain a weighted average.

Figure 2(a) shows the comparison of power consumption as well as CPU Temperature for both clusters for the TeraGen using 800 MB datasets. It can be noted, the power consumption for Xu4 devices peaks at 18.2 watts whereas RPi devices consumes at most 12.1 watts. The temperature on RPi SBC mostly stays within the range 29–32C, on the other hand Odroid Xu-4 SBC's are equipped with a cooling fan. At 45 °C the fan turns on due to the built-in hardware settings yielding in increased power consumption on the Odroid Xu-4. Since TeraGen is IO bound job, initially mappers start executing and writing to the HDFS, as the progress continues some of the mappers complete the tasks assigned. Consequently, we observe reduction in the overall power consumption of the cluster, this effect can be clearly observed in Fig. 2(a) with 800 MB Data size for both clusters.

Figure 2(b) shows the power consumption for both clusters when TeraSort is used. We observe that TeraSort requires more time for completion. Initially mappers read through the input files generated by TeraGen and stored in HDFS, as the TeraSort shuffle process for keys and values initiates, we observe increased power consumption which continues until the mappers as well as majority of reduce jobs complete. As the mappers continue to complete the tasks, the incoming results start processing in the

---

[1] Wattsup: https://www.wattsupmeters.com/secure/products.php?pn=0.

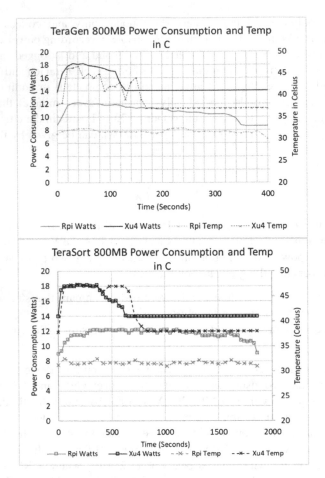

Fig. 2. Power consumption and temperature against execution time for (a) TeraGen with 800 MB dataset (b) TeraSort with 800 MB dataset.

reduce jobs. Before the completion of all map functions, the reduce functions initiate sorting and summarizing process requiring CPU as well as IO resources towards completion of the tasks.

We plot the percentage of map and reduce completion against the power consumption for RPi devices with and 800 MB data size in Fig. 3(a) and for Xu4 devices in Fig. 3(b). As can be seen, the percentage of maps and reduces completed correlates with the power consumption. In particular, when the map and reduce complete, the power consumption decreases therefore highlighting underutilized nodes in the clusters. Both TeraGen and TeraSort exhibit different power consumption. TeraSort on both sets of SBCs has a relatively long phase of higher power consumption from initialization of map jobs until about 80% of map jobs completion indicating high CPU utilization. Afterwards, the power consumption decreases slightly fluctuating while both map and reduce jobs are executing in parallel. Finally, the power consumption steadies with minor tails and peaks in the plot towards reduce jobs completion. We observe that the trends for power consumption relevant to task completion are similar for larger data sizes used in this study. Table 1 shows the comparison of completion times for various TeraGen and TeraSort jobs. It also shows the average power consumption for TeraSort Tasks in terms of kWh.

It is difficult to monitor and normalize the energy consumption for every test run over a period of time. We observed that the MapReduce jobs in particular, tend to consume more energy initially while map tasks are created and distributed across the cluster, while a reduction in power consumption is observed towards the end of the job. For the computation of power consumption, we assumed max power utilization (stress mode) for each job, during a test run.

4   Related Works

A leading incentive for adoption of cloud computing is the reduction of installation and operational cost for small businesses and enterprises. Apache Hadoop has proven to be an effective platform using the MapReduce framework allowing quick and parallel processing of data. Setting up cloud infrastructure in universities could be a very costly endeavor. Hadoop Clusters built using Single Board Computers have been presented in recent research work.

In 2016, Baun in [9] presented the design of a cluster geared towards academic research and student scientific projects building a 8-node Raspberry Pi Model 2B cluster. They develop this cluster and conduct a thorough study of quality of service parameters such as CPU execution time, Memory and IO performance etc. Qureshi et al. in [10] develop a 40 node cluster using Odroid Xu4 devices and Raspberry 2B SBCs. They utilize this cluster for image analysis using popular image processing libraries. Earlier in Tso et al. [13], researchers built a small-scale data center consisting of 56 RPi Model B boards. The Glasgow Raspberry Pi Cloud offers a cloud computing testbed including virtualization management tools. In 2013, Whitehorn [14] presented the first ever implementation of a Hadoop cluster using five Raspberry Pi Model B nodes.

Gomez in [15] use Raspberry Pi Computers as sensors in an industrial environment. They were able connect various SBCs over the network to collect sensory information. In 2016, Fernandes et al. [16] used Odroid Xu4 devices for an image processing application for matching patterns in different sketches. In both of these works, researchers demonstrate the benefit of using SBC's to accomplish application specific tasks.

To the best of our knowledge, there is a lack of literature in extensive study for evaluation of power consumption in SBC based Hadoop clusters. In this paper we present a Hadoop cluster using two kinds of SBCs, Raspberry Pi 3B and Odroid Xu4 devices. We extensively study the power consumption for data and compute intensive TeraSort and contract the average energy consumption for both sets of devices.

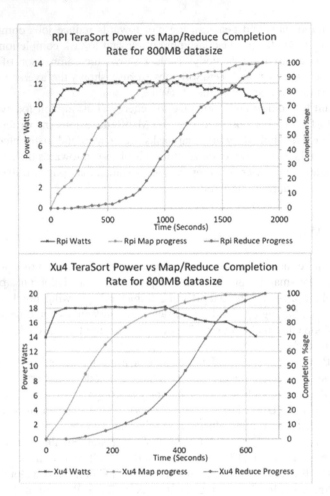

Fig. 3. TeraSort power consumption with 800 MB dataset size for (a) RPi (b) Xu4.

Table 1. Task completion time and average power consumption against various workloads for SBC devices in LoC4

	Workload (MB)	Task completion time (seconds)		Average power consumption for TeraSort task (kWh)
		TeraGen	TeraSort	
RPi devices	100	52.8	210.1	0.68 E-3
	400	122.3	681.3	2.23 E-3
	800	343.9	1873.2	6.13 E-3
Xu4 devices	100	13.2	59.2	0.29 E-3
	400	58.1	325.9	1.61 E-3
	800	124.3	692.7	3.42 E-3

5   Conclusions

In this paper, we investigate the use of SBC in a low-cost cloud computing cluster. We consider two kinds of popular platforms Raspberry Pi 3B and Odroid Xu-4 using ARM Cortex Processors. The LoC4 cluster was deployed comprising of 11 SBCs interconnected in a network topology over a gigabit Ethernet. Hadoop was installed on the cluster with configuration to suit the SBC's memory and storage requirements. Results from these studies show that while SBC based clusters are energy efficient overall, the operation cost to performance ratio can vary based on the workload. The Odroid Xu4 computers consume more energy compared to RPi computers, however the overall energy consumption for completion of a task was 91% and 72% better for workloads of 800 MB and 400 MB respectively, in favor of Xu4 Computers. We conclude that, for light to middle workload applications, SBC clusters are a very cost effective and power efficient solution for deployment in hybrid cloud environments.

Acknowledgements. This work is partially funded by the Robotics and Internet of Things Unit (RIoTU) at Prince Sultan University.

References

1. Data Center Efficiency Assessment: Scaling up energy efficiency across the data center industry, Natural Resources Defense Council, August 2014. https://www.nrdc.org/sites/default/files/data-center-efficiency-assessment-IP.pdf
2. The Apache Hadoop Project, 2017. http://www.hadoop.org
3. Feller, E., Ramakrishnan, L., Morin, C.: Performance and energy efficiency of big data applications in cloud environments: a Hadoop case study. J. Parallel Distrib. Comput. **79–80**, 80–89 (2015)
4. Conejero, J., Rana, O., Burnap, P., Morgan, J., Caminero, B., Carrión, C.: Analyzing hadoop power consumption and impact on application QoS. Future Gener. Comput. Syst. **55**, 213–223 (2016)
5. Krish, K.R., Iqbal, M.S., Rafique, M.M., Butt, A.R.: Towards energy awareness in hadoop. In: 4th International Workshop on Network-Aware Data Management, New Orleans, LA, pp. 16–22 (2014)
6. Tiwari, N., Bellur, U., Sarkar, S. Indrawan, M.: Identification of critical parameters for MapReduce energy efficiency using statistical Design of Experiments. In: 2016 IEEE International Parallel and Distributed Processing Symposium Workshops (IPDPSW), Chicago, IL, pp. 1170–1179 (2016)
7. Bilal, K., et al.: A taxonomy and survey on green data center networks. Future Gener. Comput. Syst. **36**, 189–208 (2014)
8. Deng, X., Wu, D., Shen, J., He, J.: Eco-Aware Online Power Management and Load Scheduling for Green Cloud Datacenters. IEEE Syst. J. **10**(1), 78–87 (2016)
9. Baun, C.: Mobile Clusters of Single Board Computers: An Option for Providing Resources to Student Projects and Researchers. SpringerPlus PMC. Web. **5,** 360 (2016)
10. Qureshi, B., Javed, Y., Koubâa, A., Sriti, M.-F., Alajlan, M.: Performance of a low-cost hadoop cluster for image analysis in cloud robotics environment. Procedia Comput. Sci. **82**, 90–98 (2016)

11. Odroid Xu-4 detailed specifications. http://www.hardkernel.com/main/products/prdt_info. php?g_code=G143452239825. Accessed 10 Oct 2016
12. The Raspberry Foundation. https://www.raspberrypi.org. Accessed 20 Nov 2015
13. Tso, F.P., White, D.R., Jouet, S., Singer, J., Pezaros, D.P.: The Glasgow raspberry pi cloud: a scale model for cloud computing infrastructures. In: IEEE 33rd International Conference on Distributed Computing Systems Workshops (ICDCSW). IEEE, Philadelphia, PA, USA, pp 108–112 (2013)
14. Whitehorn, J.: Raspberry flavored Hadoop. http://www.idatasci.com/uploads/1/4/6/6/ 14661274/jamiewhitehorn_raspberryflavouredhadoop_annotated.pdf
15. Gómez, A., Cuiñas, D., Catalá, P., Xin, L., Li, W., Conway, S., Lack, D.: Use of single board computers as smart sensors in the manufacturing industry. Procedia Eng. **132**, 153–159 (2015)
16. Fernandes, S.L., Bala, G.J.: ODROID XU4 based implementation of decision level fusion approach for matching computer generated sketches. J. Comput. Sci. **16**, 217–224 (2016)

Internet of Vehicles: Integrated Services over Vehicular Ad Hoc Networks

Hasan Ali Khattak[1]($\boxtimes$), Rasheed Hussain[2], and Zoobia Ameer[3]

[1] COMSATS Institute of Information Technology, Islamabad 44500, Pakistan
hasan.alikhattak@comsats.edu.pk
[2] Innopolis University, Innopolis 420500, Russia
r.hussain@innopolis.ru
[3] Shaheed Benazir Bhutto Women University, Peshawar 25500, Pakistan
zoobia.ameer@sbbwu.edu.pk

Abstract. Internet of Things (IoT) and Vehicular Ad hoc NETwork (VANET) based clouds are two emerging technologies and offer myriad of new applications in many domains of smart cities including, but not limited to, smart infrastructure and intelligent transportation. Integration of these technologies will enrich the applications and services space that will eventually stimulate the proliferation of these technologies. Nonetheless, due to their different requirements, environments, and networking models, such integration will need definitions of new communication paradigms and frameworks. To fill the voids, in this paper, we propose an architectural framework to integrate vehicular clouds (VC) and IoT, referred to as IoT-VC, to realize new services and applications that include IoT management through vehicular clouds. We particularly focus on smart city applications controlled, managed, and operated through vehicular networks. This theoretical work provides initial insights into data management in such diverse paradigm with resource constrained environment. Furthermore, we also discuss research challenges in such integration that include data acquisition, data quality, security, privacy, coverage, and so forth. These challenges must be addressed for realization of IoT-VC paradigm.

Keywords: Vehicular clouds · Internet of Things · Future internet
Vehicular social networks

1 Introduction

The emerging phenomenon of Internet of Things (IoT) has caught eyes of academia, businesses, industries, and investors a like. The main idea behind the concept of IoT is to remove the distinction layers among different objects and enable them to communicate with each other and the Internet regardless of the underlying platform and/or hardware. Similarly, concept of a connected vehicle

© ICST Institute for Computer Sciences, Social Informatics and Telecommunications Engineering 2018
R. Mehmood et al. (Eds.): SCITA 2017, LNICST 224, pp. 61–73, 2018.
https://doi.org/10.1007/978-3-319-94180-6_8

with access to Internet is replaced by a more intelligent car, equipped with a swarm of sensors, capable of communicating with other cars through vehicle-to-vehicle (V2V), vehicle-to-infrastructure (V2I), vehicle-to-cloud (V2C), and generally vehicle-to-X (V2X) communication. These communication paradigms are realized through vehicular ad hoc network (VANET) and a recent breed of VANET referred to as VANET-based clouds (VC) [1,2]. Although academia and industry has achieved remarkable research results in VANET; however, there are still challenges that need to be addressed before bringing this technology to the huge masses of vehicles. These challenges include, but not limited to, efficient resource utilization, big traffic data processing, mobility, connectivity, and so forth. For instance, normally the cars are parked in a parking lot for tens of hours which is equivalent to waste of computing, communication, and storage resources (should there be high-end vehicles). These resources could be used elsewhere and could earn revenue as well. Cloud computing is an ideal solution for such phenomena where either parked or mobile vehicles can rent out their resources, can use public cloud, and so forth. This new paradigm not only improves the resource utilization, but also enhances the applications and services sphere for intelligent transportation systems. To date, a number of services have been proposed that leverage vehicles as both services providers and consumers simultaneously, for instance data center at a parking lot [3,4], traffic information dissemination [5], vehicle witness as a service [6], visual traffic information dissemination [7], and public transport as gateways [8], to name a few.

There are range of applications and services offered by IoT, VANET, and VC that add values to our daily lives from comfort, ease of access, and safety perspective [1,9]. For instance IoT enables the realization of smart home, smart industry, and generally smartX [10], whereas VANET includes both safety and infotainment applications that enhance driving experience of the consumers. The full scale deployment of these two emerging technologies is still on its way; nevertheless, prototype implementations of both IoT and VANET have been tested by different service providers. Among other challenges, the impeded momentum in the deployment of VANET and IoT is, at least partially, caused by security and privacy issues [11–13].

VANET is based on dedicated short range communication (DSRC)[1] standard whereas IoT can opt from a bewildering choice of connectivity technologies that include well-known Zigbee, 3/4/5 G, Bluetooth, WiFi, RPL, MQTT, CoAP, Z-wave, 6LowPAN, NFC, Sigfox, Neul, and low power radio-based wide area network (LoRaWAN [14]). It is worth noting that LoRaWAN is used specifically for low power radio and long-range coverage. Therefore, LoRaWAN is ideal choice for applications that operate on long range.

There are unprecedented applications realized through IoT and the currently available management platform is android that uses Internet [9]. Since LoRaWAN operates on long range and does not need Internet connectivity, therefore in order to enhance the robustness, ease of access, safety, and personalization, it would be convenient to operate, configure, and manage the IoT services

---

[1] http://www.etsi.org/technologies-clusters/technologies/intelligent-transport/dsrc.

in an ad hoc manner. To this end, vehicular networking and VC paradigms, because of their communication setup, are ideal to integrate with IoT paradigm for service exchange, service management, and functionality enhancement.

In this paper, we propose architectural framework and design of the IoT-VC integration and envision new exciting services and applications realized through IoT-VC. We focus on the abstract level integration of these two technologies and propose a blueprint framework that will enable IoT and VC to exchange data for applications and services in a cross-platform environment. Furthermore, we also outline the envisioned applications and the research challenges faced by such integration.

The rest of the paper is organized as follows: In Sect. 2 we outline the related work followed by our proposed framework in Sect. 3 and research challenges in Sect. 4. Section 5 concludes the paper.

2   Related Work

Vehicular networks and IoT have a rich literature that covers most of the implementation aspects, services, applications, security, privacy, and data exchange, to name a few [9]. Today major car manufacturers are equipping their high-end vehicles with smart applications that are used for smart parking, cooperative cruise control, emergency warning, infotainment, partial autonomy, and so forth. The real deployment of VANET is still awaited; however, remarkable research results have already been achieved in the field of VANET. A new breed of VANET-based clouds has also been proposed to enhance the application space of pure vehicular networks [2,5]. VANET-based clouds enhance the application space of the traditional VANET and leverage the rich resources of the cloud computing for intelligent transportation and resource management in general. With VANET-based clouds more applications and services like cooperation-as-a-Service, vehicle witness as a service [6], traffic violation monitoring through VANET-clouds [15], traffic information dissemination [5], Intelligent parking system through IoT [16], and Smart Traffic Light System (STLS) [17] to name a few. Furthermore the challenges faced by this breed of VANET has been outlined in detail by Yan et al. [18].

Recently, efforts have been made to look into the possibility of using IoT services in vehicular networks. Alam et al. proposed Social Internet of Vehicles which is the extension of social IoT for vehicular networks. However, their framework does not take into account the integration of IoT and VANET for data exchange, applications and extended services [19]. It is also worth noting that IoT is no longer used only for data exchange but also the 'things' act as nodes that interact socially. Ortiz et al. discussed the clustered structure for social IoT in detail and also outlined the future research challenges [20].

Moreover, several emerging networking paradigms have been discussed in literature such as Software Defined Networks [21] in order to provide flexibility, location awareness for the cloud, scalability in order to meet the needs of the future Vehicular Cloud based services and programmability in order to manage

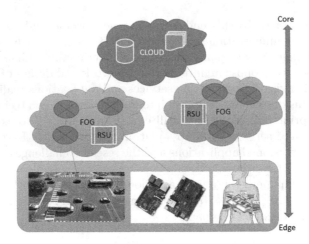

Fig. 1. Vehicular Fog: Internet of Things meet Vehicular Cloud

the network in an agile fashion. Internet in general and Cloud specifically is prone to latency, the data generated by vehicular networks is sent to the cloud for analysis, further decisive actions from cloud may get delayed which can be a problem in certain time critical scenarios. Several IoT-VC applications require cloud to respond in a timely manner in order to better cater the scenarios such as real-time traffic diversion in case of emergency situations. Fog Computing proposes that data generated by IoT be processed as near to the edge nodes as possible in order to achieve better through put of the overall system, thus overcoming the inherent latency of cloud computing and laying off the burden on core network as shown in Fig. 1. In case of Vehicles, Roadside Units (RSUs) can be leveraged to gather the data generated by Vehicular Clouds and process it locally and the analyzed data may be disseminated in a more robust manner.

Today's high-end vehicles are hosts to myriad of sensors and actuators that produce huge amount of data. Furthermore, these data are used for variety of purposes and applications. In its essence, vehicular networks and VANET-based clouds are ideal to integrate with IoT in order to get full potential of the sensory data from these technologies, and use IoT-generated data in VANET-based clouds. Nonetheless, this integration will need crafting of new middle-ware frameworks, protocol (re)design, writing new drivers that are able to talk to different technologies, and so forth. To fill the voids, we propose architectural level framework to integrate IoT with VC for huge amount of data acquisition, service and applications enhancement. Furthermore, we also outline the research challenges associated with the integration.

3 Integrated Services over IoT-VC

3.1 Baseline, LoRa, and DSRC

Vehicular clouds and networks consist of vehicular nodes (more precisely on-board units - OBUs), roadside units (RSUs), registration and management authorities and operates on DSRC/IEEE 802.11p standard. Vehicles communicate with each other, and with external entities through infrastructure. On the other hand, IoT has been realized through many technologies such as Zigbee, Bluetooth, WiFi, and so forth; however, due to the nature of our applications, we use LoRaWAN as an underlying technology for the realization of services and applications of IoT. There are twofold purposes of using LoRaWAN, it is long range and also energy-efficient. Furthermore, LoRaWAN infrastructure is relatively easy to deploy as compared to its other counterparts. Additionally, it meets the key requirements of IoT such as secure bi-directional communication, mobility and localization services and it provides seamless interoperability among smart things without complex installations. LoRaWAN network architecture usually follows star-of-stars topology where LoRaWAN gateway serves as bridge between end-things (LoRa Arduino, sensors) and a back-end network server. The Things Network has already taken initiative to deploy IoT through LoRaWAN [14]. The general baseline layered architecture of IoT is given in Fig. 2. There are two kinds of gateways in this IoT setup. 'Things' connect to the LoRaWAN gateways whereas these gateways connect to the central network routers. The routers are connected to both internet and the backend servers for data acquisition, service delivery and a number of other components. In order

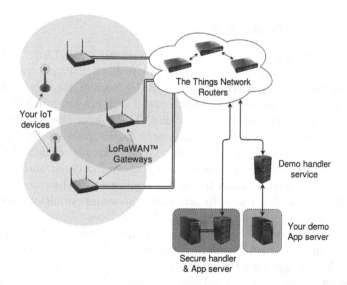

Fig. 2. The Things Network Reference architecture with LoRa (https://www.thethingsnetwork.org/)

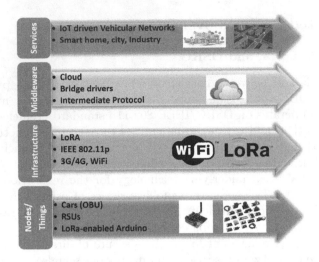

Fig. 3. Vertical IoTVC service architecture

to lay ground for our framework, the vertical service architecture for integration is shown in Fig. 3. It can be observed from the figure that in order to realize the IoT-VC applications and services, sensors and other nodes have to use both VANET infrastructure and the LoRa-based infrastructure to offload data to the cloud and receive information back from the cloud. This setup serves several-fold purposes such as increase in connectivity, multiple channels for data sharing, quality of service, and priority based communication, to name a few.

3.2   Architectural Framework

We propose a generalized infrastructural framework for IoTVC. The goal of the integration is to make sure that nodes from both IoT and vehicular networks/VC interact and share data in a seamless manner for service exchange. From bird's view, there are 3 main components of such integration, VC paradigm, IoT paradigm, and Middle-ware components. The role of the first two components is clear; however, the major component is middle-ware that is realized through the bridges, gateways, and drivers. General layout of the IoTVC design is given in Fig. 4, where IoT-generated data is stored in cloud and shared with vehicular network as well. In order to use IoT application and services in VANET through OBUs and RSUs, inter-protocol conversion and definitions are needed. It is worth noting that, as shown in Fig. 4, IoT services can be managed either directly from VANET or through clouds depending on the nature of applications. For instance a direct control of a home appliance would not need communication with cloud whereas querying the energy usage statistics at home would need a communication channel to the cloud in order to download the required statistics. In our scenario, we use Vehicles using Clouds (VuC) framework from Vehicular clouds [2].

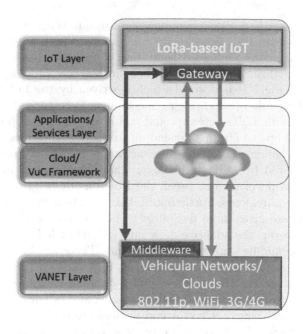

Fig. 4. Generic functional level design of IoTVC

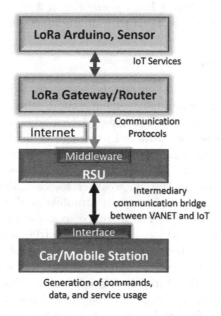

Fig. 5. Communication mechanism of IoTVC

The detailed communication mechanism for integrated IoT-VC is given in Fig. 5. We regard the RSUs as interfaces and bridges for LoRa gateways. In other words, the communication from VC paradigm will be encapsulated, tunneled, and/or converted to the LoRa communication format. With 3G capability, the bridging component in RSU can directly communicate with LoRa gateway and then route message to the intended node. Furthermore, in our extended work, we intend to formalize the security mechanism for this process as well. The upper half of the Fig. 5 is IoT world which is driven by the LoRa technology. Another important role of the bridging mechanism is to tune the communication from VC towards LoRa gateways and end-nodes. LoRa supports data rate ranging from 0.3 kbps to 50 kbps depending upon the transmission range and LoRa frequency channels. The transmission range is inversely proportional to the data rate offered by LoRa technology. Therefore, it gives more opportunity to application developers to tweak the RoRa modules in accordance with the application requirements. Furthermore, this variation in both transmission range and data rate gives more flexibility to host a diverse range of different applications. However, the adaptive data rate (ADR) of IoT end devices make the design of the middle-ware more challenging. There are basically 3 classes of end-devices in LoRaWAN (class A, class B, and class C) targeting different application requirements. These classes exhibit different characteristics on MAC layer. Communication mode, power usage, latency, and uplink/downlink capacity differentiate these classes. Class A end devices are the most energy-efficient devices at the expense of reduced data rate, class B devices are slightly moderate whereas class C devices consume more energy as compared to class A and B. However, class C has the lowest latency among all 3 classes. Therefore, LoRa can host a wide range of applications with different sets of requirements.

3.3   Application Scenarios

With the integrated IoT-VC, we target personalized IoT and envision applications that cover smart home management, smart office, smart industry, and intelligent transportation system (ITS). We particularly aim at controlling home appliances (operated based on LoRa IoT) through vehicular clouds. It is worth noting that our framework is generic; however, in our implementation phase, we target only personalized IoT. The integrated IoT-VC has applications in ITS, e-health care, smart grid, navigation, weather forecast, diagnostics, and office domains. In the smart home environment, a mobile application can be used to manage the home IoT network. For instance, controlling the temperature at home, operating washing machine, checking on refrigerator, and opening the door of garage. There are other such operations that can be performed through the integrated IoT-VC. On the other hand, through IoT network at home, one can know the current traffic situation and efficiently calculate route based on the current traffic conditions. Such information will not only save the time of commute, but also save fuel and thus-forth providing economical advantages. Furthermore, information about different sales in the market, favorite restaurants, location-based services, shopping centers, parking lots, and so forth can also be realized through IoT network. To this end, a rich spectrum of applications can be realized through such integration.

Another interesting application use case is intelligent traffic lights (ITL) which along with Vehicular Cloud and IoT leverages software defined network (SDN). In ITL, various kind of sensors are installed with Road Side Units (RSU) that continuously monitor the presence of vehicles and pedestrians, and based on the measurements, collected and/or aggregated data is sent to the gateway nodes where it is used to coordinate with the neighboring signals to maintain a constant and efficient traffic flow. Moreover, these RSUs are also capable of generating appropriate notifications in case of any incident which might be helpful for other vehicles, and if needed this analytics can be used to modify the traffic flow as well. While this information is useful locally, it can also be propagated to the cloud for long term storage and analysis in order to provide better insights on transportation needs of a smart city. Besides, intelligent parking lot management can also be realized through the collected data from different vehicles parked or mobile on the road.

4 Research Challenges

The integration of VANET-based clouds and IoT, despite of exciting applications and services, has to address key challenges that may keep the investors and key stakeholder at bay from deploying the integrated technology. Some of the research challenges are outline below:

4.1 Functional Challenges

One of the main challenges of integration is the difference in standard specifications. We have assumed LoRaWAN for IoT, and VANET follows WAVE/DSRC standard. The handshake negotiation, protocol selection, data rate, and other such factors will determine the performance of the underlying application. However, the diverse nature of both technologies advocate for in-depth analysis of the trade off among the aforementioned factors. To this end, different applications will exhibit different behavior and thus-forth require different set of parameters. The adaptation to such dynamic behavior will be a challenge for service providers and have to be dealt with in a reliable way, keeping in mind the consumer satisfaction. There exist different mechanisms that cope with the resource utilization and diversity in IoT environment [22]; however, the heterogeneity exhibited by the integrated IoT-VC calls for more insight obtain a trade-off solutions that are acceptable to both consumers and service providers.

4.2 Data Acquisition

Both VANET-based clouds and IoT generate different kind of data with relatively different goals, and with different speed and volume. Therefore, data acquisition across the different platforms will need smart pre-processing of the data locally. It is worth noting that in VANET-based clouds, there are different kind of data generated at different levels, such as in-car sensors generate data that could be useful for both owner of the car and the neighboring vehicles and auto-manufacturer for diagnostics. On the other hand, data generated by vehicles and shared with neighbors can be humongous and can be rendered as big traffic data (BTD). To be more precise, depending on the traffic regime (dense, moderate, and sparse), the data generated by each car and shared with different single-hop and multi-hop neighbors (such as beacon messages in the order of milliseconds [23]) could be so huge for the processing power of the individual vehicle. Therefore crowd-sourcing and/or offloading the data processing to the cloud could be a viable solution. Sharing VANET-generated data (which is fast and huge in volume) may have to be compressed before sharing in the IoT environment. Furthermore, the data may also need some refinement and aggregation because of the resource constraints in IoT. Similarly, using IoT data in VANET (inside car, to be more precise) must be well-presented and application specific. In our use-case environment, i.e. smart home IoT management through VANET, will require application level data sharing with in-car network and commands directed from in-car network to the IoT network at home.

4.3　Security and Privacy

Security and privacy are of prime importance in the realization of the integrated IoT-VC. It is to be noted that in personal IoT networks, the data generated can be highly privacy-sensitive and thus-forth requires privacy enhancing mechanisms for both data at rest and on the wire. Without effective measures for privacy preservation, the data shared from home IoT environment may easily cause user privacy abuse. Nonetheless, this requirement is conflicting with performance of the application. Usually privacy-preserving data sharing schemes affect the granularity of data and therefore decrease the performance. To this end, data sharing among IoT and VANET should not only be secure, but also privacy-aware, and trade off between granularity of data and performance of the application has to be made. Moreover, context aware privacy preservation techniques need to be employed in order to enable the vehicular clouds to adapt to the changing environment. Fog Computing can play an important role in preserving privacy because by design the data generated by the edge nodes is processed as near to edge nodes as possible. In case of Vehicular Clouds, Roadside Units (RSUs) can be leveraged to analyze the data locally and thus insuring that the data is not being propagated in the whole network. These roadside units may be enabled in such a way that they employ industry standard privacy preserving techniques.

4.4　Data Quality

Recent industrial advancements have enabled us to leverage the potential of millions of low cost, easily available sensors which are mostly left unattended in order to monitor certain parameters in a given environment for long periods of time. This puts question on the quality of data that these sensors are transmitting. While realizing an IoT-VC, this problem becomes more important as the mobile nature of Vehicular Clouds makes it difficult to keep check on provenance. In order to avoid such problems, it will be required to have checks in place for consistency and calibration of not only vehicular sensors but also the overall middle-ware. Moreover, different applications require different level of granularity from the same raw data. Therefore, context is an important parameter to measure while providing data to the applications. Security, integrity, and availability of data should be based on the underlying applications rather than the state of the network.

4.5 Coverage

Both IoT and VANET and its breeds are in their infancy, and a number of service providers are testing their waters for these technologies. The proliferation of these technologies is an incremental process and it will require time before we can bring these to the masses. Coverage and user satisfaction are other fronts that have to be addressed. Currently 'The Things Network' has been deployed in a number of European cities and provide partial coverage. It is also worth noting that other vendors are also competing for IoT deployment and the key market players are many. Therefore, since our envisioned framework targets only LoRaWAN, its coverage will be an important parameter in successful realization of this integration. On the other hand, VANET and its different breeds are going through legislation process in both US and Europe, therefore it is safe to assume that in a couple of years connected vehicles will pervade our highways.

5 Conclusion

In this paper, we proposed a generic abstract level framework for integrating IoT with vehicular clouds for service enhancement. Our proposed architectural framework will be a starting point towards realization of new and exciting applications in both IoT and VC domains. We particularly focused on the protocol level and functional-level integration. We also outlined the research challenges faced by such integration. In the extended version, we will work on a complete framework covering all aspects of the integration with a proof-of-concept architecture including protocols for infrastructure, communication, security, privacy, and data protocols and functional aspects such as asset management.

References

1. Hartenstein, H., Laberteaux, L.P.: A tutorial survey on vehicular ad hoc networks. IEEE Commun. Mag. **46**(6), 164–171 (2008)
2. Hussain, R., Rezaeifar, Z., Oh, H.: A paradigm shift from vehicular ad hoc networks to VANET-based clouds. Wirel. Pers. Commun. **83**(2), 1131–1158 (2015)
3. Arif, S., Olariu, S., Wang, J., Yan, G., Yang, W., Khalil, I.: Datacenter at the airport: reasoning about time-dependent parking lot occupancy. IEEE Trans. Parallel Distrib. Syst. **23**(11), 2067–2080 (2012)

4. Gu, L., Zeng, D., Guo, S., Ye, B.: Leverage parking cars in a two-tier data center. In: 2013 IEEE Wireless Communications and Networking Conference (WCNC), pp. 4665–4670, April 2013
5. Hussain, R., Rezaeifar, Z., Lee, Y.-H., Oh, H.: Secure and privacy-aware traffic information as a service in VANET-based clouds. Pervasive Mob. Comput. **24**, 194–209 (2015). Special Issue on Secure Ubiquitous Computing. http://www.sciencedirect.com/science/article/pii/S1574119215001455
6. Hussain, R., Abbas, F., Son, J., Kim, D., Kim, S., Oh, H.: Vehicle witnesses as a service: leveraging vehicles as witnesses on the road in VANET clouds. In: 2013 IEEE 5th International Conference on Cloud Computing Technology and Science, vol. 1, pp. 439–444, December 2013
7. Kwak, D., Liu, R., Kim, D., Nath, B., Iftode, L.: Seeing is believing: sharing real-time visual traffic information via vehicular clouds. IEEE Access **4**, 3617–3631 (2016)
8. Hussain, R., Abbas, F., Son, J., Kim, S., Oh, H.: Using public buses as mobile gateways in vehicular clouds. In: 2014 IEEE International Conference on Consumer Electronics (ICCE), pp. 175–176, January 2014
9. Al-Fuqaha, A., Guizani, M., Mohammadi, M., Aledhari, M., Ayyash, M.: Internet of Things: a survey on enabling technologies, protocols, and applications. IEEE Commun. Surv. Tutor. **17**(4), 2347–2376 (2015). Fourthquarter
10. Khattak, H.A., Ruta, M., Di Sciascio, E.: CoAP-based healthcare sensor networks: a survey. In: 11th International Bhurban Conference on Applied Sciences & Technology, Islamabad (2014)
11. Qu, F., Wu, Z., Wang, F.Y., Cho, W.: A security and privacy review of VANETs. IEEE Trans. Intell. Transp. Syst. **16**(6), 2985–2996 (2015)
12. Nia, A.M., Jha, N.K.: A comprehensive study of security of Internet-of-Things. IEEE Trans. Emerg. Top. Comput. **PP**(99), 1 (2016)
13. Whaiduzzaman, M., Sookhak, M., Gani, A., Buyya, R.: A survey on vehicular cloud computing. J. Netw. Comput. Appl. **40**, 325–344 (2014)
14. Mikhaylov, K., Petaejaejaervi, J., Haenninen, T.: Analysis of capacity and scalability of the LoRa low power wide area network technology. In: European Wireless 2016, 22th European Wireless Conference, pp. 1–6, May 2016
15. Mallissery, S., Pai, M.M.M., Ajam, N., Pai, R.M., Mouzna, J.: Transport and traffic rule violation monitoring service in its: a secured VANET cloud application. In: 2015 12th Annual IEEE Consumer Communications and Networking Conference (CCNC), pp. 213–218, January 2015
16. He, W., Yan, G., Xu, L.D.: Developing vehicular data cloud services in the IoT environment. IEEE Trans. Ind. Inf. **10**(2), 1587–1595 (2014)
17. Bonomi, F., Milito, R., Natarajan, P., Zhu, J.: Fog computing: a platform for Internet of Things and analytics. In: Bessis, N., Dobre, C. (eds.) Big Data and Internet of Things: A Roadmap for Smart Environments, vol. 546 pp. 169–186. Springer, Heidelberg (2014) https://doi.org/10.1007/978-3-319-05029-4_7
18. Yan, G., Wen, D., Olariu, S., Weigle, M.C.: Security challenges in vehicular cloud computing. IEEE Trans. Intell. Transp. Syst. **14**(1), 284–294 (2013)
19. Alam, K.M., Saini, M., Saddik, A.E.: Toward social internet of vehicles: concept, architecture, and applications. IEEE Access **3**, 343–357 (2015)
20. Ortiz, A.M., Hussein, D., Park, S., Han, S.N., Crespi, N.: The cluster between internet of things and social networks: review and research challenges. IEEE Internet Things J. **1**(3), 206–215 (2014)

21. Truong, N.B., Lee, G.M., Ghamri-Doudane, Y.: Software defined networking-based vehicular adhoc network with fog computing. In: IFIP/IEEE International Symposium on Integrated Network Management (IM) **2015**, 1202–1207. IEEE (2015)
22. Lin, J., Yu, W., Zhang, N., Yang, X., Zhang, H., Zhao, W.: A survey on Internet of Things: architecture, enabling technologies, security and privacy, and applications. IEEE Internet Things J. **PP**(99), 1 (2017)
23. Hussain, R., Rezaeifar, Z., Kim, D., Tokuta, A.O., Oh, H.: On secure, privacy-aware, and efficient beacon broadcasting among one-hop neighbors in VANETs. In: 2014 IEEE Military Communications Conference, pp. 1427–1434, October 2014

Secure Communication Protocol Between Two Mobile Devices Over Short Distances

Muhammad Umair Khan[1(✉)], Farhana Chowdhury[2],
Zarmina Jahangir[1], and Francis Ofougwuka[3]

[1] Department of Computer Science, Riphah International University,
Lahore, Pakistan
umair@cs.queensu.ca, zarmina.jahangir@riphah.edu.pk
[2] Department of Information and Communication Engineering Technology,
Centennial College, Toronto, ON, Canada
fchowdh3@my.centennialcollege.ca
[3] Royal Bank of Canada, Toronto, ON, Canada
francid81@gmail.com

Abstract. The security of mobile devices has become a significant issue with the increase in data and computing capacities. Such devices store security critical data such as passwords to various online services. In the event of theft of such devices, the user's credentials are at the mercy of the attacker. A secondary mobile device may be used to lock the primary mobile device if the distance between the two is larger than a specified threshold. Such proximity-based locking devices use Bluetooth and NFC technologies to communicate with the primary devices. In this paper, we propose an authentication protocol that can be used between two such mobile devices which use NFC and Bluetooth. The protocol elaborates a number of possible scenarios and how they should be implemented to maximize security of the mobile devices. The proposed protocol has been implemented and tested on Android and iOS devices.

Keywords: Software security · Security · NFC · Bluetooth
Secure communications protocol

1 Introduction

Security considerations are an integral part of today's mobile devices such as smartphones, notebooks, laptops, and tablets. The primary reason behind this consideration is that these mobile devices now have the computing and data storage capacities that were not even available on desktop computers up till recently. This computing prowess has provided users with options to conduct social and business activities on their mobile devices. However, if the data stored on the mobile devices (*e.g.*, credentials, passwords, and financial information) falls in wrong hands, the user's confidentiality and integrity may be compromised. Moreover, they may suffer emotional and financial repercussions.

Many security mechanisms have been implemented by the mobile devices' vendors to circumvent and safeguard against security threats. Such mechanisms include biometric

© ICST Institute for Computer Sciences, Social Informatics and Telecommunications Engineering 2018
R. Mehmood et al. (Eds.): SCITA 2017, LNICST 224, pp. 74–85, 2018.
https://doi.org/10.1007/978-3-319-94180-6_9

authentication and remotely deleting data (*e.g.*, Apple's "Find Your Phone" [1]). A more recent security model is to use a secondary mobile device to lock/unlock the primary one based on its proximity to the secondary one. A similar idea has successfully been implemented in high-end cars where the keys stay in the driver's pocket and the vehicle detects, based on the proximity, the presence of the key and enables functions of the car. This same idea has already been implemented by Lynk from uConekt [2] for mobile devices. The secondary mobile device does not have to be a mobile phone or tablet in itself as only limited storage and processing capabilities are required for authentication and locking purposes. The secondary device is small enough to fit in a key ring as a key fob along with other keys. As most people use and keep keys (car, office, or home) close, the secondary device will be in close range of the primary device most of the time. The range of a Bluetooth device may range be from 0.1 m to 100 m depending. Most mobile devices use Class 2 Bluetooth which has a typical range of 10 m. We consider this an effective range to implement a proximity based authentication and locking mechanism. This implies that if the secondary and primary devices are more than 10 m apart, the primary device will lock.

Proximity-based mobile authentication [4] devices use Bluetooth and Near Field Communication (NFC) technologies to communicate. These technologies are not completely secure in their handling and transfer of data. Bluetooth and NFC have various security issues such as leaking of information from the system to an unwanted party resulting into confidentiality violation, unauthorized changes of information during transmission leading to integrity violations, and resources blocked by malicious attacker resulting in availability violations. Proximity-based authentication [4] devices use NFC and Bluetooth to verify the primary device because of their short and adjustable range. However, NFC and Bluetooth are prone to attacks because they do not use a central server to authenticate and most of the time the data transferred is not strongly encrypted. We, in this paper, propose an authentication and data handling protocol that offers a secure way for these devices to communicate via Bluetooth and NFC. We discuss various security related scenarios, especially when one device (primary or secondary) is taken beyond the proximity threshold either by the legitimate user or by an attacker. We propose security safeguards that should be in implemented to secure the primary device in the event of any of these scenarios.

The remainder of this paper is organized as follows. Section 2 presents the related work in this area. Section 3 describes preliminaries. Section 4 provides the details of the proposed protocol. Section 5 concludes the paper with future works and limitations.

2   Related Work

Extended usage of the mobile computing devices (*e.g.*, smart phones) in our lives is resulting in many security issues especially regarding device-to-device communication. Numerous researchers have suggested techniques involving password based authentication, proxy based security protocols and Near Field Communications (NFC) which would ensure a secure and reliable means of communication between the devices without intervention by an unauthentic device/person.

Transport Layer Security (TLS) protocol [3] works on the transport layer which provides end-to-end security. TLS is currently being used for internet communication along with its predecessor Secure Sockets Layers (SSL) protocol. This paper proposes that the advantages of TLS protocol are much more when implemented in mobile devices domain. Implementing security protocols in mobile devices also increases maintainability and extensibility. The major technique used in this paper is to hide information from intruders using bouncy castle cryptographic packages. Object oriented technique has also been used to enhance security. The implementation did not include optional TLS specifications such as client authentication, session resumption and compression.

Key agreement protocol [5] has been used to make device-to-device communication secure. This protocol activates two mobile devices to initiate a shared secret key for both the devices. This approach specifically uses Diffie-Hellman key agreement protocol [11]. The authors claim that the proposed technique is more effective and incurs less computational cost while using device-to-device communication. This paper presents an advance integration technique that allows previous methodologies to work with the proposed method. This paper also discusses their technique with regards to a cellular network using LTE dealing power control issues and Wi-Fi based Device-to-Device communications [5]. Analysis of the technique indicates that the proposed key agreement protocol enables two mobile users to securely set up a secret key with a small computation cost and low authentication overhead. A similar approach is presented in [6] which establishes a secure key between two mobile devices.

WebBee [11, 12], another communications technique, provides a complete framework that supports security sensitive applications used in mobile devices. According to this paper, there are two possibilities in terms of time when devices are compromised: the first possibility is when the user is informed about the system being compromised. The second possibility is when the security keys are initialized. This paper introduces a new technique called Challenge Response System (CRS) that supports the WebBee system to provide overall security in the worst situation. The proposed methodology also provides support to integrate existing methodologies to minimize the impact on infrastructure by using WebBee system. One of the main constraints in the CRS is that it deals with limited numbers applications.

The authors in [10] present different mobile settings that support and provide guidance on setting up a password. Results have been compiled after comparing the strength and usability of passwords that are generated on desktops, laptops and mobile devices. The proposed methodology shows that the passwords created on mobile devices are more error prone, longer, frustrating, and weaker. It is observed that password policies vary in both mobile and desktop environments and it also suggests an easy way to enter passwords in mobile devices.

Passwords can be breached with different methods like brute force and dictionary attacks. Strings of alphanumeric characters are also more difficult to remember, Graphical passwords have been used to make passwords more easy and reliable for users. In this technique user can select different images as passwords rather than entering different alphanumeric values and characters. However, such passwords are more prone to shoulder surfing attacks. An alternative method has been proposed for authentication purposes by using graphical passwords along with alphanumeric characters [9]. It is a combination of recognition and recall based system that is more reliable and more secure than the older systems. The presented technique is also more robust and reliable against the shoulder surfing attacks on graphical passwords. Moreover, the proposed methodology is more convenient and suitable for the mobile devices.

The authors in [3] discuss the security issues of wearable gadgets and software agents. They propose two separate protocols for each of these: a separate protocol for device-to-proxy communication and another one for proxy-to-proxy communication. Using two different protocols enables us to use less computation capacity of devices. Another advantage of separate protocols is the provision of reasonable authentication in communication on more strong devices. This paper gives details on lightweight wireless devices that have been used for device-to-proxy protocol and also elaborated on simple public key infrastructure and simple distributed security infrastructure for proxy-to-proxy protocols. The authors have also developed a prototype for secure and efficient access to networks and mobile devices. A qualitative analysis was performed on this prototype whose results favor proxy based security protocols in mobile devices.

3 Preliminaries

Near Field Communication (NFC) [8] is an emerging technology in wireless short range communication. It is based on different existing standards like Radio Frequency Identification (RFID) infrastructure. NFC provides support for contactless transactions that is used in different intuitive application scenarios such as over-the-air ticketing system and mobile payment system [7].

Bluetooth is a point-to-point or point-to-multipoint radio frequency technology for data exchange requiring minimal power. For a range of ten meters, the power usage is 2.5 mW. The typical range of a Bluetooth device is 10 to 100 m. Bluetooth is also being used in to internet of things (IoT) devices in a secure manner [17].

Security is an important concern in today's software systems as security failures may lead to financial losses or physical injuries [13]. Security vulnerabilities, the root of security failures, may be introduced in requirement specification, design, or implementation phases [14–16]. While communicating between two mobile devices, the security threats increase due to the use of the wireless medium.

4 Proximity-Based Authentication and Communication Protocol

We have identified a total of ten possible scenarios where the security of the primary device may be threatened. In the following paragraphs we describe these scenarios and how the server, primary device and secondary device should communicate to safeguard against threats. We represent this communication exchange using sequence diagrams. In these diagrams, S represents the server, M_1 represents the primary device, M_2 represents the secondary device, S_{pr} represents the server's private key, M_{1pr} represents the primary device's private key, M_{2pr} represents the secondary device's private key,

S_{pu} represents the server's public key, M_{1pu} represents for the primary device's public key, M_{2pu} represents for the secondary device's public key, X represents a random number sent as a message, and K_1 and K_2 are keys generated by the server during the synchronization process. The private and public keys can be generated by any appropriate asymmetric key algorithm. The remainder of this section is organized as follows. Sections 4.1 through 4.7 describe different scenarios that the devices may come across. Section 4.8 proposes an added layer of security in the form of a local password for the primary device. Section 4.9 presents the options for storing data securely. Section 4.10 concludes the protocol by presenting the details of an experiment conducted on iOS and Android mobile devices.

4.1   Synchronizing Primary and Secondary Devices

The primary and secondary devices have to be paired to each other at the beginning. This pairing is performed by exchanging and synchronizing keys. After synchronization, the two devices keep in constant contact. However, there will be many instances when the two devices are not in contact such as when the two devices are out of range, when the devices are turned off or run out of power, or when the SIM cards are changed. In such an event, the synchronization process has to be initiated to authenticate that the two devices are legitimate ones. This process is performed every seven days, even in the absence of any of the aforementioned scenarios. During this process the primary and secondary devices come to a close range of 0.0 m. Connection to the server is mandatory for this process therefore internet connection is essential for the success of the process.

The synchronization process is initiated by M_1. It sends the sync command (which also reduces the power of both the devices). M_1 sends the profile password to the server encrypted using the server's public key S_{pu}. The server S generates two new keys K_1 and K_2 and sends them to M_1 using M_{1pu}. M_1 will decrypt the keys by using M_{1pr}. M_1 will then re-encrypt K_2 by using the same algorithm only it will use the public key M_{2pu} of M_2 and then send it to M_2. This is done to add another layer of security. K_1 will be the new private key of M_1 and K_2 will be the new private key of M_2. The method $SyncS()$ sends the username and password in an encrypted format to the server. The method $SyncM_2()$ verifies whether the distance between M_1 and M_2 is zero. This scenario is depicted in Fig. 1 in the form of a sequence diagram.

4.2   SIM Change and Device Switched ON/OFF

With the assumption that M_1 is a mobile device, SIM change is when the user removes the SIM to swap with another SIM or have the same SIM reinstated. The device has to be synchronised (sync) according to the steps defined in Sect. 4.1. Similarly, whenever the primary or secondary device is turned ON/OFF, the sync process defined in Sect. 4.1 has to be performed before the user can access the data in the primary device

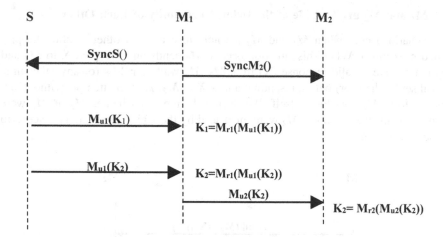

Fig. 1. Synchronizing primary and secondary.

4.3 M_1 and M_2 are Within the Defined Proximity of Each Other

To ensure a device within range is the correct device, we need a means of authenticating the two devices as part of the same pair. After every 30 s, M_1 generates a random value X and sends it to M_2. We use the M_{2pu} to encrypt the X resulting in M_{1x} before it is sent. M_2 decrypts the M_{1x} using the M_{2pr} and overwrites the X in M_2 with the new X. M_2 responds to M_1 message by sending the X to M_1 using the M_{1pu} to encrypt X resulting in M_{2x}. M_1 validates the message by decrypting the M_{2x} and checks if it matches with the initial X that was sent. If M_1 detects a discrepancy between the sent and received X, it locks M_1 deducing that the M_2 is fake or has been tampered with. When both the devices have X, then they can recognize each other as legitimate as only M_1 will have its private key. This scenario is represented in Fig. 2. If a fake or tampered device is detected, a sync process is required which involves communicating with the server S.

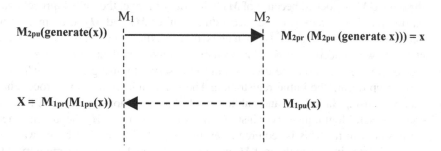

Fig. 2. Verifying proximity between M_1 and M_2.

4.4 M₁ and M₂ are Outside of the Defined Proximity of Each Other

This scenario occurs when *M₁* and *M₂* are not close to each other (within the pre-defined proximity). When this situation occurs, *M₁* sends an encrypted X to *M₂* and does not receive a valid response (X) from *M₂*. *M₁* waits for 30 s (or any other time interval set by the user) before resending a new *X* to *M₂*. After 3 attempts without any response from *M₂*, *M₁* locks itself. We do not distinguish whether *M₁* or *M₂* were stolen by an attacker or *M₁* or *M₂* were misplaced by the legitimate user. This scenario is described in Fig. 3.

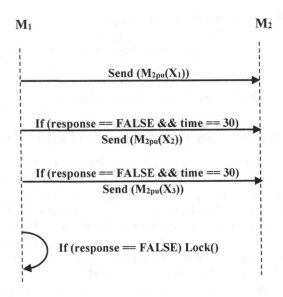

Fig. 3. Lock M₁ if proximity between M₁ and M₂ is not verified.

4.5 Unlocking M₁

Once the device *M₁* is locked because of *M₂* being out of range, the unlock process has to be carried out. This process, to be successful, requires *M₁* and *M₂* to be present in close proximity with each other (zero meters to use NFC) and with access to the internet to allow connection to **S**. This scenario is represented in Fig. 4. Using the provided software application, the user logs in to the server by using the *ServerID* and *password* set up during the initial registration. The communication in this process has to be encrypted using the private and public key of *S* and *M₁* (not shown in the figure).

Upon successful login, the server instructs *M₁* to request from *M₂* the last message *X* which is stored in its. This is required to ensure that the M₂ has not been swapped with another device since each distinct *M₂* will have different *X* store in its memory. *M₂* responds by sending the *X* value to M₁. All communication is carried out in encrypted form. *M₁* validates the *X* sent by *M₂* and when it does match with the stored *X* in *M₁*, then the sync process is initiated (Scenario I described in Sect. 4.1) with successful unlocking of *M₁*. If the *X* sent by *M₂* does not match with the *X* stored in *M₁*, then the

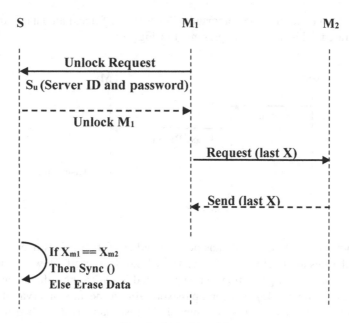

Fig. 4. Unlocking M_1.

data stored in M_1 is erased because this situation indicates that M_2 has been tampered with and someone is trying to deceive M_1.

4.6 Internet Connection not Available

There could be a scenario that the user has no internet connection and the server cannot be reached. We propose to use a session token which has been proven effective in many other applications and protocols. We propose that a token should remain valid for only one hour after the internet connection is lost. After the passage of one hour, M_1 should be locked. To unlock M_1 we need to perform the sync process defined in Sect. 4.1.

There are multiple rationales behind this lock and sync. First, consider that the legitimate user loses both M_1 and M_2. He/she may need to send an erase data command to safeguard his data. However, if M_1 not connected to the internet, it should lock itself as the erase command will not reach it. This does create a usability issue as the legitimate user will not be able to use his device in the absence of internet. However, the user can setup the time after the device locks itself.

4.7 M_1 and M_2 have been Stolen

In the unlikely case where both the devices are lost together, there are the following two possibilities:

- User is aware: When a user knows the devices are gone, he/she can login to the application server and send an erase command to M_1. If the device M_1 is still connected to the internet, the command will be successful and all data on the device will be erased. This scenario is presented in Fig. 5.

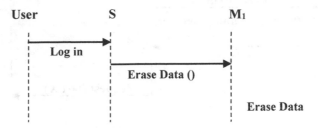

Fig. 5. Erase data.

- User is not aware: When a user has no knowledge of the devices been stolen, and both the devices are in close proximity, M_1 will not lock itself. However, to resolve this, an added layer of protection can be provided in which the software application installed on the device M_1 asks for a password after a specified interval of time and locks itself if that password is not entered. This scenario is described in detail in Sect. 4.8.

4.8   Local Password

No matter if M_1 is connected to Server or M_2 or not, in all cases M_1 will ask for a local password which will be different from the server password. The password will be at least 10 characters long. This password will work as a screen lock and will be enabled after 30 s of inactivity. The user will have only three chances to enter the right password. If the local password is not entered correctly, M_1 will let the user enter it two more times and after three incorrect attempts, M_1 will be locked and user has to go through the unlock procedure via the server. This scenario is represented in the sequence diagram in Fig. 6.

4.9   Data Storage

There are two places where data can be stored: on the cloud/server and on the device M_1. Each of them requires a process to make sure data is not compromised

- On the Cloud/Server: In this process, we synchronize M_1 with the cloud/server. M_1 only has the last values of X on it while the remaining data is on the cloud/server. M_1 encrypts the data using S_{pu} and sends it to the server S. Server decrypts the data using S_{pr}. The server then stores the data and sends "delete data" command to M_1. M_1 deletes all data and sends confirmation to the server. If M_1 requests any data, the server encrypts data using M_{1pu} and sends it. M_1 then decrypts the data using M_{1pr}.
- On M_1: For this process, all the data is stored in M_1. When M_1 needs to save any data, it requests an *EKey* from the server. The server encrypts the *EKey* with M_{1pu} and sends it to M_1. M_1 decrypts the key using M_{1pr} and encrypts the data using that

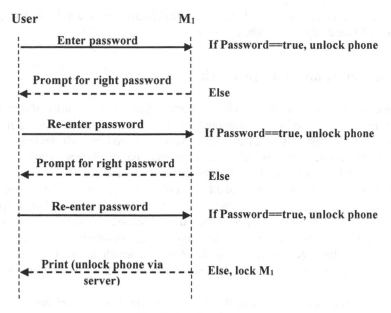

Fig. 6. Local password.

key. M_1 then deletes the **EKey** from its memory. When M_1 needs to access the data on it, it requests the **DKey** from the server. Server encrypts the **DKey** using M_{1pu} and sends that to M_1. M_1 decrypts the **DKey** using M_{1pr} and uses this key to decrypt the data. This decrypted data is only viewable and is not saved at any time in M_1. The keys are always stored in the server. This will help to mitigate the risk of the key or data been discovered when the device is lost.

4.10 Experimental Implementation

The above-mentioned communication protocol was implemented in two separate Android and iOS based primary devices. The secondary device was an embedded system in the form of a key fob. For the primary devices, JAVA was used to develop an App. This app was responsible for authentication of the user using a password, communicating with the server to verify keys and accessing user information, and locking the primary device when the secondary device was out of range.

The code for the embedded device was written in C due to space and computational restrictions. The secondary device was first registered with the server. This registered secondary device was then paired with a primary device and the pairing information was added to the user database in the server. Once the pairing was complete, the secondary device was locked to the primary one and it could not be paired with any other primary device with making changes to the secondary device database in the server.

The server was installed in the cloud and was used to host client credentials and generate keys. All of the described scenarios were tested multiple times. The results indicate that based on the discussed scenarios, the primary device was locked whenever it was out of range of the secondary device.

5 Conclusions and Future Work

With the extensive use of mobile devices in our everyday lives, security of data stored on these devices is becoming of paramount importance. Lost mobile devices may not only represent the cost of the device itself. The data stored in such devices, such as banking information, social websites' credentials, and mailboxes, maybe used to exploit the user financially, politically, socially, and emotionally.

Usually the security features available in mobile devices are not sufficient if the device is not connected to the internet (*e.g.*, erase data remotely). We propose a communication protocol in this paper which uses a secondary device as an authenticator. A similar idea has been successfully implemented in other domains such as the automobile industry. We consider multiple scenarios which the mobile device may encounter. The proposed protocol was implemented on Android and iOS devices and tested.

The only limitation observed in the protocol is the time interval between losing both the devices and the user defined time to lock the device. As a future work, this communication protocol can also be used for internet of things (IoT) devices however it may require some modification because of their distributed nature. Moreover, this protocol has to be modified and tested for devices which cannot reasonably store data on the cloud and completely depend on storing the data within itself. This will be the case when the amount of data to be protected is too large.

References

1. iCloud - Find my iPhone. https://www.apple.com/ca/icloud/find-my-iphone/. Accessed July 2017
2. uConekt. http://uconekt.com/lynk/. Accessed July 2017
3. Kayayurt, B., Tuglular, T.: End-to-end security implementation for mobile devices using TLS protocol. J. Comput. Virol. 2(1), 87–97 (2006)
4. Burnside, M., Clarke, D., Mills, T., Devadas, S., Rivest, R.: Proxy-based security protocols in networked mobile devices. In: Symposium on Applied Computing (SAC 2002), pp. 265–272 (2002)
5. Shen, W., et al.: Secure key establishment for device-to-device communications. In: IEEE Global Communications Conference (GLOBECOM), pp. 336–340 (2014)
6. Aldosari, W., El Taeib, T.: Secure key establishment for device to device communications among mobile devices. Int. J. Eng. Res. Rev. 3(2), 43–47 (2015)
7. Siira, E., Tuikka, T., Tormanen, V.: Location-based mobile wiki using NFC tag infrastructure. In: 1st International Workshop on Near Field Communication (NFC 2009), pp. 56–60 (2009)

8. Burkard, S.: Near field communication in smartphones, Department of Computer Engineering, Berlin Institute of Technology, Germany, Technical report. https://www.snet. tu-berlin.de/fileadmin/fg220/courses/WS1112/snet-project/nfc-in-smartphones_burkard.pdf. Accessed July 2017
9. Routi, S., Andersen, J., Seamons, K.: Strengthening password-based authentication. In: Symposium on Usable Privacy and Security (SOUPS) (2016)
10. Khan, W.Z., Aalsalem, M.Y., Xiang, Y.: A graphical password bases authentication based system for mobile devices. Int. J. Comput. Sci. Issues (IJCS) **8**(5)-2, 145–154 (2011)
11. Yang, B.S., Dreijer, S., Jamin, S., Mukherjee, S., Wang, L.: Secure communication framework for mobile devices. Technical report, University of Michigan at Ann Arbor, MI, USA, CSE-TR-543-08 (2008). https://www.cse.umich.edu/techreports/cse/2008/CSE-TR-543-08.pdf. Accessed July 2017
12. Upatkoon, K., Wang, W., Jamin, S.: WebBee: an architecture for web accessibility for mobile devices. In: 10th IFIP International Conference on Personal Wireless Communications, Colmar, France (2005)
13. Khan, M.U.A., Zulkernine, M.: Developing components with embedded security monitors. In: 2nd International ACM SIGSOFT Symposium on Architecting Critical Systems (ISARCS 2011), pp. 133–142 (2011)
14. Khan, M.U.A., Zulkernine, M.: Quantifying security in secure software development phases. In: 2nd IEEE International Workshop on Secure Software Engineering (IWSSE 2008), pp. 955–960 (2008)
15. Khan, M.U.A., Zulkernine, M.: On selecting appropriate development processes and requirement engineering methods for secure software. In: 4th IEEE International Workshop on Security, Trust, and Privacy for Software Applications (STPSA 2009), pp. 353–358 (2009)
16. Khan, M.U.A., Zulkernine, M.: Activity and artifact views of a secure software development process. In: International Workshop on Software Security Process (SSP 2009), pp. 399–404 (2009)
17. Hussain, S.R., Mehnaz, S., Nirjon, S., Bertino, E.: Secure seamless bluetooth low energy | connection migration for unmodified IoT devices. IEEE Trans. Mob. Comput. **PP**(99), 17 (2017)

A Theoretical Architecture for TM Through Software Defined Mobile Network in 5G Environments

Ahmed Alshaflut[✉] and Vijey Thayananthan

Department of Computer Science, Faculty of Computing and IT,
King Abdulaziz University, Jeddah, Saudi Arabia
aalshaflut@stu.kau.edu.sa, thayananthan@live.co.uk

Abstract. The 5th generations of networks have been evolved to satisfy the enormous growth of the user's requirements. To achieve the user's requirements and to assure the QoS, the traffic management (TM) of data transmission must be considered with the different network architectures. Thus, this paper presents using Software Defined Network (SDN) as well as Software Defined Mobile Network (SDMN) for (TM) purposes. Additionally, this article has analyzed the recent contributions of SDN and SDMN regarding TM within 5G environments. Moreover, we have proposed a theoretical architecture for the mobile TM systems through the SDMN controller. This architecture allows us to improve the performance enhancement through loading TM. Thus, benefits and challenging points of the proposed architecture have been presented.

Keywords: TM · Software-defined multiple access · 5G networks

1 Introduction

The massive usage of internet applications and data transportation have required tremendous demand of TM solutions. However, with the spread of various raising systems and tools, there are enormous needs for controlling the data TM. In fact, several technologies have been developed for handling traffic issues. However, some of them were not applicable for different scenarios. Traffic applications assist in managing the best service delivery requirements. Thus, each application should be able to evaluate the needed service and determine the priority behaviors. Therefore, many attempts have discussed the possible solutions to managing the massive traffic caused by large data transmissions through 5G networks. The remainder of this paper is structured as follows. Section 2 gives a brief synopsis of the relevant literature review. Section 3 covers the previous works of SDN, as well as SDMN. Furthermore, the analytical discussion is presented in Sect. 4. Consequently, a theoretical architecture has been presented in Sect. 5 for the TM using SDMN in 5G networks. Finally, the conclusion is presented in Sect. 6.

© ICST Institute for Computer Sciences, Social Informatics and Telecommunications Engineering 2018
R. Mehmood et al. (Eds.): SCITA 2017, LNICST 224, pp. 86–91, 2018.
https://doi.org/10.1007/978-3-319-94180-6_10

2 Literature Review

The term of TM can be applied to any system that permanently works for large numbers of users under different circumstances. Thus, this section briefly covers different ideas that are using TM applications in different scopes. Thus, authors in [1] have proposed fair downlink TM for enabling cell-load based on service differentiation with huge respect to the performance of different Wi-Fi networks. However, another trend has been evolved for the cloud TM. This trend has considered the importance of managing the convergence between multi-networks as in [2]. Though LTE networks have faced the traffic issues, several systems were proposed to assure reliable and efficient practices [4].

3 State of the Art

Due to the enormous applications in the increasing environments, data TM has raised as a new challenge for dealing with required network specifications. However, researchers have proposed several solutions based on their network design needs for enabling the best possible of QoS. Despite many solutions, we have studied that the TM will be better with following network and multiple access schemes.

3.1 Software Defined Network (SDN)

Mostly, SDN was proposed for enabling perfect control of network features [8] as well as for good content delivery. Other attempts are focused on the quality of service as [10, 11]. Intensely, another approach was developed in [12] for Industrial Internet of Things IIoT with excellent use of SDN. Over again, resource allocations are investigated [13]. Although, authors [14] have analyzed the shortages of current solutions, especially in data centers by proposing flexible programmability solutions.

3.2 Software Defined Mobile Network (SDMN)

Truthfully, mobility issues and features have attracted researchers in the network designing. Thus, they have increased network capabilities as in [15, 17]. However, others have used different technologies with SDMN traffic in heterogeneous networks as [16, 21]. Nonetheless, some attempts are focused on security issues [18, 19, 21]. Although, authors [22] have proposed an interference graph as an abstraction of the control. But, authors in [23] have addressed using SDN for controlled LTE network testbed with management applications.

3.3 Non-Orthogonal Multiple Access (NOMA)

Initially, NOMA is appeared to solve the access traffic problems. However, it has achieved higher loading factor. But, some approaches have investigated performance capabilities by using NOMA as in [5]. Specifically, several attempts were focused on

NOMA in LTE networks such as [6]. Recent tendencies have concentrated on energy power allocations by enabling more capacities of QoS for energy saving [7, 23].

3.4   Software Defined Multiple Access (SoDeMa)

In fact, the term of SoDeMA has been proposed for different purposes which are not only to replace NOMA but also improve the programmable capability in TM. However, it provides the main features in which several users, accessing schemas can be accepted for satisfying different services and users of different applications within 5G networks. In fact, SoDeMa has borrowed some features from NOMA but with borrowing Software Defined Radio (SDR) for multiple access schemas [25]. Thus, the use of either NOMA or SoDeMA can be chosen based on the required services capabilities. Figure 1 below illustrates the main design and use of SoDeMA [25].

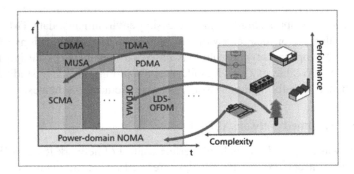

Fig. 1. SoDeMa design as presented in [25]

4   Theoretical Architecture of TM System Through SDMN in 5G

The network design plays an important role in enabling efficient TM system. Recently, several models have been proposed as architecture designs. However, they have not addressed the enormous demand for mobile solutions. Thus, this paper addresses this challenge for enabling the wider spread of mobility choices of TM systems. Thus, the mobility has been considered in this model for enabling more flexibility and usability cases. In fact, this feature is thoroughly fascinated to satisfy the continuous improvements in the mobile-based services.

The traditional SDNs have limited enabling the mobility for TM phases because of static deployments. Thus, this approach improves the mobile features for the heterogeneous networks to enable as much as required services. In fact, this architecture reduces the user's handovers since it balances the traffic loads. Initially, the loading traffic is earlier maintained before accessing the needed service. On the other side, this architecture has enabled the mobility feature for the traffic managers but, it has raised more investigations of the handover optimization mechanisms. As well as, the efficiency of interference management has required potential attentions for handling the interference issues between large numbers of users. Furthermore, this scheme requires more investigations of the network applications side to assure the fairness and his quality of service. Moreover, energy efficiency requires more attention for future deployments. Over again, the mobility management handovers should be considered before applying this schema. Finally, more security practices are required to enable secure systems with the best possible of TM (Fig. 2).

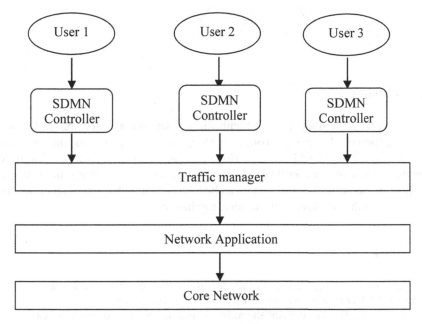

Fig. 2. The proposed architecture for TM through SDMN controllers

5   Analysis

In fact, previous works have covered many aspects of TM on 5G networks. However, different technologies have been used for meeting the requirement of the coming generations. Thus, these solutions have touched issues to solve them regarding increasing networks and number of users. Therefore, a comparison table of previous SDN works has been provided for continuous researcher's interests. Hence, these works have been classified under several considerations. In fact, these contributions have been classified based on the specific matters of their participated works. Thus, it has mainly focused on these contributions with their benefits to SDN and SDMN regarding TM solutions. An example of works that have discussed the energy efficiency can be seen in [9, 19]. However, mobility issues with performance enhancement were discussed in [24, 25] (Table 1).

Table 1. Comparison table of TM works with SDN and SDMN including covered points of these works.

Reference number	Energy efficiency	Performance enhancement	Content delivery and QoS	Mobility supporting	Security issues
[9]	✓	✓	X	X	X
[11]	X	✓	✓	X	X
[19]	✓	✓	X	X	X
[20]	X	✓	✓	X	X
[25]	X	✓	X	✓	X

6   Conclusion

In this paper, we have studied the TM with various network architectures and multiple schemes influenced by 5G networks. Further, we have proposed the theoretical architecture based on SoDeMa for TM. However, this paper has concluded that the TM can be more efficient when enabling flexible mobile controller among different users. Also, they are some restrictions of this architecture such as the interference management as well as the handover optimization mechanisms.

References

1. Li, Y., Zhou, T., Yang, Y., Hu, H., Hamalainen, M.: Fair downlink traffic management for hybrid LAA-LTE/Wi-Fi networks. IEEE Access **5**, 7031–7041 (2017)
2. Feng, C., Xu, H., Li, B.: An alternating direction method approach to cloud traffic management. IEEE Trans. Parallel Distrib. Syst. **28**(8), 2145–2158 (2017)
3. Judvaitis, J., Salmins, A., Nesenbergs, K.: Network data traffic management inside a TestBed. In: 2016 Advances in Wireless and Optical Communications (RTUWO), Riga, pp. 152–155 (2016)
4. Ambriz, S.J.G., Méndez, R.M., Ángeles, M.E.R.: 5GTraDis: a novel traffic distribution mechanism for 5G heterogeneous networks. In: 2016 13th International Conference on Electrical Engineering, Computing Science and Automatic Control (CCE), Mexico City, pp. 1–7 (2016)
5. Marcano, A.S., Christiansen, H.L.: Performance of non-orthogonal multiple access (NOMA) in mmWave wireless communications for 5G networks. In: 2017 International Conference on Computing, Networking and Communications (ICNC), Santa Clara, CA, pp. 969–974 (2017)
6. Ding, Z., et al.: Application of non-orthogonal multiple access in LTE and 5G networks. IEEE Commun. Mag. **55**(2), 185–191 (2017)
7. Zhang, Y., Wang, H.M., Zheng, T.X., Yang, Q.: Energy-efficient transmission design in non-orthogonal multiple access. IEEE Trans. Veh. Technol. **66**(3), 2852–2857 (2017)
8. Akram, H., Pascal, B.: Leveraging SDN for the 5G networks: trends, prospects, and challenges. arXiv:1506.02876, June 2015

9. Pinto, P., Cardoso, R., Amaral, P., Bernardo, L.: Lightweight admission control and traffic management with SDN. In: 2016 IEEE International Conference on Communications (ICC), Kuala Lumpur, pp. 1–7 (2016)
10. Awobuluyi, O., Nightingale, J., Wang, Q., Alcaraz-Calero, J.M.: Video quality in 5G networks: context-aware QoE management in the SDN control plane. In: 2015 IEEE International Conference on Computer and Information Technology, Liverpool, pp. 1657–1662 (2015)
11. Lin, K., Wang, W., Wang, X., Ji, W., Wan, J.: QoE-driven spectrum assignment for 5G wireless networks using SDR. IEEE Wirel. Commun. **22**(6), 48–55 (2015)
12. Wan, J., et al.: Software-defined industrial internet of things in the context of industry 4.0. IEEE Sens. J. **16**(20), 7373–7380 (2016)
13. Tajiki, M.M., Akbari, B., Mokari, N.: QRTP: QoS-aware resource reallocation based on traffic prediction in software defined cloud networks. In: 2016 8th International Symposium on Telecommunications (IST), Tehran, pp. 527–532 (2016)
14. Wang, W., He, W., Su, J.: M2SDN: achieving multipath and multihoming in data centers with software-defined networking. In: 2015 IEEE 23rd International Symposium on Quality of Service (IWQoS), Portland, OR, pp. 11–20 (2015)
15. Talli, G., et al.: Technologies and architectures to enable SDN in converged 5G/optical access networks. In: 2017 International Conference on Optical Network Design and Modeling (ONDM), Budapest, Hungary, pp. 1–6 (2017)
16. Chen, T., Matinmikko, M., Chen, X., Zhou, X., Ahokangas, P.: Software-defined mobile networks: concept, survey, and research directions. IEEE Commun. Mag. **53**(11), 126–133 (2015)
17. Jungnickel, V., et al.: Software-defined open access for flexible and service-oriented 5G deployment. In: 2016 IEEE International Conference on Communications Workshops (ICC), Kuala Lumpur, pp. 360–366 (2016)
18. Liyanage, M., et al.: Enhancing security of software defined mobile networks. IEEE Access **5**, 9422–9438 (2017)
19. Wang, G., Feng, G., Qin, S., Wen, R.: Efficient traffic engineering for 5G core and backhaul networks. J. Commun. Netw. **19**(1), 80–92 (2017)
20. Elgendi, I., Munasinghe, K.S., Jamalipour, A.: Mobility management in three-tier SDN architecture for DenseNets. In: 2016 IEEE Wireless Communications and Networking Conference, Doha, pp. 1–6 (2016)
21. Kutscher, D.: It's the network: towards better security and transport performance in 5G. In: 2016 IEEE Conference on Computer Communications Workshops (INFOCOM WKSHPS), San Francisco, CA, pp. 656–661 (2016)
22. Gebremariam, A.A., Goratti, L., Riggio, R., Siracusa, D., Rasheed, T., Granelli, F.: A framework for interference control in software-defined mobile radio networks. In: 2015 12th Annual IEEE Consumer Communications and Networking Conference (CCNC), Las Vegas, NV, pp. 892–897 (2015)
23. Costa-Requena, J., et al.: Software-defined 5G mobile backhaul. In: 1st International Conference on 5G for Ubiquitous Connectivity, Akaslompolo, pp. 258–263 (2014)
24. Hadi, A.A., Abdulkader, O.A., Al-Ardhi, S., Thayananthan, V.: Analytical model of enhancing traffic performance based on weighted nodes. In: 2016 UKSim-AMSS 18th International Conference on Computer Modelling and Simulation (UKSim), Cambridge, pp. 337–342 (2016)
25. Dai, L., Wang, B., Yuan, Y., Han, S., Chih-Lin, I., Wang, Z.: Non-orthogonal multiple access for 5G: solutions, challenges, opportunities, and future research trends. IEEE Commun. Mag. **53**(9), 74–81 (2015)

E-Governance and Transportation

II. Governance and Transportation

Smart Cities and the New Urban Analytics: Opportunities and Challenges in Urban Transport

John Polak[✉]

Urban Systems Laboratory, Imperial College London,
Exhibition Road, London SW7 2AZ, UK
j.polak@imperial.ac.uk

Abstract. This paper considers the development of urban modelling and analysis techniques over the past two decades in the context of smart cities. It identifies a number of generations of thinking and highlights the nature of the broad opportunities and challenges present in the field. It illustrates the arguments with examples drawn from the domain of urban transport planning and operations, focusing on a number of areas including the development of vehicle automation, the growth of servicized mobility, the integration between transport and other business sectors, the hyper-personalization of mobility products and the virtualization of user experience. The paper concludes by identifying the some wider implications of these developments for the governance of data and analytics.

Keywords: Smart cities · Big data · Analytics · Transport

1 Introduction

Over the past two decades the concept of a "smart city" has grown spectacularly in global prominence, and is now the focus of substantial interest from the business, government and the academic communities. Although there is no commonly agreed definition of what constitutes a smart city and many different visions have been promulgated, a common feature of almost all manifestations of the concept is an emphasis on the role of new ICT-enabled data resources as a means to achieving improvements in a range of aspects of the performance of urban systems including economic, social, environmental and health outcomes. As a result of this, in many cities, considerable effort is being devoted to creating repositories and platforms for a wide range of existing and emerging urban data resources. However, the mere accumulation of data, in and of itself, clearly achieves nothing. Data can only become the source of new value when they are linked to decision making. And this requires analysis. Moreover, if improvements are to be made in the performance of specific urban systems and functions, this analysis must be domain and context specific. It is therefore surprising that in the smart cities literature, relatively little discussion has been devoted to what forms of analysis could or should be undertaken with the data that are now increasingly populating these new repositories and platforms.

© ICST Institute for Computer Sciences, Social Informatics and Telecommunications Engineering 2018
R. Mehmood et al. (Eds.): SCITA 2017, LNICST 224, pp. 95–97, 2018.
https://doi.org/10.1007/978-3-319-94180-6_11

This paper considers the development of urban modelling and analysis techniques over the past decade in the context of smart cities. It identifies a number of generations of thinking and highlights the nature of the broad opportunities and challenges present in the field. It illustrates the arguments with examples drawn from the domain of urban transport planning and operations. The paper concludes by identifying the some wider implications of these developments for the governance of data and analytics.

2 Generations of Urban Analytics

It is possible to identify at least four overlapping generations of urban analytics that have emerged in the wake of the growth of the concept of smart cities. The first generation, still current today, is concerned with the descriptive presentation and visualization of granular and often highly dynamic spatial and temporal data relating to various aspects of urban systems and their operations, such as mobility patterns, energy consumption, air quality etc. Such analytics typically have little or no connection to actuation and little by way of actionable consequence; their role is largely as a means of communication with various stakeholders. This style of analytics is typified by the increasingly ubiquitous, *urban dashboards*.

The second generation of urban analytics consists of marginal adaptations of existing modelling and analysis tools that are designed to take advantage of specific features of newly available data sources, such as their lower cost or improved spatial and temporal granularity. In the domain of transport for example, longstanding models for strategic and tactical infrastructure planning and for real time operational control are increasingly being adapted to operate with probe vehicle or mobile network data instead of conventional survey or infrastructure based sensing data sources. The key characteristic of this style of analytics is that little or nothing is changed either in the underlying conceptualization of the problems being addressed or the modelling methods used.

A third generation of urban analytics exists that shares with the second generation a clear focus on traditional problem conceptualizations but is distinguished by the fact that it addresses these traditional problems using new modelling methods, often drawn from the burgeoning field of machine learning and data science. Again taking the domain of transport as an example, we are seeing the increasing use of machine learning based classifiers in applications such as incident detection or behavioral modelling, augmenting or supplanting more traditional physical or statistical based approaches to classification.

The fourth generation of urban analytics is distinguished by a concentration on problem definitions and solution methods that go beyond traditional frameworks and are focused on the specific opportunities and challenges that are created by the development of smart cities.

3 Opportunities and Challenges for New Urban Transport Analytics

In recent years, the domain of transport has been subject to enormous disruptions as a result of rapid change in technologies, business models, regulation and market behavior. These changes have created a new a slew of new practical and corresponding analytical challenges. We will explore examples of these opportunities and challenges as they are manifest in a number of areas including the development of vehicle automation, the growth of servicized mobility, the integration between transport and other business sectors, the hyper-personalization of mobility products and the virtualization of user experience.

Analysis of Tweets in Arabic Language
for Detection of Road Traffic Conditions

Ebtesam Alomari[1(✉)] and Rashid Mehmood[2]

[1] Faculty of Computing and Information Technology,
King AbdulAziz University, Jeddah, Saudi Arabia
EAlomari0011@stu.kau.edu.sa
[2] High Performance Computing Center, King AbdulAziz University, Jeddah,
Saudi Arabia
RMehmood@kau.edu.sa

Abstract. Traffic congestion is a worldwide problem, resulting in massive delays, increased fuel wastage, and damages to human wealth, health, and lives. Various social media e.g. Twitter have emerged as an important source of information on various topics including real-time road traffic. Particularly, social media can provide information about certain future events, the causes behind the certain behavior, anomalies, and accidents, as well as the public feelings on a matter. In this paper, we aim to analyze tweets (in the Arabic language) related to the road traffic in Jeddah city to detect the most congested roads. Using the SAP HANA platform for Twitter data extraction, storage, and analysis, we discover that Al-Madinah, King AbdulAziz, and Alharamain are the most congested roads in the city, the tweets related to the road traffic are posted mostly in the rush hours, and the highest traffic tweeting time is 1 pm.

Keywords: Twitter analysis · Traffic congestion · Arabic language
Big data analytics · SAP HANA · Smart cities

1 Introduction

Traffic congestion is a worldwide problem, resulting in massive delays, increased fuel wastage, monetary losses, and damages to human health and lives. Traditional approaches for traffic measurement have relied on road sensors. Video analysis, mobile data, and vehicular ad hoc networks (VANETs) are being used also for traffic monitoring purposes. More recently, various social media such as Twitter have emerged as an important source of information on various topics including real-time road traffic. Particularly, social media can provide information about certain future events, the causes behind certain behavior, anomalies, and accidents, as well as the public feelings on a matter.

Twitter is widely used for communication, and sharing personal status, events, news, etc. It was originally introduced in 2006, and the number of active users is growing every year. According to the sixth edition of Arab Social Media Report in 2014 [1], the number of the active Twitter users in Saudi Arabia is 2.4 million, which represent the highest number of Twitter users in the Arab region. Furthermore, the

© ICST Institute for Computer Sciences, Social Informatics and Telecommunications Engineering 2018
R. Mehmood et al. (Eds.): SCITA 2017, LNICST 224, pp. 98–110, 2018.
https://doi.org/10.1007/978-3-319-94180-6_12

Kingdom accounts for over 40% of all active Twitter users in the Arab region. By 2016, the number of Twitter users in Saudi Arabia had reached 4.99 million [2]. Saudi Arabia, hence, presents an excellent opportunity for extracting useful information from Twitter media.

Twitter provides easy-to-access APIs to enable collecting large and diverse data for analysis of valuable information such as road traffic information. Currently, road traffic congestion is one of the biggest problems in Saudi Arabia especially in large cities like Jeddah. Jeddah city is the second largest city in Saudi Arabia and arguably the most congested one. The lack of public transportation, the increasing number of vehicles, and an enormous number of pilgrim visitors all year round, have increased accidents and traffic jams in many major roads in the city.

A Large number of tweets are posted every day, by users who wish to inform their followers about current road traffic congestion condition, either to share information or to complain about the traffic problems. Also, there are official Twitter accounts, which have thousands of followers and tweets about the current road traffic conditions in Jeddah, such as @Jed_Rd1. Thus, analyzing these tweets might be useful to predict traffic congestion.

In this paper, we collect tweets in Arabic language related to traffic in Jeddah city and then analyze the data to find the most congested streets and roads. The data will be stored in *SAP HANA* database. *SAP HANA workbench* will be used to create the tables, execute the queries and analyze the data. Further, *SAP Lumira* will be used to visualize the results.

The standard text Analysis in *SAP HANA* using the *VOICEOFCUSTOMER-configuration* does not suffice. There is a need to create custom dictionaries for unknown terms in the SAP HANA system. Therefore, we will create dictionaries for Jeddah streets and roads names. Additionally, we will create dictionaries for the most popular Arabic words related to traffic jam, transportation, and the causes of traffic congestion. Finally, analysis results will be visualized using the word cloud and charts.

The main objectives and contributions of this paper can be summarized as follows:

- To discover the most congested streets and roads in Jeddah.
- To find the time periods when the number of tweets about traffic are at the highest.
- To detect the major causes of traffic congestion (accident, rains, etc.)
- To find the Arabic words that are used while tweeting about the traffic.

The Twitter data analysis carried out in this paper reveals that the most congested roads are Al-Madinah Rd, King AbdulAziz Rd, and Alharamain Rd. We also found that the most tweets related to the road traffic are posted in the rush hours and the highest traffic tweets time is 1 pm.

The rest of the paper is organized as follows. Section 2 presents brief information about SAP HANA. Section 3 reviews the related works. Section 4 illustrates the methodology. Section 5 explains the analysis process, followed by the results in Sect. 6. Finally, we draw our conclusions in Sect. 7.

2 Background: SAP HANA

SAP HANA is a relational database management system (RDBMS) developed by SAP SE. Additionally, it is an in-memory columnar database offering groundbreaking performance. It is the integration of transactional and analytical workload within the same database management system [3]. Further, SAP HANA Extended Application Services (SAP HANA XS) provides the *SAP HANA Web-based Development Workbench* that supports developing entire applications in a Web browser without the need to install any development tools.

SAP HANA Web-based Development Workbench includes a *Catalog* and *Editor* tools [4].

- Catalog: enables developing and maintaining SQL catalog objects in the SAP HANA database. It also supports creating tables, executing SQL queries and creating a remote source to collect data. Furthermore, catalog supports text analysis and text mining.
- Editor: supports running design-time objects in the SAP HANA Repository. It supports a great information view, which is a calculation view. The data foundation of the calculation view can include tables, column views, analytic views and calculation views. Also, it enables creating Joins, Unions, Aggregation, and Projections on data sources.

Moreover, SAP offers a data visualization tool for reporting on top of SAP HANA, named *SAP Lumira*[1]. It can be used to investigate GBI data stored in SAP HANA. It is a straightforward and user-friendly interface which allows users to swiftly analyze data without the need for scripting. To analyze the text in SAP HANA, there is a need to create *full-text indexing* on the text column and this results in the new table '$TA_table.' It supports tokenization, which means it decomposes word phrase or sentence into tokens. After that, it automatically specifies a type of each token such as persons, products or places.

Moreover, *catalog* supports text analysis for Arabic text. Words can be extracted and linked to the corresponding topics. Additionally, it can detect if any emoticons are used in the text. To use the default configuration, developers simply need to include *VOICEOFCUSTOMER* parameter in a query. However, if the standard configuration doesn't suffice to the requirement, developers need to customize keywords in new dictionaries.

3 Literature Review

Many traffic monitoring systems have been proposed to detect road congestion using video and image processing technologies. Wei and Dai suggested a real-time traffic congestion estimation approach based on image texture feature extraction and texture analysis [5]. A congestion detection approach using video processing has been

---

[1] http://saplumira.com/.

proposed in [6]. A congestion model based on speed and density of vehicles was proposed in [7]. Traditional approaches for traffic measurement have relied on sensors that are buried under the road (such as inductive loops) or installed on roadside [8]. However, these approaches require sensors and other equipment such as cameras and thus the deployment and maintenance are costly.

Several approaches have been proposed, particularly during the last decade, to use vehicular ad hoc networks (VANETs) for monitoring traffic [8–10], in general, and for specific purposes, such as for traffic coordination and disaster management [11–13]. Simulations have also been playing a key role in transportation planning and control [14]. A number of works on operations research related to transportation in smart cities have also been proposed, see e.g. car-free cities [15], intelligent mobility [16], big data in transport operations [17, 18], prototyping in urban logistics [19], and autonomic transportation systems [20–22],

More recently, Twitter has become a popular social platform to share real-time traffic information since numerous users tweet to report about problems that may affect traffic such as traffic accidents. Furthermore, there are specific and official Twitter accounts created to report on traffic conditions and events in particular cities. These accounts generate useful sources of information for the followers. Therefore, there is an enormous amount of traffic updates and information available in different Twitter accounts and can be freely obtained via the easy-to-access APIs [23].

Recently, some methodologies, techniques, and tools have been proposed to analyze traffic tweets. Gu et al. [24] proposed a method to collect, process and filter public tweets about traffic in Pittsburgh and Philadelphia Metropolitan. They have used Twitter REST API to collect real-time tweets using a dictionary of relevant keywords and their combinations that can indicate traffic condition. After that, the collected tweets are geocoded to define their locations. Then, the tweets are categorized into one of the five event classifications, which are Accidents, Roadwork, Hazards & Weather, Events, and Marathon. However, they mainly focused on identifying the incident categories, and they did not identify the most congested roads.

Moreover, techniques have also been proposed to analyze tweets using data mining. Kurniawan et al. [25] conducted experiments to classify real-time road traffic tweets using data mining. They collected real-time data about Yogyakarta Province, Indonesia using Twitter Streaming API. Further, they specified search parameters such as follow and track parameters. In follow parameter, they defined a list of the twitter account that reports about traffic, to get tweets from these accounts only. Furthermore, track parameter was used to identify the keywords that should be included in the retrieved data. Additionally, they compared classification performance of three machine learning algorithms, namely Naive Bayes (NB), Support Vector Machine (SVM), and Decision Tree (DT). However, they only classified tweets into the traffic or non_traffic categories.

Similar work is proposed by D'Andrea et al. [26]. They suggested an intelligent system, based on text mining and machine learning algorithms. They collected real-time tweets of several regions of the Italian road networks and then assigned the appropriate class label to each tweet, as to whether the tweet is related to a traffic event or not. Ribeiro et al. [27] analyzed tweets to detect traffic events. They manually listed the most frequent types of events that were used to indicate traffic conditions. The dataset is collected from ten twitter accounts whose primary purpose is to report traffic conditions in Belo Horizonte, Brazil. After that, they created a set of place names, called GEODICT. Subsequently, they detected the locations and streets names by using string matching technique by searching for substrings from the tweet that can be detected in GEODICT. Wongcharoen and Senivongse [28] built a congestion severity prediction model to predict traffic congestion severity level. The collected tweets are geotagged and contain traffic-related keywords. However, like previous approaches [25, 27], the tweets are fetched only from particular accounts. Finally, Suma et al. [29] have analyzed Twitter data to detect events related to road traffic and other topics for smart cities planning purposes. Their focus is on the use of big data platforms including Spark and Hadoop to analyse large amounts of data. The results are presented by analyzing 500,000 tweets about the London city.

In this paper, we execute several queries using the Arabic keywords and synonyms to fetch tweets that are posted about Jeddah traffic, and then we analyzed the tweets to identify the most congested roads. To the best of our knowledge, most papers on traffic detection using Twitter data analysis focus on languages other than Arabic, and none of them have analyzed Arabic language tweets in Jeddah for traffic related purposes. Twitter offers two categories of search APIs [30]; (a) Streaming API that gives Twitter's global stream of Tweet data, and (b) Twitter REST API or batch query API that supports access to read and write Twitter data. In this work, we use the REST API because it supports writing search queries to retrieve tweets that include the specified keywords or tweets from specific Twitter accounts. Additionally, there is a possibility to use 'OR' and 'AND' logical operations between keywords to design good quality queries. However, the search index has a 7-day limit. So, there is a need to re-execute the queries to retrieve new tweets.

Furthermore, REST API supports *geocode* parameter to restrict query by a given location using "latitude, longitude, radius". Thus, when executing the queries, the search API will first attempt to search for Tweets which have lat/long within the queried geocode. If there are no results, it will attempt to detect Tweet's location information from the location data in user's profile.

4   Methodology

We generated a list of Arabic keywords related to road traffic, transportation, and traffic reasons. In addition, we collected a list of streets and roads names in Jeddah using OpenStreetMap[2]. We searched for the most popular Twitter accounts that tweet about Jeddah and traffic conditions in the city.

As shown in Fig. 1, the main implementation steps can be summarized as follows:

1. Search queries will be executed in *SAP HANA Web-based Development Workbench Catalog* to collect tweets using twitter REST search API. The retrieved tweets will be stored in the created table 'TrafficJed'.
2. The duplicated tweets (retweets) will be deleted from the table.

---

[2] https://www.openstreetmap.org/.

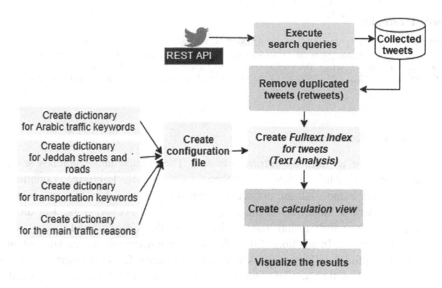

Fig. 1. Implementation Flowchart

3. The created lists of custom dictionaries will be used to create a new configuration file for analysis using *SAP HANA Web-based Development Workbench Editor.*
4. The created configuration file will be used to create the *fulltext index* on 'Tweets' column to split the text into tokens and specify the token type based on the created dictionaries.
5. Calculation view will be created.
6. In SAP Lumira, the result will be virtualized using charts and word clouds.

4.1 Search Queries

We tried to design high-quality search queries to retrieve a large number of highly related tweets about traffic in Jeddah. We have used the collected list of Arabic keywords about traffic and transportation to write a large number of queries. In addition, we have used the following accounts that tweets about Jeddah (@Jed_Rd1, @eMoroor, @SukkanJeddah, @jedgovsa, @JeddahNow and @jeddah_ar) to fetch their tweets about traffic.

Generally, there are two types of location information:

1. Tweets from geotagging enabled smartphones that carry latitude/longitude coordinates of the locations where users posted the tweets.
2. Location name referred in tweet texts.

In this work, this two location information is used to collect the tweets related to traffic and transportation in Jeddah city. To handle the problem of non-geotagged tweets, we re-execute all queries after adding the keyword 'Jeddah' and modifying the locations parameters to 'null'. However, there are still some tweets that are not included in our analysis because they do not carry any location information.

Query Example:

```
UPSERT "GBI_001"."Trafficjed" SELECT * FROM "GBI_001"." Tweets"
('@Jed_Rdl OR @eMoroor OR @SukkanJeddah OR @jedgovsa OR @JeddahNow OR
@Jeddah_ar AND ( زحام OR زحمه OR يزدحم OR مزدحم OR مزدحمة )',
1500,null, null, '21.3891, 39.8579, 35mi' , null , null , null , null );
```

4.2 Tweets Collection

We created a table to store the retrieved tweets. The created table includes several attributes such as 'UserId', 'Tweet', ' UserName', 'CreatedAt', 'Latitude', 'Longitude', 'Country', 'Place_name'. All the collected tweets will be stored in 'Tweet' column. Location fields will be important in the analysis process. However, if the user did not add information about the city and county in his/her profile, 'Country' and 'Place_name' fields would be empty. In addition, if they disable location service in their smartphones 'Latitude', 'Longitude' will be empty. 'CreatedAt' attribute refers to the time and date of posting the tweet. It will be helpful to find the top tweet time. Moreover, after we created the table, we executed all search queries. We collected tweets in the period between 13/4/2017 and 19/5/2017. Before analyzing the data, we delete all duplicated tweets in the table.

5 Tweets Analysis

5.1 Custom Dictionaries

The standard text Analysis in SAP HANA using the VOICEOFCUSTOMER-configuration does not suffice where not all Arabic tokens are classified under the right token type. Therefore, we need to add a custom dictionary for unknown terms in the SAP HANA system and then create a new configuration file. We created four dictionaries, which are:

- JeddahStreets: includes the main streets and roads in Jeddah city.
- TrafficJam: includes the collected list of Arabic traffic congestion synonyms (such as زحام, يزدحم, تزدحم, مزدحمة, مزدحمه).
- Transportation: includes the collected Arabic keywords about transportation (such as طريق, الطريق, طرق, الطرق, سيارة, سياره, السيارة).
- TrafficReasons: include the collected Arabic words about traffic congestion reasons (such as حادث,حريق, مطر).

5.2 Fulltext Index

To analyze the tweets in SAP HANA, we need to create a fulltext index for 'Tweet' column. Creating the index required executing the following SQL statement, which will lead to creating a new table containing analysis results.

```
CREATE FULLTEXT INDEX"GBI_001"."Trafficjed_Sentiment" ON
"GBI_001"."Trafficjed_001" (TWEET) TEXT ANALYSIS ON LANGUAGE COLUMN
"ISOLANGUAGECODE" LANGUAGE DETECTION ('AR') CONFIGURATION 'gbi-student-
001.CustomDictionaries:: StreetConfig_001';
```

The created table 'Trafficjed_Sentiment' will include:

– TA_token: the list of keywords extracted for the tweets.
– TA_type (token type): It will be one of the types specified in our newly created
  dictionaries, i.e., TrafficJam or TrafficReason).

5.3   Calculation View

To get the result of the text analysis, we created calculation view. We need two columns from the table 'TrafficJed', which are 'ID' the id of the tweets and 'CreatedAt', which represents the date and time of posting a tweet by the user. We also need the 'ID', 'TA_Token' and 'TA_Type' from 'Trafficjed_Sentiment'.

Therefore, we added two projections the first one for the table that includes the tweets (TrafficJed) and the second one for the table created for analysis (Trafficjed_Sentiment). Further, we need the month and hour of posting the tweets, so we calculate these data from 'CreatedAt' attribute. When we executed the created calculation view, we got result table. Figure 2 shows a sample of the results.

6   Results

To achieve the main objective of this paper, we created a chart to represent the most congested streets and roads in Jeddah, as shown in Fig. 3. However, in analysis results, we noticed that SAP HANA represents the same Arabic words that end with 'ه' or 'ة' as different words. For instance, 'طريق المدينة' and 'طريق المدينه' are the same roads, which is 'Al-Madinah Rd'. In addition, 'شارع التحلية' and 'شارع التحليه' are the same street 'Tahlia St'. Moreover, 'طريق الملك' is mostly used as an abbreviation for 'طريق الملك عبدالعزيز' 'King Abdulaziz Rd'. To handle this issue, we calculated the total tweets frequency for each street or road that appear in analysis results as different words, and then we draw a chart to represent the most congested roads and streets. As shown in Fig. 4, the top 5 congested roads are *Al-Madinah* Rd, *King Abdulaziz* Rd, *Alharamain* Rd, *Tahlia* St. and *Makkah-Jeddah* highway.

We draw a chart to find the peak time. We noticed that users post tweets about traffic at 7 am, and 1, 3, 4 pm more than any other time in the day. As shown in Fig. 5, the highest tweets time is at 1 pm. These results are expected because they represent rush hours (time to get to *work*/school or to get home from *work*/school).

We discovered the top traffic reasons that mentioned in the tweets. The results indicated that the synonyms of the word 'حادث' (accidents) are the most traffic reasons mentioned in the collected tweets in May. On the other side, the synonyms of the word

	12 HOUR	12 ID	12 MONTH	RB TA_TOKEN	RB TA_TYPE
9	13	1	4	تقاطع	transportation
10	13	1	4	شارع فلسطين	JedStreets
11	11	1	4	زحمة	trafficJam
12	14	1	4	زحمة	trafficJam
13	16	1	4	الزحمة	trafficJam
14	16	4	4	زحمة	trafficJam
15	16	2	4	الشارع	transportation
16	19	1	4	زحمة	trafficJam
17	4	1	4	الطريق	TrafficReason
18	4	1	4	لزحمة	trafficJam
19	4	1	4	طريق مكة	JedStreets
20	4	1	4	مزدحم	trafficJam
21	4	1	4	شاهدات	transportation

Fig. 2. Sample of analysis results

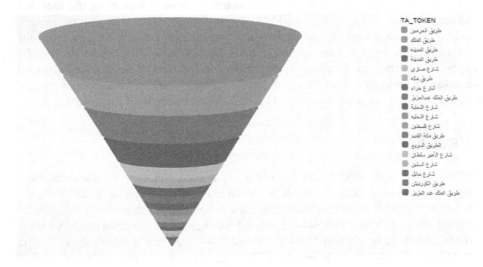

Fig. 3. Congested streets and roads

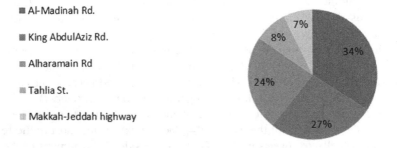

Fig. 4. Top 5 congested streets and roads in Jeddah

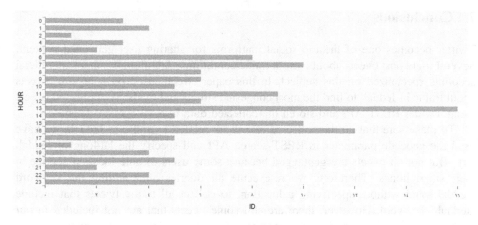

Fig. 5. Number of the posted tweets about traffic per hour

'حريق' (fire) are the most reason that mentioned in the collected tweets in April because fuel truck caught fire on the main road between Makkah and Jeddah city.

Furthermore, Fig. 6 shows the word cloud for the Arabic traffic jam, traffic reasons and transportation words and synonyms. We can notice that the most used words are the synonyms of the following three keywords 'طريق' (road), 'شارع' (street), and 'زحمة' (crowding).

Fig. 6. Traffic and transportation keywords

7 Conclusions

Twitter becomes one of the top social platforms for sharing user-generated content. Several users post tweets about current traffic conditions. Additionally, there are official accounts specialized on this subject. In this paper, we focused on analyzing tweets about traffic in Jeddah to find the most congested streets and roads. We collected tweets using Twitter REST API and stored the collected data in SAP HANA database.

To make sure that all the collected tweets are related to traffic in Jeddah, we have used the geocode parameter in REST search API and specify the lat/long of Jeddah city. But not all tweets are geotagged because some users disable location service in their smartphones. Therefore, we re-execute all queries after adding the keyword 'Jeddah' and without specifying a location, to collect all traffic tweets that include 'Jeddah' keyword. However, there are still some tweets that are not included in our analysis because they are not geotagged and not carrying location information.

Moreover, SAP HANA Web-based Development Workbench was used to create a table, execute search queries and analyze the data. While the default analysis configuration in SAP HANA is not efficient for Arabic text analysis, we created a new configuration file. We added new dictionaries for the Arabic keywords related to traffic jam, transportation, and traffic reasons. In addition, we created a dictionary for the main streets and roads in Jeddah.

Finally, we have used SAP Lumira to virtualize the results by creating charts and word cloud. We found that the most congested streets and roads in Jeddah are Al-Madinah Rd, King Abdulaziz Rd. and Alharamain Rd. We also found that the most tweets related to traffic are posted in the rush hour (at 7 am and 1, 3, 4 pm). In future, we plan to collect more tweets to analyze traffic in other cities such as Riyadh. We also plan to use other data sources to collect traffic data. Future work will also consider improving the data analyses methodology.

Acknowledgments. The work carried out in this paper is supported by the HPC Center at the King Abdulaziz University.

References

1. Mourtada, R., Salem, F., Al-Shaer, S.: Citizen Engagement and Public Services in the Arab World: The Potential of Social Media. Arab Social Media Report (2014)
2. Twitter: number of active users 2010–2016, Statista (2016). www.statista.com
3. SAP: What is SAP HANA. In Memory Computing and Real Time Analytics
4. SAP HANA Web-Based Development Workbench - Introduction to SAP HANA Development - SAP Library
5. Wei, L., Dai, H.-Y.: Real-time road congestion detection based on image texture analysis. Procedia Eng. **137**, 196–201 (2016)
6. Kanungo, A., Sharma, A., Singla, C.: Smart traffic lights switching and traffic density calculation using video processing. In: 2014 Recent Advances in Engineering and Computational Sciences (RAECS), pp. 1–6. IEEE (2014)

7. Widyantoro, D.H., Enjat Munajat, M.D.: Fuzzy traffic congestion model based on speed and density of vehicle. In: 2014 International Conference of Advanced Informatics: Concept, Theory and Application (ICAICTA), pp. 321–325. IEEE (2014)

8. Mehmood, R., Nekovee, M.: Vehicular AD HOC and grid networks: discussion, design and evaluation. In: 14th World Congress on Intelligent Transport Systems, ITS 2007, pp. 1555–1562 (2007)

9. Gillani, S., Shahzad, F., Qayyum, A., Mehmood, R.: A survey on security in vehicular ad hoc networks. In: Berbineau, M., et al. (eds.) Nets4Cars/Nets4Trains 2013. LNCS, vol. 7865, pp. 59–74. Springer, Heidelberg (2013). https://doi.org/10.1007/978-3-642-37974-1_5

10. Alvi, A., Nabi, Z., Greaves, D.J., Mehmood, R.: Intra-vehicular verification and control: a two-pronged approach. Int. J. Veh. Inf. Commun. Syst. **2**, 248–268 (2011)

11. Alazawi, Z., Altowaijri, S., Mehmood, R., Abdljabar, M.B.: Intelligent disaster management system based on cloud-enabled vehicular networks. In: Vinel, A., et al. (eds.) 2011 11th International Conference on ITS Telecommunications, ITST 2011, pp. 361–368. IEEE, St. Petersburg (2011)

12. Alazawi, Z., Abdljabar, M.B., Altowaijri, S., Vegni, A.M., Mehmood, R.: ICDMS: an intelligent cloud based disaster management system for vehicular networks. In: Vinel, A., Mehmood, R., Berbineau, M., Garcia, C.R., Huang, C.-M., Chilamkurti, N. (eds.) Nets4Cars/Nets4Trains 2012. LNCS, vol. 7266, pp. 40–56. Springer, Heidelberg (2012). https://doi.org/10.1007/978-3-642-29667-3_4

13. Alazawi, Z., Alani, O., Abdljabar, M.B., Altowaijri, S., Mehmood, R.: A smart disaster management system for future cities. In: WiMobCity 2014. International Workshop on Wireless and Mobile Technologies for Smart Cities, pp. 1–10 (2014)

14. Ayres, G., Mehmood, R.: On discovering road traffic information using virtual reality simulations. In: 11th International Conference on Computer Modelling and Simulation, UKSim 2009, pp. 411–416 (2009)

15. Mehmood, R., Lu, J.A.: Computational Markovian analysis of large systems. J. Manuf. Technol. Manag. **22**, 804–817 (2011)

16. Büscher, M., et al.: Intelligent mobility systems: some socio-technical challenges and opportunities. In: Mehmood, R., Cerqueira, E., Piesiewicz, R., Chlamtac, I. (eds.) EuropeComm 2009. LNICST, vol. 16, pp. 140–152. Springer, Heidelberg (2009). https://doi.org/10.1007/978-3-642-11284-3_15

17. Mehmood, R., Meriton, R., Graham, G., Hennelly, P., Kumar, M.: Exploring the influence of big data on city transport operations: a Markovian approach. Int. J. Oper. Prod. Manag. **37**, 75–104 (2017)

18. Mehmood, R., Graham, G.: Big data logistics: a health-care transport capacity sharing model. Procedia Comput. Sci. **64**, 1107–1114 (2015)

19. Graham, G., Mehmood, R., Coles, E.: Exploring future cityscapes through urban logistics prototyping: a technical viewpoint. Supply Chain Manag. **20**, 341–352 (2015)

20. Schlingensiepen, J., Mehmood, R., Nemtanu, F.C.: Framework for an autonomic transport system in smart cities. Cybern. Inf. Technol. **15**, 50–62 (2015)

21. Schlingensiepen, J., Mehmood, R., Nemtanu, F.C., Niculescu, M.: Increasing sustainability of road transport in European cities and metropolitan areas by facilitating autonomic road transport systems (ARTS). In: Wellnitz, J., Subic, A., Trufin, R. (eds.) Sustainable Automotive Technologies, 2013 Proceedings of the 5th International Conference ICSAT 2013, pp. 201–210. Springer, Ingolstadt (2014). https://doi.org/10.1007/978-3-319-01884-3_20

22. Schlingensiepen, J., Nemtanu, F.: Autonomic transport management systems—enabler for smart cities, personalized medicine, participation and industry grid/industry 4.0. In: Sladkowski, A., Pamula, W. (eds.) Intelligent Transportation Systems – Problems and Perspectives, pp. 3–35. Springer, London (2016). https://doi.org/10.1007/978-3-319-19150-8_1

23. Wang, S., He, L., Stenneth, L., Yu, P.S., Li, Z.: Citywide Traffic Congestion Estimation with Social Media

24. Gu, Y., Qian (Sean), Z., Chen, F.: From Twitter to detector: real-time traffic incident detection using social media data. Transp. Res. Part C Emerg. Technol. **67**, 321–342 (2016)

25. Kurniawan, D.A., Wibirama, S., Setiawan, N.A.: Real-time traffic classification with Twitter data mining (2016)

26. D'Andrea, E., Ducange, P., Lazzerini, B., Marcelloni, F.: Real-time detection of traffic from Twitter stream analysis. IEEE Trans. Intell. Transp. Syst. **16**, 2269–2283 (2015)

27. Ribeiro, S.S., Davis, C.A., Oliveira, D.R.R., Meira, W., Gonçalves, T.S., Pappa, G.L.: Traffic observatory: a system to detect and locate traffic events and conditions using Twitter Sílvio. In: Proceedings of the 5th International Workshop on Location-Based Social Networks - LBSN 2012, p. 5 (2012)

28. Wongcharoen, S., Senivongse, T.: Twitter analysis of road traffic congestion severity estimation. In: 13th International Joint Conference on Computer Science and Software Engineering (2016)

29. Suma, S., Mehmood, R., Albugami, N., Katib, I., Albeshri, A.: Enabling next generation logistics and planning for smarter societies. Procedia Comput. Sci. **109**, 1122–1127 (2017)

30. Kumar, S., Morstatter, F., Liu, H.: Twitter Data Analytics. Springer, New York (2014). https://doi.org/10.1007/978-1-4614-9372-3

Automatic Event Detection in Smart Cities Using Big Data Analytics

Sugimiyanto Suma[1(✉)], Rashid Mehmood[2], and Aiiad Albeshri[1]

[1] Department of Computer Science, FCIT,
King Abdulaziz University, Jeddah 21589, Saudi Arabia
sugimiyanto@gmail.com, aaalbeshri@kau.edu.sa
[2] High Performance Computing Center, King Abdulaziz University,
Jeddah 21589, Saudi Arabia
RMehmood@kau.edu.sa

Abstract. Big data technologies enable smart city systems in sensing the city at micro-levels, making intelligent decisions, and taking appropriate actions, all within stringent time bounds. Social media have revolutionized our societies and is gradually becoming a key pulse of smart societies by sensing the information about the people and their spatio-temporal experiences around the living spaces. In this paper, we use Twitter for the detection of spatio-temporal events in London. Specifically, we use big data and machine learning platforms including Spark, and Tableau, to study twitter data about London. Moreover, we use the Google Maps Geocoding API to locate the tweeters and make additional analysis. We find and locate congestion around London and empirically demonstrate that events can be detected automatically by analyzing data. We detect the occurrence of multiple events including the London Notting Hill Carnival 2017 event, both their locations and times, without any prior knowledge of the event. The results presented in the paper have been obtained by analyzing over three million tweets.

Keywords: Smart cities · Big data · High performance computing
Social media analysis · Machine learning

1 Introduction

Nowadays, having gadgets has become a necessity. Every electronic device is connected to a worldwide network called internet. This large network connection enables us to manage those connected devices. In another hand, the ability of managing the connected devices, and the flowing data are essential to support smart cities. Smart city application helps us to make a better life. It changes the way we work and overcome the problem of urban life, supported by various emerging technologies. Big data technologies would play a key role in support smart city systems and applications due to the need to sense the city at the micro-levels, make intelligent decisions, and take appropriate actions, all within stringent time bounds. Social media has revolutionized our societies and is gradually becoming a key pulse of smart societies by sensing the information about the people and their spatio-temporal experiences around the living

© ICST Institute for Computer Sciences, Social Informatics and Telecommunications Engineering 2018
R. Mehmood et al. (Eds.): SCITA 2017, LNICST 224, pp. 111–122, 2018.
https://doi.org/10.1007/978-3-319-94180-6_13

spaces. One of the useful application in smart city is event detection, sub-part of smart societies. For stakeholders, detecting an occurring event is important in finding out what is happening in the city for decision-making or future planning purposes. Compared with sensor-based event detection, analyzing social media data such as twitter is more cost-effective way to detect events. Sensor-based detection mines traffic data of installed sensors and cameras in certain places. It is costly, for hardware procurement and network installation, among other things. In addition, the number of installed measurement instruments limits the detection coverage. While social media event detection has wider coverage, and more efficient in terms of resources. They both have their pros and cons and could complement each other in terms of the convenience of event detection and information coverage.

In this paper, we use twitter for the detection of spatio-temporal events in London. Specifically, we use big data and AI platforms including Spark, and Tableau, to study twitter data about London. We extend our earlier work [1] of using social media data to detect spatio-temporal events in London. In this paper, we use better data analytics by implementing machine learning for contextual analysis awareness using Apache Spark MLlib. The acquired data should be truly related to traffic problem, while the acquired data is not necessary relevant to traffic problem. As well as, integrating the process with HPC to have better analysis performance. We use apache spark for parallel data processing, which is installed on top of HPC cluster. As well as, we utilize FEFS system for high-speed data distribution system. Moreover, we use the Google Maps Geocoding API to locate the tweeters and make additional analysis.

We find and locate congestion around the London city. We also empirically demonstrate that events can be detected automatically by analyzing data. We detect the occurrence of multiple events such as "Underbelly festival" and "The Luna Cinema". Underbelly festival was located at south bank, while The Luna Cinema was located in some places such as around Greenwich Park, crystal Palace Park, and National Trust-Morden Hall Park. As well as, we detect the London Notting Hill Carnival 2017 event. This is located around Notting Hill as it was the location of Notting Hill carnival [2], the Europe's biggest street festival which was organized by London Notting Hill carnival enterprises trust. We detect those event's locations and times, without any prior knowledge of the event. The results presented in the paper have been obtained by analyzing over three million tweets.

We summarize our contributions in this paper as follows:

– We design workflow of big data analytics to detect spatio-temporal events in London using Apache Spark.
– We detect the occurring events automatically by analyzing twitter data without any prior knowledge of events, both its location and time.
– We integrate big data processing with HPC technology to improve performance.

While researcher have studied social media based event detection in the recent past, the use of Apache Spark for social media based event detection has not been found in the literature. The specific data, its analysis, and event detection presented in this paper also make the contributions of this paper unique.

This paper is structured as follows. Literature review is given in Sect. 2. The used design and methodology is explained in Sect. 3. The discussion of our research results and analysis are described in Sect. 4. Finally, conclusion and future works are discussed in Sect. 5.

2 Literature Review

Research for smart cities using big data and social media analysis is becoming increasingly important. Khan et al. developed a prototype analytics as a cloud service, for managing and analyzing big data in smart cities [3]. Herrera-Quintero et al. combined big data and IoT to support transportation planning system for Bus Rapid Transit (BRT) systems [4]. Kolchyna et al. predicted spikes in sales by detecting twitter events of 150 million tweets [5]. Arfat et al. proposed an architecture for smart city as a mobile computing system with big data technologies, fogs, and clouds. In order to enable smarter cities with enhanced mobility information [6]. Other related works in smart cities are exists, such as virtual-reality-based traffic event simulations [7], location based services [8], urban logistics [9–12], and smart emergency management system [13, 14].

In another hand, for spatio-temporal event detection purpose, exploiting social media data is a cost-effective way compared with traditional method using installed sensors and cameras. There have been number of works analyzing social media data for detecting event. Gu et al. developed a real-time detector of traffic incident with five categories, including occurring events. It applies semi-naïve-Bayes classification [15]. Nguyen and Jung, proposed an approach for early event identification, by combining content-based features from the social text data and the propagation of news between viewers [16]. Unankard et al. identified strong correlations between user location and event location to detect emerging hotspot events [17].

Wang combined visual sensor (cameras) with social sensor (twitter feeds) to detect events. Images processing is applied to detect abnormal patterns indicating occurring events. Next, using social data information to derive the high-level semantic [18]. Kaleel and Abhari, proposed an algorithm to detect interesting events by matching its keywords on cluster labels of tweet (clustering). Subsequently, trend it based on time, geo-locations, and cluster size [19].

There are several event detection works related to road traffic [20–22], however, they do not use big data technologies and different analysis technique. Moreover, our work integrates big data technologies and HPC. In substance, this is an extension of our previous work [1]. In this work, we carried out a deeper analysis such as overcoming the limitation of contextual analysis of the status message, in order to ensure that the acquired data is truly related to traffic problem caused by occurring events.

3 Methodology and Design

We developed a system architecture to detect spatio-temporal events as shown in Fig. 1. First, we crawl the status message (twitter) according to a predefined keyword set and a set of social media user accounts, which is relevant to traffic. Thereafter, we store the crawled data into data pool. Secondly, we preprocess the acquired raw data before going

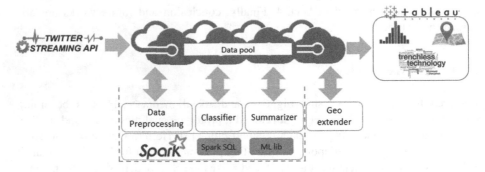

Fig. 1. Workflow of spatio-temporal events detection

to classification learning, where-upon social media data has lots of noises. It is not standardized, and there are plenty of unnecessary characters and words. Third, the status messages are classified into either traffic-related or non-traffic-related message by utilizing a supervised machine learning system. Forth, the classified status messages are extended to get more location information. Finally, the traffic-related status message with spatio-temporal information is visualized by using a map visualization.

We use apache spark platform to do heavy computation with huge data. Since spark is an in-memory computation platform, spark has better speed up to process big data in parallel, compared with other parallel data processing such as Hadoop map reduce [23]. We use spark for data processing and classifier stages. For data pool, where all machine processors take the acquired data for further processing, we utilize the power of Fujitsu Exabyte File System (FEFS). It is a parallel file storage system technology. FEFS is a software for HPC cluster systems, developed by Fujitsu Ltd. It enables high-speed parallel distributed processing of huge amounts of transactions [24]. As well as, it has superior features such as actual operational convenience, system scalability, and high reliability for zero operational downtime during a long computation. Thus, it contributes to significant improvements in system performance. Those FEFS and spark technologies are installed on top of HPC cluster.

3.1 Data Acquisition

We use social media data source (twitter) related to traffic. It is done by defining a set of keywords and a set of twitter user accounts which tend to post messages relevant to traffic such as government and media user accounts. Data crawling is performed by invoking twitter streaming API through a java based crawler application. The acquired data subsequently be stored in a data pool as raw data in FEFS system which has been described in Sect. 3. Any further data processing will pull raw data from this pool.

3.1.1 Dataset Structure

The acquired data is in raw JavaScript object notation (JSON) as a Twitter data format. It is stored in a file system as JSON file extension. In raw format, each status message contains a bunch of attributes. For our experiment purposes, we use several selected

Table 1. Raw status message data structure

Attribute	Length	Data type
Created_at	30	Time stamp
Latitude		Double
Longitude		Double
Text	140	String

required attributes for spatio-temporal event detection. The structure of raw and extended status message is shown in Tables 1 and 2 respectively.

The illustration of selected fields of raw twitter JSON data is shown in Fig. 2. It is delimited by "|" character for each attribute.

Wed Aug 21 16:54:04 +0000 2017 | 51.5131392 | -0.1397757 | Having a lovely day sitting in grid lock traffic...

Wed Aug 22 08:31:09 +0000 2017 | 51.4943053 | -0.1023826 | Traffic at this time. that's London for you...

Wed Aug 23 09:01:54 +0000 2017 | null | null | stuck in London bcose it outage i called u following...

Wed Aug 23 10:15:18 +0000 2017 | null | null | Victoria park hackney hackneytower hamlets london...

Wed Aug 23 10:29:07 +0000 2017 | 51.3898872 | 0.0421551 | Southborough, a26 London road slow moving traffic...

Wed Aug 24 15:22:41 +0000 2017 | null | null | on way home from london; been delayed in traffic...

Wed Aug 25 10:29:27 +0000 2017 | 51.5088869 | -0.1140182 | Actually hate london traffic it's taken 30 mins to go...

Wed Aug 26 12:45:32 +0000 2017 | 51.4629707 | -0.5004316 | m25 delays near j14/a3113 anticlockwise caused...

Wed Aug 28 05:09:11 +0000 2017 | null | null | fun fact london underground's logo was inspired by what is on...

Wed Aug 28 17:00:51 +0000 2017 | null | null | did you know the london chatham and dover railway opened...

Fig. 2. Illustration of raw twitter JSON data

After the data processing, classification, and geo-extender function are applied, it extends more additional attributes for spatio-temporal purposes, in order to easily plot status message's location on map visualization, as shown in Table 2.

Table 2. Extended status message data structure

Attribute	Length	Data type
Created_at	30	Time stamp
Latitude		Double
Longitude		Double
Text	140	String
Postal_code	8	String
Type	100	String

Each attribute is defined as follows:

– Created_at: the time when the status message is posted by user (timestamp)
– Latitude, Longitude: geolocation of status message

- Text: the message content posted by user
- Postal_code: the postal/zip code of status message, e.g., "SE6."
- Type: the location type of detected road name from text attribute, e.g. "route," "point_of_interest."

The illustration of data after applying data processing, classification and geo-extender function is shown in Fig. 3. It is delimited by "|" character for each attribute.

2017-08-21-16 | 51.5131392 | -0.1397757 | Having a lovely day sitting in grid lock traffic... | W1B | route	
2017-08-22-08 | 51.4943053 | -0.1023826 | Traffic at this time. that's London for you... | SE11 | route	
2017-08-23-10 | 51.3898872 | 0.0421551 | Southborough, a26 London road slow moving traffic... | BR2 | route	
2017-08-25-10 | 51.5088869 | -0.1140182 | Actually hate london traffic it's taken 30 mins to go... | SE1 | route	
2017-08-26-12 | 51.4629707 | -0.5004316 | m25 delays near j14/a3113 anticlockwise caused... | TW19 | route	

Fig. 3. Illustration of processed data after applying data processing, classification, and geo-extender function

3.2 Data Preprocessing

Data preprocessing is the first action against the acquired data in the data pool. Since it has a significant impact on accuracy and quality of learning the data by machine, hence it is an essential stage in big data analytics workflow [1]. In fact, social media status text contains lots of noise. It has plenty of unnecessary characters and words such as URL, user mention, illegal character, e.g. '&,' punctuation, and stop word. Therefore, the raw data should be preprocessed to clean those up from outliers and make it standard. We utilize spark SQL and regular expression function to preprocess the data, by referring to our defined stop word dictionary, which is adopted from stop word list website [25–27]. Data preprocessing also includes data extraction and parsing such as 'created_at' field as the date time posting to get the formatted date time, and 'coordinates' field as location precision of status message to get the spatio-temporal information. Furthermore, the preprocessed data is used to feed supervised machine learning for classification. In another hand, we ignore retweet (repost of another user's post) status message, because, it contains the same information. Thus, it leads to efficient processing. The result of data processing is stored back in data pool as cleaned data.

3.3 Classifier and Summarizer

After the status messages are clean and standard, we separate them into two categories, either they are traffic-related or non-traffic-related. At which point, the acquired data is not necessary has a meaning of traffic problem caused by occurring events, although it contains our defined keywords related to traffic. It could be a news about an accident which affected the traffic. For example, "traffic in linbro park, there has been an accident on the n3 south at the London road exit", or someone's position like "I am at London underground," or even absolutely not related to traffic such as "wanted man appeal issued human trafficking inquiry." We build a classification model by using logistic regression with stochastic gradient descent, which is available in spark MLlib. First of all, from the data pool, we take sample data to create training data to train the model. It is done by examining the status messages manually to determine its categories. Then labeling each status message by either 1 or 0. Label 1 denotes that it is traffic-related, and label 0 for non-traffic-related. Secondly, we train our model by using the training data. Thirdly, using the trained model, we classify each status message into two categories (0 and 1) iteratively. Finally, we filter out the status messages, which are not related to traffic for further processing. Furthermore, we summarize the data to get the insight by applying several data summaries such as generating buzzword (top mentioned words), counting an hourly number of tweet, and information for map plotting.

3.4 Geo-Extender

In order to plot status message's distribution in the form of map, we need to get a specific point/area location of traffic-related status messages in the form of earth cartesian coordinate (latitude, longitude). Afterwards, it will ease the user for analysis processes. This phase is done by passing latitude and longitude fields of status messages into google geocode API to get more location information such as postal code, road name, city, etc. Notably, our work uses a postal code in order to plot the location distribution of traffic-related tweet or relevant topic in the form of a map view.

3.5 Analysis Visualization

There are many ways to plot geolocation data into a map visualization for analysis phase. One of them is by using Tableau software. Tableau is a business intelligence software which helps people to see and have a better understanding of their data [28]. It enables users to explore their data with limitless visual analytics. As well as, it eases user to perform ad-hoc analysis with just a few clicks. We take the processed and geolocated data as a data source of Tableau; then we generate several visualization summaries such as a graph, word cloud, and map. With a graph, we can see the number of tweets with the time-frequency distribution in order to see the anomaly which indicates more traffic than usual. With word cloud, we can see the most mentioned words which imply the hot topic. With a map, we can depict the dissemination of traffic condition on a particular area.

By applying supervised machine learning which aims to ensure that the status message data is genuinely related to a traffic problem, we overcome the limitation of our previous work which did not consider a contextual analysis of actual traffic related problem caused by occurring events.

4   Result and Discussion

For experiment purpose, we gathered twitter data between 21st August–13th September 2017, represented as hourly data in the range (0, 576). In total, it consists of 3 million records of tweet related to our defined keyword. However, after classification process which aims to filter out non-related traffic tweet, the number of tweets are decreasing. The decrement in the tweet count is reasonable, as these status messages are not genuinely related to traffic. Even though it contains a traffic-related word, it does not mean a road traffic problem. Figure 4 shows that the time-frequency distribution of the number of tweets is varied hourly. The peak hours are around 375th and 500th hours. By looking at this, we can assume that there was an ongoing event occurring at that time which affected the traffic condition in London.

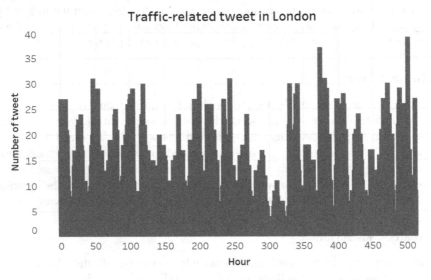

Fig. 4. Hourly number of tweet related to traffic in London

The location-intensity distribution of the number of tweets related to traffic in London is shown in Fig. 5. Red color level varies the number of distribution. The higher the intensity of red, the more traffic an area has. The figure shows that the areas around downtown had more traffic. We assume that an increase in a traffic-related tweet points to increased traffic. Grey color denotes the areas where we could not get geotagged tweets since not all acquired tweets are geotagged. There are three main areas with high-intensity red on the map. Those are in South Bank (shown as 1), around Greenwich park (shown as 2), around crystal palace park and National Trust-Morden Hall Park (shown as 3), in Fig. 5. The postal codes are SE1, SE10, SE19, and SM4, respectively.

According to London events calendar [29], in south bank, there has been an event held, called "underbelly festival." It has started from 28th April to 30th September 2017. It was a festival event held by Underbelly, which showing off cabaret, comedy, live circus, and family entertainment [30]. In another hand, around Greenwich Park, Crystal Palace Park, and National Trust-Morden Hall Park, there have been events occurred, called "The Luna Cinema," running from June to October 2017. It is an outdoor cinema for citizens or tourist to spend their warm summer evening watching a new film release or age-old classic.

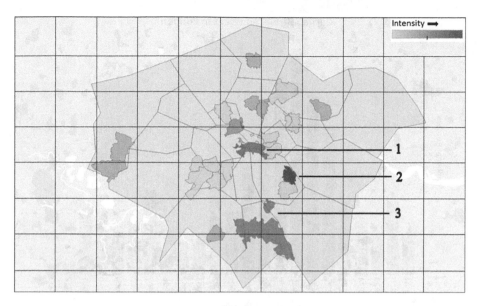

Fig. 5. Tweet intensity related to traffic in London (Color figure online)

Moreover, we analyze the hot topic among the whole tweets. Word "carnival" was among the top five most mentioned word. The location spreading of tweet related to carnival takes place is shown in Fig. 6. Most of the tweet comes from around one area, as shown in red color in the figure. By inspecting this circumstance, we can infer that there was an event related to a carnival on that area. This red colour area lies around Notting Hill London, and was the location of Notting Hill carnival [2], the Europe's biggest street festival which is organized by London Notting Hill carnival enterprises trust.

Fig. 6. Tweet intensity related to carnival in London (Color figure online)

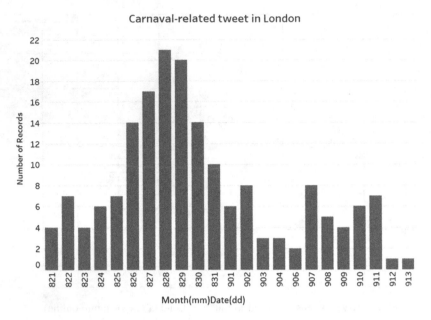

Fig. 7. Number of tweet in the period related to carnival in London

The daily frequency distribution of the number of tweets about carnival is shown in Fig. 7. We can see that the peak is on 28th August, while it is increasing gradually from 26th August and decreasing until 30th August. By observing this phenomenon, we can conclude that around those dates, there was an event related to a carnival. The carnival event was held on 26th–28th August 2017 in London [2].

This information about the event was detected automatically without any prior knowledge of the event, its location and time.

5   Conclusion

Social media has revolutionized our societies and is gradually becoming a key pulse of smart societies by sensing the information about the people and their spatio-temporal experiences around the living spaces. Analyzing social media data such as twitter has become a cost-effective way to detect events, by utilizing big data technologies such as spark, FEFS, and tableau. In this paper, we use Twitter for the detection of spatio-temporal events in London. Specifically, we use big data and AI platforms including Spark, and Tableau, to study twitter data about London. It is done by mining twitter data related to traffic problem which indicates occurring events. We have better data processing by implementing machine learning for contextual analysis awareness using spark MLlib. While the acquired data should be truly related to traffic problem.

We empirically demonstrate that events can be detected automatically by analyzing data. We detect the occurrence of multiple events such as "Underbelly festival" and "The Luna Cinema". Underbelly festival was located at south bank, while The Luna

Cinema was located in some places such as around Greenwich Park, Crystal Palace Park, and National Trust-Morden Hall Park. As well as, we detect the London Notting Hill Carnival 2017 event. This is located around Notting Hill as it was the location of Notting Hill carnival [2], the Europe's biggest street festival which was organized by London Notting Hill carnival enterprises trust. We detect those event's locations and times, without any prior knowledge of the event. The results presented in the paper have been obtained by analyzing over three million tweets. We overcome the future work of our prior work, which did not consider textual analysis to ensure that tweets are truly related to traffic problem. As well as, integrating big data technologies with HPC to enhance scalability and computational intelligence.

Although we have improved the data management and processing. It still needs improvement to have better detection accuracy, wider spatio-temporal detection, and better quality of analysis. For better detection accuracy, we plan to develop an algorithm and compared the result with actual information by associating it with events reporting such as news or media websites. For wider detection, we would acquire more social media data such as Facebook. For better quality of analysis, we hope to utilize more AI techniques. Hence, those will be the future work of our research.

Acknowledgments. The authors acknowledge with thanks the technical and financial support from the Deanship of Scientific Research (DSR) at the King Abdulaziz University (KAU), Jeddah, Saudi Arabia, under the grant number G-661-611-38. The experiments reported in this paper were performed on the Aziz supercomputer at King AbdulAziz University.

References

1. Suma, S., Mehmood, R., Albugami, N., Katib, I., Albeshri, A.: Enabling next generation logistics and planning for smarter societies. Procedia Comput. Sci. **109**, 1122–1127 (2017)
2. London.gov.uk: Notting Hill Carnival (2017). https://www.london.gov.uk/events/2017-08-26/notting-hill-carnival-2017
3. Khan, Z., Anjum, A., Soomro, K., Tahir, M.A.: Towards cloud based big data analytics for smart future cities. J. Cloud Comput. **4**, 1–11 (2015)
4. Herrera-Quintero, L.F., Banse, K., Vega-Alfonso, J., Venegas-Sanchez, A.: Smart ITS sensor for the transportation planning using the IoT and Bigdata approaches to produce ITS cloud services, pp. 3–9 (2016)
5. Kolchyna, O., Treleaven, P.C., Aste, T.: A framework for twitter events detection, differentiation and its application for retail brands (2016)
6. Arfat, Y., Aqib, M., Mehmood, R., Albeshri, A., Katib, I., Albogami, N., Alzahrani, A.: Enabling smarter societies through mobile big data fogs and clouds. Procedia Comput. Sci. **109**, 1128–1133 (2017)
7. Ayres, G., Mehmood, R.: On discovering road traffic information using virtual reality simulations. In: 11th International Conference on Computer Modelling and Simulation, UKSim 2009, pp. 411–416 (2009)
8. Ayres, G., Mehmood, R.: LocPriS: a security and privacy preserving location based services development framework (2010)
9. Mehmood, R., Graham, G.: Big data logistics: a health-care transport capacity sharing model. Procedia Comput. Sci. **64**, 1107–1114 (2015)

10. Mehmood, R., Lu, J.A.: Computational Markovian analysis of large systems. J. Manuf. Technol. Manag. **22**, 804–817 (2011)
11. Mehmood, R., Meriton, R., Graham, G., Hennelly, P., Kumar, M.: Exploring the influence of big data on city transport operations: a Markovian approach. Int. J. Oper. Prod. Manag. (2016, forthcoming)
12. Graham, G., Mehmood, R., Coles, E.: Exploring future cityscapes through urban logistics prototyping: a technical viewpoint. Supply Chain Manag. **20**, 341–352 (2015)
13. Alazawi, Z., Alani, O., Abdljabar, M.B., Altowaijri, S., Mehmood, R.: A smart disaster management system for future cities. In: International Workshop on Wireless and Mobile Technologies for Smart Cities, WiMobCity 2014, pp. 1–10 (2014)
14. Alazawi, Z., Abdljabar, Mohmmad B., Altowaijri, S., Vegni, A.M., Mehmood, R.: ICDMS: an intelligent cloud based disaster management system for vehicular networks. In: Vinel, A., Mehmood, R., Berbineau, M., Garcia, C.R., Huang, C.-M., Chilamkurti, N. (eds.) Nets4Cars/Nets4Trains 2012. LNCS, vol. 7266, pp. 40–56. Springer, Heidelberg (2012). https://doi.org/10.1007/978-3-642-29667-3_4
15. Gu, Y., Sean, Z., Chen, F.: From twitter to detector: real-time traffic incident detection using social media data. Transp. Res. Part C Emerg. Technol. **67**, 321–342 (2016)
16. Nguyen, D.T., Jung, J.E.: Real-time event detection for online behavioral analysis of big social data. Futur. Gener. Comput. Syst. **66**, 137–145 (2017)
17. Unankard, S., Li, X., Sharaf, M.A.: Emerging event detection in social networks with location sensitivity. World Wide Web **18**, 1393–1417 (2015)
18. Wang, Y.: Tweeting cameras for event detection categories and subject descriptors. In: International World Wide Web Conferences Steering Committee, pp. 1231–1241 (2015)
19. Kaleel, S.B., Abhari, A.: Cluster-discovery of twitter messages for event detection and trending. J. Comput. Sci. **6**, 47–57 (2015)
20. D'andrea, E., Ducange, P., Lazzerini, B., Marcelloni, F.: Real-time detection of traffic from twitter Stream analysis. IEEE Trans. Intell. Transp. Syst. **16**, 2269–2283 (2015)
21. Li, R., Lei, K.H., Khadiwala, R., Chang, K.C.C.: TEDAS: a Twitter-based event detection and analysis system. In: 2012 IEEE 28th International Conference on Data Engineering, Washington, DC, pp. 1273–1276 (2012). https://doi.org/10.1109/ICDE.2012.125
22. Gutierrez, C., Figuerias, P., Oliveira, P., Costa, R., Jardim-Goncalves, R.: Twitter mining for traffic events detection. In: 2015 Science and Information Conference (SAI), pp. 371–378. IEEE (2015)
23. Apache: Apache Spark. https://spark.apache.org/
24. Fujitsu Ltd.: Fujitsu Releases World's Highest-Performance File System. http://www.fujitsu.com/global/about/resources/news/press-releases/2011/1017-01.html
25. Ranks.nl: stopwords. http://www.ranks.nl/stopwords
26. Lextek.com: Stop Word List 1. http://www.lextek.com/manuals/onix/stopwords1.html
27. Github.com/Alir3z4: stop-words. https://github.com/Alir3z4/stop-words/blob/master/english.txt
28. Tableau: What is tableau - make your data make an impact. https://www.tableau.com/trial/tableau-software
29. Visitlondon.com: London Events Calendar. http://www.visitlondon.com/things-to-do/whats-on/special-events/london-events-calendar#KRbiWhui4SMAd9PT.97
30. Underbellyfestival.com: About underbelly festival. http://www.underbellyfestival.com/about

Location Privacy in Smart Cities Era

Raed Al-Dhubhani[1](✉), Rashid Mehmood[2], Iyad Katib[1],
and Abdullah Algarni[1]

[1] Department of Computer Science,
FCIT, King Abdulaziz University, Jeddah 21589, Saudi Arabia
raldhubhani@stu.kau.edu.sa,
{iakatib,amsalgarni}@kau.edu.sa
[2] High Performance Computing Center, King Abdulaziz University,
Jeddah 21589, Saudi Arabia
Rmehmood@kau.edu.sa

Abstract. In recent years, smart city concept was proposed to provide sustainable development to the cities and improve the quality of citizens' life by utilizing the information and communication technologies. To achieve that, smart city applications are expected to use IoT infrastructure to collect and integrate data continuously about the environment and citizens, and take actions based on the constructed knowledge. Indeed, identification and tracking technologies are essential to develop such context-aware applications. Therefore, citizens are expected to be surrounded by smart devices which continuously identify, track and process their daily activities. Location privacy is one of the important issues which should be addressed carefully. Preserving location privacy means that the released sensitive location data of citizens are used only for the desired purpose. In reality, adopting the citizens' for smart city applications depends on their trust on the used technologies. In this paper, we review smart city architectures, frameworks, and platforms to highlight to what extent preserving location privacy is addressed. We show that preserving location privacy in smart city applications does not get the required attention. We discuss the issues, which we think should be addressed to improve location privacy preservation for smart city applications. Accordingly, we propose a location privacy preservation system for smart city applications.

Keywords: Location privacy · Smart cities · IoT

1 Introduction

An increase in the ratio of world's population that live in urban areas is estimated to rise from 50.5% in 2010 to 59% by 2030 [1]. Due to the population growth, large cities are expected to encounter challenges, such as resources exhaustion, traffic congestion, and air pollution. The concept of smart city has emerged as a result of the need to mitigate the effects of the cities' population growth by introducing an effective management for the city's infrastructures and resources. In addition, urban planning and policy making can be optimized using such technologies. Smart city applications are

© ICST Institute for Computer Sciences, Social Informatics and Telecommunications Engineering 2018
R. Mehmood et al. (Eds.): SCITA 2017, LNICST 224, pp. 123–138, 2018.
https://doi.org/10.1007/978-3-319-94180-6_14

predicted to improve the citizens' quality of life by addressing important sectors such as healthcare [2], transportation [3], energy [4], education [5], and public safety [6].

In recent years, many smart city projects were implemented around the world, which aim to provide smart environment, smart mobility, and smart living for citizens [7]. For instance, a smart city application was developed to improve the transportation system in Singapore [8]. One of its main features is the capability to predict in advance the availability of parking spaces at the driver's destination on the expected arrival time. To get an effective management of a smart city's resources, citizens should be continuously connected to the Internet [7]. Technologies such as big data and computational intelligence are expected to play an important role in manipulating the huge amount of data collected by citizens to meet the goals of smart cities [9, 10].

According to [11], IoT is defined as "the network of physical objects that contain embedded technology to communicate and sense or interact with their internal states or the external environment". It is expected that by 2020, the number of Internet of Things (IoT) devices will be 50 billion while the world population will be 7.6 billion [12]. As expected, IoT represents the best infrastructure for smart city applications.

Despite their benefits, IoT devices are expected to significantly increase the threats of the individuals' privacy leakage. In fact, citizens will be surrounded by IoT devices which are continuously monitoring and reporting the status and activities happening in the environment. According to [13], life in a smart city is the same as life under surveillance. Therefore, the challenge is how to ensure the privacy and security of a huge amount of data gathered by a variety of autonomous devices in a heterogeneous environment through the sensing, transmitting, processing, and storing phases. In addition to that, using localization-enabled devices introduces the risk of the unauthorized tracking of citizens. Clearly, providing secure, trustworthy, and privacy-preserving IoT infrastructure is essential to the success of IoT deployment [14]. In other words, the shortcoming of addressing such issues in IoT will limit the citizens' adoption for smart city applications.

Privacy preserving is a fundamental human right which is protected by international and national laws. It represents one of the main issues which should be addressed in smart cities and IoT context. According to [14], there are two main principles which should be followed in developing any IoT system to gain the users' trust. The first principle states that the user privacy should not be violated, while the second principle emphasizes the need to maintain the user's control over his/her related operations. In smart cities, the citizens' privacy is identified in five dimensions [15]. These dimension are: owner privacy, identity privacy, location privacy, footprint privacy, and query privacy.

Location privacy is one of the important privacy dimensions which should be addressed carefully. In fact, anonymizing the location data is not enough, while using background knowledge (e.g. geographic maps) could lead to re-identify the user who produces the location data [16]. According to [17], location privacy is defined as "a special type of information privacy which concerns the claim of individuals to determine for themselves when, how, and to what extent location information about them is communicated to others". In [18], a survey was conducted to analyze to what extent the users accept sharing and trading their location data. The survey shows that the respondents realize the privacy risks resulted from sharing their location data. At the same time, the survey shows that their willingness to share the location data depends on many factors, such as the context, the expected benefits, and the trust level in the party which the data will be shared with. Therefore, preserving location privacy is essential to get the citizens' trust in IoT infrastructure and smart city applications. According to [19], privacy by design is the best practice to overcome the privacy threats. In recent years, many smart city architectures, frameworks, and platforms are proposed, which take into consideration the security and privacy issues. In many case, the goal is to provide an end-to-end security and privacy.

In this paper, we review smart city architectures, frameworks, and platforms to highlight to what extent preserving location privacy is addressed. We show that preserving location privacy in smart city applications does not get the required attention. We discuss the issues, which we think should be addressed to preserve location privacy in smart city applications. We propose location privacy preservation system for smart city applications.

2 State of the Art

In recent years, many architectures, frameworks, and platforms are developed for IoT-based applications in general, and for smart city applications in particular. They show a wide variation in addressing the privacy and security issues. In some cases, a limited support is provided, while in others the goal is to provide an end-to-end privacy and security support. In this section, we review the main works in this area, and discuss how particularly the location privacy is addressed. We show that preserving location privacy is either supported partially or supported for very specific use cases. This emphasizes that preserving location privacy does not get the required attention to address all its related requirements.

In [20], an architecture for smart cities is proposed (see Fig. 1). In this architecture, three stakeholders are identified to access the data collected by IoT devices. The stakeholders are the citizens, community service providers, and city management. The proposed architecture consists of control and services layer, network layer, and sensing layer. Using cloud computing is proposed to overcome the big data issues. The architecture is proposed to support two types of services, which are Individual services and community service. For each type of service, a control center is used, which contains a web interface, service management, database management, and knowledge discovery section. The sensing layer entities send their data through the network layer to the control center, where it is processed on the fly and then stored in the database. In this architecture, the privacy features are proposed to be implemented in the control and services layer.

In [21], a framework is proposed to address the citizen's privacy concerns regarding the smart city technologies by proposing two dimensions. The first dimension represents how the citizens classify the data by identifying it as personal or impersonal. The second dimension represents the classification according to the data collection purpose, which is either service consumption purpose or surveillance purpose. The two dimensions provides four different areas for the framework, such that each area has its own characteristics regarding the citizen's privacy concerns. The areas

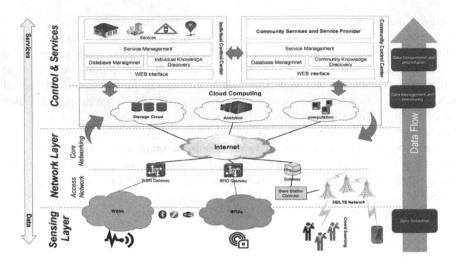

Fig. 1. The proposed smart city architecture in [20]

are: personal data for surveillance purposes, personal data for service purposes, impersonal data for surveillance purposes, and impersonal data for service purposes.

In [22], SSServProv is proposed as a security and privacy-aware framework for service provisioning in smart cities (see Fig. 2). The framework provides end-to-end privacy and security features. A detailed list of stakeholders is identified, and the contribution of each in smart city applications is modeled. Eight main roles are identified for stakeholders, which are service consumers, trusted service providers, untrusted service providers, IT specialists, data custodians, standard governing bodies, domain experts, and others. The security and privacy are addressed for all stakeholders, by

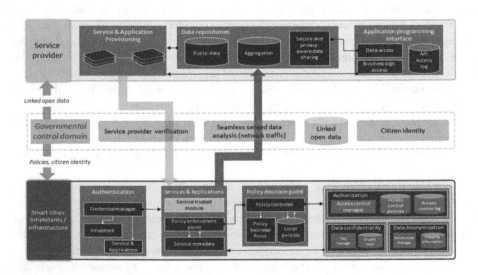

Fig. 2. SSServProv framework [22]

taking into consideration that each stakeholder could be a victim or an attacker. The governmental control domain is proposed in this framework as the controlling authority, which ensures the commitment of service providers and citizens to the defined policies and regulations. The governmental control domain has the following components: service provider verification, citizen identity, seamless sensed data analysis, and linked open data. The proposed components in the citizens and infrastructure layer are: authentication, services and applications, policy decision point, authorization, data confidentiality, and data anonymization. For the service provider layer, the components are: service and application provisioning, data repositories, and application programming interface.

In [23], a framework for smart cities is proposed (see Fig. 3). Three layers are defined in the framework, which are the information world, the communication world, and the physical world. The identified framework components are sensing components, heterogeneous network, processing unit, and control and operating components. Using existing privacy and security solutions is proposed to provide the privacy and security features, like access control, anonymity, and encryption.

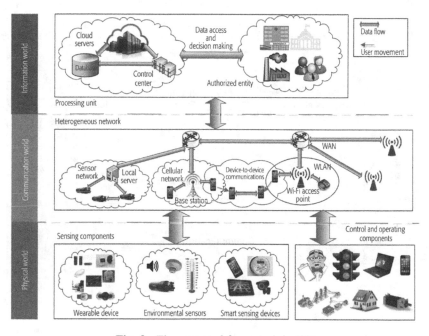

Fig. 3. The proposed framework in [23]

IoT-A was introduced by one of the European FP7 projects as an Architecture Reference Model for Internet of Things [24]. IoT-A aims to facilitate the development of IoT-related solutions by providing an efficient integration to the service layer, and hence enabling the interoperability of IoT systems. To achieve that, a set of concepts and relations are defined, which can be used to construct an abstract view for IoT entities relationships. IoT-A defines five models which are Domain Model, Functional Model,

Communication Model, Information Model, and Trust, privacy, and security model. The domain model is a structural perspective which represents the Virtual Entities and their attributes and relationships. The domain model uses the following concepts: User, Virtual Entity, Physical Entity, Augmented Entity, Resource, Device, and Service. The interaction between a User and a Physical Entity is done through a Service, where each Virtual Entity represents a Physical Entity in the digital world. Composing a Physical Entity and its associated Virtual Entity represents an Augmented Entity. The relationship between the Physical Entity and its corresponding Virtual Entity is accomplished by using one or more ICT Devices which facilitate the interaction and information gathering about the Physical Entity. There are three types of ICT Devices: Sensors, Tags, and Actuators. Resource is a software component which is used to provide data from or actuate a Physical Entity. To make the Resource accessible, it is attached to a Service. Functional model identifies a set of Functionality Groups and their interactions (see Fig. 4). Trust, security, and privacy model are addressed by using the components: Identity Management, Authentication, Authorization, Trust and Reputation, and Key Exchange and Management. To achieve the privacy, IoT-A requires the following properties:

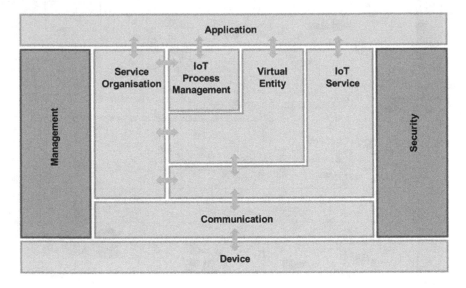

Fig. 4. Functional model of IoT-A [25]

- The subject has the option to share or not to share the data.
- The subject has full control on the used privacy mechanism.
- The subject has the option to decide the purpose for which the collected data should be used.
- The subject is notified who uses the data and when.
- Disclosing the data of the subject is kept strictly for the needed data only, and the anonymization is used whenever possible.

- Aggregating or reasoning the subject's disclosed data does not lead to infer the identity of the subject.
- The subject's data is used only for the agreed purpose and not used beyond that purpose.

In IoT-A, location privacy does not get the required attention, where it is addressed by a suggestion to use Identity management component to provide anonymization for location data.

OpenIoT is an open source IoT platform which enables the interoperability of IoT services in the cloud [26]. The aim of OpenIoT is to integrate the heterogeneous sensor networks and IoT services in one platform. The sensors middleware is one of the main components in OpenIoT which facilitates the data collection from virtually any sensor. In OpenIoT, collecting and discovering data are implemented using Publish/Subscribe principles. To provide security and privacy, OpenIoT implements following components: identity management, authentication, and authorization. In OpenIoT, location privacy is not addressed, because no specific component has been implemented to manipulate the location privacy.

COMPOSE is an open source IoT-based platform for developing smart city applications [27]. To address the privacy and security issues, COMPOSE implements the following components: Identity Management, Security Monitors, Policy Decision Points, Service Instrumentation, Static Analysis, Authentication-Authorization-Accounting (AAA) Manager, Provenance Manager, and Trust and Reputation Manager. Data Provenance is metadata which is used for logging all data transactions between different COMPOSE entities. Trust and Reputation component provides an estimation of the trustfulness of data sources within Compose based on the popularity and the data accuracy of the data sources. Policy decision points are used to enforce the security and privacy requirements. In COMPOSE, location privacy is not addressed, because no specific component has been implemented to manipulate the location privacy.

FIWARE is a European project which aims to provide the core platform of the Future Internet to facilitate the development of IoT based applications and smart city applications [28]. FIWARE platform consists of open source components called Generic Enablers which are public and open source. FIWARE platform provides many Generic Enablers to support the security and privacy requirements. For preserving location privacy, Location Generic Enabler applies authentication and authorization techniques to provide the location data using three levels of location data accuracy, which are low, medium and high.

Secure and sMARter ciTIEs data management (SMARTIE) is an IoT-based platform for smart city applications [29]. SMARTIE was developed based on IoT-A. The aim of developing SMARTIE is to provide a secure platform which has the capability to store, process, and share large volume of data collected by heterogeneous IoT devices. Security, privacy, and trust are the main issues which are considered in developing SMARTIE platform. The vision is to deliver end-to-end security and trust and meeting the privacy requirements of the data owner's. SMARTIE is a policy-enabled platform which provides functional components to provide decentralized policy-based access control and encryption to the citizen's sensitive data. The functional components in the security functional group are: identity management, authentication, authorization, key exchange & management, and trust & reputation. To preserve the location privacy in SAMRTIE, PrivLoc is introduced as a component to prevent the location tracking in the geo-fencing services by applying coordinates translation [30].

COSMOS is a IoT-based framework which introduces the decentralized and autonomous management of IoT devices motivated by social media technologies [31]. The aim is to support smart city applications by providing smart, autonomous, and reliable things. The architecture of COSMOS is based on IoT-A. The aim of COSMOS is to deliver end-to-end privacy and security. The following components are used for providing the security and privacy: authentication, authorization, key management, integrity, accountability, nonrepudiation and privacy filters (Privelets). Privelets are introduced as privacy functional components which apply the data minimization principle to preserve the privacy by controlling the data sharing to be in the minimum level. To achieve that, Privelets use Fuzzy logic to share data by supporting three levels of data accuracy, which are low, medium, and high. In COSMOS, Privelets are used to preserve location privacy.

REliable, Resilient and secUre IoT for sMart city applications (RERUM) is a project which applies the concept of privacy, security, and reliability in design to the IoT devices for the smart city context [32]. It focuses on the development of IoT devices which are considered as the weakest point in IoT systems. To achieve that, lightweight and energy efficient security and privacy mechanisms are proposed to be implemented in the IoT devices. RERUM suggests embedding and running many components in the IoT devices, like device-to-device authentication, data encryption, secure storage, geo-location privacy, and trusted routing. The project provides an IoT-based framework for smart city applications. It proposes also a smart object hardware prototype which enables embedding the security and privacy in IoT devices. RERUM focuses on four use cases, which are: smart transportation, environmental monitoring, home energy management, and indoor comfort quality monitoring. The security functional components of RERUM are: integrity generator/verifier, data encrypter/decrypter, device-to-device authenticator, credential bootstrapping client/authority, policy enforcement point, identity agent, attribute need reporter, policy decision point, policy retrieval point, and secure storage. The privacy functional components of RERUM are: consent manager, privacy policy enforcement point, privacy dashboard, deactivator/activator of data collection, privacy policy checker, anonymization/pseudonym manager, de- pseudonymizer, and privacy enhancing technologies for geo-location. The trust functional components of RERUM are: trust configurator manager, reputation rules configurator, trust engine, inaccuracy alert producer, and inaccuracy alert reactor. In RERUM, preserving location privacy is provided by the privacy enhancing technologies for geo-location component which uses the aggregation vectors scheme. Aggregation vectors scheme generates a random number of vectors with random start and end points selected from the sensed location points, such that these random vectors are shared instead of the citizen's accurate location points.

3   The Shortcomings of Existing Works and Proposed Requirements

We have reviewed the various works related to location privacy for emerging smart city environments and it is clear that the existing proposals deal with location privacy at a much abstract level such as information privacy. Some works have dealt with location privacy on detailed level; however, these have failed to take account of correlation between multiple continuous locations of an individual and the correlation of locations across multiple individuals, devices and systems.

We therefore assert that, in order to preserve the location privacy in smart city environment, two main requirements should be satisfied. The first requirement is ensuring smart city applications receive only the minimum level of location data accuracy they need to operate. The second requirement is ensuring that correlating the location data collected by smart city applications will not lead to increasing the level of location accuracy released to these applications. Satisfying these requirements need a location obfuscation mechanism which has the capability to introduce customized levels of accuracy to provide the requirements of smart city applications and also preserve citizen's location privacy. In addition, measuring the location privacy leakage resulted from the shared location data is also required.

In addition, the following issues should be addresses to preserve the citizen's location privacy in smart city applications.

- Smart city applications are context-based, so the required level of location accuracy in normal situations may vary in emergency situations.
- Citizen's IoT devices should be grouped into clusters (e.g. home, work, mobile), such that each cluster has its own location privacy characteristics and hence its own required privacy policies.
- Applying the location privacy policies for a cluster of devices should be based on its type (stationary or mobile) and the corresponding potential privacy leakage.
- For stationary clusters (like home and work), they produce sensitive data about fixed locations, and obfuscating fixed locations should not cause privacy leakage which may lead to improve the accuracy of these fixed locations.
- On the other hand, mobile clusters require addressing the potential correlation produced by the continuous reporting of different obfuscated locations.
- The possibility that a smart city application can collect the citizen's location data from more than one IoT device requires applying correlation analysis to ensure that the collected data from different IoT devices can't be used to improve the location accuracy shared with the application.
- As a result of the need of smart city applications for continuous data collection, citizens should have the capability to customize policies to manage the location data sharing when they are located in areas which are identified as sensitive.
- The contribution of citizens to build a consolidated location profile using their location data is useful to indicate the privacy leakage produced by sharing the location data of the different city areas.

- It is required to address the correlation produced by an IoT device which collects and shares location data and can be linked to more than one citizen, especially if the device is installed in shared areas (e.g. home or office).

4   The Proposed Location Privacy Preservation System

The previous section presented the shortcomings of the state-of-the-art on location privacy preservation in smart cities. We also presented the requirements for and issues surrounding location privacy preservation in smart cities. This section proposes a location privacy preservation system aimed at smart cities. Figure 5 shows the architecture of the proposed system. The architecture has the following components: Context Analyzer, Devices Clustering Manager, Correlation Manager, Policies Manager, Obfuscation Manager, Personal Location Profile Manager, and Consolidated Location Profile Manager.

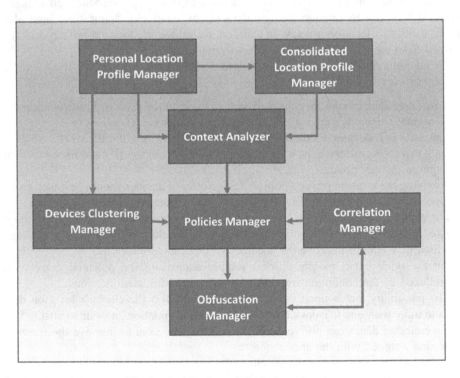

Fig. 5. Architecture of the proposed system

4.1   Context Analyzer

The purpose of this component is to notify the Policies Manager about the citizen's current context, in order to apply the corresponding policy. This component is required to identify when the citizen is located in a sensitive area, where applying specific policies with a higher level of location privacy is required. In addition, the component should identify emergency situations which requires applying specific policies for emergency situations which require sharing the citizen's location with high accuracy. The component uses Personal Location Profile to identify areas which are visited frequently by the citizen to apply a higher level of privacy policy on them. The Context Analyzer should use also Consolidated Location Profile which is created by all the citizens to identify the privacy level of the citizen's current area based on consolidated statistics.

4.2   Devices Clustering Manager

This component is responsible to manage the citizen's clusters of IoT devices that have the localization capability. Stationary and mobile clusters have different requirements in terms of location privacy, and hence require different policies. Therefore, the purpose of this component is to work with the policies manager to identify the required policies based on the cluster type which the IoT device belongs to. This component is responsible for managing the membership of IoT devices to the clusters, and when the membership of an IoT device should be changed from one cluster to another. For example, IoT devices which belong to the mobile cluster should be moved to the stationary clusters when the citizen reaches home.

4.3   Correlation Manager

This component aims to detect the potential privacy leakage produced by correlating the location data shared with smart city applications. First, sharing location data by multiple devices of a citizen to the same smart city application could produce privacy leakage. Second, sharing location data of multiple citizens sensed by the same device to the same smart city application could produce privacy leakage. This component works with the Policies Manager to ensure that the shared location data does not lead to privacy leakage.

4.4   Policies Manager

This component is responsible to manage sharing the location data by applying the required policy based on the current context, the involved cluster of IoT devices, and the detected level of privacy leakage by Correlation Manager. By specifying the suitable sharing policy, Policies Manager enforces the Obfuscation Manager to apply that policy.

4.5   Obfuscation Manager

Obfuscation Manager has the capability to apply different levels of obfuscation for citizen's location data to provide the minimum level of accuracy required to each smart city applications. Policies Manager controls the performance of Obfuscation Manager by choosing the required obfuscation level to enforce the selected policy.

4.6 Personal Location Profile Manager

This component is used to build a statistical profile about the citizen mobility. This component is used by the Context Analyzer to infer the locations which are frequently visited by the citizen, which requires applying higher levels of preserving privacy to ensure that they are not used to de-anonymize the citizen. This component works with the Policies Manager to apply policies with high level location privacy for these locations.

4.7 Consolidated Location Profile Manager

This component is used to build a consolidated profile about the mobility of all citizens to provide an overall mobility view. The objective is to provide consolidated statistics to the Context analyzer about the mobility patterns of citizens in the different areas which can be used to specify the required obfuscation levels based on the area mobility density.

5 Discussion

5.1 The Scenario

Alice and Bob are a couple who live in a smart city and have a smart autonomous vehicle. The city provides a smart transportation system for its citizens. To preserve the citizen's security and privacy, identity management and preserving location privacy systems are hosted in the secure and trusted ICT infrastructure of the city. To provide a reliable smart transportation service, the smart transportation system is hosted and operated by one of the international giant ICT service providers.

Identity management is used for three main purposes. First, it is used to ensure that the service is provided for legitimate citizens only. Second, it is used to block malfunctioned devices (e.g. as a result of a hardware failure or an attacked device) from providing the smart transportation service with invalid data. Third, it is used to provide the anonymization service for the citizens by providing pseudonyms to be used for accessing the smart transportation system.

The smart transportation system provides the traffic routing and prediction services. The routing service optimizes the trips routes of citizens in order to minimize their traveling time. In addition, it provides the priority for emergency vehicles (e.g. ambulance and firefighting) by re-routing other vehicles in the area to make space for emergency vehicles. It is used also to distribute the traffic through the city in a balanced way to keep the level of noise and air pollution within the allowed ranges. Finally, it provides instant notifications about the road status (e.g. accidents, closed roads, etc.). The predication service is used to estimate the expected travel time of trips.

The smart transportation application is installed in the smart autonomous vehicle. The application senses and shares the environment's noise and air pollution continuously. In addition, Alice and Bob use an app installed in their smart phones to connect to the smart transportation system to plan for their trips in advance and check the traffic status and the estimated travel time. The smart autonomous vehicle is equipped with a GPS sensor, noise sensor, and air pollution sensor.

Alice and Bob realize that providing their accurate locations to the smart transportation system enhance the service quality of smart transportation system. At the same time, they concern about their location privacy especially when they are at home and work, and when they visit a sensitive location (like hospitals, clinics and one of their frequent locations). Their goal is to ensure that sharing their location data with an overseas service provider will not lead to de-anonymize them by the service provider. They also concern about the privacy leakage caused by correlating their shared location data, which reduces their location privacy. They hope that their smart city provides a preserving location privacy system that enables them to configure a set of policies to preserve their location privacy.

To satisfy their location privacy needs, they propose the following policies:

- At home, the location should be obfuscated within a range of 500 m.
- At work, the location should be obfuscated within a range of 300 m.
- At sensitive and frequent locations, the location should be obfuscated within a range of 400 m.
- At low traffic density areas, the location should be obfuscated within a range of 200 m.
- In emergency cases (e.g. the existence of an ambulance in the surrounding area), the accurate location should be shared.
- Otherwise, the location should be obfuscated within a range of 30 m.
- The obfuscation process should take into consideration the potential privacy leakage resulted from correlating the shared location data.

5.2 Evaluation of the Proposed System

In this section, we discuss seven cases based on the scenario described in the previous section. We address realistic cases which happen for Alice and Bob when they go to work on any ordinary working day using their own autonomous vehicle. We show how our proposed system can manipulate these cases to preserve their location privacy.

Case 1: Alice and Bob leave home at 7 AM. Devices Clustering Manager detects that, changes the membership of their smart phones and smart vehicle from Home cluster to Mobile cluster, and finally notifies the Policies Manager to activate the proper policy. Policies Manager notifies the Obfuscation Manager to enforce the proper policy.

Case 2: On their way, the smart vehicle uses the obfuscated locations produced by the Obfuscation Manager to retrieve the routing information from the smart transportation system, and to geo-tag the sensed data before sharing them. The Obfuscation Manger cooperates with the Correlation Manager to detect and minimize the privacy leakage.

Case 3: On their way, smart transportation system detects an ambulance in their neighborhood, so the Context Analyzer receives that notification, and notifies the Policies Manager to activate the proper policy. Smart transportation system receives an accurate version of the location data, and it provides a new route for the autonomous vehicle to handle the current situation. The Context Analyzer detects the end of the emergency situation, so it notifies the Policies Manager to activate the proper policy. Hence, Policies Manager notifies the Obfuscation Manager to enforce the proper policy.

Case 4: When they reach work, the Devices Clustering Manager detects that, changes the membership of their smart phones and smart vehicle from Mobile cluster to Work cluster, and finally notifies the Policies Manager to activate the proper policy. Next, Policies Manager notifies the Obfuscation Manager to enforce the proper policy.

Case 5: Alice has an appointment in the hospital. So, on their way to return home, they go to the hospital. The Context Analyzer uses the Personal Location Profile Manager to detect that they are located in a sensitive area, so it notifies the Policies Manager to activate the proper policy. Policies Manager notifies the Obfuscation Manager to enforce the proper policy.

Case 6: On their way to return home, the road is closed for an emergency situation. So, the Smart transportation system provides the autonomous vehicle with an alternative route. In the alternative route, the Context Analyzer uses the Consolidated Location Profile Manager to detect that they are using a road with low traffic density, so it notifies the Policies Manager to activate the proper policy. Hence, Policies Manager notifies the Obfuscation Manager to enforce the proper policy.

Case 7: When they return home, Devices Clustering Manager detects that, changes the membership of their smart phones and smart vehicle from Mobile cluster to Home cluster, and finally notifies the Policies Manager to activate the proper policy.

6 Conclusion

An increase in the ratio of world's population that live in urban areas is estimated to rise from 50.5% in 2010 to 59% by 2030. As a result, large cities are expected to encounter challenges, such as resources exhaustion, traffic congestion, and air pollution. In recent years, smart city concept was proposed to provide sustainable development to the cities and improve the quality of citizens' life by utilizing the information and communication technologies. To achieve that, smart city applications are expected to use IoT infrastructure to collect and integrate data continuously about the environment and citizens, and take actions based on the constructed knowledge. Indeed, identification and tracking technologies are essential to develop such context-aware applications. Therefore, citizens are expected to be surrounded by smart devices which continuously identify, track and process their daily activities. Location privacy is one of the important issues which should be addressed carefully. Preserving the location privacy means that the sensitive location information of citizens' are released only to authorized parties, and used for the desired purpose. In reality, adopting the citizens' for smart city applications depends on their trust on the used technologies. In this paper, we reviewed smart city architectures, frameworks, and platforms to highlight to what extent preserving location privacy is addressed. We showed that preserving location privacy in smart city applications does not get the required attention. We discussed the issues, which we think should be addressed to preserve location privacy in smart city applications. We proposed an architecture of preserving location privacy system for smart city applications.

Acknowledgments. The work carried out in this paper is supported by the HPC Center at King Abdulaziz University.

References

1. United Nations Human Settlements Programme., Cities and climate change : global report on human settlements 2011. Earthscan (2011)
2. Woznowski, P., Burrows, A., Diethe, T., Fafoutis, X., Hall, J., Hannuna, S., Camplani, M., Twomey, N., Kozlowski, M., Tan, B., Zhu, N., Elsts, A., Vafeas, A., Paiement, A., Tao, L., Mirmehdi, M., Burghardt, T., Damen, D., Flach, P., Piechocki, R., Craddock, I., Oikonomou, G.: SPHERE: a sensor platform for healthcare in a residential environment. In: Angelakis, V., Tragos, E., Pöhls, Henrich C., Kapovits, A., Bassi, A. (eds.) Designing, Developing, and Facilitating Smart Cities, pp. 315–333. Springer, Cham (2017). https://doi.org/10.1007/978-3-319-44924-1_14
3. Schlingensiepen, J., Nemtanu, F., Mehmood, R., McCluskey, L.: Autonomic transport management systems—enabler for smart cities, personalized medicine, participation and industry grid/industry 4.0. In: Sładkowski, A., Pamuła, W. (eds.) Intelligent Transportation Systems – Problems and Perspectives. SSDC, vol. 32, pp. 3–35. Springer, Cham (2016). https://doi.org/10.1007/978-3-319-19150-8_1
4. Bonetto, R., Rossi, M.: Smart grid for the smart city. In: Angelakis, V., Tragos, E., Pöhls, Henrich C., Kapovits, A., Bassi, A. (eds.) Designing, Developing, and Facilitating Smart Cities, pp. 241–263. Springer, Cham (2017). https://doi.org/10.1007/978-3-319-44924-1_12
5. Wolff, A., Kortuem, G., Cavero, J.: Towards smart city education In: 2015 Sustainable Internet and ICT for Sustainability (SustainIT), pp. 1–3 (2015)
6. Coelho, J., Cacho, N., Lopes, F., Loiola, E., Tayrony, T., Andrade, T., Mendonça, M., Oliveira, M., Estaregue, D., Moura, B.: ROTA: a smart city platform to improve public safety. New Advances in Information Systems and Technologies. AISC, vol. 444, pp. 787–796. Springer, Cham (2016). https://doi.org/10.1007/978-3-319-31232-3_74
7. Khatoun, R., Zeadally, S.: Smart cities: concepts, architectures, research opportunities. Commun. ACM **59**(8), 46–57 (2016)
8. Eckhoff, D., Zehe, D., Ivanchev, J., Knoll, A.: Smart city-to-vehicle — measuring, prediction, influencing. ATZelektronik Worldw. **12**(2), 60–63 (2017)
9. Alam, F., Mehmood, R., Katib, I., Albogami, N.N., Albeshri, A.: Data fusion and IoT for smart ubiquitous environments: a survey. IEEE Access **5**, 9533–9554 (2017)
10. Suma, S., Mehmood, R., Albugami, N., Katib, I., Albeshri, A.: Enabling next generation logistics and planning for smarter societies. Procedia Comput. Sci. **109**, 1122–1127 (2017)
11. Gartner: Internet of things – Gartner IT glossary. http://www.gartner.com/it-glossary/internet-of-things/. Accessed 29 Aug 2017
12. Evans, D.: The Internet of Things How the Next Evolution of the Internet Is Changing Everything (2011)
13. Wadhwa, T.: Smart cities: toward the surveillance society? In: Araya, D. (ed.) Smart Cities as Democratic Ecologies, pp. 125–141. Palgrave Macmillan UK, London (2015). https://doi.org/10.1057/9781137377203_9
14. Porambage, P., Ylianttila, M., Schmitt, C., Kumar, P., Gurtov, A., Vasilakos, A.V.: The quest for privacy in the internet of things. IEEE Cloud Comput. **3**(2), 36–45 (2016)

15. Martinez-Balleste, A., Perez-martinez, P., Solanas, A.: The pursuit of citizens' privacy: a privacy-aware smart city is possible. IEEE Commun. Mag. **51**(6), 136–141 (2013)
16. Golle, P., Partridge, K.: On the anonymity of home/work location pairs. In: Tokuda, H., Beigl, M., Friday, A., Brush, A.J.Bernheim, Tobe, Y. (eds.) Pervasive 2009. LNCS, vol. 5538, pp. 390–397. Springer, Heidelberg (2009). https://doi.org/10.1007/978-3-642-01516-8_26
17. Duckham, M., Kulik, L.: Location privacy and location-aware computing. Dynamic and Mobile GIS: Investigating Change in Space and Time, vol. 3, pp. 35–51 (2006)
18. Cottrill, C.D., Thakuriah, P.V.: Location privacy preferences: a survey-based analysis of consumer awareness, trade-off and decision-making. Transp. Res. Part C Emerg. Technol. **56**, 132–148 (2015)
19. Federal Trade Commission: "Protecting Consumer Privacy in an Era of Rapid Change: Recommendations For Businesses and Policymakers," (2012)
20. Jalali, R., El-khatib, K., McGregor, C.: Smart city architecture for community level services through the internet of things. In: 2015 18th International Conference on Intelligence in Next Generation Networks, pp. 108–113 (2015)
21. van Zoonen, L.: Privacy concerns in smart cities. Gov. Inf. Q. **33**(3), 472–480 (2016)
22. Khan, Z., Pervez, Z., Abbasi, A.G.: Towards a secure service provisioning framework in a smart city environment. Futur. Gener. Comput. Syst. **77**, 112–135 (2017)
23. Zhang, K., Ni, J., Yang, K., Liang, X., Ren, J., Shen, X.S.: Security and privacy in smart city applications: challenges and solutions. IEEE Commun. Mag. **55**(1), 122–129 (2017)
24. Bassi, A., et al.: Enabling things to talk. Designing IoT solutions with the IoT Architectural Reference Model. Springer, Heidelberg (2013). https://doi.org/10.1007/978-3-642-40403-0
25. Bauer, M., et al.: IoT Reference Model. In. In: Bassi, A., et al. (eds.) Enabling Things to Talk, pp. 113–162. Springer, Heidelberg (2013). https://doi.org/10.1007/978-3-642-40403-0_7
26. Soldatos, J., Kefalakis, N., Hauswirth, M., Serrano, M., Calbimonte, J.-P., Riahi, M., Aberer, K., Jayaraman, P.P., Zaslavsky, A., Žarko, I.P., Skorin-Kapov, L., Herzog, R.: OpenIoT: Open Source Internet-of-Things in the Cloud. In: Podnar Žarko, I., Pripužić, K., Serrano, M. (eds.) Interoperability and Open-Source Solutions for the Internet of Things. LNCS, vol. 9001, pp. 13–25. Springer, Cham (2015). https://doi.org/10.1007/978-3-319-16546-2_3
27. Doukas, C., Antonelli, F.: A full end-to-end platform as a service for smart city applications. In: 2014 IEEE 10th International Conference on Wireless and Mobile Computing, Networking and Communications (WiMob), pp. 181–186 (2014)
28. Ramparany, F., Marquez, F.G., Soriano, J., Elsaleh, T.: Handling smart environment devices, data and services at the semantic level with the FI-WARE core platform. In: 2014 IEEE International Conference on Big Data (Big Data), pp. 14–20 (2014)
29. Bohli, J.-M., Skarmeta, A., Moreno, M.V., Garcia, D., Langendorfer, P.: SMARTIE project: secure IoT data management for smart cities. In: 2015 International Conference on Recent Advances in Internet of Things (RIoT), pp. 1–6 (2015)
30. Bohli, J.M., Dobre, D., Karame, Ghassan O., Li, W.: PrivLoc: preventing location tracking in geofencing services. In: Holz, T., Ioannidis, S. (eds.) Trust 2014. LNCS, vol. 8564, pp. 143–160. Springer, Cham (2014). https://doi.org/10.1007/978-3-319-08593-7_10
31. Voutyras, O., Gogouvitis, S.V., Marinakis, A., Varvarigou, T.: Achieving autonomicity in IoT systems via situational-aware, cognitive and social things. In: Proceedings of the 18th Panhellenic Conference on Informatics - PCI 2014, pp. 1–2 (2014)
32. Tragos. E. Z.: et al.: Enabling reliable and secure IoT-based smart city applications. In: 2014 IEEE International Conference on Pervasive Computing and Communication Workshops (PERCOM WORKSHOPS), pp. 111–116 (2014)

Disaster Management in Smart Cities by Forecasting Traffic Plan Using Deep Learning and GPUs

Muhammad Aqib[1(✉)], Rashid Mehmood[2], Aiiad Albeshri[1], and Ahmed Alzahrani[1]

[1] Department of Computer Science, FCIT, King Abdulaziz University, Jeddah 21589, Saudi Arabia
aqib.qazi@gmail.com,
{aaalbeshri,asalzahrani}@kau.edu.sa
[2] High Performance Computing Center, King Abdulaziz University, Jeddah 21589, Saudi Arabia
RMehmood@kau.edu.sa

Abstract. The importance of disaster management is evident by the increasing number of natural and manmade disasters such as Irma and Manchester attacks. The estimated cost of the recent Irma hurricane is believed to be more than 80 billion USD; more importantly, more than 40 lives have been lost and thousands were misplaced. Disaster management plays a key role in reducing the human and economic losses. In our earlier work, we have developed a disaster management system that uses VANET, cloud computing, and simulations to devise city evacuation strategies. In this paper, we extend our earlier work by using deep learning to predict urban traffic behavior. Moreover, we use GPUs to deal with compute intensive nature of deep learning algorithms. To the best of our knowledge, we are the first to apply deep learning approach in disaster management. We use real-world open road traffic within a city available through the UK Department for Transport. Our results demonstrate the effectiveness of deep learning approach in disaster management and correct prediction of traffic behavior in emergency situations.

Keywords: Smart cities · Disaster management · Deep learning
GPUs · Convolution neural networks

1 Introduction

A large amount of world's population is currently living in cities because of increased trend of urbanization. The provision of educational, health, social, cultural and other facilities is a main reason behind this trend. To provide best facilities to the citizens, companies and government authorities relies on latest technologies and use devices that collects and generates a lot of data. These devices not only include personal devices like smart phones, GPS devices etc. but also include the devices that are used by government departments like sensors to switch on and off the lights on streets, sensors and cameras to control traffic, smart health care devices and systems and many more.

© ICST Institute for Computer Sciences, Social Informatics and Telecommunications Engineering 2018
R. Mehmood et al. (Eds.): SCITA 2017, LNICST 224, pp. 139–154, 2018.
https://doi.org/10.1007/978-3-319-94180-6_15

All this together makes foundations of smart city where a tremendous amount of data is collected from devices and processed to improve the life style of its citizen and to improve their productivity by providing them a secure and peaceful environment [1, 2].

Disaster management systems or emergency response systems in a smart city are very important to efficiently handle disaster conditions in effective way, no matter the disaster was a manmade like 9/11 attacks, blasts etc. or it was natural like earthquake, tsunami etc. Traffic management in a disaster plays key role in evacuating the affected area and to monitor the traffic in other parts of the city to avoid congestion and road blockages. For efficient traffic management, traffic data could be collected from the sensors and cameras deployed on the road networks. In addition to this, data collected from GPS could also be used to monitor the traffic flow and to guide the people through different applications to take alternate routes to ensure their safety, avoid congestion and to provide the emergency services in affected area in efficient way.

In our earlier works, [3], by leveraging the advancements in the intelligent transportation systems, VANETs, and other technologies including mobile and cloud computing technologies, we proposed a disaster management systems for smart cities. This system was able to collect information from these sources and to propagate them to the vehicles, people and other components of the disaster management system in real time. In addition to this, it was able to ensure the security and safety of data and applications as well. In this work, a cloud based architecture was given and a microscopic traffic model Lighthill-Whitham-Richards (LWR) was used. The effectiveness of our model was tested by modeling the impact of a disaster on a real city and comparing it with a disaster management technique using traditional technologies. Later, this work was extended in [4] where we improved our model by introducing a message propagation through VANETs. Microscopic traffic models were used in this work as well in addition to our novel algorithm. Extended simulation results were used to demonstrate the effectiveness of newly proposed system. In continuation to these works [3, 4], we developed a model in [5] to evaluate the performance of disaster management systems on evacuation operations. In this work, microscopic models were used for the design and evaluation of our system. Two main evacuation strategies, demand strategy (DS) and speed strategy (SS) has been reported in this work.

Due to the availability of tremendous amount of data collected by devices in a smart city, many machine learning approaches could be applied on that data to get useful insights and based on the collected information from that data, the future steps taken by individuals or authorities in specific conditions could be predicted. The idea of machine learning or artificial intelligence techniques is not new but it was not applicable because it requires a huge amount of data for learning phase. Deep learning is also a machine learning approach that could be used to train the models using historic or real-time data and then those trained models could be used to predict the expected values.

In this work, we are using deep learning for traffic management in smart cities in disasters. Deep learning requires a large amount of data to train the model and therefore takes long in training process. It is more accurate but is intensive in computation, hence we need GPU [6]. Therefore, we are using GPUs to expedite the training process and to provide results in close real-time fashion. Traffic data for this purpose is collected from data.gov.uk that provides annual average vehicles flow values on roads in a city in UK.

The rest of the paper is organized as follows. Section 2 provides background material that defines the tools and technologies used in our work. Work done by others in this area is presented in Sect. 3. Our proposed framework is presented in Sect. 4. In order to find the suitable city data, we have examined a number of datasets and their details are given in Sect. 5. Performance evaluation and analysis of the proposed system is given in Sect. 6 and, finally, in Sect. 7 we have concluded the discussion with directions for future work.

2 Background Material

In this section, we will give a brief introduction to the tools and technologies used in our model in specific and some tools and simulators that are used for traffic modeling in general.

2.1 Graphical Processing Units

In this section, we will give an overview of the GPU architecture. A GPU chip contains multiple multi-processors (MP) and each MP contains many stream-processors (SP). Instructions are executed in SP like ALU in CPU. Different tasks are performed on MPs and they are mutually independent to each other whereas the SPs in an MP executes the same operations on different data items. To store data, each SP has its own register to store variables and temporal data. An SP cannot access the registers of other SPs in an MP. For this purpose, there is a shared on-chip memory that is accessible to each SP in that MP. In addition to this, an off-chip shared memory, called global memory is also available and it can be accessed by all the SPs in all the MPs. This global memory is connected externally to the GPU chip and it is much larger in size but the access to this memory is much more expensive than that of the on-chip shared memory inside the MPs.

Programs in GPU are executed with the help of Compute Unified Device Architecture (CUDA) toolkit offered by Nvidia and detailed execution flow of a CUDA, the logical structure of kernel threads and logical to physical mapping in GPU is also part of the discussion.

2.2 Deep Learning

A branch of computer science that gives the computers, the ability to learn themselves like human beings is known as machine learning. Machine learning does not require programmers to program something explicitly to tell computers to perform a specific task. Instead, machine learning algorithms train computers using different algorithms to predict the output when a specific input is given. Techniques that enable computers to learn something without explicit programming are divided into two main categories in machine learning. These are known as supervise learning and unsupervised learning techniques. Artificial neural network, clustering, genetic algorithms and deep learning etc. are some examples of machine learning techniques. In this section, we will focus on the deep learning techniques and work done in this domain.

Deep learning approaches have been classified into different categories based upon the nature and training and testing strategies. These include Convolutional Neural Networks (CNNs), Restricted Boltzmann Machines (RBMs), Autoencoders and Sparse Coding techniques [7]. In this work, we are using CNNs for training and testing purposes. So, we will discuss them in detail in the following paragraph.

2.2.1 Convolutional Neural Networks (CNNs)

In the CNNs, multiple layers including convolutional, pooling, and connected layers are used for training purpose in a robust manner. Authors in [7] have defined a general architecture of CNN for image classifications. This architecture is shown in Fig. 1. In this figure, the whole process is divided into two main phases, forward phase that include convolutional and pooling layers and backward phase where fully connected layers are used to produce the output.

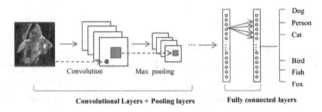

Fig. 1. General CNN architecture [7]

Convolutional neural networks are the hierarchical neural networks and their convolutional layers alternate with subsampling layers like simple and complex cells in the primary visual cortex. CNNs vary in how convolutional and sub-sampling layers are realized and how the nets are trained [8].

3 Related Work

In this section, we are presenting the work that deals with the traffic management plans during emergency conditions in smart cities. Some people focus mainly on traffic management in smart cities using any approach and some have focused on the approach i.e. deep learning with smart city scenario on low priority. As we are combining traffic management in smart cities with the deep learning approach, so both are useful for us and therefore we are presenting some approaches for better understanding of the work done in this area.

Authors in [9] have proposed an adaptive traffic management plan to ensure the provision of secure and efficient emergency services in case of disaster in a smart cities. In this work, a framework has been proposed introduces some components of traffic management system like traffic management controllers (TMC), local traffic controllers (LTC), adaptive traffic light controllers, environmental sensor controllers etc. The goal of this framework is to collect information from communication and other devices about the severity of the disaster that has been divided into three categories in this work; low, medium, and high, and then act accordingly by using these controllers. For example, in case of high emergency condition, traffic signals could be controlled to ensure the timely arrival of emergency vehicles e.g. ambulance and fire brigade and to reroute the non-emergency traffic. SUMO [10] has been used to simulate this process. In this work, focus is mainly on the provision of emergency services and their security and the plan has been simulated but no practical scenario or data has been used to handle the traffic and it also lacks the plan to manage the general traffic in case of disaster.

Smart cities are characterized by advanced and integrated ICT systems, such as smart logistics solutions [11], autonomic transportation [12]. Internet of things (IoT) could be considered as the back bone of future smart cities [13]. [14] proposes a ubiquitous learning system for smart societies. This approach can be used to educate and prepare citizens for disasters. In particular to vehicles, internet of vehicles (IoV) includes all the devices that could be used to monitor the vehicles and for inter vehicle communication as well. Data from different types of sensors placed on road networks, vehicles, and other smart devices [15] is collected to traffic management. There are many studies that use IoT and IoV to propose a traffic management plan as in [16, 17]. In addition to this, a lot work has done in the area of autonomic transport management in smart cities [18]. Work in [19] also shows the importance of Fog and other cloud technologies in dealing with emergency situations in smart cities. In [20] a parallel transportation management and control system for smart cities has been presented that not only use the artificial intelligence technologies but also uses massive traffic data and uses big data technologies or frameworks like MapReduce. Thus, shows the importance of these technologies in traffic management in smart cities.

A traffic flow prediction approach has been proposed in [21]. Authors have used the deep learning approaches for prediction purpose using a large amount of data. They have proposed a model that uses autoencoders for training and testing purpose to make predictions. The model is named as stacked autoencoder (SAE) model. To predict traffic flow at time t, traffic flow data at previous time intervals has been used. The proposed model has been used to predict 15, 30, 45 and 60 min traffic flow. Data for this purpose was collected from Caltrans Performance Measurement System (PeMS) [22]. Three months' data, collected every 30 s was used for training and testing purposes. In this data, vehicle flow was collected where two directions of same freeway were treated as different freeway. Support vector machines (SVM) have been used for comparison purpose.

Authors in [23] have proposed a deep learning based approach for traffic flow prediction and they have used unsupervised learning approach using deep belief networks. They have categorized the traffic prediction approaches into three main categories that include time-series approaches, probabilistic approaches, and non-parametric approaches such as neural network based approaches etc. Authors in this work have used Restricted Boltzmann Machines (RBMs) for training purpose which are stacked one on other. For training and testing purposes, inductive loop dataset is obtained from the PeMS [22]. In addition to this, authors have used data from highway system of China (EESH) as well. A data of 12 months has been collected and the first 10 months' data is used for training whereas the data of remaining two months has been used for validation purpose. Prediction results have been compared with other four methods for top 50 roads having high flow rates. The results shows that deep learning based architecture is more appropriate and robust in prediction and could be used for practical prediction system.

A deep learning based approach has been used in [24] to model the traffic flow. In this work, authors have developed deep learning predictors to predict the traffic flow data from the road sensors. Real-time traffic data has been used and by using the proposed model, they have predicted the traffic flow during a Chicago Bears football game and a snowstorm. They have used the number of locations on the loop detectors and traffic flow at a time (say t). They first have developed a linear vector auto regressive model for predictors selection. These predictors are later used to build a deep learning model. Stochastic gradient descent (SGC) method is used to know to structure and weights of parameters. They also have applied three filtering techniques (exponential smoothing, median filter, loess filter) on traffic data to filter noisy data from the sensors. Data for this purpose is collected from 21 loop detectors on five minutes' interval basis. This data includes speed, flow and occupancy. They have built a statistical model to capture the sudden changes from free flow (70 mph) to congestion (20 mph). In case of bottlenecks, they predict that how fast it will propagate on the network i.e. loop detectors. For predictor selection, deep learning model estimates an input-output map with the assumption that they need the recent. So, they collect last 12 readings from each sensor. The performance of DL model has been compared with sparse linear vector autoregressive (VAR). Both accurately predict morning rush hours on normal day but VAR miss-predicts congestion during evening rush hour. On the other hand, DL predicts breakdown accurately but miss-estimates the recovery time.

Authors in [25] also have used deep learning approach to predict the traffic congestion. They have used recurrent neural networks by using Restricted Boltzmann Machine (RNN-RBM). For comparison purposes, authors have used Support Vector Machines (SVMs) and found that prediction accuracy was increased by at least 17%.

4   Disaster Management System

In this section, we will discuss the proposed deep learning based disaster management system in detail. Figure 2 depicts the architecture of our proposed system. Proposed framework consists of three main layers, input layer, data processing and prediction layer and output layer.

4.1   Input Layer

Input layer manages the traffic data that is used to training and testing of deep learning model in the data processing layer. The input data could be either offline i.e. historical data or it could be real-time or streaming data. Input layer gets the traffic data and extracts the key features from it like flow, speed, occupancy, density etc. These features play a key role in prediction making using the proposed model. The role of input layer becomes more important especially when we are dealing with the real-time data. In this case, it takes the data from the source, and provides it to the processing layer for further data formatting.

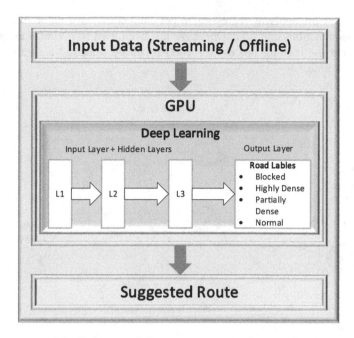

Fig. 2. Proposed disaster management framework.

4.2   Data Processing Layer

This layer is responsible to process the input data for making predictions in case of disaster. Our prediction model uses deep learning approach for this purpose. By using a deep regression model, we train a dataset which is further tested using another input dataset or a subset of the same dataset. Data processing layer, takes the data from the input layer and then process it to convert the input data into the format required by the deep learning algorithm. For example, if date attribute is included in the input dataset, it could be processed in this layer to get day, month, year, hour etc. The division of one attribute into multiple attribute could be useful in training process e.g. we can get peak hours, and can separate the data based on weekends etc. Furthermore, we may need to normalize the input data for our regression model. So, data normalization is also performed in this layer.

4.3   Deep Learning Layer

We have used deep regression model to estimate the vehicle flow value by using multiple input features. Initially we have trained our neural network by adding two hidden layers to the network. First layer is our input layer and the final one is the output layer and the two hidden layers are in between the input and output layers. Forward propagation scheme has been used for computation of weights and finally loss is calculated on the overall output.

Figure 3 shows a neural network including one input, two hidden and one output layer. In our case, we are using 9 input parameters, and output layer gives one output value because we are applying regression to get one vehicle flow value. We have used *relu* activation functions and *AdamOptimizer* has been used to optimize the generated results. We ran the training process for 1000 times by selecting a data size of 500 features at one time.

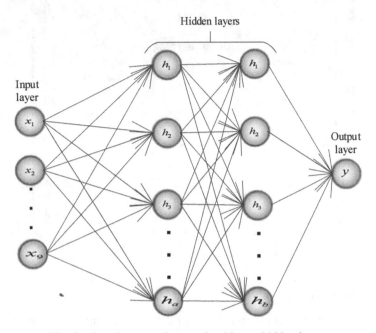

Fig. 3. Our deep neural network with two hidden layers.

5   Datasets

In this work, we are mainly working on UK traffic data. So, we have explored a variety of traffic data available through multiple sources in UK that could be used for different purposes to work on traffic management plans. Some data sources of same kind outside UK are also included in the list. In our deep learning model, we have used the data from data.gov.uk that provides the vehicles flow data for minor cities. This includes the average vehicle count or roads for different vehicle types. In Table 1, we have given some data sources that provide traffic data. Short data description and URLs to access the data are also given.

6   Analysis and Comparison

This section defines our deep model configurations and the performance metrics used for analysis purpose which is used for performance analysis of our model.

Table 1. UK traffic data sources.

	Data source	Description	URL
1	Transport for London (TFL)	Data could be accessed by using the provided API. Real-time data and status information of different sources of transportation could be accessed by using API	https://tfl.gov.uk/info-for/open-data-users/
2	London Datastore	Public data sharing portal that provides data related to different department of London government. Data from 1997 to 2015 is also available that provides number of vehicles on different roads in London	https://data.london.gov.uk/
3	Data.gov.uk	Data provided by different United Kingdom's government agencies could be accessed from this portal. Its transport data section provides many options to explore traffic data	http://data.dft.gov.uk/ https://data.gov.uk/dataset/gb-road-traffic-counts
4	Data from local government association UK	This is a research project and its purpose is to make data useful for LGA	http://www.local.gov.uk/web/guest/research/-/journal_content/56/10180/7783953/ARTICLE
5	Transit Feeds	It provides web feeds for transport data and provides updated information related to transport department of a city or state etc.	http://transitfeeds.com/
6	Department for Transport UK	It provides data for all the A class roads at city level. Data collected from data collection points on roads that fall in the selected city could be accessed from this source	
7	Transport Infrastructure Ireland (TII)	This site also provides traffic data for main roads (highways). It could be useful while dealing with the intercity traffic data. Do not provide enough data to deal with the traffic on minor roads in a city	https://www.nratrafficdata.ie/c2/gmapbasic.asp?sgid=ZvyVmXU8jBt9PJE$c7UXt6
8	Tyne and Wear Region Data	We can access the live traffic data by using the API provided by the "Open Data Service" authority	http://www.gateshead.gov.uk/Parking-roads-and-travel/planning/TADU.aspx

(continued)

Table 1. (*continued*)

	Data source	Description	URL
9	The WisTransPortal System	Hourly traffic data index page could be accessed to get a list of counties in the Wisconsin State, USA or county could be selected from the map as well. By selecting the county, it displays all the data available for different roads in that county by their names	https://transportal.cee.wisc.edu/products/hourly-traffic-data/
10	Wisconsin Department of Transport	Provides traffic flow data on weekly and/or annual basis on selected roads (say highways)	http://wisconsindot.gov/Pages/projects/data-plan/traf-counts/default.aspx
11	North East Combined Authority	Provides data for selected areas. It provides data related to special events, roadworks, incidents, journey times for key roads, car parks and CCTV images	https://www.netraveldata.co.uk/
12	Highways England	Provides three types of data: Monthly Summary Data, Journey Time Data, and Traffic Flow Data. HE also provides a conversion table that gives description of traffic data measurement sites	http://tris.highwaysengland.co.uk/
13	Developer.here.com	Provides API to get traffic flow and incidents data	https://developer.here.com/

6.1   Deep Model Setup

In this work, we have used vehicles flow data on minor roads in a city in UK. It includes six different vehicle categories ranging from cars or small personal vehicles to big trucks used for transportation of goods. Data used as input contains 70470 data flow values for all six vehicle categories for the years from 2000 to 2015 and the road names along with the road categories are also given.

We are using a deep regression model to predict the vehicle flow values. We have implemented this model using Keras deep learning library [26]. Our regressing model has four layers including one input, two hidden and one output layer. We have used the annual average flow data to predict the traffic flow in a city. Input dataset is divided in the ratio of 7, 2, 1 for training, testing and prediction purposes respectively. Batch size was set to 10 and number of epoch was set to 1000.

6.2 Dataset Schema

Dataset we have used in this work contains annual average flow data for different types of vehicles. It also provides road names, road category and other information. In Table 2, we have given the schema of input dataset that provides brief description of some important input attributes in this dataset.

Table 2. Schema of dataset used as input in our deep learning model

S.No	Attribute name	Description
1	Road	Gives character code names assigned to a road in the city
2	Road name	Name of the road
3	RCat	Roads have been divided into different categories. RCat gives character codes to define its category in city road network
4	iDir	Traffic direction on a road e.g. heading east or west
5	Year	Year for which AAFD was collected
6	dCount	Day of the year when data was collected. It is in the format dd-mm-yy h:mm
7	Hour	Hour of the day
8	CAR, BUS, LGV, HGVR2, …	A set of different types of vehicles to provide their flow values. For example, car gives the annual average flow value for cars. Similarly, Bus, provides the annual average flow value for buses and so on

6.3 Performance Analysis

In this paper, our focus is mainly on providing details of the deep learning based traffic prediction approach. Details of the overall evacuation method can be found in our earlier work [3–5]. For our deep learning model, we divided the dataset into three parts where 70% data was used for training, 20% data for testing purpose and the rest 10% data is used for prediction purposes. Our deep learning model was executed for 20 times to get results for analysis purpose. Furthermore, for all the 20 models, the batch size for training purpose was 10 and the training procedure was repeated for 2000 times in each execution.

We have used annual average vehicle flow data on different roads in a city to predict flow values on minor roads in a city in UK. We have evaluated the results of all 20 executions of our model to see the variation in the accuracy and error rate. This gives a better idea about the performance of deep learning model and we calculate the average accuracy rate. For performance analysis, we have used mean absolute error (MAE), and mean absolute percentage error (MAPE). MAE is used to shows the closeness between the actual and the predicted values and MAPE shows the relative difference between the actual and the predicted values. MAPE is not suitable to calculate error rate if the input data or actual values contain zeros because in this case it suffers from the division by zero error. MAE and MAPE values are calculated using the following equations.

$$Mean\,Absolute\,Error\,(MAE) = \frac{1}{N}\sum_{i=1}^{N} V_i - P_i$$

$$Mean\,Absolute\,Percentage\,Error\,(MAPE) = \frac{1}{N}\sum_{i=1}^{N}\frac{V_i - P_i}{V_i}$$

Here N is the size (number of values predicted by the model) of dataset used for prediction purpose, V is the set of actual values used as labels, and P is the set of values predicted by our deep learning model.

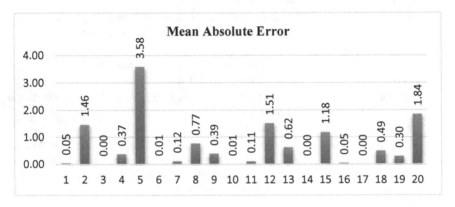

Fig. 4. Mean absolute error

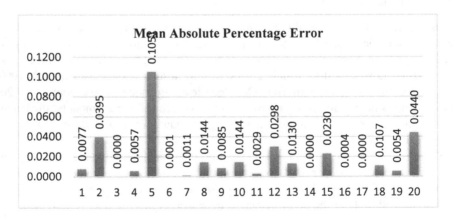

Fig. 5. Mean absolute percentage error

In Fig. 4, we have shown the results obtained by executing our deep model 20 times. In this graph, *x-axis* shows the number of model and it ranges from 1 to 20, and *y-axis* shows the MAE values calculated by using the given equation. Graph shows that error rate was very low because the maximum error value calculated was for model 5 and it was 3.58, and in some cases, it was as low as zero. Here zero does not mean that prediction was exactly the same, but it shows that the values were very close and there was not a big difference between the original and the predicted values.

In Fig. 5, we have shown the results calculated by using the mean absolute percentage error. Same as MAE, we have calculated MAPE for all 20 executions and prediction results of our deep learning model. Maximum MAPE value is 0.105 for 5th execution of our model with the same configurations. MAPE is considered a best measure to the data where there are no extremes and our data also contains a relatively balanced set of flow values. Therefore, our MAPE values describe that the predicted results have very low error rate and predicted values are very close to the original flow values.

In addition to the graphs showing error rates using MAE and MAPE, we have plotted the actual and predicted flow values to show the difference between patterns as well. Our MAE and MAPE values shows that the actual and predicted values are very close. If this is true, then the graphs of both plotted values should show the similar trends. In Fig. 6, we have plotted the first 100 actual and the predicted flow values. In this graph, *y-axis* shows the flow values. As both, actual and predicted values are very close, so graph is drawn by doubling the predicted values to avoid the overlapping of both curves. Both the curves show that these are not same but follow a similar trend. This shows that the predicted values are following the same trend that was followed by the input flow data with slight differences.

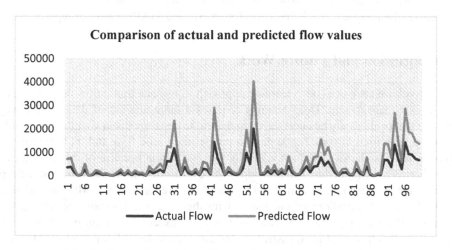

Fig. 6. Comparison of first 100 actual and predicted flow values.

Similarly, to analyze the pattern in depth, we have selected a range of actual flow values from 1 to 500, i.e. we have selected only those results where actual flow values are in the range of 1 to 500. The purpose of selecting this range is to see the trends when flow values were uniform and thus input data values were very close. This is shown in Fig. 7. Again, the predicted values are doubled to avoid overlapping of both curves representing the flow values. This graph also shows similar graph for both,

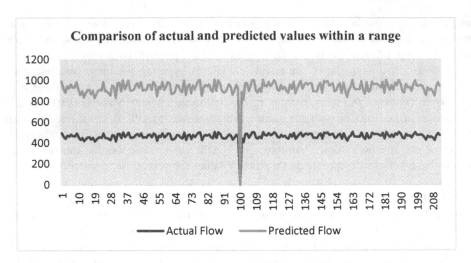

Fig. 7. Comparison actual and predicted values when flow is less than 500.

actual and predicted flow values with not big differences. In this graph, we have selected values within a range, therefor it is expected for good prediction results that the output values should also be in a specific range as shown in this graph. So, we can say that predicted values have followed the trend that was present in the input dataset. Therefore, the accuracy rate is high and low MSE and MAPE rates are reported.

7 Conclusion and Future Work

In this work we have used deep learning approach to manage traffic flow in smart cities for disaster management. Deep learning requires a large amount of data for training purpose that could easily be accessed from the traffic departments in smart cities. In this work we have used historic traffic data to predict the traffic flow and its behaviour in disaster. Results shows very high accuracy rate but this is because of the high correlation between the input data and the output values. Results may differ when same deep learning model is applied on a different type of data. We have plotted MSE and MAPE results for all 20 executions of our model with the same specification. Results shows that a specific accuracy rate was maintained in all 20 executions of our model and thus we can say that its output is consistent to a certain extent. In addition to error rates, we have plotted the original and predicted flow values to visualize the difference between the graph trends followed by actual and predicted values graphs. Graphs also show similar trends and proves that there are not big differences between the actual and the predicted values. As mentioned earlier, we mainly have focused in this paper on providing details of the deep learning based traffic prediction approach. Details of the overall evacuation method can be found in our earlier work [3–5].

Although, we have shown excellent results in this work, but this is not guaranteed while working with other traffic data with same or other deep learning models. This could be the result of high uniformity in input data that was used for training and testing purposes and therefore the same performance of deep model could not be guaranteed for other datasets. Therefore, we aim to work on different data with many other features including incidents data etc. to see its impact. This may also help us in predicting the people and other stakeholders behavior in emergency situations and we may model them collectively to present a model to not only to manage traffic by flow values but also by including other important factors in that environment as well. We can also use real-time traffic and other data to present an effective traffic management plan in the effected areas and can also use big data technologies to deal with real-time data.

Acknowledgments. The authors acknowledge with thanks the technical and financial support from the Deanship of Scientific Research (DSR) at the King Abdulaziz University (KAU), Jeddah, Saudi Arabia, under the grant number G-673-793-38. The work carried out in this paper is supported by the High Performance Computing Center at the King Abdulaziz University, Jeddah.

References

1. Gharaibeh, A., Salahuddin, M.A., Hussini, S.J., Khreishah, A., Khalil, I., Guizani, M., Al-Fuqaha, A.: Smart cities: a survey on data management, security, and enabling technologies. IEEE Commun. Surv. Tutor. **19**(4), 2456–2501 (2017)
2. Su, K., Li, J., Fu, H.: Smart city and the applications. In: 2011 International Conference on Electronics, Communications and Control (ICECC), pp. 1028–1031. IEEE (2011)
3. Alazawi, Z., Altowaijri, S., Mehmood, R., Abdljabar, M.B.: Intelligent disaster management system based on cloud-enabled vehicular networks. In: 2011 11th International Conference on ITS Telecommunications, pp. 361–368. IEEE (2011)
4. Alazawi, Z., Abdljabar, M.B., Altowaijri, S., Vegni, A.M., Mehmood, R.: ICDMS: an intelligent cloud based disaster management system for vehicular networks. In: Vinel, A., Mehmood, R., Berbineau, M., Garcia, C.R., Huang, C.-M., Chilamkurti, N. (eds.) Nets4Cars/Nets4Trains 2012. LNCS, vol. 7266, pp. 40–56. Springer, Heidelberg (2012). https://doi.org/10.1007/978-3-642-29667-3_4
5. Alazawi, Z., Alani, O., Abdljabar, M.B., Altowaijri, S., Mehmood, R.: A smart disaster management system for future cities. In: Proceedings of the 2014 ACM International Workshop on Wireless and Mobile Technologies for Smart Cities - WiMobCity 2014, pp. 1–10. ACM Press, New York (2014)
6. Alam, F., Mehmood, R., Katib, I., Albeshri, A.: Analysis of eight data mining algorithms for smarter Internet of Things (IoT). Procedia Comput. Sci. **98**, 437–442 (2016)
7. Guo, Y., Liu, Y., Oerlemans, A., Lao, S., Wu, S., Lew, M.S.: Deep learning for visual understanding: a review. Neurocomputing **187**, 27–48 (2016)
8. Cireşan, D.C., Meier, U., Masci, J., Gambardella, L.M., Schmidhuber, J.: Flexible, high performance convolutional neural networks for image classification. In: Proceedings of the Twenty-Second International Joint Conference on Artificial Intelligence - Volume Volume Two, pp. 1237–1242 (2011)
9. Djahel, S., Salehie, M., Tal, I., Jamshidi, P.: Adaptive traffic management for secure and efficient emergency services in smart cities. In: 2013 IEEE International Conference on Pervasive Computing and Communications Workshops (PERCOM Workshops), pp. 340–343. IEEE (2013)
10. SUMO | Simulation of Urban MObility. http://sumo.dlr.de/wiki/Main_Page

11. Suma, S., Mehmood, R., Albugami, N., Katib, I., Albeshri, A.: Enabling next generation logistics and planning for smarter societies. Procedia Comput. Sci. **109**, 1122–1127 (2017)
12. Schlingensiepen, J., Nemtanu, F., Mehmood, R., McCluskey, L.: Autonomic transport management systems—enabler for smart cities, personalized medicine, participation and industry grid/industry 4.0. In: Sładkowski, A., Pamuła, W. (eds.) Intelligent Transportation Systems – Problems and Perspectives. SSDC, vol. 32, pp. 3–35. Springer, Cham (2016). https://doi.org/10.1007/978-3-319-19150-8_1
13. Alam, F., Mehmood, R., Katib, I., Albogami, N.N., Albeshri, A.: Data fusion and IoT for smart ubiquitous environments: a survey. IEEE Access **5**, 9533–9554 (2017)
14. Mehmood, R., Alam, F., Albogami, N.N., Katib, I., Albeshri, A., Altowaijri, S.: UTiLearn: a personalised ubiquitous teaching and learning system for smart societies. IEEE Access **5**, 2615–2635 (2017)
15. Tawalbeh, L., Basalamah, A., Mehmood, R., Tawalbeh, H.: Greener and smarter phones for future cities: characterizing the impact of GPS signal strength on power consumption. IEEE Access **4**, 858–868 (2016)
16. Dandala, T.T., Krishnamurthy, V., Alwan, R.: Internet of Vehicles (IoV) for traffic management. In: 2017 International Conference on Computer, Communication and Signal Processing (ICCCSP), pp. 1–4. IEEE (2017)
17. Rizwan, P., Suresh, K., Babu, M.R.: Real-time smart traffic management system for smart cities by using Internet of Things and big data. In: 2016 International Conference on Emerging Technological Trends (ICETT), pp. 1–7. IEEE (2016)
18. Schlingensiepen, J., Mehmood, R., Nemtanu, F.C.: Framework for an autonomic transport system in smart cities. Cybern. Inf. Technol. **15**, 50–62 (2015)
19. Arfat, Y., Aqib, M., Mehmood, R., Albeshri, A., Katib, I., Albogami, N., Alzahrani, A.: Enabling smarter societies through mobile big data fogs and clouds. Procedia Comput. Sci. **109**, 1128–1133 (2017)
20. Zhu, F., Li, Z., Chen, S., Xiong, G.: Parallel transportation management and control system and its applications in building smart cities. IEEE Trans. Intell. Transp. Syst. **17**, 1576–1585 (2016)
21. Lv, Y., Duan, Y., Kang, W., Li, Z., Wang, F.-Y.: Traffic flow prediction with big data: a deep learning approach. IEEE Trans. Intell. Transp. Syst. **16**(2), 865–873 (2015)
22. Caltrans PeMS. http://pems.dot.ca.gov/
23. Polson, N.G., Sokolov, V.O.: Deep learning for short-term traffic flow prediction (2017)
24. Polson, N., Sokolov, V.: Deep learning predictors for traffic flows (2016)
25. Ma, X., Yu, H., Wang, Y., Wang, Y.: Large-scale transportation network congestion evolution prediction using deep learning theory. PLoS ONE **10**, e0119044 (2015)
26. Keras Documentation. https://keras.io/

D2TFRS: An Object Recognition Method for Autonomous Vehicles Based on RGB and Spatial Values of Pixels

Furqan Alam[1][(✉)], Rashid Mehmood[2], and Iyad Katib[1]

[1] Department of Computer Science, Faculty of Computing and Information Technology, King Abdulaziz University, Jeddah 21589, Saudi Arabia
fmohammed0026@stu.kau.edu.sa, iakatib@kau.edu.sa
[2] High Performance Computing Center, King Abdulaziz University, Jeddah 21589, Saudi Arabia
RMehmood@kau.edu.sa

Abstract. Autonomous driving is now near future reality which will transform our world due to its numerous benefits. The foremost challenge to this task is to correctly identify the objects in the driving environment. In this work, we propose an object recognition method known as Decision Tree and Decision Fusion based Recognition System (D2TFRS) for autonomous driving. We combined two separate feature sets, which are RGB pixel values and spatial points X,Y of each pixel to form our dataset. The D2TFRS is based on our intuition that reclassification of pre-identified misclassified objects in a driving environment can give better prediction accuracy. Results showed that D2TFRS outperformed AdaBoost classifier and performed better than C5.0 classifier in terms of the classification accuracy and Kappa. In terms of speed, C5.0 outperforms both AdaBoost and D2TFRS. However, D2TFRS outperformed AdaBoost with respect to speed. We strongly believe that D2TFRS will have better parallelization performance compared to the other two methods and it will be investigated in our future work.

Keywords: Autonomous driving · Autonomous vehicles · Object recognition
Decision tree · Decision fusion · Deep learning · Majority voting
C5.0 · SVM

1 Introduction

An autonomous vehicle (AVs) is one that can accelerate, increase and decrease speeds, put and release brakes and steer, itself avoiding any sort of accidents. Such technology has long been part of Hollywood sci-fi quixotic vision of the future. This is due to the fact that AVs will free drivers from boring side of driving during travel and reduce accident rates by providing breathtaking control over vehicles. In past, many attempts have been made but subjected to the limitation of available technologies. However, in recent years with technological advancements, the dream of AVs come very close to reality. Now we are able to manufacture them nevertheless they are in their testing phase. AVs have the potential to change how we look at our surroundings.

© ICST Institute for Computer Sciences, Social Informatics and Telecommunications Engineering 2018
R. Mehmood et al. (Eds.): SCITA 2017, LNICST 224, pp. 155–168, 2018.
https://doi.org/10.1007/978-3-319-94180-6_16

The Autonomous Driving (AD) is getting lots of attention and popularity due to its various benefits [1] and assumed to be an on-road reality soon. Most of the major industry titans which include Google, Tesla, Ford, Volvo, BMW, Microsoft, Apple, and others, are making huge investments in developing technologies which will enable AD. A new forecast by Intel and Strategy Analytics research firm estimated that AVs will be a 7$ trillion market by 2050 [2]. The competition of which company will bring its AVs first on the road to common public getting so tough, resulted in various perk luring practices to get skilled engineers from the rival companies and stealing AVs technologies from the competitors [3–5]. The core of these developments revolves around the critical question, how to perceive driving environment with higher certainties.

The key technology on which success of AVs depends is how accurately, they are able to perceive the driving environment. The initial step in this quest is to recognize the static and dynamic objects around the vehicles with higher accuracies. In a driving environment this object recognition problem in more complex due to the fact that it is multi-class problem and given the dynamic nature of the driving environment which add further complexities to it. AVs consist of several on-board and off-board sensors such as cameras, LIDAR, Radar and GPS as illustrated in Fig. 1.

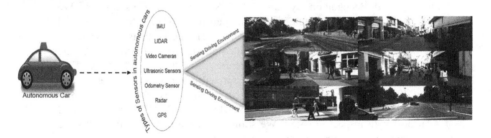

Fig. 1. General view of the autonomous driving environment.

The aim of any object recognition system is to predict with the highest degree of certainty for the given task. The result evaluation of different classification schemes can be different in terms of classification accuracies. One classifier tends to produce better predictions for a particular class, though its overall accuracy can be lower as compared to the other. The sets of patterns of rightly classified or misclassified data instances by the distinct classifiers would not certainly coincide, thus this form the basis to acquire better classification accuracies through decision fusion of predictions from various classifiers.

Supervised machine learning algorithms learn using a training dataset which contains independent variables and their response variables. They keep on learning until the minimum possible classification error achieved. In this work, our focus is to use supervised learning in a way that it enhances the object classification accuracy in a driving environment which will enable an auto-pilot to take better driving decisions.

1.1   Contributions

In this work, our main aim is to develop a methodology to achieve higher object classification accuracy by integrating supervised learning and decision fusion. The main contributions of this work are:

- We manually labeled images from a subset of KITTI city dataset [6] by using free-form selection (polygon) rather than a box or rectangular selection. This means, highly accurate pixel labeling is achieved by carefully selecting only the area of interest to enhance training of the algorithm.
- We used two feature sets together for training purposes. The first feature set consist of RGB values whereas the second feature set consist of the spatial location of each pixel i.e. x and y coordinates. The use of two feature sets increased the training accuracy considerably.
- We tried to demonstrate how pre-identification of worst data instances which are hardest to classify correctly, improves the accuracy of a classifier system.

1.2   Paper Structure

The paper is divided into seven sections. Section 2, contains literature review and in Sect. 3 we explained dataset and data preparation for this work. Further is Sect. 4, the classifiers are discussed which are used in this work, whereas in Sect. 5, the proposed method has been explained in detail. We represent results in Sect. 6 and finally, conclusions are drawn in Sect. 7.

2   Literature Review

Machine learning is mighty artificial intelligence (AI) tool which helps us to understand the complicated world around us by learning. Nowadays machine learning applied in almost every field such as biomedical, education, business, security, robotics, networking and much more [7–9]. Machine learning which eventually uses to develop AI for autonomous vehicles (AVs), ranges from infotainment systems to advanced driver assistance systems (ADAS) and further to complete self-driving auto-pilots. With machine learning, AI systems continuously learn from experience by their ability to foresee and identify the happenings in their surroundings, which is promising to be highly constructive when integrated into a software architecture of AVs. Search Engine giant Google and Tesla have been doing considerable research and development for developing the AI capabilities for their autonomous cars, albeit in a more vocal manner than their counterparts. Perceiving driving environment is the key problem for facilitating safe and smooth autonomous driving. The problem starts from recognizing static objects (road, speed breakers, traffic light, buildings) and dynamic objects (cars, cycles, trucks) around AVs. All the different objects must be classified by an object recognition system which is a multi-class problem for AVs and has been well studied in [10–12].

Identifying, tracking, and avoiding human beings is a pivotal capability of AVs. Pedestrian recognition must guarantee the safety of humans walking on footpaths and crossing the roads while auto-pilots are driving AVs which is studied in [13–15].

At Google, research scientist, Anelia Angelova introduced a novel pedestrian detection system that only requires video images [16]. Similarly to [16] in [17], the deep learning based video-only pedestrian detection system is presented which is under development at the University of California, San Diego. Works like [16, 17], could make human detection systems for AVs, to pinpoint humans using low-cost sensors like cameras alone without using expensive Lidar units which can reduce the cost of AVs considerably with high reliability. The developments in [16, 17], also support the arguments of Tesla CEO Elon Musk against using expensive Lidar technology for self-driving cars. A realistic situation can arise when AVs will have a sudden encounter with a pedestrian, to save life and avoid collision with a pedestrian is a crucial and complex problem. In [18] paper, author studies the problem of detecting sudden pedestrian encounters to aid drivers to avert any sort of accident. Road detection is a crucial problem for AVs as it decides how much space is available for driving and turning to ensure safe and smooth driving. In recent years a lot of development has been seen in this area [19–21]. For this purpose in [22], authors proposed a road detection technique using SVM which automatically updates the training data to minimize classification error. Similarly, in [23], linear SVM is used for Segment-Based Fractal Texture Analysis (SFTA) and compared with the multi-layer convolutional neural network (CNN). Both linear SVM and CNN produced very high classification accuracies. However, CNN showed slightly better specificity.

Another way to perceive driving environment is to combine multiple decisions or multiple sensor data for deducing the driving environment. This can also be defined as Data fusion which is well studied from various perspectives in one of the latest and comprehensive surveys [24]. The paper review mathematical methods for data fusion, specific sensor environments. Further authors discussed the emerging trends which would be benefited from data fusion [24]. For example combining GPS and camera images to predict safe driving distance to another vehicle on the road. Combining the multiple inputs or features into a single output is a complex problem but the outcome tends to show more certainty than single sensor data analytics as achieved in proceeding literature. For example in [25] authors fuse cameras images and LIDAR for deducing driving environment by labeling segments of images whereas in [26] object grid maps are created by combining camera images and laser. In literature such as [13, 14], the single feature set is used to identify humans. Solving the same problem, though using multi-sensor data, a smoothing-based depth up-sampling method for human detection is proposed in [27] which fuses camera images and LIDAR data. Furthermore in [28] authors uses knowledge of object classes to recognize humans, car obstacles, and bicyclists. A multi-layer perceptron (MLP) classifier is used in [29] to recognize, interpret and track autonomous moving objects. Blend of stereo vision, LIDAR and stereo vision data is used and supplied to MLP in [29] as input. Hane et, al use images from cameras with wheel odometry for drawing out static obstacles [30] whereas in [31] Dempster Shafer theory of evidence is used to integrate sensors data to classify the obstacles.

Combining results of multiple classifiers tend to produce better results, this is a well-proven concept. This sort of combination is known as Decision Fusion (DF). However, it is important to select a combination of right classifiers in order to take benefits from DF. In one of such work [32], authors critically examine the use of the ρ-correlation as a way to quantify the classifier diversity for selecting classifiers for fusion. DF methods are used successfully for image classification problems. A scheme to aggregate the results of different classifiers is proposed in [33]. Situations where the classifiers disagree with each other in [33], are solved by computing the pointwise accuracy and finding the global reliability [34]. Traditional methods for hyperspectral image classification typically use raw spectral signatures without considering spatial characteristics. In work [35], a classification algorithm based on Gabor features and decision fusion is proposed. First, the adjacent and high correlated spectral bands are intelligently grouped by coefficient correlation matrix. Following that, Gabor features in each group are extracted in PCA-projected subspaces to quantify local orientation and scale characteristics. Afterwards, locality preserving non-negative matrix factorization is incorporated to reduce the dimensionalities of these feature subspaces. Finally, the classification results from Gaussian-mixture-model classifiers are merged by a decision fusion rule. Experimental results show that the proposed algorithms substantially outperforms the traditional and state-of-the-art methods. Majority of AVs researches are based on binary classification problems and less attention has been given to challenging multi-class problems.

3 Dataset and Data Preparation

We used KITTI datasets [6] for this work. We have used two feature sets which are (R, G,B) values of the pixels and spatial values of each pixel in the image frames of dimension 1242 × 375 as depicted in Fig. 2. We create a dataset which has six attributes, namely r, g, b, x, y, class. We used Raster package [36] in R, to compute pixel values and location of each pixel in the image frame.

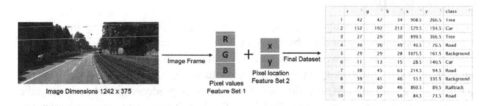

Fig. 2. Data preparation process.

Further, we manually labeled the images from a subset of KITTI city dataset [6] by using free-form selection (polygon) rather than a box or rectangular selection which is further depicted in Fig. 3. This means highly accurate pixel labeling is achieved by carefully selecting only the area of interest to enhance training of the machine learning algorithm. After selecting pixels of a particular object, we manually labeled every object pixel and spatial values to make final dataset. Our dataset contains 380000 rows and six attributes and we divided the datasets into two parts which are training 60% and 40% testing. Further, we used SMOTE algorithm on training data to overcome class imbalance problem which is discussed in proceeding section.

Box or rectangular selection of objects for labelling in a video frame.

Free-form or polygon selection of objects for labelling in a video frame.

Fig. 3. Object labeling process. The image is taken from KITTI dataset [6].

4 Algorithms

In this work, we used several supervised machine learning algorithms based on their prediction accuracy, execution time and scalability for classification and decision fusion through majority voting.

4.1 Decision Tree

C4.5 is a supervised learning algorithm which builds a decision tree using the concept of information entropy proposed by Quinlan [37]. It can handle both continuous and discrete attributes. In this work we used C5.0 which is an extension of C4.5, is also commercially sold by Ross Quinlan. The reason to use C5.0 for this work lies in the fact that it is extremely fast, several folds faster than its predecessor C4.5. It can take benefits of multi-core and multiple CPU [38]. Further, it has better memory management, which is needed because of a significant amount of data processing is required particularly in RGB image classification. It can give similar or better results to C4.5 and forms significantly smaller decision trees.

4.2 Support Vector Machine

Support vector machine (SVM) is one of the most accurate classifiers and have a sound theoretical foundation. SVM constructs hyperplane or a set of hyperplanes for performing classification and regression [39]. It can compete with far more complex modern-day classifiers in terms of accuracies and it is considered as one of the best classifiers which are listed among top 10 machine learning algorithm [38].

4.3 Deep Learning

Deep learning (DL) mimics a neural system of humans for performing learning task. It belongs to the family of artificial neural networks. It digs deep into the data and finds out the complex relationships among data elements. Widely used in image recognition, natural language processing, speech recognition and bioinformatics due to its quality of producing highly accurate predictions, though DL is computationally expensive. To develop a further understanding of various deep learning architectures, models, and their mathematical formulations in a more comprehensive manner, work such as [40–42] can be investigated.

5 Proposed Method

In this work, our prime focus is to identify data instances which are most difficult to classify for the given supervised machine learning algorithm, prior to classifying them and to reclassify the predicted misclassified data. We divide our main method into two phases. The first phase in which we carefully train our models and generate data for the training of proceeding stage because, from stage-2 onwards, machine learning algorithms need to be trained with the data specific to that stage. In the second phase, in which we test our whole method to predict its accuracy. All the experimentations are performed on R statistical machine learning platform and H2O [43], SVM [44], C5.0 [45] and Caret [46] libraries are used.

5.1 Training

Formally we can define our training process as, for the given training set (X_i, Y_i), we want to generate a classifier function to predict Y_i labels for new $X_i = (r_{i1}, g_{i2}, b_{i3}, x_{i4}, y_{i5})$. In our work, the training process is very critical and the core of the work. It serves two purposes. Firstly, identify accurate machine learning models and secondly, generate dataset for next stage. For method depicted in Fig. 4, as input we used $data_1$ to train C5.0 classifiers and to make data for training of the next stage. We predicted class labels using $data_2$.

Misclassified data instances are only 2.71% of whole data. Training C5.0 classifier for predicting misclassified (miss) and rightly classified (hit) data labels produced results with high accuracy. However, the prediction accuracy of misclassified data instances is below 50%. This is due to imbalance dataset problem. To counter this, we used SMOTE algorithm [47], to generate balanced and massive data of 1.5 million rows for training C5.0 classifier for predicting miss and hit and update $data_2$ accordingly. Then we separated miss and hit data. Further miss dataset (D_{miss_1}) is used to train classifiers for majority voting. Same steps are repeated to train classifiers n number of times. Class labels which are predicted at different stages are combined together in P_{final} based on row indexes of original input data.

```
Input:    data₁, data₂
Output:   Trained Models
  1.        ƒ = { Train M₁ = C5.0_main(data₁)
  2.            Predict P₁ ← M₁(data₂)
  3.            For(i to nrow(data₂))
  4.            {
  5.                If(data₂[class, i] ! = P₁[i])
  6.                {data₂[status, i] = "miss"}
  7.            }
  8.            MJ₁← [C5.0₁(D_miss₁), SVM₁(D_miss₁), DL₁(D_miss₁)]
  9.            # Accuracy Table of each classifier and Majority Vote
 10.            T₁←[P(MJ₁), P(C5.0₁), P(SVM₁), P(DL₁)]
 11.            # Function to select classifier or Majority vote based
               #on highest classification accuracy and named as M₂
 12.            M₂ ← maxAcc(T₁)
 13.            Predict P₂ ← M₂(D_miss₁)
 14.            For(i to nrow(D_miss₁))
 15.            {
 16.                If(D_miss₁[class, i] ! = P₂[i])
 17.                {D_miss₂ = D_miss₁[i]}
 18.            }
 20.            Repeat from line 8 to 16, n times, incrementally and save
               each trained classifier so to use them during testing
 21.            Predict P_final ← MergeRowsIndexwise(P₁, P₂, P₃, …. Pₙ)}
```

Fig. 4. Training method.

5.2 Testing

The testing process is explained in Fig. 5, which is self-explanatory in nature. We used classier function, obtained from training process, to predict Y_i label for new $X_i = (r_{i1}, g_{i2}, b_{i3}, x_{i4}, y_{i5})$. All trained classifiers are used in the testing phase. In Fig. 5, from stage-2 all the step repeated n number of times. In this work we used n = 2, however it can be more but will reduce the prediction speed.

6   Results and Analysis

To evaluate our results, we compared D2TFRS method to C5.0 and AdaBoost classifiers. We used confusion matrix, sensitivity, and specificity as the benchmarks for results evaluation.

6.1   Confusion Matrix

A confusion matrix (CM) is a table which shows actual versus predicted data labels. The sum of diagonal (SoD) of CM represents the correctly classified data label, thus can be used to compute classifier accuracy too which can be given as:

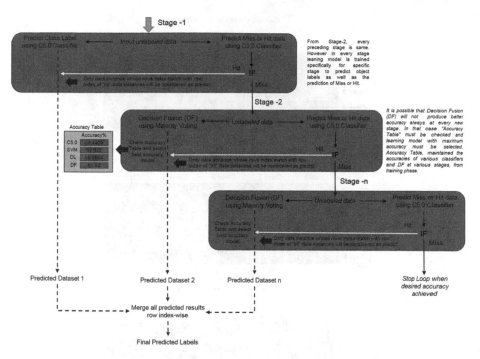

Fig. 5. Block diagram of proposed D2TFRS.

$$Accuracy\% = (SoD/Sum\ of\ all\ cells\ of\ CM) * 100 \qquad (1)$$

In Fig. 6, we visualize the CM of the D2TFRS method, C5.0 and AdaBoost classifiers. SoD which is the green color cells in Fig. 6, for each classifier represent rightly classified data labels. D2TFRS outperformed AdaBoost classifier by getting 6.48% better classification accuracy. D2TFRS performed better than C5.0 classifier which produces classification accuracy of 97.29% which is 1.33% less than classification accuracy of D2TFRS.

6.2 Sensitivity and Specificity

Sensitivity can be defined as the proportion of actual class labels which are correctly predicted by the classifier. Whereas Specificity is the ability of the classifier to identify negative results. Important terms used to calculate sensitivity and specificity are a number of true positive (TP), number of true negatives (TN), number of false positive (FP) and number of false negatives (FN) respectively.

Mathematically, these can be expressed as:

$$Sensitivity = TP/(TP + FN) \qquad (2)$$

$$Specificity = TN/(TN + FP) \qquad (3)$$

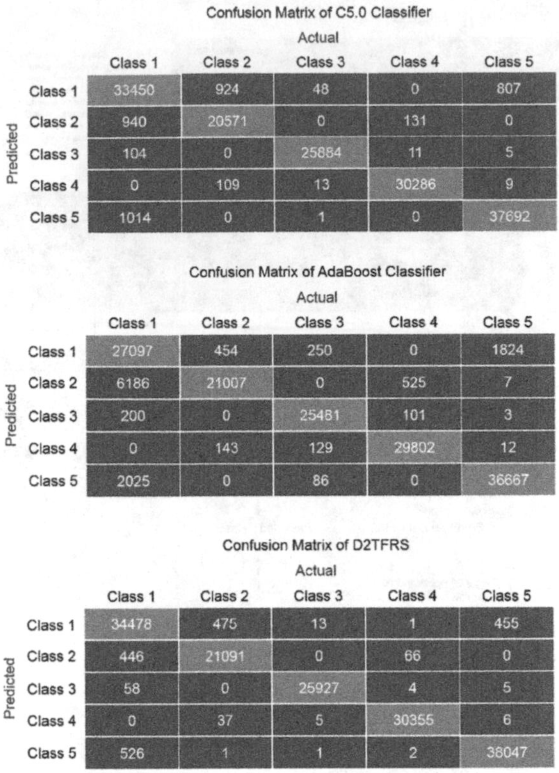

Confusion Matrix of C5.0 Classifier

Actual

	Class 1	Class 2	Class 3	Class 4	Class 5
Class 1	33450	924	48	0	807
Class 2	940	20571	0	131	0
Class 3	104	0	25884	11	5
Class 4	0	109	13	30286	9
Class 5	1014	0	1	0	37892

Predicted

Confusion Matrix of AdaBoost Classifier

Actual

	Class 1	Class 2	Class 3	Class 4	Class 5
Class 1	27097	454	250	0	1824
Class 2	6186	21007	0	525	7
Class 3	200	0	25481	101	3
Class 4	0	143	129	29802	12
Class 5	2025	0	86	0	36667

Predicted

Confusion Matrix of D2TFRS

Actual

	Class 1	Class 2	Class 3	Class 4	Class 5
Class 1	34478	475	13	1	455
Class 2	446	21091	0	66	0
Class 3	58	0	25927	4	5
Class 4	0	37	5	30355	6
Class 5	526	1	1	2	38047

Predicted

Fig. 6. Confusion Matrix of C5.0, AdaBoost, and D2TFRS.

In terms of sensitivity and specificity, D2TFRS performed better than C5.0 and AdaBoost classifiers for all classes as depicted in Figs. 7 and 8. AdaBoost performed worst among the three whereas C5.0 performed better than AdaBoost but lacks slightly behind proposed D2TFRS. Further, a graphical comparison of sensitivities and specificities are given in Figs. 7 and 8.

6.3 Kappa and Speed

Kappa (κ), is an index that considers an observed agreement with respect to a baseline agreement [48]. κ is a statistical benchmark to measure classification. There are no universal acceptability criteria on how to interpret κ. However first of its kind guidelines are given by Landis and Koch. Value of κ nearer to 1, means substantial or almost perfect agreement. Whereas the value of κ farther from 1 means no agreement or slight agreement. For more detail, characterization of κ can be found in [49].

Mathematically, κ can be expressed as:

$$\kappa = (p_o - p_e)/(1 - p_e) \tag{4}$$

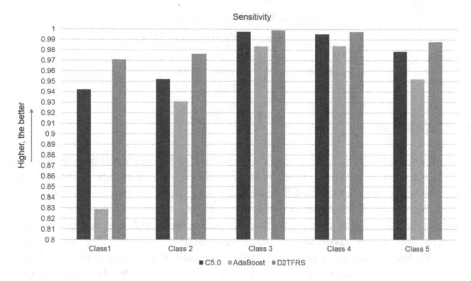

Fig. 7. Sensitivities measurement of C5.0, AdaBoost, and D2TFRS.

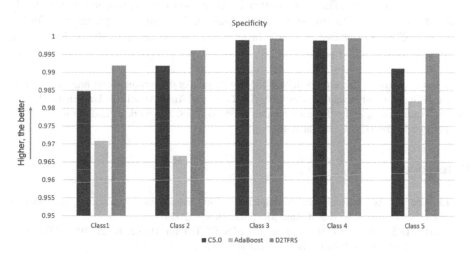

Fig. 8. Specificity measurement of C5.0, AdaBoost, and D2TFRS.

Where an observed agreement is given as p_o, and expected agreement is given as p_e. The value of κ is always ≤ 1. Values of κ are given in Table 1. Proposed method, D2TFRS, has an almost perfect agreement which is nearest to 1 as compared to C5.0 and AdaBoost classifiers.

In terms of speed, C5.0 took 5.11 s which is almost five times faster than D2TFRS which took 24.09 s and AdaBoost took 125 s with 20 iterations for which boosting is run. We strongly believe parallelization can increase the speed of D2TFRS by several magnitudes, as in this work D2TFRS implemented sequentially not in parallel. Further details of accuracy, Kappa and speeds can be found in Table 1.

Table 1. Classification statistics.

	Accuracy%	Kappa	Speed in sec
C5.0	97.29	0.9658	5.11
AdaBoost	92.14	0.9012	125
D2TFRS	98.62	0.9825	24.9

7 Conclusion

Autonomous driving is a near future reality and object recognition will play an important role in it. In this work, we proposed D2TFRS which recognize objects with higher accuracy as compared to C5.0 and AdaBoost. There are two reasons which are responsible for D2TFRS better classification accuracy. Firstly we predicted misclassified data instances prior to classification. Secondly, decision fusion through majority voting is done for reclassifying predicted misclassified data instances only. In this work, D2TFRS is implemented sequentially as a result, it is slower than C5.0. In the future, its speed can also be maximized by several magnitudes by the parallel implementation. We used a small dataset to test D2TFRS which can be considered as a drawback of this work. Therefore further investigation needed to confirm the steady performance of D2TFRS on much larger datasets. In future, we planned to further optimize D2TFRS to make it much faster with higher accuracy by training with massive datasets.

Acknowledgements. The authors acknowledge with thanks the technical and financial support from the Deanship of Scientific Research (DSR) at the King Abdulaziz University (KAU), Jeddah, Saudi Arabia, under the grant number G-661-611-38. The work carried out in this paper is supported by the HPC Center at KAU.

References

1. Litman, T.: Autonomous vehicle implementation predictions implications for transport planning. Transp. Res. Board Ann. Meet. **42**, 36–42 (2015)
2. Morris, D.Z.: Driverless cars will be part of a $7 Trillion Market by 2050 (2017). http://fortune.com/2017/06/03/autonomous-vehicles-market/
3. McGoogan, C.: Uber fires driverless car boss accused of stealing Google's trade secrets (2017). http://www.telegraph.co.uk/technology/2017/05/31/uber-fires-driverless-car-boss-failing-assist-google-lawsuit/
4. Kharpal, A.: Apple has reportedly hired ex-NASA and Tesla staffers to boost its self-driving car effort. https://www.cnbc.com/2017/04/25/apple-driverless-cars-hires-nasa-tesla.html
5. Feris, R.: Tesla sues former Autopilot director for allegedly stealing secrets, poaching coworkers. https://www.cnbc.com/2017/01/26/tesla-sues-former-exec-for-allegedly-stealing-secrets-poaching-workers.html
6. Geiger, A., Lenz, P.: Vision meets robotics: the KITTI dataset. Int. J. Rob. Res. **14**(3), 195–210 (2013)
7. Mehmood, R., Alam, F., Albogami, N.N., Katib, I., Albeshri, A., Altowaijri, S.: UTiLearn: a personalised ubiquitous teaching and learning system for smart societies. IEEE Access. **3536**, 1–22 (2017)

8. Alam, F., Mehmood, R., Katib, I., Albeshri, A.: Analysis of eight data mining algorithms for smarter Internet of Things (IoT). Int. Work. Data Min. IoT Syst. (DaMIS 2016) **98**, 437–442 (2016)

9. Alam, F., Thayananthan, V., Katib, I.: Analysis of round-robin load-balancing algorithm with adaptive and predictive approaches. In: Proceedings of 11th International Conference Control (2016)

10. Andriluka, M., Roth, S., Schiele, B.: People-tracking-by-detection and people-detection-by-tracking. In: IEEE Conference on Computer Vision and Pattern Recognition (2008)

11. Petrovskaya, A., Thrun, S.: Model based vehicle detection and tracking for autonomous urban driving. Auton. Rob. **26**, 123–139 (2009)

12. Wu, B.O., Nevatia, R.A.M.: Detection and tracking of multiple, partially occluded humans by Bayesian combination of edgelet based part detectors. Int. J. Comput. Vis. **75**, 247–266 (2007)

13. Tsukada, A., Background, A.: Road structure based scene understanding for intelligent vehicle systems. In: Proceedings of 2010 IEEE/RSJ International Conference on Intelligence Robotics System, pp. 5557–5562 (2010)

14. Hu, Q., Wang, P., Shen, C., Porikli, F.: Pushing the limits of deep CNNs for pedestrian detection. Comput. Vis. Pattern Recognit. **28**(6), 1358–1368 (2018)

15. Navarro, P.J., Fernández, C., Borraz, R., Alonso, D.: A machine learning approach to pedestrian detection for autonomous vehicles using high-definition 3D range data. Sensors **17**(1), 18 (2017)

16. Harris, M.: New pedestrian detector from google could make self-driving cars cheaper. http://spectrum.ieee.org/cars-that-think/transportation/self-driving/new-pedestrian-detector-from-google-could-make-selfdriving-cars-cheaper

17. Hsu, J.: Deep learning makes driverless cars better at spotting pedestrians. IEEE Spectrum: Technology, Engineering, and Science News. https://spectrum.ieee.org/cars-that-think/trans portation/advanced-cars/deep-learning-makes-driverless-cars-better-at-spotting-pedestrians. Accessed 3 Jul 2018

18. Xu, Y., Xu, D., Lin, S., Han, T.X.: Detection of sudden pedestrian crossings for driving assistance systems. IEEE Trans. Syst. Man Cybern. Syst. **42**, 729–739 (2012)

19. Peterson, K., Ziglar, J., Rybski, P.E.: Fast feature detection and stochastic parameter estimation of road shape using multiple LIDAR. In: IEEE/RSJ International Conference on Intelligence Robotics System, pp. 22–26 (2008)

20. Beyeler, M., Mirus, F., Verl, A.: Vision-based robust road lane detection in urban environments. In: Proceedings of 2014 IEEE International Conference on Robotics Automation, pp. 4920–4925 (2014)

21. Felisa, M., Zani, P., Dipartimento, V.: Robust monocular lane detection in urban environments. In: Proceedings of 2010 IEEE Intelligent Vehicles Symposium, pp. 591–596 (2010)

22. Zhou, S., Gong, J., Xiong, G., Chen, H., Iagnemma, K.: Road detection using support vector machine based on online learning and evaluation. In: Proceedings of 2010 IEEE Intelligent Vehicles Symposium, pp. 256–261 (2010)

23. Nair, V., Parthasarathy, N.: Supervised learning methods for vision based road detection. Stanford Univ. (2012)

24. Alam, F., Mehmood, R., Member, S., Katib, I., Nasser, N.: Data fusion and IoT for smart ubiquitous environments : A Survey. IEEE Access **3536**, 1–24 (2017)

25. Xu, P., Davoine, F., Zhao, H., Denoeux, T.: Multimodal information fusion for urban scene understanding. Mach. Vis. Appl. **27**(3), 331–349 (2014)

26. Nuss, D., Thom, M., Danzer, A., Dietmayer, K.: Fusion of laser and monocular camera data in object grid maps for vehicle environment perception. In: Proceedings of 2014 17th International Conference on Intelligent Fusion (2014)

27. Premebida, C., Batista, J., Nunes, U.: Pedestrian detection combining RGB and dense LIDAR data. In: Proceedings of 2014 IEEE/RSJ International Conference on Intelligent Robotics System IROS 2014 (2014)

28. Cho, H., Seo, Y., Kumar, B.V.K.V., Rajkumar, R.R.: A multi-sensor fusion system for moving object detection and tracking in urban driving environments. In: Proceedings of 2014 IEEE International Conference on Robotics Automation, pp. 1836–1843 (2014)

29. Chumerin, N., Van Hulle, M.M.: Cue and sensor fusion for independent moving objects detection and description in driving scenes. In: Mandic, D., Golz, M., Kuh, A., Obradovic, D., Tanaka, T. (eds.) Signal Processing Techniques for Knowledge Extraction and Information Fusion, pp. 161–180. Springer, Boston (2008). https://doi.org/10.1007/978-0-387-74367-7_9

30. Häne, C., Sattler, T., Pollefeys, M.: Obstacle detection for self-driving cars using only monocular cameras and wheel odometry. In: Proceedings of 2015 IEEE/RSJ International Conference on Intelligent Robotics System (2015)

31. Zhao, Y., Li, J., Li, L., Zhang, M., Guo, L.: Environmental perception and sensor data fusion for unmanned ground vehicle. Math. Probl. Eng. **2013**, 1–12 (2013)

32. Goebel, K., Yan, W.: Choosing classifiers for decision fusion. GE Global Research Center

33. Fauvel, M., Member, S., Chanussot, J., Member, S.: Decision fusion for the classification of urban remote sensing images. IEEE Trans. Geosci. Remote Sens. **44**, 2828–2838 (2006)

34. Yager, R.R.: A General Approach to the Fusion of Imprecise Information. Wiley, New York (1997)

35. Ye, Z., Bai, L., Tan, L.: Hyperspectral image classification based on gabor features and decision fusion. In: Proceedings of 2017 2nd International Conference on Image Vision Computing, pp. 478–482 (2017)

36. Cheng, J., et al.: Raster: geographic data analysis and modeling. CRAN (2016)

37. Quinlan, J.R.: C4.5: Programs for Machine Learning. Morgan Kaufmann Publishers Inc., San Francisco (1993)

38. Wu, X., et al.: Top 10 algorithms in data mining. Knowl. Inf. Syst. **14**, 1–37 (2008)

39. Vapnik, V.N.: The Nature of Statistical Learning Theory. Springer, New York (1999). https://doi.org/10.1007/978-1-4757-3264-1

40. LeCun, Y., Bengio, Y., Hinton, G.: Deep learning. Nature **521**, 436–444 (2015)

41. Deng, L.: A tutorial survey of architectures, algorithms, and applications for deep learning. APSIPA Trans. Signal Inf. Process. **3**, e2 (2014)

42. Bengio, Y.: Learning deep architectures for AI. Found. Trends® Mach. Learn. **2**, 1–127 (2009)

43. Candel, A., Lanford, J., LeDell, E., Parmar, V., Arora, A.: Deep Learning with H2O Deep Learning with H2O (2015)

44. Rosiers, W.: A parallel-voting version of the support-vector-machine algorithm. In: CRAN (2015)

45. Kuhn, M., Weston, S., Coulter, N., Culp, M.: C5.0 decision trees and rule-based models. In: CRAN (2015)

46. Kuhn, M., et al.: Classification and regression training. In: CRAN (2017)

47. Chawla, N.V., Bowyer, K.W., Hall, L.O., Kegelmeyer, W.P.: SMOTE: synthetic minority over-sampling technique. J. Artif. Intell. Res. **16**, 321–357 (2002)

48. Smeeton, N.C.: Early history of the kappa statistic. Biometrics. **41**, 795 (1985)

49. Landis, J.R., Koch, G.G.: The measurement of observer agreement for categorical data. Biometrics **33**, 159–174 (1977)

Enabling Reliable and Resilient IoT Based Smart City Applications

Thaha Muhammed[1]([✉]), Rashid Mehmood[2], and Aiiad Albeshri[1]

[1] Department of Computer Science, FCIT, King Abdulaziz University,
Jeddah 21589, Saudi Arabia
m.thaha.h@ieee.org, aaalbeshri@kau.edu.sa
[2] High Performance Computing Center, King Abdulaziz University,
Jeddah 21589, Saudi Arabia
rmehmood@kau.edu.sa

Abstract. Internet of Things (IoT) has emerged as a revolutionary technology that has become an integral part of smart cities. It has numerous, longstanding, economical and safety-critical smart city applications. Data acquisition for IoT applications requires sensor networks. Reliability, Resilience, and Energy conservation are the three most critical wireless sensor requirements. Fault tolerance ensures the reliability and the resilience of the sensor network in case of failures. In this paper, we propose a new taxonomy for fault tolerant technique for wireless sensor networks deployed in an IoT environment, and qualitatively compare some major existing methods and propose a new fault-tolerant routing technique for hierarchical sensor networks. The algorithm is a heterogeneous technique based on Dynamic source routing (DSR), vice cluster heads, energy thresholding and hierarchical sensor networks. The proposed technique was simulated and is compared with current techniques to evaluate its validity and performance.

Keywords: Smart-city · IoT · WSN · Reliability · Fault tolerance
Energy · Routing

1 Introduction

Urban population has increased vastly in the recent years. The United Nations Human Settlements Program (UN-Habitat) [1] has foreseen it to be 10 billion by 2050, which is two-thirds of the current population on earth. The cities will have to deal with pressing issues such as public safety, efficient transportation, energy consumption, environmental sustainability, and expense reduction. These pressing issues have led to smart city paradigm which aims to plan and develop efficient urban cities in future.

The past decade has witnessed the advancement of Internet of Things (IoT) [2] especially the sensing technology [3]; In addition to the widespread development of sensors, improvement in Big data computing infrastructure has enabled

© ICST Institute for Computer Sciences, Social Informatics and Telecommunications Engineering 2018
R. Mehmood et al. (Eds.): SCITA 2017, LNICST 224, pp. 169–184, 2018.
https://doi.org/10.1007/978-3-319-94180-6_17

the collection of huge amount of heterogeneous data produced daily by urban spaces [4]. Urban spaces produce data related to temperature, weather, pollution, traffic control, the mobility of people, resource consumption (water and electricity) which can be analyzed to improve the services provided and make the environment greener. Smart cities rely on sensors, webcams, IoT systems, wireless sensor networks, databases, ubiquitous devices, and many other frameworks that collect, process and take informed decisions based on the data [5]. A survey on Data Fusion and IoT for smart ubiquitous environments can be seen in [6].

Wireless Sensor Networks (WSNs) are one of the atomic components of IoT. Data acquisition for IoT applications require wireless sensor network and are the link between the real world and the digital world. WSNs play a major role in building interconnected urban territories and are critical to smart cities. WSNs consists of small low power sensor nodes that can sense, process, and wirelessly communicate with each other. The sensors are devices with limited battery, storage, size, and computational power. The sensors nodes sense data and forward it to a base station known as sink for further processing of data by IoT systems. Intelligent monitoring and management of smart cities are possible through IoT. WSNs are used in a number of time-critical smart city applications such as agriculture monitoring [7], intruder detection [8], disaster management, health care, mobile object tracking, environment monitoring [8], Intelligent Transport System (obstacle detection, collision warnings and avoidance, traffic monitoring) [9–11], Vehicular AdHoc Networks [12], energy monitoring in smart grids [13], and Home/Office Automation Systems (HOS) [14].

Since WSNs are deployed in harsh and hostile conditions they are susceptible to frequent errors. The occurrence of faults results in disruption of the network or worse in the failure of the network. This might lead to human, economic, environmental loss since the sensors are used in many safety critical applications. Another source of a fault in WSN is the power [3]. Since the WSNs work unattended in a hostile environment it is not feasible to replenish the batteries of the sensors. Moreover, various hazard might cause the power to run out, which results in a node failure. Data transmission consumes a major portion of energy [15]. Hence prolonging energy in WSN becomes a critical and challenging issue [16,17]. A detailed discussion on possible faults in wireless sensor networks has been discussed in [18]. It is required that the data collected by the sensors on critical events should not be of low quality [19,20] that might lead to important information loss. But often random link failures occurs that disrupt communication in the network. All these issues point to the necessity of fault tolerance techniques that would provide techniques to mask these faults and provide the expected services, in the presence of faults. Major disadvantages of existing techniques are a high dissipation of energy, large Mean Time to Repair (MTTR), and use of extra software and hardware [21].

In this paper, we propose a new fault-tolerant routing algorithm based on modified Dynamic Source Routing (DSR) on a clustered, hierarchical sensor network for IoT applications. We use a vice cluster head that takes over the duties of the CH on the failure of a CH. Moreover, we use multiple paths that have been prioritized and sorted on the basis of a cost function, that takes into consideration the total energy in a path and the distance from the source to sink. Furthermore, we use energy thresholds to decide the CHs that would participate in the routing process. One of the major advantages of the technique is that the Mean Time To Repair (MTTR) for this technique is small. We simulate our algorithm and compare our algorithm with DFTR [22], a distributed fault tolerant algorithm and LEACH [3], a well-known routing algorithm. Metrics such as the number of alive nodes, total energy consumption of the network, and total packets transmitted to the Sink are compared measured for all the three techniques. Based on these metrics it was observed that HMDSR performs better than the other techniques.

Our contributions in this article can be summarized as follows:

- We propose a new up to date taxonomy for fault-tolerant strategies for wireless sensor networks.
- We propose a new energy efficient fault-tolerant routing strategy called Heterogeneous Modified Dynamic Source Routing (HMDSR).
- We simulate the proposed technique.
- The results from the proposed technique are compared with two current techniques [3, 22] to validate the benefits of the algorithm.

The rest of the article is organized as follows. Section 2 discusses the proposed taxonomy for fault tolerant techniques in WSN. In Sect. 3, we discuss the state of art fault tolerant techniques for WSN. We also do a qualitative analysis of FT techniques in WSN. In Sect. 4, we discuss the System model and Sect. 5 introduces our proposed FT routing technique. Section 6 presents the simulation of the proposed technique. It also presents the comparison with techniques to validate our proposed technique. Section 7 concludes the paper.

2 Taxonomy

Fault tolerance techniques in wireless sensor networks can be classified according to two criteria, namely based on the phase at which the fault tolerant technique triggers and based on the origin of faults in WSN. Based on these criteria fault detection techniques in WSN can be classified as (1) Proactive and (2) Reactive as shown in Fig. 1.

2.1 Proactive Techniques

Proactive techniques in WSN proactively and sensibly uses the existing resources of the wireless sensor to extend the lifetime of the network or prevent the fault from occurring. These techniques take preemptory action against potential faults. Based on the origin of faults these techniques can be classified (1) Node based techniques, (2) Network-based techniques and, (3) Holistic techniques.

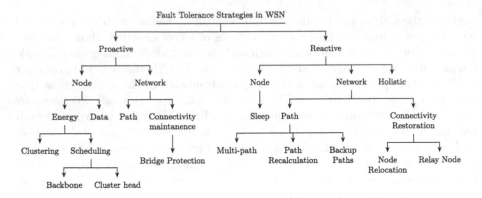

Fig. 1. Proposed taxonomy of fault tolerant techniques in WSN

Node Based Techniques. The node based proactive techniques can be further classified as (1) Energy based fault tolerance technique and (2) Data fault tolerance. Energy based fault tolerance increases the mean time to failure and the lifetime of the network. This strategy uses techniques such as clustering of sensor nodes, hibernation of nodes, and scheduling nodes and backbone of the WSN. Proactive data fault tolerant techniques helps in recovering from data faults. One of the major techniques of data fault tolerance is the dual transmission of the same value and comparison of these data to detect the faults.

Network Based Techniques. It comprises of mainly two techniques namely (1) Connectivity maintenance technique and (2) Multi-Path routing. Connectivity maintenance techniques increase the lifetime of network using various algorithms. Bridge protection algorithm is an example of connectivity maintenance algorithm that increases the lifetime of WSNs comprising bridged nodes. Data is sent through multiple paths to increase the redundancy and tolerate network fault in multi-path techniques.

2.2   Reactive Techniques

Reactive techniques trigger the fault tolerant strategy on the occurrence of the faults. This strategy waits for the faults to occur and then adjusts or reacts to the faultby starting the recovery process. These techniques can also be further classified based on the origin of the faults as (1) Node based, (2) Network-based and, (3) Holistic based technique.

Node Based Techniques. Node based reactive techniques are used to recover from node failures. It consist of strategies like switching to the sleeping backup node on the occurrence of node failure.

Network Based Faults. Network-based reactive techniques consist of using multiple paths, backup paths, and path recalculation in case of network/link failure. Moreover, for restoring the connectivity, extra nodes are deployed or the existing nodes are repositioned.

Holistic Techniques. These are the techniques that can deal and recover from both network and node based faults. They provide a complete fault tolerance for various faults.

3   Previous Work

In this section we shall discuss the existing work related to WSN fault tolerance techniques.

Zhao et al. [23] proposes a sleep scheduling technique called virtual backbone scheduling (VBS). Multiple backbones that overlap with each other are used to transmit data to the sink. The other nodes does not participate in the transmission to save energy. Selection of the backbones is an NP-hard problem. However, node failures might require recalculating the backbones.

Khan et al. [24] propose a fault-tolerant algorithm for bridge protection in WSNs. The authors propose a bridge protection algorithm to prevent the bridge node(s) from prematurely exhausting the energy and to maintain the minimal functionality of the network with minimal interference. But this technique has a trade of between time and residual energy.

Boucetta et al. [25] propose an energy efficient fault tolerant scheduling algorithm called PASC_AR. The network is clustered geographically based on node location. The cluster head is selected in rotation from the nodes based on a TDMA schedule. The rest of the nodes are put to sleep. However, the sensing accuracy is reduced due to the sleep mode of majority nodes.

Azharuddin et al. [22] propose an energy saving and FT routing technique called DFTR that not only deal with energy utilization of cluster heads but also their fault-tolerance. The routing is done based on following criteria: (1) gateway to next hop gateway distance, (2) next-hop gateway to base station distance, (3) energy remaining at the next-hop gateway. But, fixed gateways are not always suitable or plausible. Moreover, clustering is difficult when there are fixed gateways.

Rana [26] proposes a modified dynamic source routing algorithm (DSR) offering energy-efficient, fault-tolerant routing. The major features of this technique are (1) non-usage of nodes below certain energy threshold in the routing process, and (2) two routes cached between source and destination. There is a reduction in throughput of network for any given time period as all nodes are not involved in transmission

Gupta et al. [27] propose an energy-efficient fault tolerant clustering algorithm named B^3FT. In this technique, the authors discuss fault tolerance for cluster heads without the redundant usage of cluster heads. This scheme requires the use of extra hardware as gateways.

Azharuddin *et al.* [28] discuss a fault tolerant clustering based routing algorithm based on particle swarm optimization. They maximize the lifetime of the gateway with minimum lifetime by minimizing the routing load over the gateway. This is achieved with the help of particle swarm optimization. However, this scheme does not handle fault tolerance if no gateway is in range.

Hezaveh *et al.* [29] propose a technique called Fault-Tolerant and Energy Aware Mechanism (FTEAM). They put overlapped nodes with highest residual energies to sleep so they can be used as a cluster head (CH) in case of CH failures. It is only reliable when rate of change of sensed value is small inside the cluster.

Dima *et al.* [30] propose an integrated fault tolerance framework (IFTF) which holistically detects and diagnose application level faults, network layer faults, and establish the cause of the fault. However, there is a 4% increase in message overhead and does not consider the computation overhead.

4   Network and Radio Model

We consider a clustered WSN which consists of a single base station/sink and multiple clusters of sensor nodes. The sensor nodes in each cluster are normal nodes that are responsible for sensing and transmitting the data to their respective clusterheads (CH). All the nodes and the clusterheads are considered to be homogeneous with identical initial energy levels. The CHs are also normal nodes with the same energy constraints as that of sensing nodes. The CHs receive the sensed data, aggregates the data and forwards it to the base station. Direct data transmission occurs if the base station is one hop away from the CH else the aggregated data is forwarded to the CH closer to the base station. The nodes are deployed randomly as in smartdust model. The sensor nodes and CHs are considered immobile. There is only a single base station which is stationary and has an inexhaustible power supply. All sensor nodes have equivalent bi-directional communication range. All the wireless links are assumed to be symmetric so as to compute the distance between the nodes based on the received signal strength [31]. CSMA/CA MAC protocol is used by the CHs for communicating with base station [31]. For energy consumption analysis we only consider the energy used due to transmission and receiving of data since radio is the most power consuming parte as the consumption due to sensing and computing is negligible.

In this technique we use a radio model that is used in [3]. The energy dissipated E_T due to the transmission of a message of size l-bit, between two nodes separated by a distance d is given by

$$E_T(l,d) = \begin{cases} l(E_{elec} + \varepsilon_{FS} \times d^2) & for\ (d < d_0) \\ l(E_{elec} + \varepsilon_{MP} \times d^4) & for\ (d > d_0) \end{cases} \tag{1}$$

where $d_0 = \sqrt{\varepsilon_{FS}/\varepsilon_{MP}}$, E_{elec} is the electronic energy required by the circuit, ε_{FS} and ε_{MP} are the transmit amplifier parameters that represents the energy required by the amplifier in free space and multipath models respectively. The energy dissipation at the receiver sensor node for a message of size l-bit is given by

$$E_R(l) = l \times E_{elec} \tag{2}$$

Moreover, the energy consumed for fusing $l-$bits can be given by

$$E_F(l) = l \times E_{df} \tag{3}$$

where E_{df} is the energy incurred due to fusing of one bit data.

5   Proposed Technique

The proposed technique has two phases: (1) Setup phase, (2) Route determination phase, (3) Data communication phase and (4) Fault recovery phase.

5.1   Network Setup

Initially the network will be in setup phase. Initially all the sensor nodes send a HELLO message to the sink. The sink then assigns an ID to all sensor nodes. During the setup phase, we use any of the standard clustering algorithm to cluster the network and assign a cluster head to each cluster. The cluster head in each of the cluster sends a HELLO message to all its node with specific power and based on the strength of the signal received, it finds the nearest node to itself. The nearest node to the cluster head in each cluster is assigned as the vice cluster head. The sink then broadcasts a HELLO message using specific amount of power to all the cluster heads. The sink calculates the distances to each sensor node using the radio strength and this distance is send back to the cluster head. The setup phase ends and the communication phase starts wherein the nodes sends their data to the cluster heads and the cluster heads will fuse multiple identical values into a single value [3]. After certain amount of time the network switches back to the setup phase so as to balance the energy of the nodes in the network. Subsequently, it enters the communication phase and this process continues until the network encounters a fault.

5.2   Route Discovery and Routing Algorithm

We develop our routing technique on top of the foregoing medium access control (MAC) layer. The major steps in our routing technique is given below:

Step 1: Initially in the route determination phase, each cluster head broadcasts an REQ packet similar to that of Dynamic Source Routing (DSR). The REQ initially consists of the source ID, destination ID, the energy of the each cluster head and, the distance to the sink that was obtained during the bootstrap process.

Step 2: This REQ packet is flooded among other cluster heads, and each cluster adds to the packet their respective ID, energy level and, the distance to the base station.

Step 3: We define an energy threshold level. Any cluster head that has energy level below this threshold will not participate in the flooding process.

Step 4: The broadcasted REQ packets reaches the destination. For each cluster head, the sink starts a timer on the arrival of the first REQ packet from that cluster head. The sink will wait for more packets till timer expiry. Once the timer expires the sink will analyze and select the routes for each cluster head based on the remaining energy level and the sum of distance of the all cluster heads in the path to the sink. Based on this the routes for each cluster head is prioritized and are given priority numbers P1, P2,..., Pn.

Step 5: Thereafter, the sink sends a REP message to the cluster heads through all the discovered routes for the cluster heads. The REP message consists of the ID of the nodes that are in the path and the priority of that path.

Step 6: Once all REP messages reach the cluster heads they save the routes on basis of their priority and the route with priority P1 will be used for sending data to base station. The intermediate nodes between the source and destination also saves the routes.

Step 7: Once the routes are selected, the cluster heads pass the route information to their respective vice cluster heads and the vice cluster head resume their sleep state after storing this information.

The routing algorithm has been given in Algorithm 1.

5.3   Fault Tolerance

In this technique we only consider faults in routing especially disruption of route due to failure of cluster heads. We can consider the following cases of failures:

Failure of the source cluster head. When the source cluster head fails, the vice cluster head takes over the job of the cluster head. The routing table is already present in the vice cluster head as explained before.

Failure of the intermediate cluster head. When the data from the source cluster head is send ahead and one of the intermediate cluster head fails then the failed cluster head sends an error message (ERR) to the preceding cluster head. The preceding cluster head will switch its route from primary to secondary route and the faulty cluster head will be replace by the vice cluster head. if the secondary route also fails then it will use the tertiary route and so on. Since the routes have been stored this will save us from recalculating the routes again.

Failure of vice cluster head. On the instance of vice cluster head failure, we go back to the network setup phase we recluster the network and determine new routes.

The fault tolerance algorithm has been given in Algorithm 2.

Algorithm 1. Proposed routing algorithm

Input: $\forall CH_k,\ Energy_k,\ Distance\ to\ Sink_k$
Output: $All\ paths,\ from\ Source\ CH_i\ to\ Sink$

```
 1: procedure CH–ROUTESELECTION
 2:     Node_i receives REQ_i packet from it NeighborNode(i)
 3:     if Node_i! = sink then
 4:         if Energy(i) < E_thresh then
 5:             REQ_i ← REQ_i + (Id_i, Energy_i, Dist_i)
 6:             Forward REQ_i to NeighborNodes(i)
 7:         else
 8:             Node_i does not broadcast
 9:         end if
10:     else if Node_i is == Sink then
11:         Start timer_j
12:         while timer_i < Time_thresh do
13:             if REQ == REQ_i then
14:                 REQSet(i) ← REQSet(i) ∪ REQ_i
15:             end if
16:         end while
17:         for each Request REQ_i ∈ REQSet(j) do
18:             Cost(j, i) ← 0.3 × Dist(Source, Sink) + 0.7 × Energy(Source, Sink)
19:         end for
20:         for each row Cost(j, :) do
21:             Sort Cost(j, :)
22:             Set Priority in Descending Order in Cost(j, :)
23:         end for
24:         for each REQ_i in REQSet(j) do
25:             REP_i ← REP_i + (Id_i, Path_i, Priority_i)
26:             Forward REP_i to Source_i
27:         end for
28:         Node N_i creates routing table using REP messages.
29:     end if
30: end procedure
31:
32: procedure CH–ROUTING
33:     Use the Path with Priority = 1
34: end procedure
```

6 Simulation Results and Discussion

6.1 Experimental Setup

Th proposed protocol was simulated using MATLAB R2015a on an intel i5 machine with 2.40 GHz and 16 GB RAM running on Ubuntu 15.10. We deployed 400 sensor nodes in a square area of size 300×300 square meters. The topology of the simulated network is illustrated in Fig. 2. The sensor nodes were considered to have a starting energy of 2 J. When the energy level of the node reached 0 J

Algorithm 2. Fault tolerance Algorithm

```
1: procedure CH–FAULTTOLERANCE
2:     for i ∈ Priority do
3:         if Path with Priority = i fails due to CH failure then
4:             if Vice CH not used then
5:                 Awake Vice CH
6:                 Replace CH with Vice CH
7:                 Update routing Tables
8:             end if
9:         else
10:             Use path with Priority = i + 1
11:         end if
12:     end for
13: end procedure
```

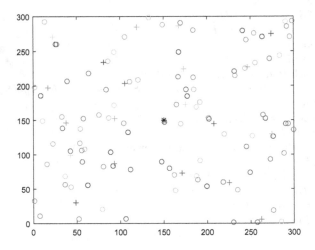

Fig. 2. The simulated network topology

the node was considered dead. We use Weibull reliability function [32] to model the faults in the cluster heads in our network which is given by

$$R(t) = e^{-\left(\frac{t-\gamma}{\eta}\right)^{\beta}} \tag{4}$$

where γ is the location parameter, η is the scale parameter, and β is the shape parameter. We set the values of $\gamma = 0$, $\beta = 3$, and $\eta = 3000$. If β is greater than 1 then the rate of failure increases with time else if β is less than 1 then the rate of failure decreases with time. Moreover, of $\beta = 0$ the rate of failure is constant. β is chosen as per the analysis provided in [33] where it is established that the failure of cluster heads can be represented using a weibull distribution with $\beta = 3$. Furthermore, [22] uses $\beta = 3$ for gateway faults in WSN. The simulation parameters used in the simulation are shown in Table 1. The parameters used are similar to [3].

Table 1. The simulation parameters

Simulation parameters	
Network size	400
Number of clusters	300×300
Initial sensor node energy	$2.0\,\mathrm{J}$
E_{elec}	$50\,\mathrm{nJ/bit}$
E_F	$5\,\mathrm{nJ/bit}$
Communication range	$100\,\mathrm{m}$
ε_{FS}	$10\,\mathrm{pJ/bit/m^2}$
ε_{MP}	$0.0013\,\mathrm{pJ/bit/m^4}$
d_0	$88\,\mathrm{m}$
Packet size	4,000 bits
Message size	200 bits
E_{thresh}	20%

The proposed algorithm is compared with DFTR [22] and LEACH [34] in terms of residual energy, number of packets received at sink, number of dead cluster heads, and network lifetime. We discuss the results of the experiments in the following sections.

6.2   Analysis of HMDSR

A wireless sensor network consisting of 120 nodes were simulated and was clustered initially into 20 clusters. These 120 nodes were deployed in a sensing field of size 300×300. The sink was placed at the center of the sensing field at the coordinates (150, 150). The simulated network is depicted in Fig. 2. The total number of alive nodes is compared in Fig. 4. We can see that the total alive nodes after 5000 rounds for the proposed technique are more than the LEACH and DFTR. Nodes are considered dead when their energy reaches 0 J or due to the simulation of faults following the Weibull distribution. We can observe in our proposed technique that initially there is a decrease in alive nodes that stabilizes after a certain amount of rounds.

The stability of alive nodes is due to the Energy threshold that was applied which resulted in many cluster heads with lower energy not to participate in the clustering. Whereas in LEACH protocol, we can observe that the rate of dead nodes increases after a certain number of rounds. The DFTR protocol that does not provide an Energy threshold has the least amount of total energy in the network. This is because once the cluster head dies in DFTR technique and nodes of clusters becomes orphan they have to send it to a longer distance. Since DFTR uses special fixed gateways, a failure in cluster head means another normal node doesn't take its place as a replacement, unlike the proposed technique. Figure 3 shows the total energy in the network per round for each of the technique. It is

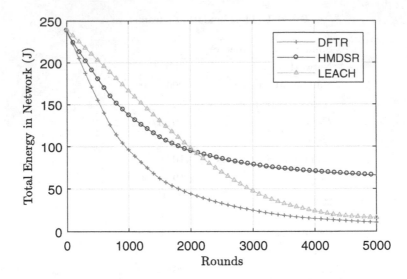

Fig. 3. Comparison of total energy in the simulated network per round among DFTR, LEACH, and HMDSR.

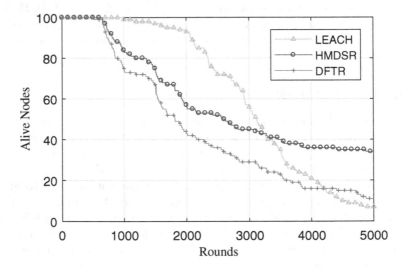

Fig. 4. The number of alive nodes per round in the simulated network among DFTR, LEACH, and HMDSR

also similar to the previous graph where the total energy at the end of 5000 round is highest in the proposed technique. Hence, we can clearly say that the proposed technique increases the overall lifetime of the network as compared to LEACH and DFTR.

The total number of packets that has been transmitted to the sink for 5000 rounds have been compared in Fig. 5. We can see that the proposed technique

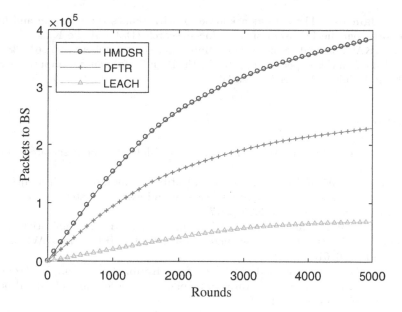

Fig. 5. The total number of data packets received at sink per round among DFTR, LEACH, and HMDSR

transmits the maximum amount of packets. This is due to the presence of vice cluster heads which replaces the failed cluster heads unlike LEACH protocol or DFTR protocol. A Higher number of packets transmitted to the base station indicates the longer life of gateways. We can see that the proposed algorithm performs better than both DFTR and LEACH.

7   Conclusions

In this article, we have proposed a reliable and resilient routing technique for wireless sensor networks that forms the atomic component of IoT, for smart city applications. We have proposed a taxonomy for fault tolerant techniques in WSN. Furthermore, we proposed a new fault-tolerant routing algorithms for hierarchical WSN networks based on modified DSR (Dynamic Source Routing) and vice cluster heads. Multiple routes are identified and these routes are prioritized on the basis of residual energy in the path and the distance of the source from the sink. In addition, the proposed technique uses vice cluster heads to tolerate faults during routing. We have shown through simulation that the proposed technique is better than LEACH and DFTR in terms of total energy in the network, the total number of packets transmitted to the sink and the number of alive nodes. Our future work will be based on the mobility of the sensor nodes and the interaction with other IoT components.

Acknowledgments. The authors acknowledge with thanks the technical and financial support from the Deanship of Scientific Research (DSR) at the King Abdulaziz University (KAU), Jeddah, Saudi Arabia, under the grant number G-651-611-38. The work carried out in this paper is supported by the High Performance Computing Center at the King Abdulaziz University, Jeddah.

References

1. United Nations Human Settlement Programme: Global Urban Observatory (GUO) UN-Habitat
2. Mehmood, R., Alam, F., Albogami, N.N., Katib, I., Albeshri, A., Altowaijri, S.M.: UTiLearn: a personalised ubiquitous teaching and learning system for smart societies. IEEE Access **5**, 2615–2635 (2017)
3. Heinzelman, W.B., Chandrakasan, A.P., Balakrishnan, H.: An application-specific protocol architecture for wireless microsensor networks. IEEE Trans. Wirel. Commun. **1**(4), 660–670 (2002)
4. Arfat, Y., Aqib, M., Mehmood, R., Albeshri, A., Katib, I., Albogami, N., Alzahrani, A.: Enabling smarter societies through mobile big data fogs and clouds. Procedia Comput. Sci. **109**, 1128–1133 (2017)
5. Alam, F., Mehmood, R., Katib, I., Albeshri, A.: Analysis of eight data mining algorithms for smarter internet of things (IoT). Procedia Comput. Sci. **98**(Supplement C), 437–442 (2016)
6. Alam, F., Mehmood, R., Katib, I., Albogami, N.N., Albeshri, A.: Data fusion and IoT for smart ubiquitous environments: a survey. IEEE Access **5**, 9533–9554 (2017)
7. Pantazis, N., Nikolidakis, S.A., Vergados, D.D.: Energy-efficient routing protocols in wireless sensor networks: a survey. IEEE Commun. Surv. Tutorials **15**(2), 551–591 (2013)
8. Casey, K., Lim, A., Dozier, G.: A sensor network architecture for tsunami detection and response. Int. J. Distrib. Sens. Netw. **4**(1), 27–42 (2008)
9. Wang, R., Zhang, L., Sun, R., Gong, J., Cui, L.: EasiTia: a pervasive traffic information acquisition system based on wireless sensor networks. IEEE Trans. Intell. Transp. Syst. **12**(2), 615–621 (2011)
10. Nikam, S.S., Mane, P.B.: Swarm intelligent WSN for smart city. In: Satapathy, S.C., Bhateja, V., Joshi, A. (eds.) Proceedings of the International Conference on Data Engineering and Communication Technology. AISC, vol. 469, pp. 691–700. Springer, Singapore (2017). https://doi.org/10.1007/978-981-10-1678-3_66
11. Bottero, M., Chiara, B.D., Deflorio, F.: Wireless sensor networks for traffic monitoring in a logistic centre. Transp. Res. Part C Emerg. Technol. **26**, 99–124 (2013)
12. Mehmood, R., Nekovee, M.: Vehicular ad hoc and grid networks: discussion, design and evaluation. In: Proceedings of the 14th World Congress on Intelligent Transport Systems (ITS), Beijing, October 2007
13. Morello, R., Mukhopadhyay, S.C., Liu, Z., Slomovitz, D., Samantaray, S.R.: Advances on sensing technologies for smart cities and power grids: a review. IEEE Sens. J. **17**, 7596–7610 (2017)
14. Cetinkaya, O., Akan, O.B.: Use of wireless sensor networks in smart homes. In: Emerging Communication Technologies Based on Wireless Sensor Networks: Current Research and Future Applications, pp. 233–258, April 2016

15. Shnayder, V., Hempstead, M., Chen, B.r., Allen, G.W., Welsh, M.: Simulating the power consumption of large-scale sensor network applications. In: Proceedings of the 2nd International Conference on Embedded Networked Sensor Systems, SenSys 2004, pp. 188–200. ACM, New York (2004)

16. Abbasi, A.A., Younis, M.: A survey on clustering algorithms for wireless sensor networks. Comput. Commun. 30(14–15), 2826–2841 (2007). Network Coverage and Routing Schemes for Wireless Sensor Networks

17. Li, Y., Xiao, G., Singh, G., Gupta, R.: Algorithms for finding best locations of cluster heads for minimizing energy consumption in wireless sensor networks. Wirel. Netw. 19(7), 1755–1768 (2013)

18. Muhammed, T., Shaikh, R.A.: An analysis of fault detection strategies in wireless sensor networks. J. Netw. Comput. Appl. 78(Supplement C), 267–287 (2017)

19. Gillies, D., Thornley, D., Bisdikian, C.: Probabilistic approaches to estimating the quality of information in military sensor networks. Comput. J. 53(5), 493–502 (2010)

20. Gelenbe, E., Ngai, E.: Adaptive random re-routing for differentiated QoS in sensor networks. Comput. J. 53(7), 1052–1061 (2010)

21. Ramanathan, N., Kohler, E., Girod, L., Estrin, D.: Sympathy: a debugging system for sensor networks [wireless networks]. In: Proceedings of the 29th Annual IEEE International Conference on Local Computer Networks, Washington, DC, USA, pp. 554–555. IEEE Computer Society, November 2004

22. Azharuddin, M., Jana, P.K.: A distributed algorithm for energy efficient and fault tolerant routing in wireless sensor networks. Wirel. Netw. 21(1), 251–267 (2015)

23. Zhao, Y., Wu, J., Li, F., Lu, S.: On maximizing the lifetime of wireless sensor networks using virtual backbone scheduling. IEEE Trans. Parallel Distrib. Syst. 23(8), 1528–1535 (2012)

24. Khan, S.A., Bölöni, L., Turgut, D.: Bridge protection algorithms - a technique for fault-tolerance in sensor networks. Ad Hoc Netw. 24, 186–199 (2015)

25. Boucetta, C., Idoudi, H., Saidane, L.A.: Adaptive scheduling with fault tolerance for wireless sensor networks. In: 2015 IEEE 81st Vehicular Technology Conference (VTC Spring), pp. 1–5. IEEE (2015)

26. Ahmed, R.E.: A fault-tolerant, energy-efficient routing protocol for wireless sensor networks. In: 2015 International Conference on Information and Communication Technology Research (ICTRC), pp. 175–178, May 2015

27. Gupta, S.K., Kuila, P., Jana, P.K.: E3BFT: energy efficient and energy balanced fault tolerance clustering in wireless sensor networks. In: 2014 International Conference on Contemporary Computing and Informatics (IC3I), pp. 714–719. November 2014

28. Azharuddin, M., Jana, P.K.: A PSO based fault tolerant routing algorithm for wireless sensor networks. In: Mandal, J.K., Satapathy, S.C., Sanyal, M.K., Sarkar, P.P., Mukhopadhyay, A. (eds.) Information Systems Design and Intelligent Applications. AISC, vol. 339, pp. 329–336. Springer, New Delhi (2015). https://doi.org/10.1007/978-81-322-2250-7_32

29. Hezaveh, M., Shirmohammdi, Z., Rohbani, N., Miremadi, S.G.: A fault-tolerant and energy-aware mechanism for cluster-based routing algorithm of WSNs. In: 2015 IFIP/IEEE International Symposium on Integrated Network Management (IM), pp. 659–664, May 2015

30. Hamdan, D., Aktouf, O.E.K., Parissis, I., El Hassan, B., Hijazi, A.: Integrated fault tolerance framework for wireless sensor networks. In: 2012 19th International Conference on Telecommunications (ICT), pp. 1–6. IEEE (2012)

31. Xu, J., Liu, W., Lang, F., Zhang, Y., Wang, C.: Distance measurement model based on RSSI in WSN. Wirel. Sens. Netw. **02**(08), 6 (2010)
32. Antle, C.E., Bain, L.J.: Weibull distribution. In: Encyclopedia of Statistical Sciences, July 2004
33. Lee, J.J., Krishnamachari, B., Kuo, C.C.J.: Aging analysis in large-scale wireless sensor networks. Ad Hoc Netw. **6**(7), 1117–1133 (2008)
34. Balakrishnan, H., Heinzelman, W.R., Chandrakasan, A.: Energy-efficient communication protocol for wireless microsensor networks. In: 2014 47th Hawaii International Conference on System Sciences, vol. 08, p. 8020 (2000)

Preserving Privacy of Smart Cities
Based on the Fog Computing

Adnan Ahmed Abi Sen[(✉)], Fathy Albouraey Eassa, and Kamal Jambi

Department of Computer Science, College of Computing and Information
Technology, King Abdul-Aziz University, Jeddah, Saudi Arabia
adnanmnm@hotmail.com, {feassa,kjambi}@kau.edu.sa

Abstract. The Smart city is a modern day technological concept which uses sensors, advanced communication technologies and data analysis for maximizing operational efficiency of services offered by the government to its citizens. Mobile devices are the backbone of the smart cities. These mobile devices rely heavily on clouds or fog computing to compensate their low processing capabilities. This brings new challenges to security and privacy of the users of mobile devices. In this paper we focused on the idea of utilizing fog computing properties like caching, cooperating between themselves, playing as a broker between users and cloud. We presented three novel approaches for satisfying the required privacy of the mobile devices in smart cities using fog computing. This paper is the preliminary stage of our work in progress. In future we will present this research in a comprehensive manner.

Keywords: IOT · Smart city · Privacy · Security · Cloud · Fog computing

1 Introduction

Internet of Things (IOT) paradigm is changing our life and facilitating several services which are beyond imagination a few years back. Smart city uses IOT infrastructure to provide several sophisticated services to its users such as smart homes, smart disaster management systems, smart teaching, smart navigation with Location-based Services (LBS), smart energy, smart education and smart health, etc. [1–3]. These services use IOT infrastructure and computing models as a third party (TP) to facilitate many of tasks and features like storing, processing, availability [4, 5].

Substantial progress has been made, addressing security and privacy issues in smart cities, though new challenges keep adding. Privacy and protection issues related to sensitive data of the mobile device users is a source of concern, which depends on collecting data and analyzing it to enhancing services. The sensitive data of the users can be leaked or hacked. For example, services which rely on LBS can perform tracing for the customer by a malicious party, which can reveal many sensitive issues about the user, his habits, beliefs, job, and even personal life information [6, 7].

There are several approaches which are focused on protecting privacy, which is different from security. Privacy means that every person has the right to determine the degree of his/her interaction with the environment and the amount of data allowed to be accessed by other party. While in the security it is enough to detect an information as

© ICST Institute for Computer Sciences, Social Informatics and Telecommunications Engineering 2018
R. Mehmood et al. (Eds.): SCITA 2017, LNICST 224, pp. 185–191, 2018.
https://doi.org/10.1007/978-3-319-94180-6_18

"password", in addition, security is between two trusted parties, while in privacy, server provider (SP) may be an adversary.

The different aspects of privacy and security are given in Table 1 [8, 9]:

Table 1. Difference aspect of security and privacy.

Security	Privacy
Encryption, authentication, confident, integrity, availability, accountability, digital signature, threat, hacking, virus, validity, safety, access control	Authorization, hidden identity, access control, unlink-ability, profiling, tracing, trust, data misusing, localization

Finally, all the current approaches still suffer from several open problems (the need to trust, performance, the accuracy of the result, and privacy level). Also, they didn't take care of the recent models of fog and edge computing [10, 11] as a tool to enhancing the traditional techniques of privacy. For that, this paper presents the idea of "how to employ the fog computing, which already addressing some limitations of the conventional clouds, to protect the privacy in smart cities applications, and solving open problems".

2   Literature Review

Most of the research developments of the privacy in smart cities only confirm the importance of this issue and called for addressing it in Smart applications [12–17]. A few papers referenced to some traditional methods [18], while others focused on security privacy [19–21]. About the traditional privacy approaches we found that an anonymity approach tried to hide the identity of the user through Pseudonyms, Nickname or Hash value [11]. The second approach focused on data, and used Encryption, Steganography, Perturbation, moving data, deleting periodically, or minimizing data by Data Mining or Statistical techniques [4].

Access Control and Requests also were methods to give the user ability to access, edit or lock his data on the server [22]. Other approach confirmed the importance of awareness, policy, and laws to help the user to know about his privacy and rights, in addition, to forcing SP to respect them [23]. All previous ones aren't effective, so Obfuscation and Land-marking are proposed, it used mathematical and transformation functions to change or hide the sensitive information of locations, but there is a tradeoff between privacy level vs. accuracy of results and overhead [24, 25].

Mix Zone enhanced the anonymity, it divided the area into many zones and user has to take a new nickname in each zone [26], While Cloaking area and K-anonymity created homogeneity clusters between k-users to prevent discrimination them, but these techniques relied on Third Trust Party (TTP) [27]. Peers Cooperation relied on users themselves without TTP as sharing answers or creating special area [28], anyways the trust among peer was required too.

In Dummies approach, the user sends a group of queries (K) to disguise the real one from SP, however generating smart dummies in addition to overhead still problem [29]. The caching approach is used in each cell to store some answers of queries for future ones, which reduced the number of connection with SP [30].

Finally, Private Information Retrieval (PIR) allowed a user to retrieve a particular record from database without revealing its identity by requesting a set of records instead of one, which means it is very costly especially with encryption [31].

3   Proposed Approaches

Fog Computing is a modern computing model that can be seen as an extension of cloud computing to serve network parties, is developed with a smaller storage, smaller processing power, and closer to the peripherals to perform processing on data before it reaches the cloud and respond quickly to emergencies cases [8, 9].

The most important features of fog computing are [32, 33]:

1. Processing location is close to ending user which means minimum latency time.
2. Supports distributed processing, real-time apps, mobility, and caching.
3. Uses wireless connectivity with smart objects.
4. Fog computing can cooperate among themselves which increases the availability.

The proposed approaches are the preliminary part of our work in progress. In this research, we introduce three approaches. Each approach deals with more than one of the existing problems with the previous approaches and enhances the privacy level. The three approaches rely on the fog computing to achieve their goals. The proposed research is dependent on these properties of fog computing. Our three approaches are Foggy Dummies, Blind Trust Party, and Double Foggy Cache for preserving privacy in smart cities. Proposed approaches provide solutions for current open problems. Moreover, we will also get the benefits that are related to the fog computing.

3.1   Foggy Dummies

The main idea is to generate very smart dummies to protect the privacy of the user. In this approach, we perform swapping of queries between the fogs before sending to SP and after that swapping the answers. This will be achieved by cooperation between fogs to exchange this data before releasing it to server provider (SP).

The advantages of this technique are:

1. A un-trusted SP will aggregate false data for each user and that will increase the level of privacy because the entropy metric of the user data will be a maximum.
2. No overhead on a user for generating dummies, as in the work [34].
3. No network overheads because each user sent just one query as dummy instead of a set of queries plus the real one in the traditional dummies technique.
4. This dummy is smart because it is not random and SP cannot detect it.
5. It is possible to integrate this approach with a traditional caching approach to increase the cache hit ratio and decrease the connections with SP.

6. There is no loss in accuracy of the results as that is in Obfuscation techniques. In addition, the level of privacy will be higher in this approach.

3.2   Blind Third Party (BTP)

The main idea is why we have to trust the third party (TP) to protect the user from SP. That means we shift the problem from server to another one. This approach depends on the role of fog in each area as a broker between the user and SP. The difference here is we prevent the fog from seeing the user data by using the steps as given in Fig. 1, which are:

1. User encrypts his query (location, data plus the new key UK) by SP public key.
2. The user sends his query to the Fog in the same cell.
3. Fog will be as an Anonymizer to hide ID of the user and resend his query to SP.
4. SP cannot detect UID; it just answers the query and encrypts the answers by UK.
5. SP sends the result to Fog which cannot read it, only resend it to the user.

So the advantages are:
There is no need to trust party fully, and very less overhead comparing to PIR.

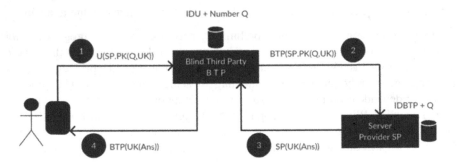

Fig. 1. BTP approach

3.3   Double Foggy Cache

The main idea here is to solve the trust issue between peers with traditional cooperation approach. Meanwhile achieve privacy protection from SP. Particularly this approach can be seen as the improvement of the work [35].

To achieve this, we suggested putting two caches in the Fog, which will act as the brokers between peers. First one is for queries and other for answers. This prevented the direct connection between peers.

The steps of this approach are (first scenario):

1. The answers to queries for each cell will be stored in the first cache (C1).
2. User A will search for an answer to his query (AQ) in C1, if it is found that's fine, else A will put his query in the second cache (C2). In the same time, he must draw another query for another user (unknown) from C2 and send it to SP.
3. When the result returned from SP, A will put it in C1.

4. Now A will research for AQ answer in C1 because it will be sent to SP by user B.

The advantages of this approach are:

1. Decrease the connections to SP by using cache and enhance the performance.
2. The user does not need to trust another user to protect himself.
3. The SP cannot collect any data about the behavior of the user.
4. Increase the cache hit-ratio because it will not contain answers of dummies.

4 Conclusion

This is the preliminary study of our work in progress. We presented a new concept of using the fog computing for creating and developing new methods to protect privacy in smart cities, in addition, to getting advantages of fog computing for enhancing services and functions in the applications of smart cities.

Three new ideas have been presented with limited working details as this is work in progress. Each one will be comprehensively explained, implemented in our next work with results evaluation.

References

1. Lu, C.: Overview of security and privacy issues in the internet of things. Washington University (2014)
2. Kumar, J.S., Patel, D.R.: A survey on internet of things: security and privacy issues. Int. J. Comput. Appl. **90**(11) (2014)
3. Mehmood, R., Alam, F., Albogami, N., Katib, I., Albeshri, A., Altowaijri, S.: UTiLearn: a personalised ubiquitous teaching and learning system for smart societies. IEEE Access **5**, 2615–2635 (2017)
4. Serbanati, A., Medaglia, C.M., Ceipidor, U.B.: Building blocks of the internet of things: state of the art and beyond. INTECH Open Access Publisher (2011)
5. Ukil, A., Bandyopadhyay, S., Pal, A.: IoT-privacy: to be private or not to be private. In: 2014 IEEE Conference on Computer Communications Workshops (INFOCOM WKSHPS), pp. 123–124. IEEE April 2014
6. Schrammel, J., Hochleitner, C., Tscheligi, M.: Privacy, trust and interaction in the internet of things. In: Keyson, D.V., et al. (eds.) AmI 2011. LNCS, vol. 7040, pp. 378–379. Springer, Heidelberg (2011). https://doi.org/10.1007/978-3-642-25167-2_59
7. Cirani, S., Picone, M., Gonizzi, P., Veltri, L., Ferrari, G.: IoT-Oas: an OAuth-based authorization service architecture for secure services in IoT scenarios. IEEE Sens. J. **15**(2), 1224–1234 (2015)
8. Dastjerdi, A.V., Gupta, H., Calheiros, R.N., Ghosh, S.K., Buyya, R.: Fog computing: principles, architectures, and applications. arXiv preprint arXiv:1601.027522016))
9. Roman, R., Lopez, J., Mambo, M.: Mobile edge computing, fog et al.: a survey and analysis of security threats and challenges. Future Comput. Syst. **78**, 680–698 (2016)
10. Hu, P., Ning, H., Qiu, T., Zhang, Y., Luo, X.: Fog computing-based face identification and resolution scheme in internet of things. IEEE Trans. Ind. Inform. **13**, 1910–1920 (2016)

11. Gudymenko, I., Borcea-Pfitzmann, K., Tietze, K.: Privacy implications of the internet of things. In: Wichert, R., Van Laerhoven, K., Gelissen, J. (eds.) AmI 2011. CCIS, vol. 277, pp. 280–286. Springer, Heidelberg (2012). https://doi.org/10.1007/978-3-642-31479-7_48

12. Zhang, K., Ni, J., Yang, K., Liang, X., Ren, J., Shen, X.S.: Security and Privacy in smart city applications: challenges and solutions. IEEE Commun. Mag. **55**(1), 122–129 (2017)

13. Vattapparamban, E., Güvenç, İ., Yurekli, A.İ., Akkaya, K., Uluağaç, S.: Drones for smart cities: issues in cybersecurity, privacy, and public safety. In: 2016 International Wireless Communications and Mobile Computing Conference (IWCMC), pp. 216–221. IEEE, September 2016

14. Martínez-Ballesté, A., Pérez-Martínez, P.A., Solanas, A.: The pursuit of citizens' privacy: a privacy-aware smart city is possible. IEEE Commun. Mag. **51**(6), 136–141 (2013)

15. Mulligan, C.E., Olsson, M.: Architectural implications of smart city business models: an evolutionary perspective. IEEE Commun. Mag. **51**(6), 80–85 (2013)

16. Li, Y., Dai, W., Ming, Z., Qiu, M.: Privacy protection for preventing data over-collection in smart city. IEEE Trans. Comput. **65**(5), 1339–1350 (2016)

17. Bartoli, A., Hernández-Serrano, J., Soriano, M., Dohler, M., Kountouris, A., Barthel, D.: Security and privacy in your smart city. In: Proceedings of the Barcelona Smart Cities Congress, pp. 1–6, December 2011

18. Srinivasan, R., Mohan, A., Srinivasan, P.: Privacy conscious architecture for improving emergency response in smart cities. In: 2016 Smart City Security and Privacy Workshop (SCSP-W), pp. 1–5. IEEE, April 2016

19. Jin, J., Gubbi, J., Marusic, S., Palaniswami, M.: An information framework for creating a smart city through internet of things. IEEE Internet Things J. **1**(2), 112–121 (2014)

20. Ding, D., Conti, M., Solanas, A.: A smart health application and its related privacy issues. In: 2016 Smart City Security and Privacy Workshop (SCSP-W), pp. 1–5. IEEE, April 2016

21. Suomalainen, J., Julku, J.: Enhancing privacy of information brokering in smart districts by adaptive pseudonymization. IEEE Access **4**, 914–927 (2016)

22. Kung, A., et al.: A privacy engineering framework for the internet of things. In: Leenes, R., van Brakel, R., Gutwirth, S., De Hert, P. (eds.) Data Protection and Privacy: (In)visibilities and Infrastructures. LGTS, vol. 36, pp. 163–202. Springer, Cham (2017). https://doi.org/10.1007/978-3-319-50796-5_7

23. Weber, R.H.: Internet of things-new security and privacy challenges. Comput. Law Secur. Rev. **26**(1), 23–30 (2010)

24. Bhattasali, T., Chaki, R., Chaki, N.: Study of security issues in pervasive environment of next generation internet of things. In: Saeed, K., Chaki, R., Cortesi, A., Wierzchoń, S. (eds.) CISIM 2013. LNCS, vol. 8104, pp. 206–217. Springer, Heidelberg (2013). https://doi.org/10.1007/978-3-642-40925-7_20

25. Duckham, M., Kulik, L.: A formal model of obfuscation and negotiation for location privacy. In: Gellersen, H.-W., Want, R., Schmidt, A. (eds.) Pervasive 2005. LNCS, vol. 3468, pp. 152–170. Springer, Heidelberg (2005). https://doi.org/10.1007/11428572_10

26. Palanisamy, B., Liu, L.: Mobimix: protecting location privacy with mix-zones over road networks. In: 2011 IEEE 27th International Conference on Data Engineering (ICDE), pp. 494–505. IEEE, April 2011

27. Liu, X., Li, X.: Privacy preserving techniques for location based services in mobile networks. In: 2012 IEEE 26th International Parallel and Distributed Processing Symposium Workshops & Ph.D. Forum (IPDPSW). IEEE (2012)

28. Domingo-Ferrer, J., Bras-Amorós, M., Wu, Q., Manjón, J.: User-private information retrieval based on a peer-to-peer community. Data Knowl. Eng. **68**(11), 1237–1252 (2009)

29. Kido, H., Yanagisawa, Y., Satoh, T.: An anonymous communication technique using dummies for location-based services. In: Proceedings of International Conference on Pervasive Services, ICPS 2005, pp. 88–97. IEEE, July 2005
30. Niu, B., Li, Q., Zhu, X., Cao, G., Li, H.: Enhancing privacy through caching in location-based services. In: 2015 Conference on Computer Communications (INFOCOM), pp. 1017–1025. IEEE, April 2015
31. Song, D., et al.: A privacy-preserving continuous location monitoring system for location-based services. Int. J. Distrib. Sens. Netw. **2015**, 14 (2015)
32. Saharan, K.P., Kumar, A.: Fog in comparison to cloud: a survey. Int. J. Comput. Appl. **122** (3) (2015)
33. Suryawanshi, R., Mandlik, G.: Focusing on mobile users at edge and internet of things using fog computing. Int. Sci. Eng. Technol. Res. **4**(17), 3225–3231 (2015)
34. Alrahhal, M.S., Ashraf, M.U., Abesen, A., Arif, S.: AES-route server model for location based services in road networks. IJACSA **8**(8), 361–368 (2017)
35. Yamin, M., Abi Sen, A.A.: Improving privacy and security of user data in location based services. Int. J. Ambient Comput. Intell. **9**, 19–42 (2017)

Healthcare

Toward the Genomic-Information Society

Takashi Gojobori[(✉)]

Computational Bioscience Research Center (CBRC), King Abdullah,
University of Science and Technology (KAUST),
Thuwal 23955-6900, Kingdom of Saudi Arabia
takashi.gojobori@kaust.edu.sa

Abstract. In life science, strong needs for big data analysis and its related data-oriented methodologies such as AI (Artificial Intelligence) are acutely increasing in the recent years. These needs are recognized in not only medical sciences but also other disciplines in which genomic information plays a crucial role in understanding phenomena of interest and in conducting their innovative application to practical usages in the society. It eventually leads us to significant implication that our society will have undergone totally new experiences with enormous benefits from various advancements by research and development of genome information. On the basis of such observations, I would like to propose a future vision of our society as a "Genome-Information-Oriented Society (G-Society)" or "Genomic Information Society".

Keywords: Big data · AI · Metagenomics

1 Metagenomics as an Example

Taking a methodology called "metagenomics" as an example, I would like to discuss how our society changes with advancements of big data analyses of genomic information.

Metagenomics is an approach of understanding the whole features of microbes existing in a given sample by directly conducting extensive sequencing almost all the DNA fragments of microbial genomes without any microscopic observations. In particular, this approach can be applied to all the microbes including non-culturable bacterial species.

When this approach can be used for seawater samples, we will know all the microbial communities in that seawater, which will be useful to monitor marine environments and further to explore fishing grounds. This may be called as "Marine Metagenomics".

When this approach is conducted for soil samples, it will be very useful for improvements of agricultural efficiencies and conservation of ecological habitation. It has huge potential to change the way of conventional agriculture. This may be called as "Soil Metagenomics" or "Agricultural Metagenomics".

This approach can be applied for air samples, by which we can identify pathogens such as detrimental bacteria and viruses present in an air sample. In particular, immediate application to the sand storms may lead to understanding of etiological

R. Mehmood et al. (Eds.): SCITA 2017, LNICST 224, pp. 195–196, 2018.
https://doi.org/10.1007/978-3-319-94180-6_19

agents that can be brought into a human society. This is called as "Airborne Metagenomics".

Moreover, metagenomics has been applied to human cavities such as human guts. For example, intestinal bacteria have been understood in a variety of aspects in an enormous speed. It is getting known that some bacterial species are deeply associated with human disease such as not only diseases associated with adult lifestyle habits but also cancers and even mental diseases.

Although we have already known how beneficial human complete genome information is for curing the diseases and maintaining our health, the state-of-art methodologies of metagenomics are surely changing our society, as stated above.

2   Big Data Analyses as Crucial Tools

The data produced from genomic approaches including metagenomics is really huge: It is literally "big data". In order to extract useful knowledge from such big data as genomic information, it is obvious that informatics of big data analyses is crucial. Database construction, functional annotation with appropriate ontology of controlled vocabularies, and AI (artificial Intelligence) such as machine learning, text mining and deep learning will be key elements of big data analyses.

How usefully we can utilize genetic information depends heavily upon successful developments of those IT (Information Technology) elements. It follows that our future vision of the so-called "G-Society" will come true only if such big data analyses can be applied, in a timely and appropriate fashion, to genome information that will be hugely produced further in the coming years.

3   Conclusion

In the situation that a huge amount of genomic information has been produced by the recent advancements of genomic approaches such as metagenomics, it is pointed out that our human society may be faced by new experiences including benefits from useful knowledge extracted from big data of genomic information. This vision of new human society may be called "Genome-Information-oriented Society (G-Society)" or "Genome Information Society". To make this vision come true, developments of various IT elements for big data analyses must be crucial.

A Lightweight and Secure Framework for Hybrid Cloud Based EHR Systems

Basit Qureshi[1]([⊠]), Anis Koubaa[1,2,3], and Mohammad Al Mhaini[1]

[1] Prince Sultan University, Riyadh, Saudi Arabia
{qureshi,akoubaa}@psu.edu.sa, malmhaini@gmail.com
[2] Gaitech Robotics, Hong Kong, China
[3] CISTER, INESC-TEC, ISEP, Polytechnic Institute of Porto, Porto, Portugal

Abstract. Recently Cloud based Electronic Health Records Systems have been developed and are being used in the healthcare industry. Albeit the various benefits of the technology, security, trust and privacy are a major concern. In this paper, we present a secure and affordable framework for EHR storage, leveraging the properties of hybrid cloud in securing data in addition to building low power back-end cluster constructed using low cost single board computers (SBC). We detail requirements for a secure cloud based EHR framework and present the system architecture based on the publisher/subscriber model. The framework is developed and tested on a Hadoop based cloud cluster using SBCs as nodes. Efficiency of the framework is measured in terms of response time for various sizes of Data Blocks containing EHRs.

Keywords: Hybrid cloud computing · EHR systems · Encryption

1 Introduction

Over the last few years, cloud computing has grown to be a new service model and has had a tremendous impact on the establishment of several cost-effective platforms for hosting largescale service applications in data centers. Nonetheless, notwithstanding the considerable benefits and services, the issue of security and privacy has been at the forefront of consumer confidence in the availability of confidential information in public domain [1]. There are many Electronic Health Records Management (EHR) systems available, most of these follow a client server model where the service provider maintains data centers hosting data while clients can access these data. The variety and size of these data systems challenge researchers to accurately and effortlessly integrate data from various sources while maintaining integrity, security and availability using reliable channels [4, 8].

Several researchers have concentrated their efforts in developing various architecture for healthcare based applications in the cloud [1–6]. Fang et al. [9] present a survey on Health informatics in the cloud. Authors in [10, 11] investigate privacy preserving secure communication in cloud assisted e-healthcare systems. Researchers in [3, 12] present a security aware cloud enabled eco-system for healthcare data storage and analytics. Shrestha et al. in [4] present a eHealth Framework for security and privacy. Suresh in [5] detail a secured cloud based health record model for storage of

© ICST Institute for Computer Sciences, Social Informatics and Telecommunications Engineering 2018
R. Mehmood et al. (Eds.): SCITA 2017, LNICST 224, pp. 197–206, 2018.
https://doi.org/10.1007/978-3-319-94180-6_20

medical records in the public cloud domain. In most of the aforementioned works, the mechanism of security heavily involves cryptographic algorithms and application of various encryption techniques. As pointed out in [1, 2], a major concern in these mechanisms is the quality of service issue; as the size of the records grow, the time to encrypt and decrypt large records increases significantly consequently affecting the latency in data transfer thus affecting the QoS parameters. Another major issue is the search keywords and access control mechanisms where certain users in the EHR system have privileges to access certain parts of data records. In such systems, based on the search keywords, the entire data blocks matching the query results are downloaded, decrypted based on access control parameters and served to the consumer which is very inefficient in terms of performance.

In this work, we address the aforementioned issues by detailing a lightweight framework utilizing hybrid cloud for preservation of security and privacy. The proposed framework takes inspiration from the work presented in [6] vertical partitioning of EHRs to decrease the latency costs incurred in keywords search. The data is encrypted using an access control policy based on credentials. The access control policy is defined as joints and disjoints with various attributes allowing the users with appropriate credentials to have access to the data. The resulting framework is evaluated in the hybrid cloud environment using a Hadoop based cluster. Data is stored in Hbase and served based on queries and access control information. Initial results demonstrate successful implementation of the framework for lightweight data control.

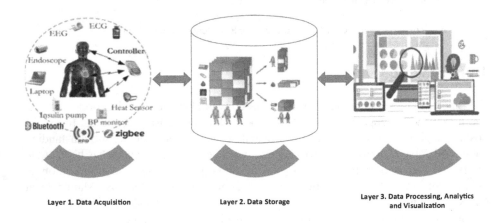

Layer 1. Data Acquisition   Layer 2. Data Storage   Layer 3. Data Processing, Analytics and Visualization

Fig. 1. Layout of 3 layers in the proposed framework

2   Framework Requirements and Design

In this section, we reflect on the requirements for a hybrid cloud based design and architecture of secure and power efficient framework for cloud based Electronic Health Records System. A mainstream cloud based EHR system consists of three layers, (i) Data acquisition, (ii) Data storage in Cloud, (iii) Data Processing, analytics and visualization.

Data acquisition layer collects data in any of the various mechanisms for data entry. It could be as complex as a Wireless Body Area Network (WBAN) [13] consisting of various wireless wearable sensors for specific medical applications such as blood pressure, thermometer etc. These sensors and devices can connect to a data collection device using Bluetooth, Zigbee protocols or similar wireless communication medium, and transmit the information to an intermediate cloudlet for synchronizing and processing information.

Cloud Storage Layer provides a reliable, scalable and secure storage that is perhaps the most important functionality of Cloud based PHR systems. Due to large volumes of data being generated, it is critical to provide a secure, efficient and reliable storage and retrieval system for personal records. To enable searching over the data, the customer must either store an index locally, or download all the (encrypted) data, decrypt it and search locally. Both approaches negate the benefit of cloud computing and are therefore poor choice for processing of large scale data thus increasing the overhead of security and volume of communications.

Processing Data is the third important aspect of cloud based PHR systems. Data analytics requires processing of large volumes of data to be used in decision support for Health care providers. Furthermore, visualization of data can be of much benefit to the stakeholders.

The Health Insurance Portability and Accountability Act (HIPAA) [7] states that data privacy must be protected within every layer of a EHR system. Here we detail the requirements for each layer of the system.

(i)   Data acquisition Layer. The acquisition layer in Fig. 1 is composed of Wireless Body Area Network sensor devices. These devices have limited computational capacities and operate on finite battery power. Encryption schemes used to protect the communication within BAN sensors and BAN-to cloudlet communications should not be computationally intensive.

(ii) Data Storage Layer. There can be various stakeholders involved in storage, retrieval and sharing of data from the system including, patient, doctor/nurse, emergency unit staff etc. Conventional encryption techniques may not work and would not be able to handle multiple keys from multiple parties.

(iii) Data Processing, Analytics and Visualization Layer. To process data, it must first be decrypted. Decryption of this data in the intermediate stage requires trusted storage infrastructure possibly at the site of the HCP necessitating a private cloud infrastructure.

Further to the above, in an enterprise environment many stakeholders may have access to various kinds of data. Doctors, patients, nurses, emergency unit staff, medical insurance personnel etc. to name a few, require strict access control mechanisms in place. For any efficient solution, it is imperative to address the above-mentioned issues thoroughly and effectively.

3 Hybrid Cloud Based Architecture

Storage services based on public clouds provide consumers with scalable, reliable and dynamic storage at the cost of security trust and privacy. Privacy critical data such as personal health records need to be secured on the public cloud, whereas data with low privacy requirements such as data dictionaries etc. or intermediary data such as data generated from health analytics or visualization, may not require stringent security measures. Figure 2 shows an overview of the public and private cloud domains of the framework.

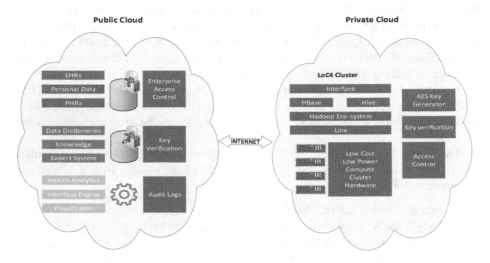

Fig. 2. Hybrid cloud architecture

Large volumes of data generated at the Data acquisition layer needs to be stored and shared with appropriate consumers with valid credentials. Access Control parameters are defined in the private cloud service and are periodically updated in the public service. Public cloud service affords reliable and fast processing of data due to large amounts of compute power available at the service provider. However due to privacy concerns it is not feasible to decrypt data in the public cloud domain, process it and then re-encrypt for further storage. Consequently, a publisher/subscriber model of the system may need to download the encrypted data on a local machine, decrypt, process and upload it to the cloud service after re-encrypting this data. Salient features and components of the proposed publisher/subscriber model is given in Fig. 3. We develop a custom encryption approach that is efficient and reliable and is described further in this section.

The private cloud service essentially hosts a cluster of machines realizing a small data center at the premises of the enterprise. The infrastructure is secured in the enterprise locale with physical, data and network security measures in place. The data center hosts low cost, efficient and eco-friendly Hadoop cluster. Access control information for the enterprise is stored in HBase and Hive data warehouse which are

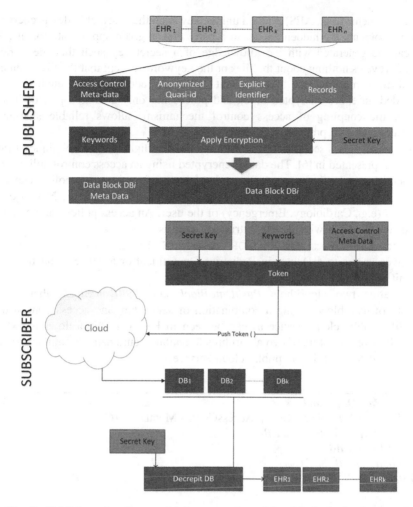

Fig. 3. Publisher subscriber model for encryption of data blocks in the framework

encrypted using commonly available encryption techniques. Additional modules for encryption key generation and verification are implemented in the private cloud. These are necessary for efficient and reliable storage and sharing of data. Communication takes place through the interface which implements a light weight communication protocol for data transmission between the public and private cloud services.

Communicating devices must agree on a secret-key before using AES encryption by using generic key exchange algorithm such as Diffie-Hellman (DH) [14]. Irrespective of the kind of encryption scheme, a consumer must agree on key(s) to encrypt/decrypt messages with a service provider. Advanced Encryption Standard (AES) is one of the most widely used symmetric key encryption algorithms and is accepted as an industry and a government applications standard. AES is optimized for speed, low memory footprint and energy efficiency. Data is encrypted using symmetric encryption scheme (e.g., AES) under a unique key such that a search index is encrypted so that its contents are hidden except to a party that is given appropriate tokens. The token can be generated with the knowledge of a secret key such that the retrieval procedure reveals nothing about the files or the keywords except that the files contain a keyword in common. This light weight technique addresses the inefficiency of downloaded an entire encrypted block and processing only a limited part of it. Furthermore, the coupling of access control mechanisms allows reliable sharing of appropriate data with proper stakeholders.

To implement this security mechanism, we define a light weight technique inspired by the work presented in [6]. The data is encrypted using an access control policy based on credentials. Only the user whose credentials satisfy the access policy can have access to the data. The attributes can be the profession (e.g., Doctor, Nurse) or the department (e.g., Cardiology, Emergency) of the user. An access policy can be defined as joints and disjoints with various attributes such as

(Doctor AND Pediatrics) OR (Nurse OR Intensive-Care-Unit)

which gives access to a Doctor in Pediatrics Department or a Nurse or an Intensive-Care-Unit staff member.

We define two algorithms *PushDataBlock* and *PullDataBlock*, that control read/write of data blocks using a combination of secret key and access control meta data, in the public cloud service as can be seen in Fig. 4. In the following text, we describe the working of these two algorithms to enable secure data communication and storage of a data block in the public cloud service.

---

algorithm **PushDataBlock**
input: DataBlock B_i, SecretKey S_k, AccessControlMetaData AC_{MDi}
output: Encrypted DataBlock EB_i
  for $i = 1$ **to** $n - 1$ **do**
    $KeyGenerator(B_i, S_k, AC_{MDi})$
    $PushCloud(EB_i)$
  end

algorithm **PullDataBlock**
input: SecretKey S_k, *Keyword*
output: Decrypted DataBlock DB_i
  for $i = 1$ **to** $n - 1$ **do**
    $RequestToken(AC_{MD}, S_k, Keyword)$
    $AcquireToken(S_k)$
    $PushToken(token, S_k)$
    $PullDataBock(DB_i)$
    $VerifyDataBlock(DB_i)$
  end

Fig. 4. The PushDataBlock and PullDataBlock algorithms.

Each subscriber is allocated a Secret Key S_k to facilitate access to the private cloud service, these keys are managed by the administrators at the enterprise and assigned to stakeholders with appropriate access control credentials.

Assuming a data block B_i was generated (data acquired from WBAN cloudlet etc.) consisting of one or many records/files and is ready to be uploaded to the public cloud storage, the publisher would call the PushDataBlock with an access control meta data AC_{MDi} for this data block B_i.

The *KeyGenerator* is responsible for properly indexing and encrypting the data block. KG is responsible for encrypting various data blocks using access control information provided and appends metadata for identification of datablocks such as timestamp, size, keywords, ownership etc. It encrypts the data block in such a way that given a *token*, a subscriber can retrieve pointers to the encrypted records/files that contain a *keyword*. Without appropriate *token*, the data block would not be decrypted. The tokens cannot be generated without a secret key S_k. It must be noted that the retrieval procedure does not reveal any details within the data block except only the searchable keywords. Once the *KeyGenerator* has encrypted the DataBlock B_i, *PushCloud(B_i)* is called to push the data block to the public cloud storage.

When a subscriber intends to access a data block for processing or sharing, it needs to call the *PullDataBlock* with the secret key S_k, and the access control meta data AC_{MD}. *RequestToken* call is made for a search keyword term to the private cloud service. Based on the access control policy, the *AcquireToken(S_k, AC_{MD})* generates a token which is then sent to the public cloud service using the *PushToken(token)*. The public cloud service uses the token to find the appropriate encrypted documents. The *PullDataBlock* call returns the selected documents as data blocks to the subscriber. At any point and time, the subscriber can verify the integrity of the data blocks by calling the *VerifyDataBlock* call.

A prototype of the proposed framework is built and successfully tested. The next section presents experimental results.

4 Results

The implementation of the proposed framework is based in a SBC based cluster reported in [15]. This cluster is composed of 40 nodes consisting of Raspberry Pi Model 2B and Odroid Xu-4 computers. All nodes are interconnected using gigabit Ethernet. Hadoop 2.6.2 is installed on all nodes with additional installations for HBase and Hive. To optimize the performance of the RPi Cluster, yarn-site.xml and Mapred-site.xml were configured with 852 MB of resource size allocation. The Master node is installed on a regular PC running Ubuntu 14.4 and Hadoop. The default container size on the Hadoop Distributed File System (HDFS) is 128 MB.

A light weight middleware is written using bash script which is responsible for executing *KeyGenerator*, *PullDataBlock*, *RequestToken* and *AcquireToken*. The middleware is executed taking various parameters including EHR (as xml File of various sizes) along with associated Meta-Data for the file. Access Control parameters were generated for four users (Doctor, Nurse, Manager and Patient). We use AES for encryption of records before it is stored in the cluster. All operations including encryption and decryption time, cost of key generation are linear to the number of attributes. For this experimentation about 100 DataBlocks were pre-loaded in the cluster composed of various EHRs (as xml files). The middleware is executed to simulate the subscriber aspect of the framework with various request sizes and access control parameters. We measure the response time of the *PullDataBlock* request in terms of milliseconds as shown in Table 1.

Table 1. Response time for PullDataBlock request

Number of parallel requests	Total DataBlock(s) size in MB	Response time in milliseconds
1	1.8	6009.9
2	3.6	6101.2
3	5.1	6108.1
5	9.7	6204.8
8	14.9	6208.0
10	18.2	6410.0
15	37.8	7022.6
20	51.7	9514.0
30	108.4	11089.1
50	394.6	28223.1
70	728.4	42188.2
100	1352.5	92579.5

Our results show that the Framework is successfully implemented with reasonable response times from the Hadoop cluster. It must be noted due to the settings in the SBC based cluster the minimum response time for executing Hadoop jobs is approximately 6 s, given these conditions the response time for smaller workloads i.e. less than 50 MB is within one second. As the size of the DataBlocks increases, the time also increases linearly.

5 Conclusions

In this paper, we presented a secure framework for EHR storage based on a hybrid cloud computing architecture. We detail requirements for a secure cloud based EHR framework and present the system architecture based on the publisher/subscriber model. The framework is developed and tested using Hadoop based cloud cluster using SBCs as nodes. Efficiency of the framework is measured in terms of response time for various sizes of Data Blocks containing EHRs. Results show successful deployment of the proposed framework on the testbed. We intend to extend the implementation of the framework in the public cloud domain which has not been completed as of now. We intend to develop Microsoft Azure web services for the publishers' part of the framework. Both parts of the framework would be thoroughly tested.

Acknowledgements. This work is partially funded by the Robotics and Internet of Things Unit (RIoTU) at Prince Sultan University.

References

1. Yang, J.J., Li, J., Niu, Y.: A hybrid solution for privacy preserving medical data sharing in cloud computing. Future Gener. Comput. Syst. **43**(44), 74–86 (2015)
2. Manoj, R., Alsadoon, A., Prasad, P.W.C., Costadopoulos, N., Ali, S.: Hybrid secure and scalable electronic health record sharing in hybrid cloud. In: 5th IEEE International Conference on Mobile Cloud Computing, Services, and Engineering (MobileCloud), pp. 185–190 (2017)
3. Arora, A., Khanna, A., Rastogi, A., Agarwal, A.: Cloud security ecosystem for data security and privacy. In: 7th International Conference on Cloud Computing, Data Science and Engineering, pp. 288–292 (2017)
4. Shrestha, M.N., Alsadoon, A., Prasad, C.P., Houran, L.: Enhanced eHealth framework for security and privacy in healthcare. In: 6th International Conference on Digital Information Processing and Communications (ICDIPC), pp. 75–79 (2016)
5. Suresh, S.: Highly secured cloud based personal health record model. In: International Conference on Green Engineering and Technologies (IC-GET), pp. 1–4 (2015)
6. Liu, Z., Weng, J., et al.: Cloud-based electronic health record system supporting fuzzy keyword search. Soft Comput. **20**(8), 3243–3255 (2016)
7. US Department of Health and Human Services: Health Insurance Portability and Accountability Act (2017). http://www.hhs.gov/ocr/privacy
8. Bahga, A., Madisetti, V.K.: Healthcare data integration and informatics in the cloud. Computer **48**(2), 50–57 (2015)
9. Fang, R., et al.: Computational health informatics in the big data age: a survey. ACM Comput. Surv. **49**(1), 12 (2016)
10. Zhou, J., Cao, Z., Dong, X., Lin, X.: PPDM: a privacy-preserving protocol for cloud-assisted e-healthcare systems. IEEE J. Sel. Top. Sig. Process. **9**(7), 1332–1344 (2015)
11. Zhou, J., et al.: PSMPA: patient self-controllable and multi-level privacy-preserving cooperative authentication in distributed m-healthcare cloud computing system. In: IEEE Transactions on Parallel and Distributed Systems, vol. 26, no. 6, pp. 1693–1703, 1 June 2015
12. Qureshi, B.: Towards a digital ecosystem for predictive healthcare analytics. In: 6th International Conference on Management of Emergent Digital EcoSystems (MEDES 2014), pp. 34–41 (2014)

13. Page, A., et al.: QT clock to improve detection of QT prolongation in long QT syndrome patients. Heart Rhythm **13**(1), 190–198 (2016)
14. Diffie, W., Hellman, M.: New directions in cryptography. IEEE Trans. Inf. Theor. **22**(6), 644–654 (2006)
15. Qureshi, B., et al.: Performance of a low cost Hadoop cluster for image analysis in cloud robotics environment. Procedia Comput. Sci. **82**, 90–98 (2016)

Big Data Enabled Healthcare Supply Chain Management: Opportunities and Challenges

Shoayee Alotaibi[1(✉)] and Rashid Mehmood[2]

[1] Computer Science Department, Faculty of Computing and Information Technology, King Abdulaziz Univeristy, Jeddah, Saudi Arabia
shoayee@gmail.com
[2] High Performance Computing Center, King Abdulaziz University, Jeddah, Saudi Arabia
RMehmood@kau.edu.sa

Abstract. It is estimated that healthcare spending in the world's major regions will increase from 2.4% of GDP to 7.5% during 2015 to 2020. Healthcare providers are required to deliver high quality medical services to their customers. Since most of their budgets are spent on high cost medical equipment and medicines, there is a pressing need for them to optimize their supply chain activities such that high-quality services could be provided at lower costs. Relatedly, medical equipment and devices generate massive amounts of unused data. Big data analytics is proven to be helpful in forecasting and decision-making, and, hence, can be a powerful tool to improve healthcare supply chains. This paper presents a review on the use of big data in healthcare supply chains. We review the various concepts related to the topic of this paper including big data, big data analytics, and the role of big data in healthcare, and in healthcare supply chain management. The opportunities and challenges for big data enabled healthcare supply chains are discussed along with several directions for future developments. We conclude that the use of big data in healthcare supply chains is of immense potential and demands further investigation.

Keywords: Big data · Data analytics · Healthcare · Supply chain management

1 Introduction

The healthcare sector is considered one of the main economic pillars worlwide, to which significant proportions of countries' budgets are allocated. It is estimated that healthcare spending in the world's major regions will increase from 2.4% to 7.5% of GDP between 2015 and 2020 [1]. Despite this massive expenditure, healthcare organizations are required to deliver high-quality medical services at lower costs to their patients. However, spending hundreds of millions does not alone guarantee high quality services. Hence, most of healthcare organizations nowadays are faced with incremental challenges, including limited budget, daily increases in patient numbers and increasing costs of medical equipment and pharmaceuticals [2]. As much as 45% of a hospital's typical total operating expense is committed to its supply chain, including suppliers, drugs and consumables.

© ICST Institute for Computer Sciences, Social Informatics and Telecommunications Engineering 2018
R. Mehmood et al. (Eds.): SCITA 2017, LNICST 224, pp. 207–215, 2018.
https://doi.org/10.1007/978-3-319-94180-6_21

The healthcare supply chain is an essential area that should be considered and improved. It would be incorrect to understand it as only relating to purchasing and managing contracts, as it is a very complex concept, and could free up huge revenues within healthcare sectors once managed properly [3]. Consequently, healthcare organizations will likely increasingly need to employ recent technological developments to deliver efficient services at lower costs and high quality. Moreover, such improvements are required to reduce the waste and loss that threaten sustainability.

In the current era of increasingly advanced technologies in medical devices and medical equipment, the size of data generated by their use is growing exponentially. The immense growth in the volume of electronic medical records (EMRs) stored by healthcare organizations is also significant and undeniable. Exploring the possibility of investing this big data in improving services has become attractive to researchers and practitioners. A lot of fruitful business applications and network search engines have been developed using Business Intelligence (BI) for extracting knowledge from big data [4]. Some researchers have been investigating how to transfer and where to store this amount of data, while others have been focusing on big data utilization. Big data utilization involves analysing it to seek a solution for existing issues, exploring trends, and supporting decision-making.

A plethora of literature has been produced that explores to what extent big data can be beneficial in the healthcare industry. Malik and his colleagues [5] noted that big data analytics seems to have been frequently used for the diagnosis, prognosis or planning of treatment, for example, disease management for oncology to anticipate heart attacks and identify and classify at-risk people. However, a very limited work has been done in applying big data to healthcare supply chains. Existing published survey papers focus on reviewing the significant applications of big data to supply chains in manufacturing generally.

In this paper, our main aim is to review the use of big data in the healthcare supply chains. To the best of our knowledge, only three peer-reviewed works have been published on this topic. We will investigate the opportunities, challenges and future directions of big data in this field.

The paper is organized as follow: Sect. 2 gives brief definitions for the basic concepts that are mentioned in this paper. Big data analytics in supply chain and healthcare opportunities and challenges are discussed in Sect. 3. Section 4 concludes the work and suggests possible future directions.

2 Background

This section introduces the work by defining the basic terminologies that are mentioned in this paper. Supply chain, big data and big data analytics are illustrated based on the reviewed references. Then, some examples of how the big data been used in healthcare and supply chain individually are given in the last two sub sections below.

2.1 Supply Chain

Malik et al. define the supply chain process as "having the right item in the right quantity at the right time at the right place for the right price in the right condition to the right customer" [6]. In the meantime, supply chain managers can legitimately claim to have played a major role in spreading the information technology revolution. E-SCM (e-supply chain management) was a great transformation as supply chain activities were integrated with the Internet [7]. Smarter supply chains [8] and smart factories [9] are further examples of intelligent systems developments. Sustainability (triple bottom line, TBL) has become a crucial consideration in business, government and academia. Therefore, the concept and practice of green or sustainable supply chains have become a vital part of industrial and government operations, see e.g. [10, 11].

2.2 Big Data

According to [4], big data refers to "the datasets that could not be perceived, acquired, managed, and processed by traditional IT and software/hardware tools within a tolerable time". However, researchers and scientists have defined the term "big data" according to several different aspects. Apache Hadoop in 2010, defined big data as "datasets which could not be captured, managed, and processed by general computers within an acceptable scope."

In 2011, an IDC report characterized big data as "large information innovations depict another era of advancements and structures, intended to financially extricate an incentive from substantial volumes of a wide assortment of information, by empowering the high-speed catch, disclosure, as well as examination". Big data technologies have also been defined as "the emerging technologies that are designed to extract value from data having four Vs characteristics; volume, variety, velocity and veracity." [12]. Accordingly, the key attributes of big data can be outlined as the 'four Vs', i.e., Volume (extraordinary volume), Variety (different modalities), Velocity (quick era), and Value, as shown in Fig. 1.

2.3 Big Data Analytics

Big data analytics has become a key buzzword these days. It is not just a buzzword but is making a fundamental impact on all spheres of our life, transport [13], planning and operations [14, 15], smart cities [16], teaching and learning [17], to name but a few. According to Feki and Wamba [18] and Hogarth and Soyer [19], the term 'analytic' can be defined as transforming big data into meaningful intelligent information. This transformation of big data is usually done using two main steps: Data management, then Data Analytics using specific techniques [20]. Data management implies "processes and supporting technologies to acquire and store data and to prepare and retrieve it for analysis" while analytics means "techniques used to analyse and acquire intelligence from big data" [18].

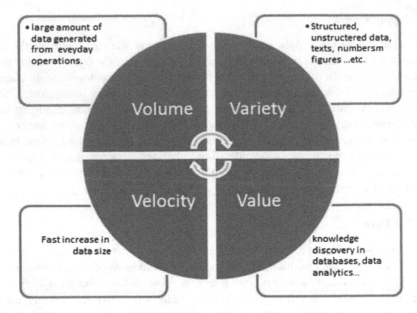

Fig. 1. Big Data Characteristics.

2.4   Big Data in Supply Chain Management

Big data has been widely used in supply chain management in many industries. According to Waller and Fawcett [21], despite the operational influence of big data in supply chains, traditional approaches and standard activities are affected, too. They identified the potential opportunities that big data could offer in enhancing supply chain processes.

Carriers, manufacturers and retailers, the main users of logistics, are also the main beneficiary of big data. They could obtain actionable information about many of their daily activities, such as inventory, transport, and human resources management. DHL and UPS, two leading companies who are pioneer investors in big data initiatives to enhance their services and increase their profits [22].

2.5   Big Data in Healthcare

The use of big data is not limited to industrial fields. It is playing a key role in enhancing critical service sectors such as healthcare. Healthcare systems and applications have long been considered computationally intensive [23]. However, the focus on data—i.e., big data—has only began in the last few years. It As noted in [12], "the cost of healthcare, according to World Health Organization is mostly due to system and operational inefficiencies, and missed disease-prevention opportunities. Big data analytics can minimize these efficiencies and improve the clinical processes resulting in better, preventive, personalized healthcare; estimated to save billions in the healthcare sector alone with virtually unquantifiable impact".

Collaborations between big data platform providers and scientific research centres have generated remarkable and noticeable successes. In Australia, two innovative applications for big data have been developed by Srinivasan and Arunasalam [24]. They have utilized the massive data extracted from hospital discharge reports and insurance claims to detect fraud, abuse, waste and errors in insurance claims.

Similarly, in 2014, Raghupathi and Raghupathi [25] reported that in healthcare more than $300 billion could be saved annually through big data analytics utilization, as estimated by McKinsey. Big data utilization could be applied in two vital areas: Clinical Operations and Research & Development [26]. A practical example of using big data analytics has been undertaken by developers [27] in US health care sector. They built predictive systems based on big data that could help in early identification of six critical cases: high cost patients, readmissions, triage, decompensating (once a patient's situations get worse), adverse events, and treatment optimization for diseases affecting multiple organ systems.

Several works exist that use big data to improve healthcare ICT systems efficiencies. For example, the use of cloudlets and big data to improve mobile healthcare systems response and experience is proposed in [28, 29]. A capacity sharing model for healthcare using big data is proposed in [30]. The use of big data to improve the performance of networked (integrated) healthcare systems is proposed in [12].

3 Big Data in Healthcare Supply Chains

In this section, we demonstrate the possible opportunities of using big data as a solution in healthcare supply chains. The opportunities are summarized based on the previous works that have been published. Unfortunately, very limited work has been found. However, the application of big data in this regard is unlimited and further investigations are required. In the last sub section, the challenges that might be considered are listed.

3.1 Opportunities

Nowadays, big data has in many ways become a solution looking for a problem to solve. Rozados and Tjahjono saw that "Major business players who embrace Big Data as a new paradigm are seemingly offered endless promises of business transformation and operational efficiency improvements" [31]. This has attracted researchers and practitioners in many industries to explore the possibilities of using big data. Abundant research has been done in both healthcare and in supply chain management generally. The healthcare industry is considered as an essential and critical sector within services, but there is a lack of information about the current state of research into healthcare operations management (OM) and supply chain management (SCM) [32]. At the time of writing this paper, only three peer reviewed papers have been found in this area, and we can summarize the opportunities of using big data in healthcare supply chains as follows.

Demand Forecasting. At management level in many industries, demand forecasting is widely used in order to decision-making reinforcement and to promote other management tasks. In China, historical recorded data from transaction datasets has been successfully used to build a predictive model based on data mining algorithms [33]. This model is supposed to work as a prediction tool to estimate future needs within the healthcare supply chain process in China. They used real datasets from 2014 to build the prediction tool, to predict the next year's needs. Since the nature of the collected data set is heterogeneous, and in order to empower the prediction tool, they combined a classification decision tree and regression algorithm in CRT modelling. The efficiency of their model was proven and gained better results than other traditional statistical approaches.

Improving Safety and Quality Assurance in the Pharmaceutical Supply Chain. In the pharmaceutical industry, counterfeiting and illegal export and import of medicines is a major issue. Moreover, transferring medicines and medical equipment in inappropriate environmental conditions, such as at high temperature and humidity, can affect quality. Thus, the challenge is to guarantee the delivery of shipped medicines safely. Further, medical care providers (hospitals, clinics etc.) need to verify that they have obtained the right medicine from the right source. In Germany XQ in [2] made use of the data stored by their RFID-based system about tracked and traced shipments, such as ID, location, temperature, humidity etc. Tracking and tracing are widely-known terms in the supply chain management context, which may offer opportunities to ensure quality of medicines and prevent counterfeiting.

Indoor Monitoring. For healthcare organizations, the benefits of track and trace systems are not limited to ensuring medicines' quality. Data generated from these systems can also offer an opportunity to improve the safety of special needs patients and new-born babies. A healthcare unit's administrators can retrieve real time locations and other necessary information, such as vital signs for Alzheimer's patients, at any moment, to ensure that they are safe. Intelligent applications can offer monitoring without restricting patients' movements. Also, new-born babies can be saved from kidnapping and theft. A real application for this opportunity was delivered by Sultanow and Chircu [2] when they launched the track and trace system and reported its significant benefits.

3.2   Challenges

While big data could offer a wide range of opportunities, it has characteristics that could be considered as important challenges, both generally as well as in the case of healthcare, specifically. The criticality of the healthcare industry and its standards of confidentiality might create difficulties too. The key challenges of applying big data in the healthcare supply chain can be summarized as follows.

Data Related Issues. Due to big data's characteristics, such as data volume, variety, and heterogeneity, some issues may arise. According to Tan et al. the variations of data require finding special techniques for handling and storing, as claimed by Burghin et al. [34]. Moreover, the traditional data mining techniques may not be longer sufficient for such kinds of data [35]. Alongside (and sometimes as a result of) the variety and volume, incompleteness, incorrectness and uselessness are also commonly reported difficulties.

Healthcare Related Issues. The main resources of big data in the healthcare industry are electronic medical records (EMRs) [25]. Practitioners use EMRs to record patient's medication histories every time the patient visit the clinic. According to [6], data ownership, governance and standardization are the main challenges that should be considered in this area.

Knowledge Related Issues. Deep knowledge is needed in order to understand the variety of data forms and analyse the relationship between different kinds of data [24]. Moreover, the topic is complexly multidisciplinary, since sufficient knowledge of big data analytics techniques, healthcare data and supply chain processes are required, too.

4   Conclusion and Future Research Directions

In conclusion, healthcare supply chains are an essential area that should be considered and improved. Healthcare organizations will likely need to employ recent developments in technology to deliver efficient services at reasonable cost and high quality. Improved data analysis is also required to reduce the waste and loss that threaten sustainability. Big data analytics is a powerful tool that is usually concerned with large-scale data and high-performance computing environments; it has emerged as a revolution that is able to contribute in different ways to many field, such as through data analysis, knowledge extraction, and advanced decision-making. We recommend some future directions for the use of big data in healthcare supply chains in the following.

1. Data driven inventory can enhance prediction tools through several optimization methods. This includes studying how to get benefits from "data patterns" that are extracted at the analysis step, and how to use them to support decision-making.
2. Further reviews of how big data is used in manufacturing, unrelated to patients, is another possible direction, informing how we might use patient-centric data in estimating hospitals' needs or logistic operations such as scheduling, staff scheduling, resources allocation, and hospital design layout.
3. Using social media in addition to EMRs can assist in determining the best locations for future clinics and services.

An important step to enable optimised supply chains in healthcare sector would be the networking and integration of healthcare and other smart world systems [28]. Such integration would give rise to a plethora of useful data where the systems integration would allow automatic collection, storage, and analyses of data. Moreover, the integration would also enable optimised decisions to be taken and enforced automatically leading to optimised supply chains in the healthcare sector.

Acknowledgments.   The work carried out in this paper is supported by the HPC Center at the King Abdulaziz University.

References

1. Deloitte: 2017 Global Health Care Sector Outlook 2015 (2017)
2. Sultanow, E., Chircu, A.M.: Improving healthcare with data-driven track-and-trace systems. In: Strategic Data Based Wisdom in the Big Data Era, pp. 65–82 (2015)
3. Kwon, I.W.G., Kim, S.H., Martin, D.G.: Healthcare supply chain management; strategic areas for quality and financial improvement. Technol. Forecast. Soc. Change **113**, 422–428 (2016)
4. Chen, M., Mao, S., Liu, Y.: Big data: a survey. Mob. Netw. Appl. **19**, 171–209 (2014)
5. Malik, M.M., Abdallah, S., Ala'raj, M.: Data mining and predictive analytics applications for the delivery of healthcare services: a systematic literature review. Ann. Oper. Res. **247**, 1–26 (2016)
6. Naoui, F.: Customer service in supply chain management: a case study. J. Enterp. Inf. Manag. **27**, 786–801 (2014)
7. Akyuz, G.A., Rehan, M.: Requirements for forming an "e-supply chain". Int. J. Prod. Res. **47**, 3265–3287 (2009)
8. Butner, K.: The smarter supply chain of the future. Strateg. Leadersh. **38**, 22–31 (2010)
9. Hessman, T.: The dawn of the smart factory. IndustryWeek **14**, 14–19 (2013)
10. Ahmad, N., Mehmood, R.: Enterprise systems: are we ready for future sustainable cities. Supply Chain Manag. Int. J. **20**, 264–283 (2015)
11. Ahmad, N., Mehmood, R.: Enterprise systems and performance of future city logistics **27**, 500–513 (2016). http://dx.doi.org/10.1080/09537287.2016.1147098
12. Mehmood, R., Faisal, M.A., Altowaijri, S.: Future networked healthcare systems: a review and case study. In: Information Resources Management Association (ed.) Big Data: Concepts, Methodologies, Tools, and Applications, pp. 2429–2457. IGI Global (2016)
13. Mehmood, R., Meriton, R., Graham, G., Hennelly, P., Kumar, M.: Exploring the influence of big data on city transport operations: a Markovian approach. Int. J. Oper. Prod. Manag. **37**, 75–104 (2017)
14. Suma, S., Mehmood, R., Albugami, N., Katib, I., Albeshri, A.: Enabling next generation logistics and planning for smarter societies. Procedia - Procedia Comput. Sci. **104C**, 1–6 (2017)
15. Enabling Smarter Societies through Mobile Big Data Fogs and Clouds. http://www.sciencedirect.com/science/article/pii/S1877050917311213
16. Alam, F., Mehmood, R., Katib, I., Albogami, N.N., Albeshri, A.: Data fusion and IoT for smart ubiquitous environments: a survey. IEEE Access **5**, 9533–9554 (2017)
17. Mehmood, R., Alam, F., Albogami, N.N., Katib, I., Albeshri, A., Altowaijri, S.M.: UTiLearn: a personalised ubiquitous teaching and learning system for smart societies. IEEE Access **5**, 2615–2635 (2017)
18. Feki, M., Wamba, S.F.: Big data analytics-enabled supply chain transformation : a literature review. In: 49th Hawaii International Conference on System Sciences, pp. 1123–1132 (2016)
19. Hogarth, R.M., Soyer, E.: Using simulated experience to make sense of big data. MIT Sloan Manag. Rev. **56**, 49–54 (2015)
20. Gandomi, A., Haider, M.: Beyond the hype: big data concepts, methods, and analytics. Int. J. Inf. Manag. **35**, 137–144 (2015)
21. Waller, M.A., Fawcett, S.E.: Data science, predictive analytics, and big data: a revolution that will transform supply chain design and management. J. Bus. Logist. **34**, 77–84 (2013)

22. Zhong, R.Y., Newman, S.T., Huang, G.Q., Lan, S.: Big data for supply chain management in the service and manufacturing sectors: challenges, opportunities, and future perspectives. Comput. Ind. Eng. **101**, 572–591 (2016)
23. Altowaijri, S., Mehmood, R., Williams, J.: A quantitative model of grid systems performance in healthcare organisations. In: ISMS 2010 - UKSim/AMSS 1st International Conference on Intelligent Systems, Modelling and Simulation, pp. 431–436 (2010)
24. Srinivasan, U., Arunasalam, B.: Leveraging big data analytics to reduce healthcare costs. IT Prof. **15**, 21–28 (2013)
25. Raghupathi, W., Raghupathi, V.: Big data analytics in healthcare: promise and potential. Health Inf. Sci. Syst. **2**, 3 (2014)
26. Feldman, B., Martin, E.M., Skotnes, T.: Big Data in Healthcare - Hype and Hope (2012). http://www.riss.kr/link?id=A99883549
27. Bates, D.W., Saria, S., Ohno-Machado, L., Shah, A., Escobar, G.: Big data in health care: using analytics to identify and manage high-risk and high-cost patients. Health Aff. **33**, 1123–1131 (2014)
28. Tawalbeh, L.A., Mehmood, R., Benkhlifa, E., Song, H.: Mobile cloud computing model and big data analysis for healthcare applications. IEEE Access **4**, 6171–6180 (2016)
29. Tawalbeh, L.A., Bakhader, W., Mehmood, R., Song, H.: Cloudlet-based mobile cloud computing for healthcare applications. In: 2016 IEEE Global Communications Conference (GLOBECOM), pp. 1–6. IEEE (2016)
30. Mehmood, R., Graham, G.: Big data logistics: a health-care transport capacity sharing model. Procedia Comput. Sci. **64**, 1107–1114 (2015)
31. Varela, I.R., Tjahjono, B.: Big data analytics in supply chain management: trends and related research. In: 6th International Conference on Operations and Supply Chain Management, 1, 2013–2014 (2014)
32. Dobrzykowski, D., Saboori Deilami, V., Hong, P., Kim, S.C.: A structured analysis of operations and supply chain management research in healthcare (1982–2011). Int. J. Prod. Econ. **147**, 514–530 (2014)
33. Xu, S., Tan, K.H.: Data-driven inventory management in the healthcare supply chain (2016)
34. Bughin, J., Chui, M., Manyika, J.: Clouds, big data, and smart assets: ten tech-enabled business trends to watch. McKinsey Q. **56**, 75–86 (2010)
35. Tan, K.H., Zhan, Y.Z., Ji, G., Ye, F., Chang, C.: Harvesting big data to enhance supply chain innovation capabilities: an analytic infrastructure based on deduction graph. Int. J. Prod. Econ. **165**, 223–233 (2015)

DNA Profiling Methods and Tools: A Review

Emad Alamoudi[1]($\boxtimes$), Rashid Mehmood[2], Aiiad Albeshri[1],
and Takashi Gojobori[3]

[1] Department of Computer Science, Faculty of Computing
and Information Technology (FCIT), King Abdulaziz University,
Jeddah, Kingdom of Saudi Arabia
ealamoodi0003@stu.kau.edu.sa, aaalbeshri@kau.edu.sa
[2] High-Performance Computing Center, King Abdulaziz University,
Jeddah, Kingdom of Saudi Arabia
RMehmood@kau.edu.sa
[3] Computational Bioscience Research Center (CBRC),
King Abdullah University of Science and Technology (KAUST),
Thuwal 23955-6900, Kingdom of Saudi Arabia
Takashi.Gojobori@kaust.edu.sa

Abstract. DNA typing or profiling is a widely used practice in various forensic laboratories, used, for example, in sexual assault cases when the source of DNA mixture can combine different individuals such as the victim, the criminal, and the victim's partner. DNA typing is considered one of the hardest problem in the forensic science domain, and it is an active area of research. The computational complexity of DNA typing increases significantly with the number of unknowns in the mixture. Different methods have been developed and implemented to address this problem. However, its computational complexity has been the major deterring factor holding its advancements and applications. In this paper, we review DNA profiling methods and tools with a particular focus on their computational performance and accuracy. Faster interpretations of DNA mixtures with a large number of unknowns and higher accuracies are expected to open up new frontiers for this area.

Keywords: DNA profiling · Bioinformatics · Forensic science
Likelihood computations · High-performance computing

1 Introduction

According to The American Heritage Medical Dictionary, DNA profiling is "the identification and documentation of the structure of certain regions of a given DNA molecule, used to determine the source of a DNA sample, to determine a child's paternity, to diagnose genetic disorders, or to incriminate or exonerate suspects of a crime [1]." DNA profiling (also named DNA typing, DNA fingerprinting, or DNA testing) which was first introduced in 1985 by Alec Jeffreys has changed the area of forensic science significantly [2]. Dr. Jeffreys has found that there are several regions in the human DNA that contain repeated DNA sequence. He found that these DNA sequence areas may differ from one person to another. Dr. Jeffreys was able to measure

© ICST Institute for Computer Sciences, Social Informatics and Telecommunications Engineering 2018
R. Mehmood et al. (Eds.): SCITA 2017, LNICST 224, pp. 216–231, 2018.
https://doi.org/10.1007/978-3-319-94180-6_22

the variation in these DNA sequences by developing a unique identity test called Restriction Fragment Length Polymorphism (RFLP). The repeated DNA areas are called Variable Number of Tandem Repeats (VNTRs).

Today, DNA profiling is helping in many cases to identify an innocent from guilty. Human Identity test can also be used in contexts such as missing people investigation, parentage test, ancestry test, and disaster victim identification.

The DNA typing is considered today to be the most useful tool in the hand of law enforcement. Moreover, computer databases which contain DNA information of criminals which was taken from crime scenes had helped to associate a crime to an offender. Due to having a specific set of Short Tandem Repeat (STR) loci in these massive databases, it is unlikely to see a new set of DNA markers to be introduced shortly [2].

In order for DNA sample to be processed, several steps should be involved [2]. First, obtaining the DNA from a biological source. Second, assessing the amount of DNA recovered. Third, isolating the DNA from its cells and using Polymerase Chain Reaction (PCR), which is a technique for copying specific DNA areas. Finally, the STR alleles which have been generated from the previous step will be examined.

However, many difficulties may occur during the procedure of producing a DNA profile that affects the analysis of a sample. One of these problems is the stochastic effects, which arise during DNA extraction. Other challenges are allele dropout, PCR process, allele sharing, and PCR amplification artifacts. Such difficulties hardened the accurate interpretation of the DNA profile [3].

The result of the DNA sample processing will be compared to other sample or databases to check the similarity. If there is a match or 'inclusion,' this indicates that both samples were taken from the same source. On the other hand, if there is no match, the result would consider as 'exclusion,' which means there is no biological relation between the two samples [2]. A case report will be made by a forensic specialist explaining the result and containing random match probability answering the similarity question.

The Scientific Working Group on DNA Analysis Methods (SWGDAM) advise forensic report to contain a prediction of the number of contributors to the mixture that is under examination [3]. Usually, the number of contributors of a sample that taken from a crime scene is unknown. Therefore, an analyst should estimate it according to the electropherogram obtained. This assumption affects the final weight of DNA evidence [3].

In this paper, we review DNA profiling methods and tools with a particular focus on their computational performance and accuracy. To the best of our knowledge, this is the first review paper on DNA profiling tools. Faster interpretations of DNA mixtures with a large number of unknowns and higher accuracies are expected to open up new frontiers for DNA profiling. In the coming years, the complete genome sequencing technologies in a single or only a few cells will be easily available. These technologies may change the situation of DNA profiling completely. In this case, it is obvious to prepare appropriate statistical methods for that. It will be, therefore, important to prepare the mathematical and statistical algorithms for complete-genome-sequencing-based DNA profile. Emerging computational and big data developments [4], along with

Internet of Things (IoT) [5] and smart society environments [6], will provide opportunities for new services related to DNA profiling.

The rest of the paper is organized as follows. Section 2 describes background concepts related to this paper. Section 3 provides information regarding DNA profiling methods and technologies that are being used to obtain a DNA sample. Section 4 describes a number of approaches that rely upon the calculation of Likelihood ratio to interpret DNA profile. We further discuss the importance of the Number of Contributors (NoC) in profiling a DNA mixture in Sect. 5. Some implementations that estimate the NoC was mentioned in the same section. Section 6 then illustrate notable DNA profiling applications. We conclude and give an outlook for the future of DNA profiling in Sect. 7.

2   Background Material

We now give a brief background of the various concepts and methods related to DNA profiling.

2.1   Forensic Science

Forensic DNA tests had a major influence on the evolution of the criminal justice system. Yet, the advancement of new technologies is enabling forensic labs to expand its capabilities and improved the sensitivity of the DNA interpretation.

Butler [7] thinks that this area would develop in the future in three main areas; DNA technologies will become faster, the sensitivity of extracting relative information will increase, and higher volume of data will be expected due to that sensitive nature. He argued that STR will remain the dominant genetic marker.

According to Butler [7], key challenges in the forensic science field are the subjectivity, inconsistency of the complex DNA mixture interpretations between different laboratories and analysts, and the need for training forensic analyst to enhance interpretation of DNA profiles.

2.2   DNA Mixture

A sample is called a DNA mixture when two or more individuals contribute to it. Under some circumstances, the interpretation of a mixture could be more challenging. Allele sharing is one of the factors that increase the difficulty of interpreting a profile [2].

If we have a two-person mixture, then we expected to observe only four alleles per locus. However, this rule may change if we have alleles overlapping or if we have heterozygous individuals. If we have more than four alleles per locus, then we might deal more than two people mixture [8].

DNA mixtures interpretation is a very demanding task [9]. Perez et al. define the DNA mixtures as when two or more people contribute to the same sample. They added that contributors include victims, perpetrators, or other people who interact with the crime scene. Yet, the mixture can be complex when it became a subject of allele drop-in or/and allele drop-out [10]. A detailed introduction to the DNA analysis on the forensic science domain was given by [2, 11]. Butler gives a historical overview that explaining the evolution of the area. He also explains the structure of the DNA and its fundamental component. Moreover, how this structure can be different among species which enable us to use it in the identity test. DNA profiling can use in identity tests such as parentage analysis, and disaster victim identification [2].

2.3 Technologies for DNA Profiling

The topic of DNA profiling was improved by the new advances in the technology. Weedn and Foran [11] gave a general overview of the latest updates and challenges in the forensic science domain related to DNA profiling. STR followed by PCR amplification is one of the most used methods that regularly used in forensic labs [11]. Other markers such as Single Nucleotide Polymorphisms (SNP), Y chromosome STRs, and mitochondrial DNA are also considered. Weedn and Foran argued that the forensic DNA typing is the most dominant method in the forensic science laboratory. They mentioned that the forensic test usually performed with taking into consideration the court challenges. Therefore, the forensic science only uses a well-validated procedure, and all the laboratory process should be documented. The protocols should be ready to defend against legal attack.

New technologies had not only increases the quality of profiling the DNA mixture, but also amplified artifacts such as stutter, variabilities, and baseline noise. Monich et al. [12] had introduced a quantitative signal model which forms the variability in a stutter, baseline noise, and allele peak height. They had also applied the chi-squared and Kolmogorov-Smirnov (KS) tests on the true peak heights and noise to test the fitness of various probability distribution classes. They argued that the interpretation of signal measured from a DNA sample used to be accomplished by using thresholding. Nonetheless, using thresholds during DNA analysis yield problem of losing valuable information. For that reason, new methods that don't rely on threshold were developed.

2.4 Factors Increasing the Complexity of DNA Profiles

Different phenomena affect the complexity of interpreting a DNA profile. These factors include: number of contributors, peak heights, stutter, a major peak masking, a stutter peak masking, population, drop-out probability, drop-in probability, analytical threshold. No software had yet considered all these factors in its calculation [13]. Therefore, it is part of the challenges that face people who develop DNA profiler to select which factor to model in their implementation.

2.5 Likelihood Estimator

Likelihood ratio (LR) is the probability comparison between evidence under two propositions [2]. One is called the prosecution hypothesis, which assumes that the DNA collected from a crime scene goes to the suspect, whereas the other is the defendant hypothesis, which assumes that the matches between the suspect and the questioned sample happened coincidentally. The two considered propositions are mutually exclusive.

The Likelihood ratio is calculated by putting the prosecution hypothesis as a numerator while putting the defendant hypothesis as a denominator [2]. The LR equation is:

$$LR = Hp/Hd \tag{1}$$

If we assume that the suspect commits the crime (100% probability), which is the prosecution hypothesis, then $Hp = 1$. Additionally, if the STR typing result is heterozygous, the probability of the defendant hypothesis would be $Hd = 2pq$, where p and q are the occurrences of the allele one and two for a locus in a relevant population [2]. If we have a homozygous STR typing, then the probability of the defendant hypothesis would be $Hd = p^2$. Therefore, the equation would become:

$$LR = Hp/Hd = 1/2pq \tag{2}$$

Butler [2] said that if the final result was greater than one, then this result would support the prosecution side. While if it is less than one, then the defendant theory would be in favor.

Typically, the LR will have higher ratio if the STR genotype is rear because of the reciprocal relationship. LR is the inverse of the locus estimated frequency [2]. Note that the likelihood ratio can be more complex depending on the mixture of the evidence.

The strength of the result of the likelihood ratio in terms of the prosecution's case can be interpreted numerically as presented in Table 1. Column 1 represents the LR value, while Column 2 is showing the corresponding strength of evidence.

Table 1. The strength of evidence according to LR result [2]

Likelihood ratio	Corresponding evidence
1 to 10	Limited support
10 to 100	Moderated support
100 to 1000	Moderated strong support
1000 10,000	Strong support
10,000 or greater	Very strong support

3 DNA Profiling: General Methods

Several methods had been proposed to statistically evaluate a DNA mixture. Likelihood ratio, the combined probability of inclusion/exclusion (CPI/CPE), and a modified random match probability (mRMP) are some examples of these methods [14]. In February 2000, the FBI's DNA Advisory Boar had strongly recommended the first two methods to be used [2]. Moreover, in 2006, the International Society of Forensic Genetics (ISFG) had emphasis the value of likelihood ratio [14]. There are six steps to interpreting a DNA mixture which was first described by Tim Clayton in 1998 [2]. First, we need to identify the existence of a mixture. Second, the Allele peaks should be selected. Third, we need to determine the possible number of contributors. Fourth, an approximation of the ratio of the people who contribute to the sample. Fifth, we need to calculate all potential genotype combinations. Finally, a reference sample comparison should be made.

In CPI approach, an equal weight is given to all possible genotype combinations. Therefore, a lot of information is being wasted when using this approach which makes it inefficient when working with distinct genotypes [14]. This approach does not require prior knowledge of the number of contributors because it is evaluating all genotypes' combination based on the evidence profile [14].

The Random Match probability (RMP) is usually used with single-source samples; therefore, a modified random match probability (mRMP) is used to refer to the method when it is used with more than single-source sample [14]. Unlike CPI, this approach requires a prior knowledge of the number of contributors in the mixture and will not work well with low-level profiles. An example of two- and three-person mixtures calculations using mRMP was described in [15].

According to Bille et al. LR is the most dominant method of evaluating a DNA mixture. However, both mRMP and LR make use of the available information in the sample where CPI does not tend to do so.

More detailed analysis of the three methods and their advantages and weaknesses can be seen in butler's book "Advanced Topics in Forensic DNA Typing: Interpretation" [14].

4 DNA Profiling Using Likelihood Ratio

LR is considered as the most appropriate and powerful approach for calculating the weight of DNA evidence. There are three methods using LR that are widely described in the literature. The first model is the Binary model, which is the simplest yet it cannot handle complex mixture [16]. Second, the semi-continuous, which is the most used by scientists since it is easy to understand and explain, but it still neglects relevant information [17]. This result in losing information that could be precious. Finally, the continuous which overcomes most of the previous models' shortcomings. It utilizes most of the available information provided by the sample, yet it is harder to be accepted and explained in a courtroom [16]. These models may involve a human or computerized process, depend on of the complexity of the approach. Kelly et al. [17] had made a comparison between these three approaches which are suggested by the DNA Commission of the ISFG.

Many frameworks that interpret complex DNA profiles rely on the likelihood ratios approach such as [10]. Gill and Haned had mentioned set of guidelines which can help to evaluate any complex mixture. In addition, they provide some features for any model that might be dealing with complex interpretation such as the ability to incorporate several contributors. They emphasize the fact that the calculation must be provided in a fast manner.

Most of the likelihood ratio based analysis require the number of contributors be given before to analysis Number of contributors. For instance [18–23] rely on the number of contributors on their analysis.

However, others had tried to avoid using it in their interpretation, such as [24, 25]. Russell et al. had developed a semi-continuous method that can calculate the likelihood ratios without previous knowledge about the contributor's number. Their simple model has the abilities to calculate the statistical weight to inclusions. They had also provided a limit test which will guarantee the absence of any false inclusion by chance. To test the proposed unconstructed likelihood ratio (UCLR) model, researchers had collected a set of DNA mixtures with known contributors in different ratios. The result shows good performance on three people mixture. However, the performance becomes worse as the number of contributors increased.

5   Estimating Number of Contributors for DNA Profiling

Today, most applications that interpreted the DNA profile require the number of contributors to available as an input [24]. Different methods have been developed to conclude the number of contributors in a DNA mixture. One of these methods called Maximum Allele Count (MAC). This approach calculates the minimum number of contributors who might contribute to a sample by counting the observed alleles at each locus. Nevertheless, this method may not be valid to work in a complex mixture because of the complexity of allele-sharing [26]. New methods were proposed that do not only rely on the number of observed alleles, but also on the frequencies of observing the allele in the population. Biedermann et al. [27] had developed a probabilistic method that a perform a Bayesian network to conclude the number of contributors to DNA mixture. The new approach performs better than MAC with degraded DNA sample and a higher number of contributors. Maximum Likelihood Estimator (MLE) is another method used to estimate the number of contributors. It tries to maximize the likelihood value of the DNA profile [28].

Haned et al. [29] had compared MAC and MLE. The efficiency of both methods had been analyzed and compared for identifying two to five-person mixtures. Three different situations used to test both methods. First, when all contributors belong to the same population and when allele occurrences are known. Second, when allele occurrences are not known, which may occur in population subdivision. Finally, a condition of partial profiles and how it could affect the estimation accuracy. MAC method is used to set the lower bound that can clarify the number of alleles in a mixture. Haned et al. believe that MAC is unreliable since there is a chance for allele sharing between people which called the masking effect. The result of the comparison supports the use of MLE when a mixture contains more than three contributors. However, when three or two people contribute to a mixture, MAC would perform better.

However, as the number of contributors increased the risk would increase. Haned et al. [30] Had analyzed the risk of dealing with three-, four-, and five-person mixture. They have done that by comparing the gold standard LR to the casework LR. The gold standard LR is when the number of contributors and genotypes are known which mean the availability of all required information to compute LR per contributor. Authors showed the result and the implied thoughts of analyzing high order mixture in the forensic domain. Haned et al. argued that the low template DNA mixture of three-, four-, and five-person are common in forensic casework, yet it is hard to interpret.

Many methods are used today to evaluate the number of contributors in a sample such as [3, 8, 9, 31]. Perez et al. had created a strategy that could find out the number of contributors from two to four-person mixtures for both low template and high template DNA amounts. The proposed strategy helped to provide a useful tool to differentiate between high and low template two-, three-, and four-person mixtures. The four-person mixtures show some difficulties due to the allele sharing phenomena.

Egeland et al. focus on calculating the number of contributors in a mixture by maximizing the likelihood. The proposed approach is based on single SNP. The method tried to answer two questions: Is it a mixture? And if yes, then how many markers are required and how they should be selected. One of the recommendations that driven from the result was regarding the number of markers needed to calculate the number of contributors which is 100 markers.

A typical algorithm for finding the best allele pair in a locus to interpret a mixture is presented in Algorithm 1. Such a process is essential when calculating the number of contributors in a DNA profile. Moreover, it is a performance bottleneck.

6 Software Tools for DNA Profiling

A number of tools are available that implement various DNA profiling methods. These include DNA MIX [32], Euroformix [18], LRmix [20], LRmix studio [33, 16], TrueAllele [19], LikeLTD [22], LabRetriever [13], CeesIt [21], NOCIt [3], DNAMixture [34], Forensim [35], MixtureCalc, Mixture Analysis [36], FamLink kinship [37], DNA Mixture Separator [38], and STRmix [39]. We will review the most notable of these in this section. We shall describe them here and explain their differences.

6.1 DNAMIX

There were three versions of this software, and all of them are open sources. The third version is the most notable and powerful one among the three, and was based on [32]. This version was written in Java and are appropriate for complex mixtures as well as single-contributor stains. The software will ask for the database, stains, genotype, and hypothesis to be inputted as external files. A simple GUI has been developed in this version.

6.2 LRmix Studio

LRmix Studio is a software designed to interpret complex DNA profiles. It was built on its previous version, which called LRmix; however, LRmix Studio is much faster and more flexible. It can measure the probative value of any (autosomal STR-based) DNA profile [33]. This software is following the semi-continuous model of interpreting DNA profiles. Moreover, it was written in Java, and it is open-source.

Algorithm 1	calculate locus's best allele pair that give best interpretation of the sample

```
1:  procedure GeneProbCalc(stepSize, noc, lname, revLoci, forLoci, DNAmass, AlleleAtLoci, LDO)
    //noc=number of contributors, lname=locus name, LDO= Locus Drop Out
2:      locAlleles = AlleleAtLoci[locusname]
3:      MeanAndStd = Meanstd(locusname) //find mean and stddev
4:      for i=0 to stepSize do
5:          g=random array between 0 and 1 with size noc
6:          for j=0 to noc do
7:              for k=0 to 2 do
8:                  r=Generate random number that does not exceed the interval of the locus
9:                  allele = AlleleRange[r] //get the allele in the selected interval for a specific locus
10:                 Add allele to Peakscumulative
11:                 contMass=g[i-1]*DNAmass
12:                 if Rand() < ExpVal(locusName, LDO, contMass) then
13:                     ValidAlleles.add(allele)
14:                     weight[allele] = weight[allele] + contMass
15:                 end if
16:             end for
17:         end for
18:         for aName=ValidAlleles.start to ValidAlleles.end do //aName=Allele Name
19:             if locAlleles contains allele then
20:                 (mean, variance) =Meanstd(weight[allele]) //find the mean and stddev
21:                 if revLoci[lName] && Rand()<ExpVal(lname, RevStutDropO, weight) then
22:                     rMu=ExpVal2(lName, mean, weight[allele]) * allele.height
23:                     rSigma=ExpVal2(lName, Stddev, weight[allele]) * allele.height
24:                     revAlleleStut = aName - 10 // get the reverse
25:                     fowStutPeak = Peakscumulative[allele]
26:                 end if
27:                 means[revAlleleStut] = means[revAlleleStut] + rMu
28:                 variances[revAlleleStut] = variances[revAlleleStut] + rSigma * r
29:                 if forLoci[lName] && Rand()>ExpVal(lName, forStutDropO, weight) then
30:                     fMu=ExpVal2(lName, Mean, allele.weight) * allele.height
31:                     fSigma=ExpVal2(lName, Stddev, allele.weight) * allele.height
32:                     fowAlleleStut = aName + 10 // get forward
33:                     fowStutPeak = Peakscumulative[allele]
34:                 end if
35:                 means[fowAlleleStut] = means[fowAlleleStut] + rMu
36:                 variances[fowAlleleStut] = variances[fowAlleleStut] + rSigma * rSigma
37:             end if
38:         end for
39:         for temp=Peakscumulative.start to Peakscumulative.end do
40:             mean.add(temp.allele, MeanAndStd[0])
41:             variances.add(temp.allele, MeanAndStd[1] * MeanAndStd[1])
42:         end for
43:         locusProb=calcLocusPeakHeightsProb(Peakscumulative, means, variances)
44:         Summation+ = locusProb
45:         if locusProb > currMax then
46:             currMax = locusProb
47:             for alleleName=selectedValidAlleles.start to selectedValidAlleles.end do
48:                 currMaxAlls.add(alleleName)
49:             end for
50:         end if
51:     end for
52:     result.add(Summation, currMax, currMaxAlls)
53:     Return result
54: end procedure
```

Algorithm 1: A typical algorithm for calculating locus's best allele pair that gives the best interpretation which helps in finding the number of unknowns in a DNA mixture (algorithm inspired by NOCIt tool [3]).

6.3   TrueAllele

It is a software that computes DNA interpretation automatically. It can infer genetic profiles from all sorts of DNA samples. The software applies the continuous model; however, no open source version of the code is available. It was written in Matlab. Analysis followed by a comparison of TrueAllele is presented on [19] using a real information that has been taken from actual cases.

6.4   LabRetriever

LabRetriever is a free software developed to estimate the likelihood ratios that combine a probability of drop-out. It was built on another software called LikeLTD which was written in R language. Authors rewrote the code using C++ to acquire more speed. The software uses the semi-continuous model. It computes likelihood ratios for up to four unknown contributors to a DNA sample.

6.5   CeesIt

CeesIt is a method that integrates two features of the continuous approach to calculate the LR and its distribution which are conditioned on the defense hypothesis and the linked p-value. It combines stutter, dropout, and noise in its calculation. It uses a single source sample with known genotypes. It calculates the LR for a selected POI on a questioned sample, together with the p-value and LR distribution. The software was Witten in Java and is available in a (.jar) format. A deep analysis of the software was presented on [21].

6.6   LikeLTD

LikeLTD is a software that used to computing likelihoods for DNA profile evidence, including complex mixtures. It has been written in R. However, since the fifth version, the computation-intensive areas in code have been rewritten in C to be executed in parallel. This software applies the continuous model of calculating the Likelihood ratio. These areas include the computation of genotype combinations for unknown contributors, computing allele doses for each genotype combination, dose adjustments for relatedness, heterozygosity, dropout, and power.

The runtime of the Peak height model is much slower than the runtime of the discrete model, yet it yields a higher evidence weight (see Table 2). The time complexity of the peak height model scales up with the number of unknown contributors, the number of observed peaks, and the number of replicates in the profile. Other parameters that increase the runtime are the modeling double-stutter or over-stutter. A parallelism was achieved on the C++ code by using shared memory parallelism (OpenMP).

Table 2. The runtime of calculating the Weight of Evidence (WoE) using both the two different models for the laboratory case [18]

Hypothesis	Model	WOE	Runtime (minutes)
Q/X + K1 + U1	Discrete	2.3	14
	Peak height	8.2	23
Q/X + U1 + U2	Discrete	0.5	38
	Peak height	7.8	200

The runtime of the algorithms was recorded using node with eight Intel Core I7 processors (3.1 Hgz per core) and with 15 Gb of RAM. The result is presented in Table 2. The first column describes the hypothesis that was applied. Two hypotheses were used. Q is a contributor to the crime scene profile under the Hp while X is the unknown individual under Hd that assumes to contribute to the profile instead of Q. The hypotheses may specify the number of K is representing the known contributors whereas U is the unknown contributors. The second column indicates the used model whether it uses discrete or peak height. The last two columns are showing the weight of evidence and the corresponding running time.

6.7   DNAMixture

DNAMixture is a statistical model that calculates and analyze DNA sample for one or more contributors [34]. This software has been written in R and follows the "fully continuous" statistical model. Its author claims to develop all methodology within his framework for consistent analysis and transparency. However, the application does not have a graphical user interface, which requires a basic experience with R. The parallelism was applied onto the Bayesian network package that used by this software which called "Hugin." In Hugin package, they used Pthread in the C code.

6.8   EuroForMix

EuroForMix is a software based on the fully continuous approach to estimate STR DNA profiles from a complex DNA sample of contributors with artifacts. It is available as an open source. EuroForMix was written in R language. Nonetheless, the likelihood function was written in C++. The software added a parallel processing, since the 0.5.0 version, using snow R-package. The parallel implementation will only be considered when a number of unknowns are at least 3 (not performed yet for database searching or non-contributor simulation). A number of processes will be similar to the number of random start points required in the optimization.

Euroformix requires a significant amount of computational time when the number of unknown contributors is four or more. Table 3 gives an approximation time complexity for each number of unknown contributors. From the table, it was clear that the time consumed when we have four unknown contributors was too much. A good idea would be to parallelize the code over distributed memory system to reduce that time. The runtime is given in Table 3. Column 1 is showing the number of contributors while Column 2 gives the corresponding time taken.

Table 3. An approximate overview of the time taken to calculate the LR depend on the number of unknown contributors [40]

Number of unknown contributors	Runtime
1	~1 s
2	~1 min
3	~30 min
4	~24 h

6.9   NOCIt

NOCIt [3] analyzes the DNA sample to calculate the number of contributors in a mixture. Java programming language was used to write the software. It determines the number of contributors (from 1 to 5). NOCIt can only interpret an autosomal STRs data which are independent of each other. Moreover, the software is not developed to deal with a stutter.

The execution time of [3] depends on the maximum number of contributors, the number of loci/alleles considered and the processing speed of the computer. It is also dependent on whether multiple runs of NOCIt are occurring at the same time, i.e., two NOCIt interfaces are open at once and running two separate samples. Table 4 provides the runtime of NOCIt. The first column gives the number of contributors, whereas the second column describes the range of time taken to analysis that number. The result was collected from a dual-core laptop with Intel® CoreTM i5-3380 CPU @ 2.9 GHz.

Table 4. The runtime using a different maximum number of contributors [25]

Number of contributors	Range of time (mode)
1	<1 min (0.2 min)
2	15 min–30 min (17 min)
3	30 min–1.5 h (1 h)
4	1 h–5 h (4 h)
5	5 h–20 h (14 h)

6.10   STRmix

STRmix is a probabilistic genotyping application which performs the continuous model of interpreting the DNA profile. It was built to interpret single and mixed DNA profiles. Moreover, it follows the SWGDAM recommendations. It utilizes information that extracts from a DNA sample, such as peak height, to calculate the probability of a DNA profile for all possible genotype combinations. The software considers aspects such as allele drop-in, allele dropout, and stutter. The software has been written in Java, and it's only available for purchase.

6.11   A Comparison of the DNA Profiling Tools

Table 5 compares different software that we had reviewed in this section. The first column gives the names of the software. Columns 2–8 provide information about various features of the software. Column 2 gives information whether the software has a GUI or not. Columns 3 and 4 are illustrating if the selected software considers the phenomena of drop-in and stutter on its interpretation or not. Column 5 gives the model that used to the calculation of LR. The sixth column describes the programming language that used to build the selected software. Column 7 indicates the availability of source code. The last column describes the used parallel framework. The table is missing some information due to either the lack of resource for some software or because of the inability to access the software's source code.

Table 5. A general comparison between the review softwares

	GUI	Drop-in	Stutter	Calculation model	Language	Source code	Parallelism
LRmix studio [13, 16, 33]	Yes	Yes	–	Semi continuous	Java	Yes	Thread pool
TrueAllele [18, 19]	Yes	Yes	Yes	Continuous	Matlab	No	–
DNAMIX V.3 [32]	Yes	–	–	–	Java	Yes	No
Euroformix [18]	Yes	Yes	Yes	Continuous	R, C ++	Yes	Snow package
CeesIt [21]	Yes	Yes	Yes	Continuous	Java	No	Thread pool
NOCIt [3]	Yes	Yes	Yes	Continuous	Java	No	Thread pool
DNAMixtures [34]	No	Yes	Yes	Continuous	R	Yes	No
LikeLTD [22]	No	Yes	Yes	Continuous	R, C	Yes	OpenMP
LabRetriever [13]	Yes	Yes	–	Semi continuous	C ++	Yes	No
STRmix [23, 39]	Yes	Yes	Yes	Continuous	Java	No	–

7 Conclusion

Interpreting DNA mixture is a common practice in forensic science domain. It is a complicated process that requires an extended period of time. We gave an overview of the field of DNA profiling. A historical background, along with its application was mentioned. We, then, discuss the needed steps to sample a DNA mixture and what are the required technologies. After that, we reviewed the literature based on their classification into describing DNA profiling in general. We focus later on approaches that follow the Likelihood Ratio model. We also reviewed the various tools and compared their performance and accuracy

In the end, we would suggest the use of Euroformix and LikeLTD for DNA profiling since they are already performing parallelism. They both utilize most of the available information in the DNA sample because they follow the continuous model for calculating the LR value. The source code for the two software is available for assessment and modification. However, Euroformix provides a GUI which gives it a slight advantage over LikeLTD for users who have no technological expertise.

A frequent necessity to apply these tests might raise the need to speed up the run time of such analysis. The computational complexity has been the major deterring factor holding the area advancements and applications. An improvement would give a chance to interpret mixtures with a larger number of unknowns and within a shorter timeframe. The investigation of the relevant literature reveals that the current approaches for parallelization of DNA profiling rely on shared memory parallelization. A distributed implementation is needed to speed up the computations allowing for the use of a large number of cores/processors. This is our ongoing research, which will be reported in the near future. Faster interpretations of DNA mixtures with a large number of unknowns and higher accuracies are expected to open up new frontiers for DNA profiling.

In the coming years, the complete genome sequencing technologies in a single or only a few cells will be easily available. These technologies may change the situation of DNA profiling completely. In this case, it is obvious to prepare appropriate statistical methods for that. It will be, therefore, important to prepare the mathematical and statistical algorithms for complete-genome-sequencing-based DNA profile. High performance computing (HPC) will play a key role in speeding up DNA profiling methods, particularly those HPC techniques which exploit domain specific data and algorithmic patterns [41], system heterogeneity (e.g. disks for space, and accelerators for speed) for its advantage [42], and virtual organization models (similar to grids [43]) for information sharing across organizational boundaries. Hierarchical system structures will be needed to localize and optimize data and computations [44]. Internet of Things (IoT) would be integrated in smart city systems to create innovative services [6] and deal with big data-related challenges [5]. Mobile, fog and cloud computing [4, 45, 46] will enable dynamic system environments, seamlessly connecting users and systems.

Acknowledgments. The work carried out in this paper is supported by the HPC Center at the King Abdulaziz University.

References

1. The American Heritage Medical Dictionary. Houghton Mifflin Co., Boston (2007)
2. Butler, J.M.: Fundamentals of Forensic DNA Typing. Academic Press/Elsevier (2010)
3. Swaminathan, H., Grgicak, C.M., Medard, M., Lun, D.S.: NOCIt: a computational method to infer the number of contributors to DNA samples analyzed by STR genotyping. Forensic Sci. Int. Genet. **16**, 172–180 (2015)
4. Arfat, Y., Aqib, M., Mehmood, R., Albeshri, A., Katib, I., Albogami, N., Alzahrani, A.: Enabling smarter societies through mobile big data fogs and clouds. Procedia Comput. Sci. **109**, 1128–1133 (2017)
5. Alam, F., Mehmood, R., Katib, I., Albogami, N.N., Albeshri, A.: Data fusion and IoT for smart ubiquitous environments: a survey. IEEE Access. **5**, 9533–9554 (2017)
6. Mehmood, R., Alam, F., Albogami, N.N., Katib, I., Albeshri, A., Altowaijri, S.M.: UTiLearn: a personalised ubiquitous teaching and learning system for smart societies. IEEE Access. **5**, 2615–2635 (2017)
7. Butler, J.M.: The future of forensic DNA analysis. Philos. Trans. R. Soc. Lond. B Biol. Sci. **370**, 577–579 (2015)
8. Paoletti, D.R., Krane, D.E., Raymer, M.L., Doom, T.E.: Inferring the number of contributors to mixed DNA profiles. IEEE/ACM Trans. Comput. Biol. Bioinforma. **9**, 113–122 (2012)
9. Perez, J., Mitchell, A.A., Ducasse, N., Tamariz, J., Caragine, T.: Estimating the number of contributors to two-, three-, and four-person mixtures containing DNA in high template and low template amounts. Croat. Med. J. **52**, 314–326 (2011)
10. Gill, P., Haned, H.: A new methodological framework to interpret complex DNA profiles using likelihood ratios. Forensic Sci. Int. Genet. **7**, 251–263 (2013)

11. Weedn, V.W., Foran, D.R.: Forensic DNA typing. In: Leonard, D.G.B. (ed.) Molecular Pathology in Clinical Practice, pp. 793–810. Springer, Cham (2016). https://doi.org/10.1007/978-3-319-19674-9_54

12. Monich, U.J., Grgicak, C., Cadambe, V., Wu, J.Y., Wellner, G., Duffy, K., Medard, M.: A signal model for forensic DNA mixtures. In: 2014 48th Asilomar Conference on Signals, Systems and Computers, pp. 429–433. IEEE (2014)

13. Inman, K., Rudin, N., Cheng, K., Robinson, C., Kirschner, A., Inman-Semerau, L., Lohmueller, K.E.: Lab retriever: a software tool for calculating likelihood ratios incorporating a probability of drop-out for forensic DNA profiles. BMC Bioinf. 16, 298 (2015)

14. Butler, J.M.: Advanced Topics in Forensic DNA Typing: Interpretation. Academic Press (2014)

15. Bille, T., Bright, J.-A., Buckleton, J.: Application of random match probability calculations to mixed STR profiles. J. Forensic Sci. 58, 474–485 (2013)

16. Garofano, P., Caneparo, D., D'Amico, G., Vincenti, M., Alladio, E.: An alternative application of the consensus method to DNA typing interpretation for Low Template-DNA mixtures. Forensic Sci. Int. Genet. Suppl. Ser. 5, e422–e424 (2015)

17. Kelly, H., Bright, J.-A., Buckleton, J.S., Curran, J.M.: A comparison of statistical models for the analysis of complex forensic DNA profiles. Sci. Justice 54, 66–70 (2014)

18. Bleka, Ø., Storvik, G., Gill, P.: EuroForMix: An open source software based on a continuous model to evaluate STR DNA profiles from a mixture of contributors with artefacts. Forensic Sci. Int. Genet. 21, 35–44 (2016)

19. Perlin, M.W., Dormer, K., Hornyak, J., Schiermeier-Wood, L., Greenspoon, S.: TrueAllele casework on Virginia DNA mixture evidence: computer and manual interpretation in 72 reported criminal cases. PLoS ONE 9, e92837 (2014)

20. Gill, P., Haned, H., Eduardoff, M., Santos, C., Phillips, C., Parson, W.: The open-source software LRmix can be used to analyse SNP mixtures. Forensic Sci. Int. Genet. Suppl., Ser (2015)

21. Swaminathan, H., Garg, A., Grgicak, C.M., Medard, M., Lun, D.S.: CEESIt: A computational tool for the interpretation of STR mixtures. Forensic Sci. Int. Genet. 22, 149–160 (2016)

22. Balding, D.J., Steele, C.: The likeLTD software: an illustrative analysis, explanation of the model, results of performance tests and version history. UCL Genet. Inst. 1, 1–49 (2014)

23. Moretti, T.R., Just, R.S., Kehl, S.C., Willis, L.E., Buckleton, J.S., Bright, J.-A., Taylor, D. A., Onorato, A.J.: Internal validation of STRmix^{TM} for the interpretation of single source and mixed DNA profiles. Forensic Sci. Int. Genet. 29, 126–144 (2017)

24. Taylor, D., Bright, J.-A., Buckleton, J.: Interpreting forensic DNA profiling evidence without specifying the number of contributors. Forensic Sci. Int. Genet. 13, 269–280 (2014)

25. Russell, D., Christensen, W., Lindsey, T.: A simple unconstrained semi-continuous model for calculating likelihood ratios for complex DNA mixtures. Forensic Sci. Int. Genet. Suppl. Ser. 5, e37–e38 (2015)

26. Paoletti, D.R., Doom, T.E., Krane, C.M., Raymer, M.L., Krane, D.E.: Empirical analysis of the STR profiles resulting from conceptual mixtures. J. Forensic Sci. 50, JFS2004475-6 (2005)

27. Biedermann, A., Bozza, S., Konis, K., Taroni, F.: Inference about the number of contributors to a DNA mixture: comparative analyses of a Bayesian network approach and the maximum allele count method. Forensic Sci. Int. Genet. 6, 689–696 (2012)

28. Haned, H., Pène, L., Sauvage, F., Pontier, D.: The predictive value of the maximum likelihood estimator of the number of contributors to a DNA mixture. Forensic Sci. Int. Genet. 5, 281–284 (2011)

29. Haned, H., Pène, L., Lobry, J.R., Dufour, A.B., Pontier, D.: Estimating the number of contributors to forensic DNA mixtures: does maximum likelihood perform better than maximum allele count? J. Forensic Sci. **56**, 23–28 (2011)

30. Haned, H., Benschop, C.C.G., Gill, P.D., Sijen, T.: Complex DNA mixture analysis in a forensic context: evaluating the probative value using a likelihood ratio model. Forensic Sci. Int. Genet. **16**, 17–25 (2015)

31. Egeland, T., Dalen, I., Mostad, P.F.: Estimating the number of contributors to a DNA profile. Int. J. Legal Med. **117**, 271–275 (2003)

32. Curran, J.M., Triggs, C.M., Buckleton, J., Weir, B.S.: Interpreting DNA mixtures in structured populations. J. Forensic Sci. **44**, 987–995 (1999)

33. Haned, H., De Jong, J.: LRmix Studio 2.1 user manual (2016)

34. Lauritzen, S.L.: Statistical and computational methodology for the analysis of forensic DNA mixtures with artefacts (2014)

35. Haned, H.: Forensim: an open-source initiative for the evaluation of statistical methods in forensic genetics. Forensic Sci. Int. Genet. **5**, 265–268 (2011)

36. Gill, P., Sparkes, R., Pinchin, R., Clayton, T., Whitaker, J., Buckleton, J.: Interpreting simple STR mixtures using allele peak areas. Forensic Sci. Int. **91**, 41–53 (1998)

37. Kling, D., Egeland, T., Tillmar, A.O.: FamLink – A user friendly software for linkage calculations in family genetics. Forensic Sci. Int. Genet. **6**, 616–620 (2012)

38. Tvedebrink, T., Eriksen, P.S., Mogensen, H.S., Morling, N.: Evaluating the weight of evidence by using quantitative short tandem repeat data in DNA mixtures. J. R. Stat. Soc. Ser. C (Appl. Stat.) **59**, 855–874 (2010)

39. Developmental validation of STRmixTM: Expert software for the interpretation of forensic DNA profiles. Forensic Sci. Int. Genet. **23**, 226–239 (2016)

40. Bleka, Ø.: An introduction to EuroForMix (v1.8) **2016**, 1–59 (2016)

41. Mehmood, R., Crowcroft, J.: Parallel Iterative solution method for Large Sparse Linear Equation Systems, vol. 22 (2005)

42. Mehmood, R.: Serial disk-based analysis of large stochastic models. In: Baier, C., Haverkort, Boudewijn R., Hermanns, H., Katoen, J.-P., Siegle, M. (eds.) Validation of Stochastic Systems. LNCS, vol. 2925, pp. 230–255. Springer, Heidelberg (2004). https://doi.org/10.1007/978-3-540-24611-4_7

43. Altowaijri, S., Mehmood, R., Williams, J.: A quantitative model of grid systems performance in healthcare organisations. In: 2010 International Conference on Intelligent Systems, Modelling and Simulation, pp. 431–436. IEEE (2010)

44. Mehmood, R., Crowcroft, J., Hand, S., Smith, S.: Grid-level computing needs pervasive debugging. In: The 6th IEEE/ACM International Workshop on Grid Computing, 2005, p. 8. IEEE (2005)

45. Tawalbeh, L.A., Mehmood, R., Benkhlifa, E., Song, H.: Mobile cloud computing model and big data analysis for healthcare applications. IEEE Access. **4**, 6171–6180 (2016)

46. Tawalbeh, L.A., Bakhader, W., Mehmood, R., Song, H.: Cloudlet-based mobile cloud computing for healthcare applications. In: 2016 IEEE Global Communications Conference (GLOBECOM), pp. 1–6. IEEE (2016)

A Smart Pain Management System
Using Big Data Computing

Waleed Al Shehri[1(✉)], Rashid Mehmood[2], and Hassan Alayyaf[3]

[1] Department of Computer Science, Faculty of Computing and Information
Technology, King Abdulaziz University, Jeddah 21589, Saudi Arabia
Waleed.ab2@gmail.com
[2] High Performance Computing Center, King Abdulaziz University,
Jeddah, Saudi Arabia
RMehmood@kau.edu.sa
[3] Al Hada Military Hospital, Taif, Saudi Arabia
dr.alayyaf@hotmail.com

Abstract. Pain is a universal experience and there is hardly a human being who
has never experienced pain at one time or another. Managing pain is of high
priority for healthcare organizations given the increasing incidence of pain
among patients and the costs associated with it. The current standards and
practices in pain management are limited to mostly manual processes hindering
innovations in this area. This paper proposes a smart pain management system
based on big data computing technologies. The system devises pain management strategies based on the relevant standards and patients' data, and these
strategies are identified, applied, and monitored by the system in real-time.
A perpetual feedback loop is created among the system components and the
outcomes are communicated to the stakeholders to enable reflections and continuous improvements in the pain management standards, strategies, and processes. The system architecture and its architectural components are described.
A preliminary analysis is provided using handwritten and digital pain management related data.

Keywords: Big data computing · Apache spark · HealthCare
Pain management · Numeric Pain Rating Scale (NPRS)
Electronic Health Records (EHRs) · Patients' data

1 Introduction

Generating valuable information was always the idea behind the processing and
manipulation of data. In the last many decades we have seen systems that process data to
extract valuable information that sometimes is used in real-time to make right decisions.
In addition, the expansion of the systems was enormous and this has resulted in the
increase of amount of data and also decision making on this data has become prob-
lematic. Accordingly, big data technologies emerged to provide analysis on this large
quantity and high velocity data sources. Purpose is still the same to generate valuable
information and insight into the data to see what is really happening. This information is
needed to set the course of actions to produce right results. Many field of science like

© ICST Institute for Computer Sciences, Social Informatics and Telecommunications Engineering 2018
R. Mehmood et al. (Eds.): SCITA 2017, LNICST 224, pp. 232–246, 2018.
https://doi.org/10.1007/978-3-319-94180-6_23

economics, computer science, mathematics, and statistics have contributed in the processes of solving complex data to simplified understandable information.

Applying scientific ways to analyze data require resort to computer sciences as most of the fields like meteorology, social computing, astronomy, computational biology and bioinformatics are heavily dependent on computer sciences. In consequence, there is a number of problems but the most prominent being various resources generating huge volumes data with structures of differing nature [1]. A related example comes from the healthcare data collected in 2012 amounting to 500 petabytes which may rise to 25 exabytes in 2020 [2]. Challenges of the sort require extensive labor for being able to know more from large volumes of data.

There are various sources of data in healthcare sector. Mostly the data comes from physicians' memos, laboratory information, patients' records, Electronic Health Records (EHRs), national health registry, doctors and nurses employed, etc. Data coming from paper and other non-digital resources must be converted to digital form for enabling healthcare service providers to provide top rated health services. The data that is being collected now can be used to do analysis of different problems in healthcare. This data is sometimes too large to be analyzed so we need big data technologies to analyze data.

Analyzing huge data in healthcare is highly important because it helps to improve the level of service provided to patients by suggesting the right remedies thus avoiding any chance of error in diagnostic and prescription while at the same the process is cost effective. Moreover, such analysis can help in early detection of diseases and early prevention. In addition, a major benefit of the process is its use as a tool for quality measurement regarding different organizations and the employees therein [3].

It has been observed that due to high amount of data generated because of unexpected growth in biomedicine and the types of data being generated is not always in relational format; the storage and processing of data obtained is becoming increasingly complex [4]. For this reason, big data analytics are required to deal with enormous amounts of data. The most well-known fields include bioinformatics [5–7], health informatics [8–10], imaging informatics [11, 12], and sensor informatics [13, 14].

A branch of healthcare services is pain management and data being generated by the pain management practices is mostly stored in patient records. The patient records are stored in transactional databases and to analyze the data on a large scale, many databases should be combined to get a large enough database to do analysis of the pain management data. The improvement of the pain management practices depends on the correct analysis of the practices and their results, this combined data is too large and too complex to be placed in a simple database and the analysis has to be done through the tools and techniques used in big data analytics. Such an analysis will help develop technologies based on smart solution criteria to improve pain management through standardized assessment procedures.

This paper proposes a smart pain management system based on big data computing technologies. The standards and practice in pain management are turned by the proposed system into strategies that can be tested and improved in real-time. The system devises pain management strategies based on the relevant standards and patients' data. These strategies are identified, applied, and monitored by the system in real-time. A perpetual feedback loop is created among the system components and the outcomes are communicated to the stakeholders to allow reflections and continuous improvements in the pain management standards, strategies, and processes. The system architecture and its architectural components are described. A preliminary analysis is provided using handwritten and electronic pain management related data.

In Sect. 2 of this paper, we provide background on big data and pain management. In Sect. 3, notable related works on pain management are reviewed. In Sect. 4, we describe the architecture of our proposed smart pain management system. Section 5 provides the results and analysis. Conclusions are drawn in Sect. 6.

2 Background

2.1 Big Data, Big Data Analytics, and Healthcare

Big data has been defined in the literature differently based on the researchers' and practitioners' views of the term. For example, in [15], big data technologies are defined as *"the emerging technologies that are designed to extract value from data having four Vs characteristics; volume, variety, velocity and veracity"*. The definition refers to the four "V" characteristics of big data, which have been referred to widely in the literature.

In simple words, big data is sets of data analysis, management, and realization of which is not possible by conventional IT methods. Two implications are obvious from this definition; firstly, volume of data is increasing and changing on continuous basis and secondly, increasing data volume differs according to applications involved in analytics [16]. Another method used in defining big data is multi Vs model volume implying that generated data and its analysis has a velocity related to timeliness of big data. Variety in data signifies different data types whether structured or not. These include audio, video, webpage, text, and customary structured data. Getting value from huge volumes of data is the major objective of big data analysis and this characteristic is an important aspect of multi Vs model. The four cycles involved in life cycle of big data are; generation, acquisition, storage, and analysis.

To achieve efficiency in operations, notifying strategic route, improving customer services, developing innovative products, identifying new markets, and achieving other important objectives, big data analytics have an indispensable role to play. However, it must be borne in mind that achieving these advantages is not possible unless proper procedures are followed to benefit from big data analytics. The usual challenges appear when capturing, storage, searching, sharing, analysis, and visualization of data is to be done. Other problems include inconsistent and incomplete data, scalability, timeliness, and data security. Additionally, a critical challenge is to deal with big data of different nature that comes from a variety of sources.

The healthcare sector has adopted the developments in ICT for long. Some of the most powerful supercomputers have been commissioned for the sole purpose of healthcare research including computational grids [17]. Naturally, big data and other emerging technologies such as cloud computing and Internet of Things (IoT), have found there uses in Healthcare [15, 18–20], to provide personalized and preventive healthcare. The integration of healthcare systems with other smart city systems such as transportation and logistics have also been proposed, see e.g. [21]. The emerging technologies indeed are set to revolutionize healthcare.

2.2 Pain Management

Pain is a universal experience and there is hardly a human being who has never experienced pain at one time or another. Understanding pain and the way to manage it is essential for healthcare professionals. Managing pain is an issue of high priority for healthcare organizations and their employees given the increasing incidence of pain among patients [22]. In fact, often it is hard for doctors to comprehend the exact feelings of a patient in pain but healthcare professionals cannot ignore a patient in pain.

One of the primary objectives of any healthcare organization is preventing and managing pain. Pain is categorized according to its intensity and duration. There are two types of pain. One is acute pain which is of short duration usually not more than six months and the other is chronic pain which is permanent, continuous, and lasts for longer periods of time. Acute pain is usually sudden in onset and is better termed as a warning signal that there is something wrong with the body. On the other hand, chronic pain can be mild or severe in intensity and may develop rapidly. Moreover, pain is classified as neuropathic or non-neuropathic depending upon the comprehension of Healthcare providers (HCPs) [22].

To assess neuropathic pain, National Health Service (NHS) of UK has developed a questionnaire known as DN4 (Douleur Neuropathique 4). The DN4 questionnaire is a useful tool in diagnosing neuropathic pain with all the necessary components about assessing how much pain the patient is feeling and for how long [23]. However, health experts are expected to examine the patient and form an opinion whether pain has been reduced or increased. Moreover, it is also important to know the incidence, intensity, recurrence, duration, and level of pain. The questionnaire has proved its efficacy and validity in numerous cases of neuropathic pain and related clinical research.

Another effort in assessment of pain is the development of Numeric Pain Rating Scale (NPRS) with the purpose of measuring intensity of pain in adults with chronic pain. NPRS is a numeric form of visual analog scale (VAS) where respondent has to select between 0 and 10 to inform the intensity of pain being felt [24]. As in the case of VAS, NPRS is a description of pain severity. The digit is the reference point of no pain and the digit 10 is for expressing the extremity of pain. Patients are to respond on the basis of pain intensity felt in the last 24 h on an average basis [24].

The administration of NPRS can be verbal, through telephone, or by a graphic portrayal. Patient has to respond by attaching a numeric value to the questions being asked indicating the intensity of pain. Patient responses help clinicians in choosing best remedies from the available ones to manage pain [24]. NPRS is a speedy and easy way to assess the condition of patients no matter the language or cultural belonging of the patients. It has proved its reliability and validity in measuring intensity of pain. The measuring method of NPRS is advantageous over VAS because it can be used in writing or through verbal communication. Moreover, NPRS is simple as regards scoring and analysis of the results is concerned. However, one obvious weakness of NPRS is its inability to give a complete picture of pain experiences [24]. Moreover, it cannot handle the fluctuations in intensity of pain and the variable nature of pain.

3 Related Work

Every healthcare organization works for welfare of patients striving to provide the best of care with continuous attempts for improvements. To make it possible various models and theories have been proposed in the last few decades [25]. The emphasis during the last decade has been on "personalized medicine" whereby each patient is dealt with individually with the purpose to provide efficient and personalized healthcare on priority basis [26]. In 2009, Hood and Friend proposed the P4 model where P4 stood for personalized, predictive, preventive, and participatory [27]. The intent of P4 model is to focus on patients by doing away with reactive care methods to be replaced with proactive treatment methods and also reduce healthcare expenses [27]. Of recent, a new model has been proposed named "precision medicine." This model extends personalized medicine model with emphasis on classifying patients according to subgroups of diseases categorized on biological basis [28, 29]. The essential requirement of precision medicine model is utilizing data right from the start till the application of analytic techniques [30].

In 2005, for examining the complexity of human body through collaborative efforts using established methods and technologies, the phrase virtual physiological human (VPH) was coined [31]. VPH is explained as follows. For simplifying the study of living beings, the necessary parts such as cells, tissues, organs, and organ systems can be isolated and studied independently for better understanding. In this way, a specialist will examine one part and the other expert will study the part related to personal expertise. On the contrary, such a method will be an impediment towards diseases related to multi-organs or systemic diseases. Further, it will be difficult to know how genotype-phenotype interacts with treatment methods related to multiple diseases treatment. A proposed solution to overcome this challenge is to use computer models for rearranging the known data and related information to see how body parts interact with each other and then observe the final results.

The above-stated understanding of VPH may appear simple but developing an efficient and effective mathematical model for the accurate understanding of biological systems is a massively complicated task. For the purpose of overcoming problem involved, extensive research is required in knowing medical imaging and sensing technologies so that quantitative information is obtained regarding anatomy and physiology of a patient. To know the unknown information, it is imperative that all the available data should be processed. In the end, biomedical modeling is the reliable way to develop predictive models using known information with aid from computational skills and related engineering sciences for simplifying huge volumes of data.

Analyzing big data is vital in understanding of VPH applications and plays a key role in enabling this approach to handle complex issues in clinical applications. The purpose is better achieved if researchers working on big data devise appropriate methods in the field of computational biomedicine and propose problem solving methods to deal with emerging issues in the field. Moreover, a proposition to give a research platform for future needs is urgently needed.

Designing of clinical systems and their support is done very effectively when data mining procedures are used. The procedure has been found capable of finding the requisite non-obvious patterns and related relationships that are highly relevant in healthcare data. To analyze heart related issues, data mining techniques and their classification are in use in recent times. As a follow up, clustering data mining techniques of diverse nature are proposed for predicting the incidence of heart disease [32]. Of these techniques, k-mean, EM, and the farthest first algorithm are well known. The most important one among all the known algorithms is the farthest first algorithm with clustering properties.

Ramia et al. [33] aim to describe the intensity of acute pain felt by patients. The assessment involves patients' description of pain, management of pain, and to see whether patients are satisfied with their treatment procedures.

For the purpose of research, three medical centers in Lebanon were chosen and patients were to answer a questionnaire prepared on the basis of cross-sectional study. The period of study was between October 2014 and March 2015. Once answered, excel sheets were used to codify the patients' reply and analysis of data was done through SPSS version 21 software. Specific steps were taken not to mix up the data collected from different units thus assuring accuracy of records and simplifying the analysis procedures. All relevant variables such as demographic information, intensity of pain, and patients' reaction about pain management were summed up through descriptive statistical procedures.

The noteworthy fact is that cases of acute pain must be treated with extreme care in accordance with the expectation of patients. The quality of treatment requires proper assessment of pain following proper treatment procedures which includes complete patient participation. The intent is to administer treatment in a way that patients feel thoroughly satisfied. In cases where patients have been through surgery, the condition of pain before and after is a serious issue requiring special attention. There should be remedies to handle known issues in treatment of pains.

The major objective of the research in [34] is to see the effect of using big data in reducing problems of healthcare systems. The known issues in this regard include: accurate diagnosis, selection of correct treatment method, improving healthcare systems, and many more. The methods used provides general impressions about applying big data in healthcare and studying the challenges as well as opportunities involved in the usage of big data for public and private healthcare systems. The authors conclude that there are positive indications for applying big data to determine and solve healthcare issues for all interested parties. In fact, the use of big data by public or private healthcare systems can enable them to excel the health service provision. What is needed is the careful analysis of essentials.

Kononenko [35] present an outline of advances in the analysis of intelligent data especially where machines are involved. Such analyses are of concern where medical diagnosis has to be done. In historical perspective, the focus is on Bayesian classifier, neural networks and decision trees. Herein, a comparison of modern systems and various aspects of machine learning are given when emphasis is on medical diagnosis. Two case studies are illustrative of future tendencies. The first study depicts good prospects for analysis of intelligent data through a method showing consistent decisions by classifiers. With second study, the verification of complicated occurrences in complementary medicine through machine learning is attempted though there are reservations by medical community. However, in future, such an approach can be fruitful for diagnostic purposes.

4   The Proposed System and Its Architecture

In this section, we discuss our proposed system using its architecture depicted in Fig. 1. The system is composed of three layers: Big Data Computing layer, Data Integration layer, and Pain Management Strategy Improvement layer. These layers interact with the stakeholders and various databases to acquire and provide data and feedback related to pain management.

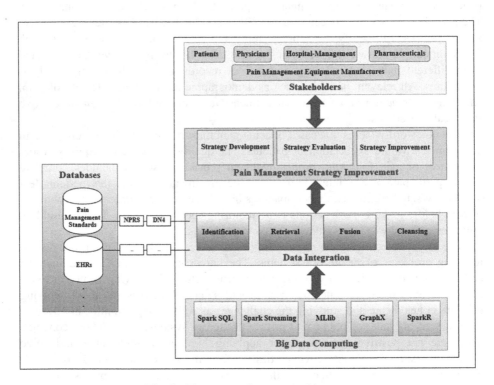

Fig. 1. The proposed system architecture.

The Big Data Computing layer comprises Apache Spark platform and tools. These include Spark SQL for performing SQL queries, Spark Streaming to enable live processing streams of data, MLlib which is a library of different machine learning algorithms, GraphX library to manipulate graphs and perform parallel computation, and SparkR that enables using spark within R. The Data Integration layer compromises of some components to identify and retrieve a suitable pain management strategy and do some data cleansing functions. The Pain Management Strategy Improvement layer focuses on developing strategies of pain management and considers any required improvement based on the evaluation process.

The system interacts with the various stakeholders to acquire and provide feedback about various pain management standards, strategies and processes. The stakeholders include pain management standards bodies, patients, physicians, hospital management, pharmaceuticals, manufacturers of pain management equipment, etc. The stakeholders could use the outcomes of the proposed systems to improve pain management standards, which then can become part of the proposed system databases. Additionally, the various databases that our system acquired data from include patient health records databases and pain management standards databases.

4.1 Improvements in Pain Management Standards, Strategies, and Processes

The system we propose here should have an evaluation criterion to measure the change in the effectiveness and efficiency in managing the pain. There are many ways to establish a criterion to measure this. We will discuss some ideas here. One way is to perform analysis on data about different types of methods for pain management, like DN4 and NPRS methodology. These types of comparative studies will provide a basis for many types of analyses with the proposed architecture.

With the proposed system, we are able to monitor the outcome for the changes in the pain management standards. The architecture allows the system to get new data as it arrives, as it imports data from different transactional data sources.

The evaluation mechanisms would be included in the system as workflows, which will communicate with the Big Data Computing Layer, Data Integration Layer, and the stakeholders. This will allow the developed analysis tests to be included automatically into the processes of evaluation of the architecture and system. The analysis provides the basis for the changes in the methodologies being applied to the pain management techniques. This way evaluation of the system can also be automated.

The usage of the apache spark layer also requires us to evaluate the performance of the system, the system can be evaluated on the basis of amount of data and value it generates from the analysis. The measurement of the pain score that the system generates can be elaborated by the health sector and uploaded into the Identification and Retrieval functions within the Data Integration Layer, from the pain management standards.

In summary, the system workflow for the evaluation and improvement of a pain management strategy can be summarized as follows. The system receives a patient for pain management. In addition to the current symptoms of the patient, the system acquires any data related to the patient, such as EHRs, from the associated databases. Based on the patient information and circumstances, the system identifies and retrieves an appropriate pain management strategy (including pain management standards) to be executed. The patient's condition is monitored and alternative strategies are used if the patient's condition does not improve. These strategies are selected and all decisions are made based on machine learning intelligence. The outcomes of the patient management workflows are updated in the databases resulting in the improvements of the pain management strategies. These outcomes are also made available to the stakeholders through textual and graphical interactive reports to allow discussion and improvements in the standards and processes for pain management.

5 System Analysis and Results

This section provides a preliminary analysis of the proposed system. We have collected some data related to pain management in both electronic forms and handwritten notes on paper. We converted the paper notes to digital form before the analysis.

One of the most important challenges that has hindered the implementation of the proposed architecture is that most of the patients' data that has been collected are paper documents. These data need to be digitized to fulfill the requirements of the proposed architecture. Some of the patients' information that will be considered as a pain management case includes *Case Number, History, Exam, Numeric Pain Score Before Treatment, Treatment,* and *Numeric Pain Score After Treatment.*

Table 1 shows statistics found from original data for few patients following with some descriptive charts. Column 1 in the table gives six different patient cases with different pain types. Columns 2 to 4 give details related to patients, their age, gender, and the effected body part. Columns 5 and 7 list the numeric pain score before and after the treatment. Column 6 gives the particular treatments offered to each patient such as Occipital nerve block for the first patient in the second row.

Figures 2, 3 and 4 depict patients pain related data in a graphical form. The aim here is to show that our proposed system can provide reports in tabular form and the visualization of data for quick insights. Figure 2 provides age and gender wise diseases distribution. The chart shows that the Males have major issues in their middle and lower body parts, as they grow older, while females in their 30's get lower body problems.

The chart in Fig. 3 shows that the oldest age people were involved in two major diseases cerebral facet join osteoarthritis and peripheral neuropathy. Chronic abdominal pain and Discogenic low back pain were the most common diseases found in middle-aged patients.

Figure 4 shows that the Numeric Pain Score after treatment was dramatically lower than the Numeric Pain Score before treatment. The remarkable downfall in the upper body and the middle body Numeric Pain Score can easily be seen. The decreased value in the lower body is also visibly low from the 7 points down to 2.

We have also used a sample of pain management data for Queensland Ambulance Service to reflect how big data analytics can benefit pain management field [36]. Figures 5, 6, and 7 depict the results from this data. The figures plot different types of patients that have used various pain management strategies and their responses against these strategies.

Table 1. A sample of pain management data

Case #	Age	Gender	Effected body part	Numeric Pain Score before treatment	Treatment	Numeric Pain Score after treatment
1- Occipital neuralgia.	45	Female	Upper body	9/10	Occipital nerve block	2/10
2- Cerebral facet join osteoarthritis	65	Male	Upper body	8-9/10	Nonsteroidal anti-inflammatory drugs (NSAIDs) - Celebrex 200 mg P.O B:D	3-4/10
3-Discogenic low back pain	38	Male	Middle body	10/10	- Lumbar Epidural - Steroid injection	3/10
4- Chronic abdominal pain	35	Female	Middle body	9/10	Celiac plexus block	0/10
5- Chest wall pain	52	Male	Middle body	10/10	- Intercostal nerve block - pregabalin 150 mg P.O B:D	3/10
6- Peripheral neuropathy	58	Male	Lower body	7-8/10	- Pregabalin 150 mg P.O B:D - Tramadol 50 mg P.O B:D	2/10

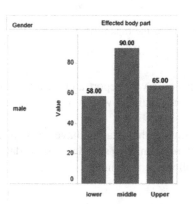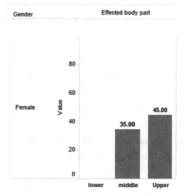

Fig. 2. Age/gender wise diseases distribution

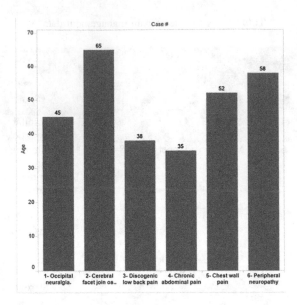

Fig. 3. Disease wise age statistics

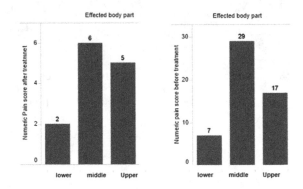

Fig. 4. Stats before and after the treatment

Figures 5 and 6 indicate proportion of patients who report a clinically meaningful decrease in pain rating, while Fig. 7 depict total patients with a lower last pain value than first recorded pain value.

For the future work, we are working to convert the data that have been collected to the digital format and use our Spark architecture to analyze such large-scale data, which will help to automate the process of data collection and analysis.

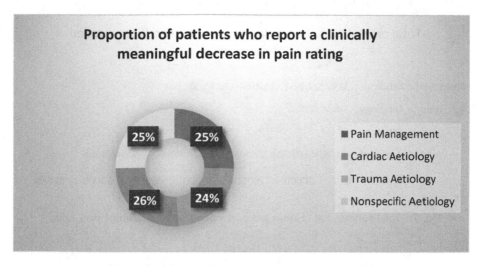

Fig. 5. Proportion of patients who report a clinically meaningful decrease in pain rating.

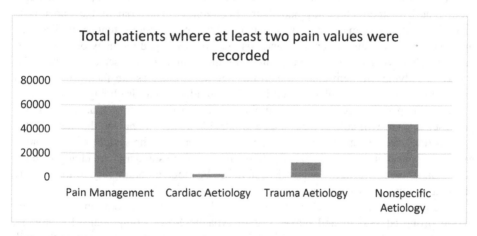

Fig. 6. Proportion of patients who report a clinically meaningful decrease in pain rating.

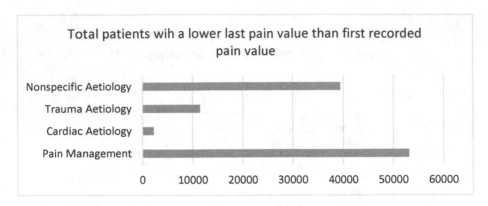

Fig. 7. Total patients with a lower last pain value than first recorded pain value.

6   Conclusion

The Proposed smart pain management system may provide insight into the management practices, their efficiency and their effectiveness. The goal of the paper is to provide smart way of managing patients' pain. The current systems that are in place can only provide pain management on standards that are developed by many organizations, but their effectiveness and efficiency cannot be monitored at microscales. We provides a way of solving problem that the pain management practices are facing in terms of data management and feedback handling. The standards that are being developed to manage the patient's pain are only limited to the patient record management, the proposed system will collect these data and provide a way to analyze this data so that the practices can be categorized and analyzed. Furthermore, the system will be able to monitor the change in the records of patients if any of the standards are changed in the pain management practices. This will enable the healthcare community to make more efficient standards for pain management.

The paper provides overview and details of the architectural components involved in the proposed system and makes use of Apache Spark components for storage, manipulation and analysis of data. In addition, it provides other components that will interact with external entities and Apache Spark to make use of the resources that are already under use in the healthcare industry.

To conclude, the system can provide a basis for testing the pain management standards and the results from the practice of these standards, and the data then can be analyzed in comparison with the standards and the results using large quantities of different types of data from different sources. The standards and practice are turned by the proposed system into strategies that can be tested and improved in real-time. The strategies and their outcomes are also made available to the stakeholders through textual and graphical interactive reports to allow informed discussion and improvements in the standards and processes for pain management. Future work will focus on a detailed implementation and analysis of the proposed system using real-life big data.

Acknowledgments. The work carried out in this paper is supported by the HPC Center at the King Abdulaziz University.

References

1. Philip Chen, C.L., Zhang, C.Y.: Data-intensive applications, challenges, techniques and technologies: a survey on Big Data. Inf. Sci. (Ny) **275**, 314–347 (2014)
2. Kechadi, M.-T.: M-Tahar: healthcare big data. In: Proceedings of the International Conference on Big Data and Advanced Wireless Technologies - BDAW 2016, p. 1. ACM Press, New York (2016)
3. Archenaa, J., Anita, E.A.M.: A survey of big data analytics in healthcare and government. Procedia Comput. Sci. **50**, 408–413 (2015)
4. Chute, C.G., Ullman-Cullere, M., Wood, G.M., Lin, S.M., He, M., Pathak, J.: Some experiences and opportunities for big data in translational research. Genet. Med. **15**, 802–809 (2013)
5. Dai, L., Gao, X., Guo, Y., Xiao, J.: Bioinformatics clouds for big data manipulation. Biol. Direct **7**, 43 (2012)
6. Marx, V.: Biology: the big challenges of big data. Nature **498**, 255–260 (2013)
7. O'Driscoll, A., Daugelaite, J., Sleator, R.: "Big data", Hadoop and cloud computing in genomics. J. Biomed. Inf. **46**, 774–781 (2013)
8. Murdoch, T., Detsky, A.: The inevitable application of big data to health care. JAMA **309**, 1351–1352 (2013)
9. Raghupathi, W., Raghupathi, V.: Big data analytics in healthcare: promise and potential. Heal. Inf. Sci. Syst. **2**, 3 (2014)
10. Bates, D., Saria, S., Ohno-Machado, L., Shah, A.: Big data in health care: using analytics to identify and manage high-risk and high-cost patients. Heal. Aff. **33**, 1123–1131 (2014)
11. Hsu, W., Markey, M., Wang, M.: Biomedical imaging informatics in the era of precision medicine: progress, challenges, and opportunities (2013). https://academic.oup.com/jamia/article-abstract/20/6/1010/2909178
12. Clark, K., Vendt, B., Smith, K., Freymann, J., Kirby, J.: The Cancer Imaging Archive (TCIA): maintaining and operating a public information repository. J. Digit. **26**, 1045–1057 (2013)
13. Banaee, H., Ahmed, M., Loutfi, A.: Data mining for wearable sensors in health monitoring systems: a review of recent trends and challenges. Sensors **13**, 17472–17500 (2013)
14. Da Xu, L., He, W., Li, S.: Internet of things in industries: a survey. IEEE Trans. Ind. Inf. **10**(4), 2233–2243 (2014). https://doi.org/10.1109/TII.2014.2300753
15. Mehmood, R., Faisal, M.A., Altowaijri, S.: Future networked healthcare systems: a review and case study. In: Information Resources Management Association (ed.) Big Data: Concepts, Methodologies, Tools, and Applications, pp. 2429–2457. IGI Global (2016)
16. Chen, M., Mao, S., Liu, Y.: Big data: a survey. Mob. Netw. Appl. **19**, 171–209 (2014)
17. Altowaijri, S., Mehmood, R., Williams, J.: A quantitative model of grid systems performance in healthcare organisations. In: ISMS 2010 - UKSim/AMSS 1st International Conference on Intelligent Systems, Modelling and Simulation, pp. 431–436 (2010)
18. Tawalbeh, L.A., Mehmood, R., Benkhlifa, E., Song, H.: Mobile cloud computing model and big data analysis for healthcare applications. IEEE Access. **4**, 6171–6180 (2016)
19. Tawalbeh, L.A., Bakhader, W., Mehmood, R., Song, H.: Cloudlet-based mobile cloud computing for healthcare applications. In: 2016 IEEE Global Communications Conference (GLOBECOM), pp. 1–6. IEEE (2016)

20. Zhang, J., Zhang, Y., Hu, Q., Tian, H., Xing, C.: A big data analysis platform for healthcare on apache spark. Presented at the 24 December (2017)
21. Mehmood, R., Graham, G.: Big data logistics: a health-care transport capacity sharing model. Procedia Comput. Sci. **64**, 1107–1114 (2015)
22. FDA Education Blueprint for Health Care Providers Involved in the Management or Support of Patients with Pain Section 1: The Basics of Pain Management I. DEFINITIONS AND MECHANISMS OF PAIN Section 2: Creating the Pain Treatment Plan (2017)
23. The DN4 Questionnaire – GHNHSFT. http://www.gloshospitals.nhs.uk/en/Wards-and-Departments/Departments/Pain-Management/Different-Pains/Nerve-Pain/Assessment-of-Nerve-Pain/DN4-Draft/
24. Numeric Pain Rating Scale – Physiopedia. http://www.physio-pedia.com/Numeric_Pain_Rating_Scale
25. Wu, P., Cheng, C., Kaddi, C.: Omic and electronic health record big data analytics for precision medicine. IEEE Trans. **64**, 263–273 (2017)
26. Fernald, G., Capriotti, E., et al.: Bioinformatics challenges for personalized medicine. Academic.Oup.Com (2011). https://academic.oup.com/bioinformatics/article-abstract/27/13/1741/186256
27. Hood, L., Friend, S.: Predictive, personalized, preventive, participatory (P4) cancer medicine. Nat. Rev. Clin. Oncol. **8**, 444 (2011)
28. NR Council: Toward precision medicine: building a knowledge network for biomedical research and a new taxonomy of disease (2011)
29. Katsnelson, A.: Momentum grows to make 'personalized' medicine more 'precise' (2013)
30. Mirnezami, R., Nicholson, J., Darzi, A.: Preparing for precision medicine. Engl. J. Med. **366**, 489–491 (2012)
31. Viceconti, M., Hunter, P., Hose, R.: Big data, big knowledge: big data for personalized healthcare. IEEE J. Biomed. Heal. Inf. **19**, 1209–1215 (2015)
32. Singla, M., Singh, K.: Heart disease prediction system using data mining clustering techniques. Int. J. Comput. Appl. **136**, 975–8887 (2016)
33. Ramia, E., Nasser, S.C., Salameh, P., Saad, A.H.: Patient perception of acute pain management: data from three tertiary care hospitals. Pain Res. Manag. **2017**, 1–12 (2017)
34. Jee, K., Kim, G.-H.: Potentiality of big data in the medical sector: focus on how to reshape the healthcare system. Heal. Inf. Res. **19**, 79–85 (2013)
35. Kononenko, I.: Machine learning for medical diagnosis: history, state of the art and perspective. Artif. Intell. Med. **23**(1), 89–109 (2001). https://doi.org/10.1016/S0933-3657(01)00077-X
36. Queensland Ambulance Service Pain Management Data - Queensland Ambulance Service Pain Management Data | Data | Queensland Government. https://data.qld.gov.au/dataset/queensland-ambulance-service-pain-management-data/resource/e3372ccf-3a2c-469f-a8d5-0562b43b840b

Towards a Semantically Enriched Computational Intelligence (SECI) Framework for Smart Farming

Aasia Khanum[1(✉)], Atif Alvi[1], and Rashid Mehmood[2]

[1] Department of Computer Science, Forman Christian College (A Chartered University), Lahore, Pakistan
{aasiakhanum,atifalvi}@fccollege.edu.pk
[2] High Performance Computing Center, King Abdul Aziz University, Jeddah, Saudi Arabia
RMehmood@kau.edu.sa

Abstract. This paper advocates the use of Semantically Enriched Computational Intelligence (SECI) for managing the complex tasks of smart farming. Specifically, it proposes ontology-based Fuzzy Logic for dealing with inherent imprecisions and vagueness in the domain of smart farming. The paper highlights various characteristics of SECI that make it a suitable computational technique for smart farming. It also discusses a few aspects out of the huge number of possible applications in smart farming that we are planning to implement with the help of SECI. Further, it shares in detail the implementation and some preliminary results obtained by applying SECI to one specific aspect of smart farming.

Keywords: Smart farming · SECI · Intelligent agriculture · Knowledge-based agriculture

1 Introduction

Smart Farming (SF) is based on the idea of harnessing Information and Communication Technologies (ICT) for improving the efficiency, productivity, and efficacy of agricultural operations. SF has several aspects with the most important being smart sensing, smart planning/analysis, and smart control. Smart sensing employs advanced sensing technologies to obtain accurate and up-to-date information on soil and climatic conditions in a crop field. Smart planning/analysis uses data analytic and predictive tools for making optimal decisions depending on actual data obtained from the field. Smart control refers to reconfiguration of smart sensing devices on the field depending on real time data. A number of technologies act as enablers of SF including Internet of Things (IoT), Big Data, robots, drones, and Cloud Computing among others.

Computational Intelligence (CI) deals with representation and reasoning schemes for domains where accurate models are not feasible. Examples of CI techniques are Artificial Neural Networks (ANN), Fuzzy Logic (FL), Case Based Reasoning (CBR) and Genetic Algorithms (GA). These techniques aim at making optimal

© ICST Institute for Computer Sciences, Social Informatics and Telecommunications Engineering 2018
R. Mehmood et al. (Eds.): SCITA 2017, LNICST 224, pp. 247–257, 2018.
https://doi.org/10.1007/978-3-319-94180-6_24

decisions in face of problems that are not precisely defined and where the search space is so large that any optimal decision is as good as the best but elusive decision. Agriculture is one such field where quantitative modeling is not possible due to the huge number of parameters related to climate, temperature, soil, humidity, crop appearance etc. There are complex interactions between the parameters which are difficult for analytical reasoning. Many of the parameters are qualitative in nature e.g. crop color, pest size etc. Due to this, the parameters do not take on a crisp definite value in a decision situation. For example, not all leaves that are brown are diseased, but sometimes this color maybe a warning sign of disease. Moreover, as SF becomes available at scale, the sheer number of parameters for decision-making becomes non-trivial. Managing SF with large number of parameters can benefit a lot from linguistic reasoning techniques offered by CI. Data representation in qualitative, relative terms also makes sense because the data in real time is also continuously changing due to the dynamic nature of agriculture domain.

Agricultural scientists and experts, through years of experience, have accumulated reserves of heuristic knowledge that has shown to get results in face of vague and incomplete data. This knowledge ought to be part of any smart solution, but is difficult to model mathematically. A knowledge-base and computable ontology is the most appropriate tool to encapsulate such semantically rich, qualitative knowledge.

This paper proposes the novel idea of using a specialized branch of CI, namely Fuzzy Logic (FL) in combination with semantically representative ontology for smart farm management. FL comes in as a strong technique because we need to make inferentially strong decisions in presence of approximate data and relying on expert knowledge. This expert knowledge gets its expression in the form of a semantic ontology. The link between expert knowledge and inference framework is established by defining computable mappings between semantic terminology and computable features in the domain.

This paper has three primary contributions:

- It proposes a novel Fuzzy Logic based SECI framework for smart farming.
- It discusses attributes of SECI that make it applicable to various dimensions of smart farming.
- It describes three possible applications of SECI in smart farming that we are planning to implement and explains one of these application in detail.

Rest of this paper is organized as follows. Section 2 is a brief introduction to various CI and semantics technologies. Section 3 is the literature review. Section 4 gives some possible applications of SECI in smart farming. Section 5 covers the application that we are currently working on. Section 6 presents the experimental setup and results. Finally, Sect. 7 concludes the paper with options for future work.

2   Computational Intelligence and Semantic Technologies

Here we give a brief introduction to the CI and Semantic technologies directly relevant to our work:

2.1   Fuzzy Sets

A fuzzy set [14] allows for graded membership of its elements. A fuzzy set A is defined as: $A = \{\mu_A(x)|x \in X\}$ where $\mu_A(x)$ is the membership function for any $x \in X$, X is the domain of discourse and $\mu_A(x) : X \rightarrow [0, 1]$. The essential characteristic of Fuzzy Sets is the absence of sharp boundaries between members and non-members of the set which is not possible in classical set theory.

2.2   Fuzzy Logic (FL) and Fuzzy Rule Based Systems (FRBS)

Fuzzy Logic is an extension of classic Boolean logic with provision for graded truth values. FL is used to make inference where exact modeling of the domain is not possible due to imperfect knowledge or imperfect measurement of domain parameters. It allows to reason with qualitative and approximate data by making use of linguistic variables and approximate reasoning. Linguistic variables employ fuzzy sets to represent linguistic terms like hot, cold, humid etc. An FRBS uses linguistic variables belonging to the domain of discourse in the form of fuzzy if-then rules to make inferences. A typical fuzzy rule looks like:

$$if \langle fuzzy\, proposition\, with\, linguistic\, variables \rangle\, then\, \langle \begin{array}{c} fuzzy\, proposition \\ with\, linguistic\, variables \end{array} \rangle$$

During fuzzy inference the fuzzified input is provided to all rules in the FRBS. As a consequence, various rule "fire" up to various degrees depending on the degree to which their antecedents match the input fuzzy data. The output from all the fired rules is aggregated using aggregation operators to obtain the final output, which may then be defuzzified using various defuzzification operators.

2.3   Ontologies

An ontology in Computer Science is a tool for expressing knowledge about a concept or a domain. Ontologies provide a convenient formalism for expressing concepts of the domain and their inter-relationships. They are a powerful tool for creating knowledge based systems.

3   Literature Review

Smart Farming is increasingly gaining importance as a research area. Several papers have discussed the application of CI in agriculture. Here we are discussing only the representative ones according to the approach used. We would like to mention that to the best of our knowledge no paper has discussed the use SECI as an integration of FL and semantics so far.

Many papers describe approaches using computationally intensive techniques relying image data. For instance, in [1] a series of deep convolutional neural networks (CNN) is used to estimate disease severity from plant images. Likewise, in [6] CNN is used to classify disease types from leaf images. The deep learning systems are reliant on a large set of annotated images for its learning and tuning. There is no feature engineering, so the system results are difficult to interpret.

In [2] a fitness function based metaheuristic approach is used to adjust the amount of pest control spray based on predicting the weather conditions impacting deposition.

Neural Networks as a CI technique have been used in a number of smart farming use cases including yield prediction [3] and site specific herbicide management (SSHM) [4]. The black box nature of neural networks however precludes their use as expert knowledge representation.

In [5] the authors present a decision-making framework for aquaculture sites using Case Based Reasoning (CBR). The system utilizes sensor based data to make semantic inferences about conditions and operations related to fish farming.

Flourish [7] is a European Union (EU) project that uses CI in the form of decision trees to coordinate smart farming actions between Unmanned Air Vehicle (UAV) fitted sensors and ground based Unmanned Ground Vehicle (UGV) mounted actuators.

4   Possible Applications of SECI in Smart Farming

Here we are discussing various applications of SECI in smart farming that we are exploring at present.

4.1   SECI in Smart Sensing and Monitoring

Smart sensing and monitoring ensures that the crop is always under surveillance and any change in field parameters is effectively responded to. Natural conditions for various hazardous situations are not precisely defined. For instance, different stages of a foliar disease may show multiple symptoms on different plants. The color and distribution of disease spots may be similar across different pathologies. Since a clear demarcation of deciding parameters and their values is not possible, CI techniques can help in establishing frameworks for representation of seemingly disparate data. A number of CI techniques have in fact been employed for smart sensing of agriculture, e.g. [10]. These frameworks can be further strengthened by integrating with semantic knowledge about the specific application domain. Work is being done on agricultural ontologies e.g. AGROVOC by Food and Agriculture Organization (FAO) [11] and GRIN ontology by US Department of Agriculture (USDA) [12]. However, work is needed to integrate these ontologies/thesauri with computable frameworks.

4.2   SECI in Smart Planning/Analysis

This aspect is concerned with setting objectives for quantity, quality, and timing etc. of farm inputs. It is also concerned with measuring actual behavior against planned one, and initiating appropriate interventions if needed. An SECI based farm manager can maintain objectives, as well as rules regarding control adaptation in case of divergences between anticipated and observed conditions. Beyond the production, SECI can also be used to maximize marketing profits from crop [13]. We anticipate semantically enriched Fuzzy Logic based smart planners for optimal balancing of all resources against performance objectives.

4.3 SECI in Smart Control

Smart Farming is increasingly reliant on large amounts of data from disparate sources. Sudden changes in weather conditions or disease alerts demand intelligent and agile adaptation on part of farm control [9]. SECI can be used effectively for rapid reconfiguration of smart devices based on agile composition and analysis of real time data. We anticipate the use of SECI techniques in representing context-sensitive response to such changes in operational conditions. Since a lot of decision parameters may be involved requiring different responses in different contexts it will be efficient to coalesce seemingly separate but logically similar decision boundaries to economize on computational resource for control and management decisions.

5   SECI in Smart Sensing and Monitoring

Smart sensing and monitoring ensures that the farm conditions are properly monitored to avoid any hazard to crop, e.g. to protect against pest and pathogen attacks. Crop diseases are a major reason for agricultural under-productivity, especially in underdeveloped countries where knowledge barriers further hinder the framers from timely and accurate detection of disease. Accurate disease detection is crucial for correct management action on part of the farmer. Disease detection and classification however is a complicated challenge due to non-specificity of disease symptoms. It is known that many symptoms are common to multiple diseases. Likewise, a single disease may exhibit multiple variations of symptoms in various cases. Human experts do not face great difficulty in identifying the diseases if visiting the fields; however, the presence of an expert on field is not always possible. We are developing an SECI based disease classification framework where which can replace the human expert for disease classification in-situ. The framework works on cheap sensor-based images of the crop parts to intelligently classify the disease. Due to space constraints, we are describing here only part of the system that identifies leaf diseases. The framework is built around two primary parts: (1) an ontology of visually perceptible (phenotype) features used by experts for diagnosing a disease (Fig. 1) and (2) a classifier that maps the computable representations of ontology features to disease (Fig. 2).

The purpose of ontology is to map sensor based image features to the features employed by experts in identifying diseases. As shown in Fig. 1 the phenotype ontology is divided into three levels; each disease at the top level is expressed as a pattern of phenotype attributes at the intermediate or semantic level. We divide these phenotype attributes into categories as shown in Table 1.

At the lowest level of ontology are sensor generated features that pass through various Digital Image Processing (DIP) procedures (not discussed here). As shown in Table 2 these features are quantitative and numeric by nature e.g. intensity, hue, entropy etc. The innovative aspect about our approach is how we map these features to

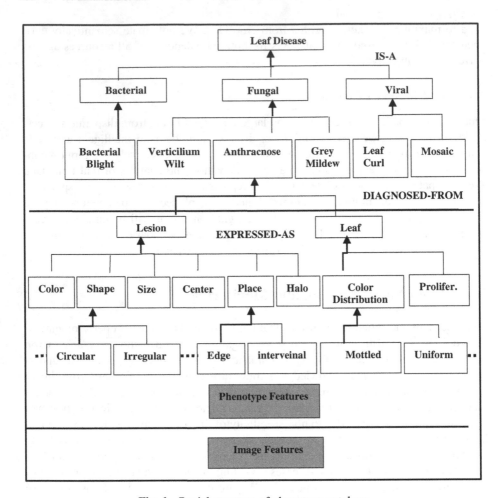

Fig. 1. Partial structure of phenotype ontology

knowledge-based semantic features in the disease ontology. At the next higher level lies the phenotype layer which represents semantic description of disease as understood by the experts. The joint contribution of phenotype expressions leads to inference of a specific disease as expressed by top layer in the ontology.

The classifier takes as input a collection of leaf lesions detected through DIP techniques. First the lesion extraction module executes, giving as output all potential candidates or disease lesions. An image is represented as $x = \{v_1, v_2, v_3, ..., v_N\}$ where N is the number of potential lesions detected. For disease classification, each potential lesion is represented by a feature vector $v_i = \{f_1, f_2, f_3, ..., f_M\}$ where $i = 1, 2, ..., N$.

We model the lesion classes using a proposed hybrid of state of the art classifiers including Logistic Regression Model and Fuzzy Rule Based classifier. First, the image features are mapped to semantic categories using a Multinomial regression model. The

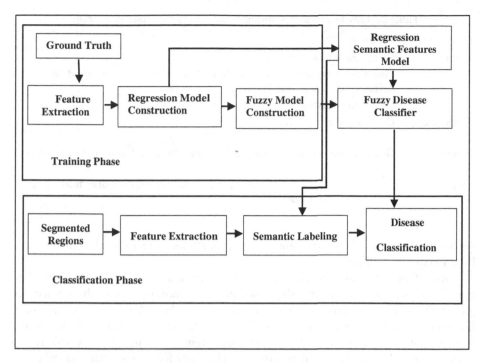

Fig. 2. Classifier architecture

Table 1. Semantic features for disease identification

Category	Phenotype	Possible values
Lesion	Color	{Yellow, green, brown, black, gray, white, purple}
	Size	{Small, medium, large}
	Shape	{Round, polygonal, complex}
	Center structure	{Water-soaked, Sunken, raised}
	Place	{Edge-neighboring, vein-neighboring}
	Halo	{Present, absent}
Leaf	Proliferation	{Dense, sparse}
	Color distribution	{Mottled, Uniform}

output of this model is then used as input to a Fuzzy Rule Based System (FRBS) classifier to decide the disease based on the semantic categories.

We use a Multinomial Logistic Regression (MLR) at first stage of our classification process. Logistic Regression is an extension of ordinary regression with allowance of categorical and ordinal variables as dependent variable. MLR can be used to model dependence on any number of ordinal, continuous, or categorical variables. Since the semantic categories in our framework are categorical in nature, we model them with help of MLR. The MLR model assigns probabilities to each of the semantic classes on

Table 2. Low level features obtained through digital image processing

Category	Phenotype
Color	Global color histogram
	First 4 moments for each channel in HSV color space (mean, standard deviation, skewness, and kurtosis)
	Global color histogram
Shape and size	Centroid, area, perimeter
Statistical	GLCM features (energy, contrast, homogeneity, correlation) at 4 different offsets
Transform	Gabor wavelet responses: mean and standard deviation of Gabor features in 4 orientations and 3 scales

the basis of calculated image features. The probabilities are forwarded to the next FRBS classifier as input.

First of all, the semantic class probability values are fuzzified with help of a fuzzifier on basis of fuzzy membership functions of the form $\mu_F(c)$ such that c is a crisp probability value, F is a fuzzy set and $\mu_F(c) : c \rightarrow [0, 1]$. We use Gaussian membership functions for fuzzification. All fuzzy linguistic variables corresponding to each specific semantic category are processed by an Inference Engine, working on Fuzzy Rule Base, to deduce membership values of all diseases. The rules for disease detection take the form:

$$Ru^l : IF\ S_1\ is\ s_1^l\ AND\ S_2\ is\ s_2^l\ AND\ \dots\ S_n\ is\ s_n^l\ THEN$$
$$D_1\ is\ d_1^l\ AND\ D_2\ is\ d_2^l\ AND\ \dots\ D_m\ is\ d_m^l$$

where l is the rule index.

There are M rules with K input parameters, each divided into a number of fuzzy terms. Likewise, m output variables are used to express the disease, represented by Gaussian membership functions of the form:

$$\mu_F(c) = \frac{1}{\sigma\sqrt{2\pi}} e^{-\frac{1}{2}\left(\frac{c-\bar{c}}{\sigma}\right)^2}$$

where σ and $\bar{c}$ are standard deviation and mean respectively.

We measure the degree of relevance of each rule to possible diseases using the AND-rule:

$$\mu_{Ru^l}(.) = \mu_{S_1}(.) \cap \mu_{S_2}(.) \dots \cap \mu_{S_n}(.)$$

where $\cap$ is a t-norm and (.) denotes the semantic categories. We interpret t-norm operation as min operation, i.e.:

$$\mu_{Ru^i}(.) = \min[\mu_{S_1}(.), \mu_{S_2}(.), \ldots, \mu_{S_n}(.)]$$

We use fuzzy implication operator to determine the firing strength each rule. The implication process yields a fuzzy vector with diseases Di, truncated at $\mu_{Ru^i}(.)$. All rule outputs are aggregated using Mamdani's combination. This yields a fuzzy membership vector: $s = [s_1, s_2, \ldots, s_n]$ in which the entries indicate the degree of membership of each of the n diseases. The membership function for each disease is defuzzified to yield a single membership score for that disease. We use a Center Average (COA) method for defuzzification:

$$o = \frac{\sum_{m=1}^{M} c^m w^m}{\sum_{m=1}^{M} w^m}$$

where o is the output crisp value, M is the number of output fuzzy sets being aggregated, c^m is the center of mth output fuzzy set and w^m is the height of mth output fuzzy set.

The above modeling framework makes it possible to map any combination of image features to corresponding diseases in a manner consistent to expert knowledge.

6 Experimental Setup and Results

The SECI based disease classification system is flexible and can accommodate any number of diseases and features. Currently we have implemented it for three diseases of the cotton leaf: Bacterial Blight, Anthracnose and Verticillium Wilt. Anthracnose is a

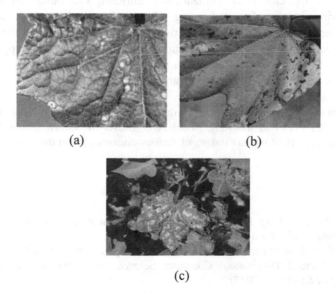

(a)   (b)

(c)

Fig. 3. (a) Anthracnose (b) Bacterial Blight (c) Verticillium Wilt (Color figure online)

fungal disease that appears as pinkish spots on leaf surface. Areas around veins turn yellow to brown and eventually die out. Bacterial blight starts as scattered small dark green translucent spots on under surface of the leaf. Gradually the spots turn dark brown to black, enlarge and appear on the upper surface as well. The spots also become angular in shape due to veination on the leaf. In case of Verticillium Wilt the leaves develop a characteristic yellow (diffuse or angular) mottle on the edges and around veins. Eventually tissue on the leaf edges may die down and replace the mottle as a dark brown border. Figure 3 shows an example of each disease.

The system is implemented using MATLAB 2015 on an Intel i5 processor. There are 50 images of each kind of disease in the dataset. In Table 3 we present the results of classification using average accuracy over 3-fold cross-validation. It can be seen that the use of more informative features improves accuracy of the system.

Table 3. Experimental results

Feature based accuracy (%)	Accuracy (%)
Color	83
Size	46
Shape	66
Distribution	64
Color, size, shape, and distribution	94

7   Conclusions and Future Work

Smart Farming involves complex data processing and decision making. We have discussed three applications of Semantically Enriched Computational Intelligence (SECI) to various aspects of smart farming. We also discussed one of the applications that we are currently implementing. Experimental results indicate that the idea holds promise and can be explored further. In future, we will explore other applications of SECI in smart farming as discussed in this paper. We will also experiment with other CI approaches in semantically enriched frameworks for agriculture.

Acknowledgments. The work presented in this paper is supported by High Performance Computing (HPC) Center at the King Abdul Aziz University Jeddah (Saudi Arabia). We acknowledge all sources of internet images of various diseases used in this study.

References

1. Wang, G., Sun, Y., Wang, J.: Automatic image-based plant disease severity estimation using deep learning. Comput. Intell. Neurosci. (2017)
2. Faical, B.S.: The use of computational intelligence for precision spraying of plant protection products. Doctoral Dissertation, Computer Science and Computational Mathematics, University of Sau Paolo (2017)

3. Baral, S., Kumar Tripathy, A., Bijayasingh, P.: Yield prediction using artificial neural networks. In: Das, V.V., Stephen, J., Chaba, Y. (eds.) CNC 2011. CCIS, vol. 142, pp. 315–317. Springer, Heidelberg (2011). https://doi.org/10.1007/978-3-642-19542-6_57

4. Eddy, P., Smith, A.M., Hill, B.D., Peddle, D.R., Coburn, C.A., Blackshaw, R.E.: Hybrid segmentation – artificial neural network classification of high resolution hyperspectral imagery for site-specific herbicide management in agriculture. Photogramm. Eng. Remote Sens. **74**, 1249–1257 (2008)

5. Tidemann, A., Bjørnson, F.O., Aamodt, A.: Operational support in fish farming through case-based reasoning. In: Jiang, H., Ding, W., Ali, M., Wu, X. (eds.) IEA/AIE 2012. LNCS (LNAI), vol. 7345, pp. 104–113. Springer, Heidelberg (2012). https://doi.org/10.1007/978-3-642-31087-4_12

6. Sladojevic, S., Arsenovic, M., Anderla, A., Culibrk, D., Stefanovic, D.: Deep neural networks based recognition of plant diseases by leaf image classification. Comput. Intell. Neurosci. (2016)

7. Liebisch, F., Pfeifer, J., Khanna, R., Lottes, P., Stachniss, C., Falck, T., Sander, S., Siegwart, R., Walter, A., Galceran, E.: Flourish – a robotic approach for automation in crop management. In: Workshop Computer-Bildanalyse und Unbemannte autonom fliegende Systeme in der Landwirtschaft, at Wernigerrode, Volume: Bornimer Agrartechnische Berichte (2016)

8. Anwer, F., Azeem, R., Alvi, A., Khanum, A.: A framework for interpreting crop leaf lesions in tele-agriculture. In: Multi-Disciplinary Student Research Conference (MDSRC) (2015)

9. Wolfert, S., Goense, D., Sorensen, C.G.: A future internet collaboration platform for safe and healthy food from farm to fork. In: Annual SRII Global Conference (SRII) (2014)

10. Mustafa, N.B., Ahmed, S.K., Ali, Z., Yit, W.B., Abidin, A.A.Z., Sharrif, Z.A.: Agricultural produce sorting and grading using support vector machines and fuzzy logic. In: IEEE International Conference on Signal and Image Processing Applications (2009)

11. http://aims.fao.org/vest-registry/vocabularies/agrovoc-multilingual-agricultural-thesaurus. Accessed Sept 2017

12. https://data.nal.usda.gov/dataset/germplasm-resources-information-network-grin_140. Accessed Sept 2017

13. Wolfert, S., Ge, L., Verdouwa, C., Bogaardt, M.: Big data in smart farming – a review. Agric. Syst. **153**, 69–80 (2017)

14. Zadeh, L.A.: Fuzzy sets. Inf. Control **8**(3), 338–353 (1965)

Towards a Mobile Cloud Framework for First Responder Teams in Smart Emergency Management

Aakash Ahmad[1($\boxtimes$)], Numra Saeed[2], Ahmed B. Altamimi[1],
and Abdulrahman Alreshidi[1]

[1] College of Computer Science and Engineering, University of Ha'il,
Ha'il, Saudi Arabia
{a.abbasi,altamimi.a,ab.alreshidi}@uoh.edu.sa
[2] School of Electrical Engineering and Computer Science, NUST,
Islamabad, Pakistan
14msitnsaeed@seecs.edu.pk

Abstract. Smart city systems integrate multiple information and communication technologies (ICTs) to enhance the efficiency of urban services and quality of citizen's life while decreasing operational costs and efforts. To manage smart city infrastructure, Mobile Cloud Computing (MCC) has emerged as a disruptive technology that facilitates its users to exploit portable and context-aware computation with pay-per-use software/hardware resources. We propose to exploit the MCC technologies to develop a framework that facilitates first responder teams to operate smartly in emergency situations.

Keywords: Smart infrastructure · Mobile cloud system · Software engineering

1 Introduction

In recent years, smart city systems have emerged as solutions that transform the conventional cities and societies into information and communication (ICT) driven metropoles [1]. Smart city systems offer improved and digitized urban services such as smart health, transportation and emergency management to the stakeholders and empowers citizens, public administration and organizations to utilize such services efficiently and cost-effectively [1, 2]. Mobile Cloud Computing (MCC) represents the state-of-the-art mobile computing technology that exploits mobility and context-awareness to support the operations and infrastructure of smart cities based on portable computation and location-aware communication [3]. In smart cities, disaster and emergency management needs an effective coordination and mobilization of the first responder teams to respond to the catastrophic scenarios in a smart way [4, 5].

First responder teams refer to a group of people who are responsible for providing services and operations in case of emergency scenarios such as fire fighters, emergency medical paramedics or rescue workers [5]. For a successful completion of their tasks, the individuals in the first responder team needs to establish an effective coordination and task allocation among them [6]. In this paper, we propose a framework that

© ICST Institute for Computer Sciences, Social Informatics and Telecommunications Engineering 2018
R. Mehmood et al. (Eds.): SCITA 2017, LNICST 224, pp. 258–263, 2018.
https://doi.org/10.1007/978-3-319-94180-6_25

facilitates and empowers first responder teams to operate and coordinate efficiently in different emergency situations. The proposed framework utilizes the MCC technologies as the unification of mobile and cloud computing can benefit from the mobility and context awareness (of mobile computing) and the computation and storage services (of cloud computing) to provide systems that are portable, yet resource sufficient [5].

Framework Overview: Our proposed framework consists of two main layers namely mobile computing layer and cloud computing layer as illustrated in Fig. 1. Cloud computing layer is used for data storage and computation of data intensive task – referred to as machine centric layer. Mobile computing layer utilizes the services of mobile device such as context awareness and mobility services to capture and share contextual information of an emergency scenario. Mobile computing layer acts as the interface for the first responder teams – referred to as human centric layer. Mobile and cloud layer communicate with each via the network connectivity that has challenges such as latency and availability of communication between the layers [11].

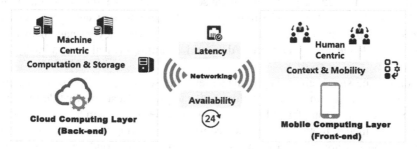

Fig. 1. A layered representation of the proposed framework.

Assumptions and Contributions: Our solution is based on assumptions of high network availability to maintain an effective coordination between the first responder teams. Moreover, a secure public or private cloud server and resource efficient mobile devices are central to the framework. We highlight the primary contributions as:

- *Unification of Mobile and Cloud Computing* technologies to enable first responder teams for emergency management in smart city context. The proposed solution aims at timely application and acquisition of the contextual information to facilitate collaborative activities of the first responders in emergency management.
- *Smart City Infrastructure* is specifically focused based on provisioning of emergency services. In contrast to [8, 9], the proposed solution utilizes mobility but also combines the cloud computing that facilitates a cost-effective implementation of ICT infrastructure for emergency management in smart city context.

The rest of the paper is organized as follows. Related research is presented in Sect. 2. Framework architecture and its implementation plan are presented in Sect. 3. Conclusions and dimensions of future research are discussed in Sect. 4.

2 Related Research

In this section, first we present some of the relevant research on event management in smart city systems (Sect. 2.1) that follows a discussion of the platform for first responder teams (Sect. 2.2). Highlighting the most relevant research justifies our proposed contribution and helps us to define the scope of our presented framework.

2.1 Event Management in Smart City Systems

Event management such as disaster recovery, traffic planning and emergency handling are becoming commonplace in smart city systems. Specifically, in [7] the authors proposed a critical infrastructure response framework for Smart cities. This research highlights the needs to gather real-time information from different urban services (e.g.; firefighting, surveillance and monitoring) within the city environment to make right decisions in critical situations. The proposed framework aims to provide a response approach to first responders based on the flows of information in smart cities and support efficient and timely responses in critical scenarios. The role of cloud computing is vital in managing smart city infrastructure. In [4], the proposed emergency event management system controls the coordination between emergency management and local first responder teams by collecting data and handling critical events easily in smart cites.

Considering the smart emergency management, the studies [8, 9] proposed emergency management platforms. These platforms aim to provide a support while making decision in critical situations for public protection via the use of wireless sensor networks and social media. In smart emergency context, considering the research state-of-the-art, we propose a novel approach by unifying mobile and cloud computing. The benefit of our proposed approach is to empower the first responder teams with mobile and context-aware infrastructure that lacks in the existing research.

2.2 Platform for First Responder Teams

To support platforms for the first responder teams, some of the recent research have focused on the simulation and experimental training of the first responder teams. Specifically, the research in [5] provides a simulated environment (as virtual reality) to simulate a medical emergency case where a critical thinking is needed for the right response by the team. Similarly, the authors in [6] conducted an experiment to allow first responders including police officers to securely access the information in a mobility-driven environment. It is vital to mention about the studies [7, 8] that exploit mobile and service oriented computing respectively to empower first responder teams to be aware of critical emergency scenarios and coordinate effectively as a team.

Our proposed solution advances the research state-of-the-art by unifying mobile and cloud computing technologies for smart emergency management. In our solution, mobile cloud computing is exploited as state-of-the-art mobile computing technology. Our proposal compensates for resource poverty of a mobile device by offloading computation and memory intensive tasks to back-end cloud servers – maintain system's efficiency for first responder teams.

3   Architecture and Implementation of the Framework

First, we present the architectural overview (in Sect. 3.1) and then discuss the proposed implementation of the framework (in Sect. 3.2).

3.1   Layered Architectural View for the Proposed Framework

A. Front-End – Context-Aware Mobile Computing Layer

As the bottom layer of the solution that supports the operations of the on-field activities by the first responder teams as in Fig. 2. The layers support the interaction and orchestration of the mobile devices (coordinator to peer setup) to communicate and share the context specific information in a given emergency management scenario. This layer acts as a context sensitive user interface that allows the human driven first responder teams to capture, process and share the information from the emergency scene. From a technical point of view, this layer consists of a number of software services that exploits a mobile device to enable the interaction of the emergency management workers in the first responder teams.

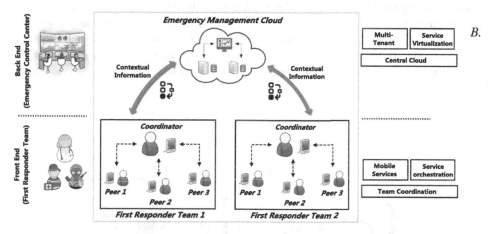

Fig. 2. Layered architecture view for the proposed framework.

Back-End – Computation-Specific Cloud Computing Layer

It is the top layer of the solution that primarily supports the storage and computation specific operations of the first responder teams to support the on-field emergency management activities as in Fig. 2. The technical combination, i.e.; mobile and cloud computing layers can facilitate the computation and data intensive operations away from (resource-efficient) mobile systems to (resource-sufficient) cloud servers [1, 2]. We aim to exploit the elasticity and resource provisioning of cloud computing to offer computational, resource and energy efficiency of context-aware and portable (mobile) systems for emergency operations. Software services at this layer ensures multi-tenant and virtualized resources for collaborative, on-field activities of the first responders.

3.2 Proposed Implementation for the Framework

The architecture of the framework as illustrated in Fig. 2 represents a blueprint for the system to be implemented by relying on reuse of architectural knowledge [10]. We are in process to develop the framework as a prototype for validations and proof of concept. We highlight the tools/technologies to implement the framework as in Fig. 3.

A. Implementing Mobile Computing Layer

It primarily depends on the *Ionic framework* to gather the context information in the emergency scenario. Moreover, the *JavaScript* based user interfacing allows the emergency teams to work with customized and intuitive interface(s) for collection of the contextual information as in Fig. 3. The front-end mobile layer aims to notify the first responder team when certain incident happens and provide a platform for coordination and task management.

B. Implementing Cloud Computing Layer

This layer is responsible to receive and provide data to the on-field mobile devices. The data exchange is enable with the *REST API* to transfer states of a device as software services. Cloud layer has two primary functions that include (i) data processing managed by the *Amazon EC2*, and (ii) data storage using *MongoDB* as in Fig. 3. The front-end service calls the backend services with amazon cloud processing and storage for data retrieval and storage.

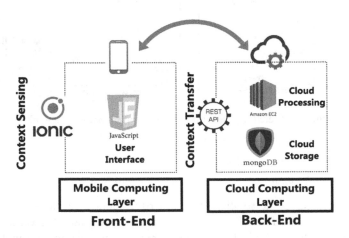

Fig. 3. Overview of tools and technologies for framework implementation

4   Conclusions and Dimensions of Future Research

We have proposed a framework that unifies the mobile and cloud computing technologies to deliver a solution that empowers the first responder teams to coordinate and operate in an emergency situation. The solution aims to incorporate mobility, context-awareness and computational efficiency to enable data and knowledge driven smart emergency management for smart city based systems.

As part of the future research, we are in process to develop the framework's prototype as the proof of concept that can be evaluated and deployed to support smart systems, i.e., smart cities in general and smart emergency management in particular. Furthermore, in future we aim to rely on the ISO/IEC-9126-1 qualitative and multi-level validation of the framework to assess its usefulness/applicability in real context.

References

1. Su, K., Li, J., Fu, H..: Smart city and the applications. In: 2011 International Conference on Electronics, Communications and Control (ICECC). IEEE Press (2011)
2. Nam, T., Pardo, T.A.: Conceptualizing smart city with dimensions of technology, people, and institutions. In: 12th Annual International Digital Government Research Conference: Digital Government Innovation in Challenging Times. ACM (2011)
3. Khan, A.R., Othman, M., Madani, S.A., Khan, S.U.: A survey of mobile cloud computing application models. IEEE Commun. Surv. Tutor. **16**(1), 393–413 (2014)
4. Palmieri, F., Ficco, M., Pardi, S., Castiglione, A.: A cloud-based architecture for emergency management and first responders localization in smart city environments. Comput. Electr. Eng. **26**, 810–830 (2016)
5. Sawyer, S., Tapia, A., Pesheck, L., Davenport, J.: Mobility and the first responder. Commun. ACM **47**(3), 62–65 (2004)
6. Kopena, J., Sultanik, E., Naik, G., Howley, I., Peysakhov, M., Cicirello, V.A., Kam, M., Regli, W.C.: Service-based computing on manets: enabling dynamic interoperability of first responders. IEEE Intell. Syst. **20**(5), 17–25 (2005)
7. Attwood, A., Merabti, M., Fergus, P., Abuelmaatti, O.: ScCCIR: smart cities critical infrastructure response framework. In: Developments in E-systems Engineering (DeSE), pp. 460–464. IEEE (2011)
8. Bartoli, G., Fantacci, R., Gei, F., Marabissi, D., Micciullo, L.: A novel emergency management platform for smart public safety. Int. J. Commun. Syst. **28**(5), 928–943 (2013)
9. Asimakopoulou, E., Bessis, N.: Buildings and crowds: forming smart cities for more effective disaster management. In: Fifth International Conference on Innovative Mobile and Internet Services in Ubiquitous Computing. IEEE (2011)
10. Ahmad, A., Jamshidi, P., Pahl, C.: Classification and comparison of architecture evolution reuse knowledge - a systematic review. J. Softw. Evol. Process **26**(7), 654–691 (2014)
11. Ahmad, A., Altamimi, A., Alreshidi, A.: Towards establishing a catalogue of patterns for architecting mobile cloud software. In: 9th International Conference on Software Engineering and Application (SEAS) (2017)

Applications

The Application of Geographic Information System (GIS) on Five Basic Indicators of Sustainable Urban Transport Performance

Puji Adiatna Nadi[(✉)] and AbdulKader Murad

Department of Urban and Regional Planning, Faculty of Environmental Design,
King Abdulaziz University, Jeddah 21589, Saudi Arabia
padiatna@stu.kau.edu.sa

Abstract. As the era of information technology today, the use of digital information is very useful in the process of data collection, analysis and modeling. A Geographical Information Systems (GIS) is not only a tool, but it is also has a powerful ability in the analysis process, included to measure the performance of transportation in sustainability issues. The purpose of this study is to show how GIS can be used to analyze Sustainable Urban Transport performance based on its basic indicators. This paper used literature review in the field of GIS approach in sustainable urban transport studies with using classification methods from the sources with certain procedure. The paper shows the GIS application in urban transport performance studies on five basic indicators: traffic congestion, traffic air pollution, traffic noise pollution, traffic accident and transport infrastructure. The study found that the use of GIS in urban transport performance studies is dominant on traffic congestion indicator and the tool of GIS which used to measure transport performance mainly by the shortest path. It is interesting how to measure the performance of Sustainable Urban Transport (SUT) to be more comprehensive with involves all basic indicators i.e. traffic congestion, traffic air pollution, traffic noise pollution, traffic accident and transport infrastructure.

Keywords: GIS · Sustainable urban transport · Basic indicator
Performance

1 Introduction

As a system with a computer-based methodology for collecting, managing, analyzing, modeling, and presenting geographic or spatial data, GIS has a powerful ability to analyze a variety of planning problems [1]. This capability makes it easy for planners to determine decisions more effectively and efficiently. The problem of transportation that continues to grow requires an effective remedy. The role of GIS as an analysis tool gives a big influence in providing solutions to solve the problems of transportation. The advantages of GIS in data integration and map display provides comprehensive analysis and information with very accurate and convincing results. GIS has functions that support the transportation system through statistics analysis, charting, decision support systems, modeling and databases, also encoding, management, analysis and reporting [2].

© ICST Institute for Computer Sciences, Social Informatics and Telecommunications Engineering 2018
R. Mehmood et al. (Eds.): SCITA 2017, LNICST 224, pp. 267–281, 2018.
https://doi.org/10.1007/978-3-319-94180-6_26

The natural environment is a human dwelling to live in the world that was inherited and will continue to be inherited in the future. The existence of a comfortable habitat necessary to establish events life for the residents. These events are characterized by movement in the form of transport as the backbone of community activities. Transportation plays a vital role in keeping human activity vibrant, therefore careful attention must be given to it in order to support sustainability. There is a trend that growth is ever so rapid in all countries now and more so in the future to come. Therefore, the attention in sustainability development becomes important. The increase of urban population is directly proportional to the increase in needs of the movement in urban transportation. The performance of urban transport should be measured in an effort to prepare future community. There are several analytical techniques to assess relationship between land use and transport i.e. descriptive statistics, spatial mapping, spatial statistics, travel preference functions, regression analysis, selection of suitable predictive models based on-time series census data and application of travel models scenarios for land use distribution [3]. As for this study, the GIS will be explored as tool to analyze the performance of urban transport to be sustainable.

Trends and issues in sustainability and urban transport has become more popular in rapidly growth city, especially developing countries which have bigger population with middle-income and where the rate of ownership of private vehicle is significantly high. The purpose of this paper is to review the GIS application to measure sustainable urban transport performance based on its basic indicators. To achieve this purpose which in other words is the research objective, let us start with by way of determining the research question: what are the trends of use of GIS for analyzing urban transport performance and sustainability in current practices? The structure of this paper consists of several parts: first, to find all papers related to the study of Sustainable Urban Transport using the GIS approach; second, to perform specifications to measure the performance of Sustainable Urban Transport based on five basic indicators; third, to classify into five main categories; finally, the results and findings.

2   Materials and Methods

The sustainability of transportation needs to be improved. The scope of the regional and local objectives in sustainable transportation consists of five indicators i.e. air pollution, noise pollution, congestions, accidents and land consumption [3]. Similarly, basic concern must be focused in environment, economy and society i.e.: traffic congestion, emission/air pollution, noise pollution, non-renewable resource consumption, and road safety/traffic accidents [4]. Also, the common issues of transportation (specifically in Asia Region) need more to be explored is about traffic congestion, traffic accidents and air pollution [5]. Land consumption by transport infrastructure and noise pollution as interesting issues for the future problems. Based on previous research, this paper focuses in five basic indicators of sustainable transportation i.e. traffic congestion, traffic air pollution, traffic accident, transport infrastructure and traffic noise pollution. The GIS analysis also arranged to focus in these issues.

This paper based on a review of international journal studies, thesis, textbooks, and conference proceeding papers. The journals were selected through electronic search topics on the field. During the electronic search, the authors used key words or terms: GIS and urban transport, sustainable urban transport, and sustainable urban transport performance. The first term is utilized to generate all papers that treat the relationship topic between GIS approach and Urban Transport sector, including papers referring to this subject in different methods and techniques used. The second term aims to find all papers related to Sustainable Urban Transport studies, this attempt was to delimit papers that were related in the transportation sector. Finally, the last terms are adopted to generate more specific search result about how to measure the performance of Sustainable Urban Transport based on the five basic indicators.

The electronic sources that the authors used were from Science Direct, Springer Link, and Scholar Google. Also the authors examined some references cited in each relevant literature source to obtain additional sources of knowledge. The research covers a period of more than ten years between 2000 and 2016. Next step, the authors excluded all papers that were not related to the GIS approach and Urban Transport sector, through identification on the title of journals, abstract and introduction section. As a result, the papers with only specific in GIS approach and urban transport performance based on the five basic indicators were analyzed in this study. In this study, the authors used literature review and research of GIS in the field sustainable urban transport. In contrast to previous studies that had discussed GIS and the transport sustainability in general, this study will focus on 5 basic indicators of sustainable urban transport (SUT) only. The studies will be classified into five major categories: (i) publications with year and number of articles, (ii) scientific institutions-country case studies, (iii) types of studies, (iv) types of GIS application in analyzing of five basic indicators of SUT, and (v) types of GIS tools in measuring of five basic indicators of SUT.

3   Results and Discussion

The result of the search extrapolated studies related to utilizing of GIS tools for measure urban transport performances especially in 5 indicators i.e. traffic congestion, traffic air pollution, traffic noise pollution, transport infrastructure, and traffic accident. Based on years of publication from 2000, generally the research that discussed the SUT had a tendency to in-crease until 2016. Based on Fig. 1 shows that the interest of researchers is high and increasingly related to GIS analysis for measure urban transport performance. Results of exploration in the search engine revealed 33 studies that specifically deals with GIS analysis in Urban Transport. Based on the search results it shows that at the beginning of the year's trend up to 2004, but in the year between 2005 and 2006 it experienced a drastic decline and then again showed a trend of trend to increase beginning in 2007 until 2016.

The area of study represents countries in all the continents of the world from Africa, Asia, Australia, America and Europe. Some studies showed a significant result by 5 studies in UK, 4 studies in Saudi Arabia and 3 studies in USA. The overall picture of the distribution of case studies on the theme of GIS analysis in Urban Transport can be seen in Fig. 2.

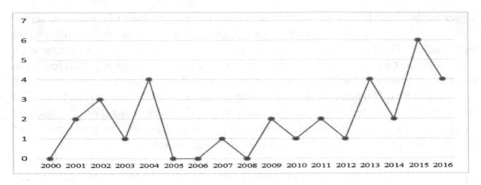

Fig. 1. Papers by year of publication of urban transportation in 5 basic indicators performance using GIS

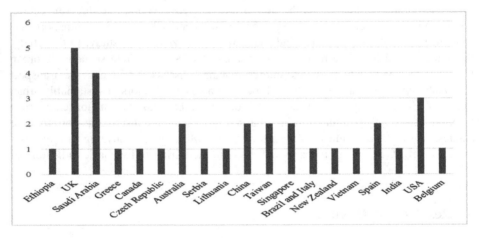

Fig. 2. Country of publishers on urban transportation studies in 5 basic indicators using GIS over period 2000–2016

The previous studies relating concern between GIS analysis and Urban Transport journals searches with the time period 2000 to 2016 shows in this paper. The results indicate that Scholar Google provides the highest results of 20 studies, followed by Science Direct were 9 studies, 10 studies by Elsevier and other Springer Link as a study, as shown by Fig. 3. It shows how far the ability of each researcher to contribute in improving the dissemination of knowledge, especially through the media publisher, and the level of success of the study search engine in providing services to researchers in the quest the desired study.

The results of searching process also shows the discovery of several types of studies related to the SUT. Studies in the type of a paper as the highest by 29 studies. Furthermore, the form of proceeding by 2 studies, theses and book section respectively of a study. It can be seen in Fig. 4.

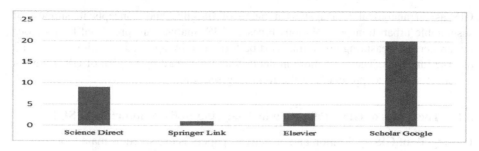

Fig. 3. Results of study search engine in urban transport performance studies using GIS topic

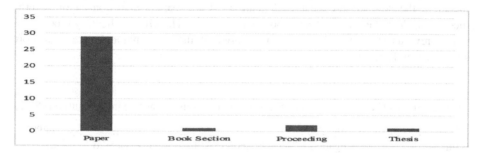

Fig. 4. Type of study in urban transport through five basic indicators using GIS

On the criteria of journal titles, found some journals as choice of the researchers to publish their research. On the many titles in studies found five titles journal is a journal title chosen most researchers in the topic of the SUT i.e. Accident Analysis and Prevention, Applied Acoustics, International Journal of Geo-Information, Journal of Transport Geography and Journal of Geographic Information System (Table 1).

The findings of previous studies generally illustrate the use of GIS analysis to measure the performance level of urban transport. Increasing the researcher's attention to transport performance from various disciplines and point of view through the use of

Table 1. Journal titles, total citations and average annual number of citations

Journals title	Paper numbers	Total citations*	Ave. cit. per year*	H index*
Accident Analysis and Prevention	2	2879	2.25	94
Applied Acoustics	2	933	1.85	49
International Journal of Geo-Information	2	931	2.57	79
Journal of Transport Geography	2	1333	2.49	58
Journal of Geographic Information System	2	1502**	No data	15**

*Source: www.scimagojr.com, **Source: http://www.scirp.org

GIS as an analytical tool spawns a range of findings and concepts in support of sustainable urban transport. Various types of GIS analysis are presented by previous researchers in measuring urban transport performance by optimizing various tools with diverse functions. There are more in-depth findings regarding the use of GIS in urban transport studies as presented in the following section.

3.1   The Types of GIS Application in Analyzing of Basic Indictors of SUT

In category of GIS application and objectives, papers is classified as main topic of GIS application in urban transport research. As the urban transport knowledge very large, especially how to measure its performance, the authors filtered of the papers in main objects of the studies and what is depend on. Each papers also consist of several objective to describe the urban transport performance. The GIS application types used in the previous studies in five basic indicators of the Sustainable Urban Transport summarize in Table 2.

Table 2. GIS application in analyzing of 5 basic indictors in sustainable urban transport (SUT)

Indicators	Objectives	Authors
Traffic congestion	- Investigation of network shortages that are an obstacle to accessibility	[6]
	- Development of social needs index of composite public transport	[7]
	- Identification of lacking facilities in vital areas within the capital's ring road	[8]
	- The development of simple GIS-based methods to analyze rapid accessibility with different modes of transport	[9]
	- Analyze accessibility and other indicators to show troubled transport zones	[10]
	- Integrated GIS development on accessibility analysis	[11, 12]
	- The depiction of two public transport access measurements: a combination of public transit and access indexes and transit frequency sizes	[13]
	- Evaluation on the contribution of 'major' land use in the region to traffic congestion in certain corridors and to test how relocation can reduce traffic congestion	[14]
	- Measurement of congestion using fuzzy logic and create strategies to reduce congestion	[15]
	- Modelling dynamic congestion spread effects	[16]
	- Evaluation of traffic congestion during working hours in accordance with road direction	[17]

(*continued*)

Table 2. (*continued*)

Indicators	Objectives	Authors
Traffic air pollution	- Improved efficiency of transport supply in improving the environment	[18]
	- Analyze the emission implications to reduce motor vehicle emissions in urban transport	[19]
	- The depiction of air pollution consequences to the environment as a result of road transport	[20]
	- Present a preliminary study to evaluate the air pollution situation related to urban transport	[21]
	- Modeling temporal and spatial variability of traffic air pollution	[22]
	- Characterization of intra-urban distributions NO_x and NO_2, and land-use regression (LUR) to assess NO_x and NO_2 outdoor concentrations	[23]
Traffic noise pollution	- The depiction of GIS-based modeling systems in assessing the environmental impact of road traffic plans	[24]
	- Development of road traffic noise maps day and night	[25]
	- Modeling to assess TRAffic Noise EXposure (TRANEX)	[26]
	- Testing of the adequacy of data to generate urban noise maps and verifying the application of environmental noise mapping disturbance models	[27]
Transport infrastructure	- Assessment of territorial effects from new linear transport infrastructure	[28]
	- Identification with sustainability metrics on environmental, economic, and social factors of the transport project	[29]
	- Development of appropriate methodologies that explicitly link transportation infrastructure with the impact of strategic sustainability	[30]
Traffic accident	- An investigation of the use of GIS tools in assessing traffic accidents/transport system safety performance integrating spatial parameters and indicators	[2]
	- Use of a methodology using GIS and Kernel Density Estimates to study the spatial patterns of road accidents related to injury	[31]
	- The clustering methodology uses environmental data and results from the first section to create a road accident hotspot classification	[31]
	- Establish procedures to evaluate traffic accident groups and arrange them according to their significance	[32]
	- Depiction of trends in Road Traffic Accident (RTA) and to raise consciousness of RTA issues in developing countries	[33]
	- Determination of the location of the area marked by the concentration of traffic accidents (black zone) involving Vulnerable Road Use (VRU)	[34]
	- Identify traffic accidents through integration between NetKDE and local Moran'I for hot spot detection	[35]

The research objective in SUT performance using GIS is dominantly by traffic congestion indicators with 12 studies, secondly by traffic accident indicators with 8 studies, thirdly about traffic air pollution with 6 studies, following by traffic noise pollution with 4 studies and transport infrastructure with 3 studies. Figure 5 shows the papers number used GIS approach in five basic indicators of transport performance studies.

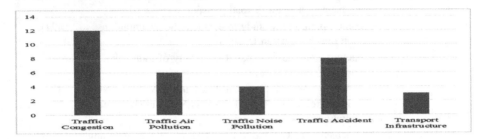

Fig. 5. Number of studies in 5 basic indicators of SUT using GIS

Figure 6 describe a number of studies with its research methods. Found about 8 types of methods used by previous researchers on the GIS for SUT theme. Modelling method widely used as many as 24 studies. Then followed by decision support system and literature review methods as much as 2 studies.

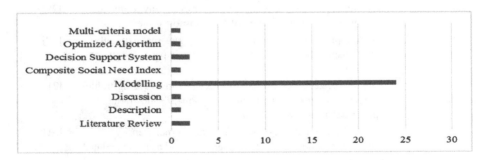

Fig. 6. Types of research methods in urban transport performance using GIS

From the survey between 2000 and 2016 above, we find the fact that the methods used by the researchers in sustainable urban transport (SUT) studies using GIS are mostly using one indicators of SUT, still rare using more than one indicators. Of course this is an interesting finding that needs to be studied more comprehensively by involving more than one indicators or all of the five indicators as a basic indicators. Modelling methods dominantly used by earlier researchers as convincing methods to be use in future research.

3.2   The Types of GIS Tools in Measuring of Five Basic Indicators of SUT

Previous researchers used a variety of tools from GIS analysis to measure the performance level of indicators on urban transport each researcher has a way of exploring the information and analyzing it by involving certain scenarios resulting in reliable research. The papers is classified based on GIS tools was used in research to analyse urban transport performance. The GIS has many type of tools as instrument to be used in analysis process of the research. The function of GIS tools in each research according focus of the object research. Each function have unique function depend on creativity of the researchers to measure performances of urban transport. Based on the results of a review in previous research, the following describes several types of GIS tools and their functions summarize in Table 3.

Table 3. The classification GIS use by tools in transport performance studies

Indicators	GIS tools	Function	Authors
Transport congestion	Buffer analysis	- To measure the range of the route/stop - To represent the impact area	[6] [8]
	Quantities analysis	- To measure routes number per segment of road	[6, 7]
	Shortest path analysis	- To produce the shortest route between proposed interactive project points - To estimate the volume of traffic contributed by these primary land uses in the corridor during peak hours	[8, 11, 12, 14, 15, 17]
	Deficiency analysis	- To identify the lack of facilities, the relationship between link capacity and estimated volume	[8]
	Allocation of resources	- To identify the distance and travel period of various points of interest on the street GIS network map	[8]
	Simple additive weighting/SAW	- To measure with the greatest value which means the best transport situation in a particular traffic analysis zone	[10]
	Network analyst	- To create a multi-modal network that combines transit mode and runs using travel time as network impedance	[13, 15, 17]
	What If questions	- To create strategic planning and tactical management of unplanned network disruptions	[16]
	Overlay analysis	- To determine the congestion point according to the direction of the road	[17]

(*continued*)

Table 3. (*continued*)

Indicators	GIS tools	Function	Authors
Traffic air pollution	Geo-database	- To generate thematic diagrams, tables and maps	[18]
	Geocoding	- To input the field data to the GIS attribute	[19]
	Network analyst	- To test transport policies in terms of emission effects at the link level and merged to the regional level	[19]
	KDE	- To present the center of air pollution in area	[19]
	Dispersion model (grid cells)	- To integrate the outputs of transport planning activities with land use information based on user-defined grid sizes	[21, 24]
	Transport Add-on Env. Model. Syst./TRAEMS	- To integrate traffic information from the travel forecasting model for input data used in various models in estimating pollution	[20]
	Buffer	- To calculate the path length of the total traffic variable of the day and the distance to the nearest road	[22]
	Geostatistical analyst	- To present the spatial distribution of NOx and NO2 in urban areas drawn by ordinary kriging method	[23]
Traffic noise pollution	Dispersion model (grid cells)	- To model the noise impact of different road traffic scenarios	[24]
	What If question	- To model noise calculations, environmental noise presentations, noise reduction design	[36]
	PostGIS	- To handle large vector data sets to be more effective	[26]
	Geocoding	- To produce a measurable acoustic parameter noise map	[27]
Transportation infrastructure	Spatial analyst	- To create sustainability metrics for the selection of transit infrastructure projects	[29]
	Spatial classification	- Modeling as a graph with a set of vertices and an arc	[30]
	The TITIM	- Evaluation of accessibility improvement, landscape connectivity, and impact on other local area variables	[28]

(*continued*)

Table 3. (*continued*)

Indicators	GIS tools	Function	Authors
Traffic accidents	Network analyst	- To measure the level of traffic accidents - To present transport performances - To measure safety level caused by traffic accidents	[2] [37]
	Kernel density estimation (KDE)	- To know the spread of accident risk - To identify dangerous locations on the road - To calculate the probability density function of each crash site	[31, 33] [32, 35] [34]
	K-means clustering	- To create a road accident hotspot classification	[31–33]

The use of GIS tools in reviewed papers is dominant by the shortest path analysis, kernel density estimation (KDE) and network analyst as shows in Fig. 7. Urban Transport Performance is how well urban transport to serve the society activities as navigation tools to achieve the goals. An essential topic for sustainable development is to encourage efficient urban transportation systems while decreasing their negative impacts [38]. A sustainable transportation system is one that: tolerates the elementary access needs of individuals and societies, to be met safely and in a manner consistent with human and ecosystem health, and with equity within and between generations; operates efficiently, offers choice of transport mode, and supports a vibrant economy; and limits emissions and waste within the planet's ability to absorb them, minimizes consumption of non-renewable resources, limits consumption of renewable resources to the sustainable yield level, reuses and recycles its components, reduces the use of land and minimizes the production of noise [39]. According the literature, there is a need for comprehensive analysis using basic indicators of sustainable urban transport

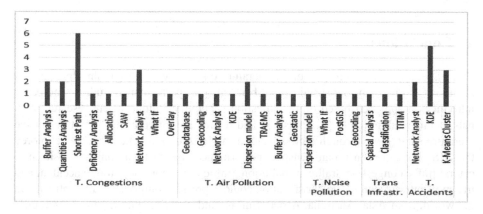

Fig. 7. The use of GIS tools to measure sustainable urban transport studies

performance as instruments to measure performance of sustainability includes economy factors, environment factors and social factors.

GIS is considered as a useful tool for transport planners in defining how well the movement of people or goods from one place to another place, also measure, predict, evaluate and monitor the degree to which the transportation system accomplishes adopted public objectives [40]. The interesting function of indicators are used for a variety of purposes including measurement, policy formulation, and project assessment [41]. Performance measures are measurable criteria that are utilized to evaluate progress towards goals [42]. According [43] also suggest that indicators should be used to measure progress, inputs, and outputs of a transport project. Furthermore, [44] that selecting the indicators can greatly influence the analysis results. Therefore, the steps of selecting indicators must be with carefully actions. As this study results that the use of GIS in SUT performance studies dominantly by traffic congestion, traffic accidents and traffic air pollution. For methods type of the research, in previous research mostly by modelling methods. Then GIS tools which used to measure SUT performance indicate that dominantly by shortest path, Kernel Density Estimation (KDE) and Network Analysis.

According the result of this study result, in measuring sustainable urban transportation performance, dominantly with traffic congestion indicator using shortest path analysis. Indicator of traffic air pollution generally using dispersion model (grid cells) to measure the performances. For traffic noise pollution, the previous study also used dispersion model (grid cells) and other tools such as What If?, PostGIS, and Geocoding. In measuring transport infrastructure three GIS tools used i.e. spatial analysis, classification and TITIM. Also in analyzing traffic accidents using three GIS tools i.e. network analyst, KDE and K-Means Cluster. Based on observations in previous research, it was found that in general the research topic only discusses one or two aspects of the basic indicator of sustainable urban transport. Whereas the performance of sustainable urban transport based on the scope of the study needs to be comprehensive or at least can meet the basic indicators. Therefore this is an interesting gap knowledge to be explored more deeply based on five basic indicators using GIS approach, such as congestion, traffic air pollution, traffic noise pollution, land consumption for transport infrastructure and traffic accidents.

4   Conclusions

This paper objectives to review of the literature on the use of Geographic Information System (GIS) in analysing sustainable urban transport performance studies. The paper introduce an approach based on classification scheme technique where research journals in this field are collected, classified and results are interpreted. A comprehensive literature study done through a classification model adoption. The study has explored the GIS application in urban transport performance studies focus on five basic indicators: traffic congestion, traffic air pollution, traffic noise pollution, traffic accident and transport infrastructure. The classification could represent countries on all continents in the world, from Asia, Australia, Africa, Europe and America within period 2000 until 2016 and found that UK country as dominantly in this case. Scholar Google provides the highest productive search engine and also found that paper type as majority in SUT studies. In category of journal name, Accident Analysis and Prevention, Applied Acoustics, International Journal of Geo-Information, Journal of Transport Geography and Journal of Geographic Information System as the most chosen by the previous researchers. For category of studies numbers in five basic indicators of SUT, traffic congestion as mostly concern by previous research, following with traffic accident, traffic air pollution, traffic noise pollution, and transport infrastructure. In the category of research method, modelling as dominant in previous research, and for category of GIS tools, mostly researcher used i.e. Shortest Path, Network Analyst, KDE and K-Means Cluster. The use of GIS in previous research still focus in one or several indicators in measuring performance Sustainable Urban Transport. According to the literature, there is interesting for future research to know GIS application with comprehensive analysis using all of the five basic indicators i.e. traffic congestion, traffic air pollution, traffic noise pollution, traffic accident and transport infrastructure as instruments to measure sustainable urban transport performance.

References

1. ESRI: What is GIS? http://www.esri.com/what-is-gis
2. Al-Ali, M.M.: Applicability of GIS tools in assessing performance of the transportation systems in urban areas. World J. Sci. Technol. Sustain. Dev. **13**, 120–127 (2016)
3. Black, J.A., Paez, A., Suthanaya, P.A.: Sustainable urban transportation: performance indicators and some analytical approaches. J. Urban Plan. Dev. **128**, 184–209 (2002). 733-94534
4. Mitropoulos, L.K.: Sustainability framework for urban transportation modes and exploratory applications (2011)
5. Fujiwara, A., Zhang, J.: Sustainable Transport Studies in Asia. Springer, Hiroshima (2013). https://doi.org/10.1007/978-4-431-54379-4
6. Abreha, D.A.: Analysing public transport performance using efficiency measures and spatial analysis: the case of Addis Ababa, Ethiopia (2007)
7. Aljoufie, M.: Development of a GIS based public transport composite social need index in Jeddah. J. Geogr. Inf. Syst. **8**, 470–479 (2016)
8. Alterkawi, M.: Application of GIS in transportation planning: the case of Riyadh, the Kingdom of Saudi Arabia. GBER **1**, 38–46 (2001)
9. Ford, A.C., Barr, S.L., Dawson, R.J., James, P.: Transport accessibility analysis using GIS: assessing sustainable transport in London. Geo-Information **4**, 124–149 (2015)
10. Jakimavičius, M., Burinskiene, M.: A GIS and multi-criteria-based analysis and ranking of transportation zones of Vilnius city. Technol. Econ. Dev. Econ. **15**, 39–48 (2009)
11. Liu, S., Zhu, X.: Accessibility analyst: an integrated GIS tool for accessibility analysis in urban transportation planning. Environ. Plan. B Plan. Des. **31**, 105–124 (2004)
12. Liu, S., Zhu, X.: An integrated GIS approach to accessibility analysis. Trans. GIS **8**, 45–62 (2004)
13. Mavoa, S., Witten, K., Mccreanor, T., Sullivan, D.O.: GIS based destination accessibility via public transit and walking in Auckland, New Zealand. J. Transp. Geogr. **20**, 15–22 (2012)
14. Nguyen, N.Q., Zuidgeest, M., Brussel, M.: Development of an integrated GIS-based land use and transport model for studying land-use relocation in Hanoi, Vietnam, pp. 1–16 (2011)

15. Narayanan, R., Udayakumar, R., Kumar, K., Subbaraj, L.: Quantification of congestion using fuzzy logic and network analysis using GIS. In: Presented at the Transportation (2003)
16. Wu, Y., Miller, H.J., Hung, M.: A GIS-based decision support system for analysis of route choice in congested urban road networks. J. Geogr. Syst. **3**, 3–24 (2001)
17. Al-enazi, M.: Traffic congestion evaluation using GIS case study: Jeddah City. Int. J. Comput. Appl. **138**, 7–11 (2016)
18. Arampatzis, G., Kiranoudis, C.T., Scaloubacas, P., Assimacopoulos, D.: A GIS-based decision support system for planning urban transportation policies. Eur. J. Oper. Res. **152**, 465–475 (2004)
19. Armstrong, J.M., Khan, A.M.: Modelling urban transportation emissions: role of GIS. Comput. Environ. Urban Syst. **28**, 421–433 (2004)
20. Gharineiat, Z., Khalfan, M.: Using the geographic information system (GIS) in the sustainable transportation. Int. J. Soc. Behav. Educ. Econ. Bus. Ind. Eng. **5**, 1425–1431 (2011)
21. Lin, M.Der, Lin, Y.C.: The application of GIS to air quality analysis in Taichung City, Taiwan, ROC. Environ. Model Softw. **17**, 11–19 (2002)
22. Dons, E., Poppel, M.Van, Kochan, B., Wets, G., Panis, L.I.: Modeling temporal and spatial variability of traffic-related air pollution: hourly land use regression models for black carbon. Atmos. Environ. **74**, 237–246 (2013)
23. Lee, J., Wu, C., Hoek, G., Hoogh, K.De, Beelen, R., Brunekreef, B., Chan, C.: Land use regression models for estimating individual NOx and NO2 exposures in a metropolis with a high density of traffic roads and population. Sci. Total Environ. **472**, 1163–1171 (2014)
24. Brown, A.L., Affum, J.K.: A GIS-based environmental modelling system for transport planners. Pergamon **26**, 577–590 (2002)
25. Cai, M., Zou, J., Xie, J., Ma, X.: Road traffic noise mapping in Guangzhou using GIS and GPS. Appl. Acoust. **87**, 94–102 (2015)
26. Gulliver, J., Morley, D., Vienneau, D., Fabbri, F., Bell, M., Goodman, P., Beevers, S., Dajnak, D., Kelly, F.J., Fecht, D.: Development of an open-source road traffic noise model for exposure assessment. Environ. Model Softw. **74**, 183–193 (2015)
27. Zytoon, M.A.: Opportunities for environmental noise mapping in Saudi Arabia: a case of traffic noise annoyance in an urban area in Jeddah City. Environ. Res. Public Health **13**, 496 (2016)
28. Ortega, E., Otero, I., Mancebo, S.: TITIM GIS-tool: a GIS-based decision support system for measuring the territorial impact of transport infrastructures. Expert Syst. Appl. **41**, 7641–7652 (2014)
29. Beiler, M.R.O., Asce, A.M., Treat, C.: Integrating GIS and AHP to prioritize transportation infrastructure using sustainability metrics, vol. 4014053, pp. 1–11 (2015)
30. Elena, L., Monzon, A.: Integration of sustainability issues in strategic transportation planning: a multi-criteria model for the assessment of transport infrastructure plans. Comput.-Aided Civ. Infrastruct. Eng. **25**, 440–451 (2010)
31. Anderson, T.K.: Kernel density estimation and K-means clustering to profile road accident hotspots. Accid. Anal. Prev. **41**, 359–364 (2009)
32. Bíl, M., Andrá˘, R.: Identification of hazardous road locations of traffic accidents by means of kernel density estimation and cluster significance evaluation. Accid. Anal. Prev. **55**, 265–273 (2013)
33. Çela, L., Shiode, S., Lipovac, K.: Integrating GIS and spatial analytical techniques in an analysis of road traffic accidents in Serbia. Int. J. Traffic Transp. Eng. **3**, 1–15 (2013)
34. Machado, C., Giannotti, M., Neto, F., Tripodi, A., Persia, L., Quintanilha, J.: Characterization of black spot zones for vulnerable road users in São Paulo (Brazil) and Rome (Italy). ISPRS Int. J. Geo-Inform. **4**, 858–882 (2015)

35. Xie, Z., Yan, J.: Detecting traffic accident clusters with network kernel density estimation and local spatial statistics: an integrated approach. J. Transp. Geogr. **31**, 64–71 (2013)
36. Li, B., Tao, S., Dawson, R.W., Cao, J., Lam, K.: A GIS based road traffic noise prediction model. Appl. Acoust. **63**, 679–691 (2002)
37. Al-ali, M., Saleh, W.: GIS as a tool for assessing transportation system: a case study from Saudi Arabia. In: World Association for Sustainable Development, pp. 329–337. Edinburgh Napier University, Edinburgh (2015)
38. Chen, S., Tan, J., Claramunt, C., Ray, C.: Multi-scale and multi-modal GIS-T data model. J. Transp. Geogr. **19**, 147–161 (2011)
39. Centre for Sustainable Transportation: Sustainable Transportation Performance Indicators (2005)
40. USEPA: Guide to Sustainable Transportation Performance Measures, pp. 1–55 (2011)
41. Joumard, R., Nicolas, J.-P.: Transport project assessment methodology within the framework of sustainable development. Ecol. Indic. **10**, 136–142 (2010)
42. Ramani, T., Zietsman, J., Eisele, W., Rosa, D.: Developing sustainable transportation performance measures for TxDOT's strategic plan, vol. 7. Technical report. Security (2009)
43. Bongardt, R.D.D.: Financing Sustainable Urban Transport (2012)
44. Litman, T., Burwell, D.: Issues in sustainable transportation. Int. J. Glob. Environ. Issues **6**, 331–347 (2006)

Designing PID Controller Based Semi-active Suspension System Using MATLAB Simulink

Mohsin Jamil[1,2], Salman Zafar[3], and Syed Omer Gilani[1(✉)]

[1] School of Mechanical and Manufacturing Engineering,
National University of Sciences and Technology (NUST), Islamabad, Pakistan
{mohsin,omer}@smme.nust.edu.pk
[2] Department of Electrical Engineering, Faculty of Engineering,
Islamic University Madinah, Medina, Saudi Arabia
[3] College of Electrical and Mechanical Engineering,
National University of Sciences and Technology (NUST), Islamabad, Pakistan
salman.zaffar@gmail.com

Abstract. The suspension system of any vehicle is responsible for not only to support the weight of the vehicle, but also to improve ride comfort and vehicle handling by damping out the roughness of the road before transferring it to the passengers. When the vehicle experiences an uneven road profile, the suspension should not generate too large oscillations, and even if it does, then these oscillations must be removed as quickly as possible. In this paper, we have investigated the functioning of a semi-active suspension system of a vehicle by modelling it as a quarter car semi-active suspension system. The model is designed as a PID controller based semi-active suspension system. MATLAB Simulink has been used in the process. The system considered in the paper is a linear system, which can apprehend basic performance parameters of a suspension system like body and suspension travel and give results in terms of rise time, settling time and over-shoot. The performance of the system is taken as better ride quality given by body travel. The lesser body displacement (over-shoot) in earlier time (settling time) are used to depict these performance standards. These performance indicators are also compared with a passive suspension system of similar specifications. The results achieved through the simulation show that the semi - active suspension system, using the designed PID controller to adjust its damping parameters, demonstrates much better performance than the passive system, having fixed damping. The designed controller can be used to design more comfortable and stable suspension systems.

Keywords: Semi-active suspension system · PID controller
Quarter car model · MATLAB Simulink

© ICST Institute for Computer Sciences, Social Informatics and Telecommunications Engineering 2018
R. Mehmood et al. (Eds.): SCITA 2017, LNICST 224, pp. 282–295, 2018.
https://doi.org/10.1007/978-3-319-94180-6_27

1   Introduction

The objectives of the vehicle suspension system is to ensure the comfort of the passengers, maximize the road grip of the tyres and to provide maximum stability for the steering. An efficient suspension has to maintain balance among all these factors. Vehicle suspensions can be categorized in three types, passive systems, semi-active systems and active suspensions systems (Fig. 1). The conventional suspension system [1], utilizing un-controlled shock-absorbing dampers and springs with constant parameters are the passive suspension [2,3]. They have fixed specifications which are designed for a specific range of operating conditions and hence cannot re-adjust these parameters with the variations in the conditions [4]. This causes the passive suspension system to generate fixed response for all types of road profiles. Passive system possesses an element to absorb energy; a damper, and an element to store energy; a spring. Since there is no source for any additional energy in the system, therefore the system is called a "passive suspension system". This system is subject to multiple trade-off when it experiences a large bandwidth of oscillating frequencies. To get the most optimized response for all these frequencies, passive systems are designed for such an operating condition, which the vehicle is experiencing the most, utilizing a constant stiffness spring and a fixed damping coefficient damper. This spring and damper cannot adjust their coefficients to suit the variations in the operating conditions [5]. An adjustable system is ideally required to cater for the variety of road disturbances that a vehicle can encounter while on road, which should have varying response for different conditions. A semi active suspension system does exactly this. It offers a remarkable upgrade in the suspension of the vehicle by utilizing fluid dampers, which can change their damping coefficient per the variations in the road disturbances. This system has the capacity to adapt either its damping coefficient, and/or the stiffness of the spring to cater for the continuously changing profiles of the road [6]. This auto-controlled adjusted system is especially beneficial for the suspensions due to its low energy requirements. Normally, in semi active systems, the spring already in use of the passive suspension is kept, while an added system is introduced to modulate the damping force of the damper to achieve a range of damping force for multiple operating conditions. "Electro Rheological (ER)" and "Magnetic Rheological fluid dampers" [7] are favoured for the fact that they can change their damping stiffness coefficient [5].

In an active suspension system, the conventional (passive) components are supplemented with the help of actuators which can provide extra force to pull or push the sprung mass of the vehicle to achieve the required level of comfort [8]. An active shock absorber may be used as an active control which can generate force instantaneously, to support the body weight and to provide stability and comfort in varying road disturbances [9]. The biggest drawback of this type of system is the increase in the cost caused by the added apparatus (external source) to provide the required actuation energy to the system [10]. Although there is a variety of options for actuators, like electromagnetic and hydraulic, the electromagnetic actuators are generally favoured due to their speed of actuation and rapid response. In short, the active suspension system can give better performance over a wide-ranging road disturbances. However, this active system is handicapped by being more complex, heavy in weight and requiring high external energy [5].

In current paper the concept of a semi active suspension system is studied due to its advantage of providing better driving experience and safety without adding any additional burden on the power requirements or overall vehicle weight [11]. A PID controller is designed for controlling the parameters of a semi active suspension system to demonstrate its advantages over the conventional passive approach. The paper tries to analyse the proposed system in the application of a quarter car model. The response of the proposed system and a passive system, caused by multiple road disturbances is simulated with fixed system parameters and their performances are compared to establish the better solution.

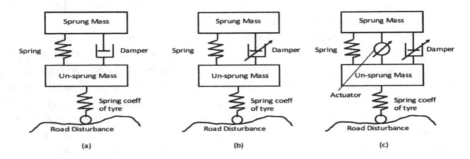

Fig. 1. (a) Passive system, (b) Semi-active system (c) Active suspension system [5]

2 Problem Statement

The semi-active suspension system has been considered for the paper due to its clear edge over the conventional passive suspension. The semi-active system demonstrates added adjustment in the stiffness of the damping force against multiple kinds of road disturbances, which enhances the drive comfort and increases the stability of the vehicle. The semi-active system is at an advantageous position as compared to active suspension system as well, which although possess much superior adjustment capabilities against the road disturbances, but also adds extra weight on the vehicle and at the same time requires extra external power to activate the actuators. This is where the semi-active suspension system gets its edge over active system. It is for the same reason such system is advised to be implemented on normal commercial cars. In the paper the suggested model is tested for a normal passenger car. A PID controller has been designed to control the damping force or stiffness of the adjustable damper of a semi-active suspension. For the ease of the simplicity, a quarter car model is taken to model and simulate the system. The quarter car model considers the working of a single tire and associated suspension components of a normal road car. The effects of various forces acting on one tire are considered and studied. The same results can be expected to be effecting all the tyres separately, considering the uniformity of the car.

3 Mathematical Modelling

The mathematical model for a quarter car passive and semi-active suspension system Fig. 2 has been derived by using the basic Newton's laws of motion and the free body diagram approach. The modelling has been done considering certain assumptions to keep the model simple yet effective [12].

- Two degree of freedom system has been considered for the suspension system modelled here. Moreover, the overall vehicle design is assumed to be a linear or uniform to support the quarter car model.
- For the ease of the design, certain minor factors, like backlash and movement in various gear systems, linkages and joints and the vehicle chassis flex have been disregarded to reduce the complexity. As the effect of these forces is negligible, therefore, these have been neglected in the model.
- The tyre is considered to act as having both damping and spring properties.

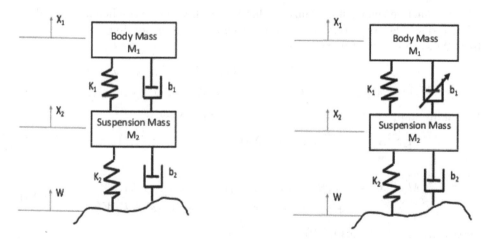

Fig. 2. (a) Quarter car passive suspension system model, (b) Semi-active suspension model

3.1 Passive Suspension System Model

The equation for quarter car passive suspension system are

$$M_1\ddot{x}_1 + b_1(\dot{x}_1 - \dot{x}_2) + k_1(x_1 - x_2) = 0 \qquad (1)$$
$$M_2\ddot{x}_2 + b_1(\dot{x}_2 - \dot{x}_1) + k_2(x_2 - x_1) + b_2\dot{x}_2 + k_2x_2 = b_2\dot{w} + k_2w \qquad (2)$$

Taking Laplace transform of Eqs. (1) and (2), we get

$$M_1 S^2 X_1(s) + b_1 S(X_1(s) - X_2) + K_1(X_1(s) - X_2(s)) = 0 \tag{3}$$

$$M_2 S^2 X_2(s) + b_1 S(X_2(s) - X_1(s)) + k_2(X_2(s) - X_1(S))$$
$$+ b_2 S X_2(s) + k_2 X_2(s) = b_2 S W(s) + k_2 W(s) \tag{4}$$

by separating variable in (3)

$$X_1(s)\{M_1 S^2 + b_1 S + k_1\} = X_2(s)\{b_1 S + k_1\} \tag{5}$$

Substituting in (4) to get transfer function

$$G(s) = \frac{X_1(s)}{W(s)} =$$

$$\frac{b_1 b_2 S^2 + (b_1 k_2 + b_2 k_1)S + k_1 k_2}{m_1 m_2 s^4 + \{m_1(b_1 + b_2) + b_1 m_2\}S^3 + \{m_1(k_1 + k_2) + b_1 b_2 + k_1 m_2\}S^2} \tag{6}$$
$$+ \frac{1}{(b_1 k_2 + b_2 k_1)S + k_2^2}$$

3.2 Semi-active Suspension System Model

The semi-active suspension utilizes a damper with variable coefficient instead of a linear one. The equations for quarter car semi-active suspension system derived from Newton's laws of motion are:

$$M_1 \ddot{x}_1 + \bar{b}_1(\dot{x}_1 - \dot{x}_2) + k_1(x_1 - x_2) = 0 \tag{7}$$
$$M_2 \ddot{x}_2 + \bar{b}_1(\dot{x}_2 - \dot{x}_1) + k_2(x_2 - x_1) + b_2 \dot{x}_2 + k_2 x_2 = b_2 \dot{w} + k_2 w \tag{8}$$

By taking Laplace transform of Eqs. (7) and (8), we get,

$$M_1 S^2 X_1(s) + \bar{b}_1 S(X_1(s) - X_2) + K_1(X_1(s) - X_2(s)) = 0 \tag{9}$$

$$M_2 S^2 X_2(s) + \bar{b}_1 S(X_2(s) - X_1(s)) + k_2(X_2(s) - X_1(S))$$
$$+ b_2 S X_2(s) + k_2 X_2(s) = b_2 S W(s) + k_2 W(s) \tag{10}$$

Separating the variables in (9)

$$X_1(s)\{M_1 S^2 + \bar{b}_1 S + k_1\} = X_2(s)\{\bar{b}_1 S + k_1\} \tag{11}$$

Substituting in (10) to get transfer function

$$G(s) = \frac{X_1(s)}{W(s)} =$$

$$\frac{\bar{b}_1 b_2 S^2 + (\bar{b}_1 k_2 + b_2 k_1)S + k_1 k_2}{m_1 m_2 s^4 + \{m_1(\bar{b}_1 + b_2) + \bar{b}_1 m_2\}S^3 + \{m_1(k_1 + k_2) + \bar{b}_1 b_2 + k_1 m_2\}S^2} \tag{12}$$
$$+ \frac{1}{(\bar{b}_1 k_2 + b_2 k_1)S + k_2^2}$$

where :

M_1 = Bodymass/Sprung mass (kg)

M_2 = Suspension mass/Un − Spring mass (kg)

x_1 = Body mass displacement (m)

x_2 = Suspension mass displacement (m)

b_1 = Suspension damping coefficient (N.s/m)

b_2 = Tyre damping coefficient (N.s/m)

k_1 = Suspension spring coefficient (N/m)

k_2 = Tyre spring coefficient (N/m)

w = Road profile

$\bar{b_1}$ = Variable damper stiffness coefficient for semi − active system (N.s/m)

The semi-active suspension system utilizes a varying damping stiffness coefficient damper, and is operated by an external power source and an embedded controller with a set of sensors. The level of damping required as per the road profile is selected by the controller, which then adjusts the damper to achieve the optimized damping. A Proportional Integral Derivative (PID) controller was designed and tested for various types of road disturbances and the results were compared with a similar passive suspension system. The values of proportionality constants i.e. kp, ki and kd, for the designed PID controller, are determined using the trial and error method.

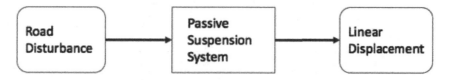

Fig. 3. Block diagram of passive suspension system

4   Simulation Model

The derived mathematical model, given in Eqs. (1), (2), (7) and (8), were simulated using MATLAB Simulink software. Separate models were developed for both, the passive suspension system (Fig. 3) and the semi-active suspension system (Fig. 4). The block diagram of the passive suspension system shows a road disturbance, the suspension system and the vehicle body mass displacement (output).

The semi-active suspension system has a feedback mechanism to control the damping coefficient of the damper. This feedback is fed to a PID controller which generates its response and as a result adjusts the damping stiffness of the damper

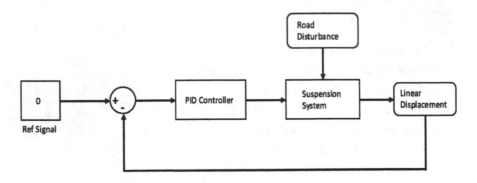

Fig. 4. Block diagram of semi-active suspension system

used. All other components of the system remain the same. Figure 4 shows the block diagram of a semi-active suspension system.

Basing on the block diagrams of the passive and the semi-active suspension system and the Eqs. (1), (2), (7) and (8), the Simulink models designed and used for the simulation are shown in Figs. 5 and 6.

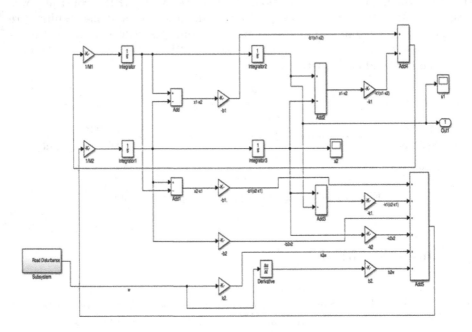

Fig. 5. Simulink model for passive suspension system

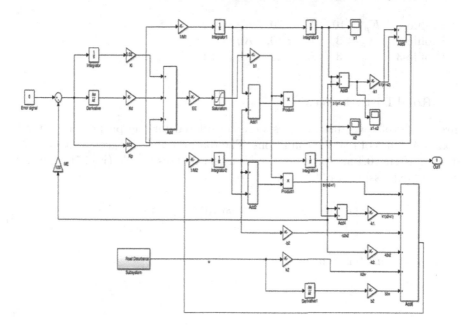

Fig. 6. Simulink model of semi-active suspension system having a PID controller

5   System Parameters and Conditions

Following parameters and conditions were set for dynamical modelling.

5.1   Parameters

Parameters of a normal passenger car considered for the simulated analysis are given in Table 1 [13].

Table 1. System parameters

Parameters	Value
M_1 (Sprung mass)	350 kg
M_2 (Un − Sprung mass)	40 kg
K_1 (Suspension spring coefficient)	18000 N/m
K_2 (Tyre spring coefficient)	1950000 N/m
b_1 (Suspension damper coefficient)	600 N.s/m
b_2 (Tyre damping coefficient)	800 N.s/m

The tuning of the PID controller was carried out manually to reduce overshoot and minimize settling time. The optimal gain values for various road profiles achieved were;

Profile-1: $K_p = 10,$ $K_i = 70,$ $K_d = 0.2$
Profile-2: $K_p = 3,$ $K_i = 10,$ $K_d = 0.2$
Profile-3: $K_p = 3,$ $K_i = 23,$ $K_d = 0.1$

5.2 Road Disturbances

Three kinds of road disturbances were considered for the purpose to cater for maximum types of real life conditions. The road profile-1 is taken as a sinusoidal bump of 10 cm (0.1 m) spread over a 5 s interval. This profile (Fig. 7) is given by following expression [14, 20].

$$w = 1 \begin{cases} a[u(t-5) - (t-10)]sin(0.2\pi t) & 5\,\mathrm{s} \leq t \leq 10\,\mathrm{s} \\ 0 & \text{otherwise} \end{cases} \tag{13}$$

where: $a = 0.1\,\mathrm{m}$ (bump height).

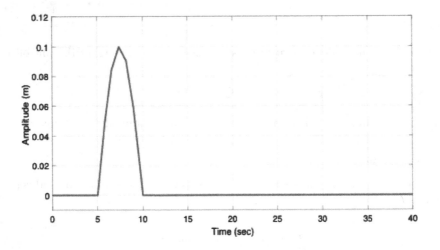

Fig. 7. Road disturbance profile-1

The profile-2 is taken as a single step of 10 cm. It is considered as a sudden step on the road surface [15]. The response of the suspension on this sudden step was also evaluated. This profile (Fig. 8) is expressed by the following expression

$$w = \begin{cases} 0 & 5\,\mathrm{s} \leq t \leq 10\,\mathrm{s} \\ 0.1 & t \geq 5\,\mathrm{s} \end{cases} \tag{14}$$

The road disturbance profile-3 is taken as a series of two consecutive jerks within a time period of 3 s. The bumps are sharp and depict the disturbance

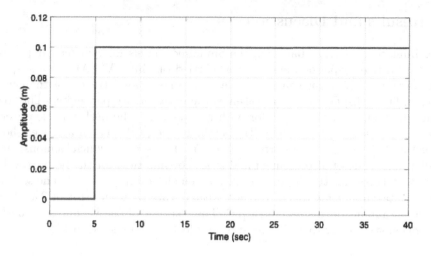

Fig. 8. Road disturbance profile-2

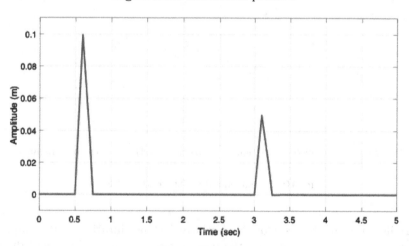

Fig. 9. Road disturbance profile-3

experienced by tyres at relatively faster speeds. The profile (Fig. 9) details are taken from [16,19] and the expression is given by:

$$w = a\{\frac{1 - cos(8\pi t)}{2}\} \tag{15}$$

$$a = \begin{cases} 0.11\,\mathrm{m} & 0.5\,\mathrm{s} \leq t \leq 0.75\,\mathrm{s} \\ 0.55\,\mathrm{m} & 3.0\,\mathrm{s} \leq t \leq 3.25\,\mathrm{s} \end{cases} \tag{16}$$

6   Results and Discussion

The simulation analysis, based on the Simulink models for quarter car passive and semi active suspension system, was carried out in MATLAB. The suspension travel and the displacement of the body mass (body travel) of the car in terms of linear displacement was taken as the performance parameter. The road disturbance was taken as input for both the systems. The performance criteria were taken in terms of rise time (Tr), settling time (Ts), percentage over-shoot (%OS) and the steady state error (eSS) [15]. The system which demonstrates smaller amplitude of displacement and lesser settling time for the body travel is considered better for the drive comfort and vehicle stability [16,17]. The settling time was taken as time taken to reach steady state with an error of 2% of the referenced amplitude/displacement [18]. The response of passive and semi-active suspension system for road disturbance profile-1 is as depicted in Fig. 10.

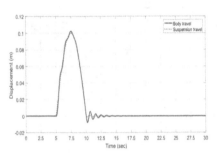
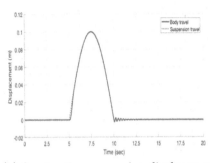

(a) Passive suspension displacement   (b) Semi-active suspension displacement

Fig. 10. Displacements with road profile-1

Profile-1 represents a smooth and relatively long duration (5 s) bump. It is observed from Fig. 10a that even the passive suspension (body travel) displays smooth response and experiences a percentage over-shoot of 2.3% and has a settling time of 7.05 s. The body travel for the designed PID controller based semi active suspension system (Fig. 10b), however, shows 0.1% over-shoot and a settling time of 5.22 s.

Figure 11 shows the response of passive and semi-active suspension system, for the road disturbance profile–2. Here the sharp step of 0.1 m in this disturbance, indicates the effectiveness of PID controller based semi-active system. Figure 11a shows the percentage over-shoot and settling time of body travel of passive system which is equal to 73.8% and 5.49 s. On the contrary, the body travel of semi active system (Fig. 11b) has over-shoot of just 6.1% and a settling time of 0.82 s.

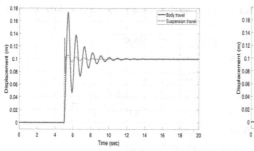 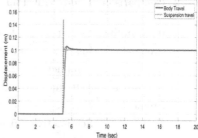

(a) Passive suspension displacement   (b) Semi-active suspension displacement

Fig. 11. Displacements with road profile-2

The comparison of passive and semi-active system for road profile-3 is given in Fig. 12 respectively. The percentage over-shoot of body travel of passive system (Fig. 12a) is 27.45% with settling time of 6.99 s. The body travel of semi-active system (Fig. 12b) shows much improved response with over-shoot of 11.98% and settling time of 3.07 s.

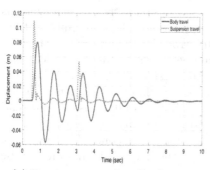 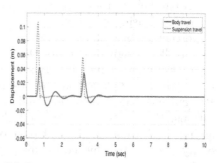

(a) Passive suspension displacement   (b) Semi-active suspension displacement

Fig. 12. Displacements with road profile-3

The complete comparison of both passive and semi active suspension simulated models is carried out in Table 2. The analysis clearly demonstrates the efficiency of PID controller based semi active suspension system to be much higher in terms of the performance parameters considered in this paper.

Table 2. Comparison of body travel for passive and semi-active suspension system

Road profile	System	Tr (sec)	Ts (sec)	%OS	eSS (m)
Profile-1	Passive	2.49	7.05	2.3	0
	Semi-active	2.50	5.22	0.1	0
%Improvement/Reduction		−0.4%	25.96%	%95.65	0
Profile-2	Passive	0.42	5.49	73.8	0
	Semi-active	0.44	0.82	6.1	0
%Improvement/Reduction		−4.76%	85.06%	%91.73	0
Profile-3	Passive	0.31	6.99	27.45	0
	Semi-active	0.13	3.07	11.98	0
%Improvement/Reduction		58.06%	56.08%	%56.36	0

7   Conclusion

Passive and Semi-active suspension systems have been reviewed in this paper and a comprehensive simulated comparison has been done among them. A PID controller for a controller based semi active suspension system was designed and tested in parallel with a conventional passive suspension system. Their analysis was compared using common performance parameters like rise time, settling time, percentage over-shoot and steady state error. The results reveal that the PID controller designed here, for the semi active system is highly efficient and shows a lot of improvement in terms of body/suspension oscillations and settling time. Hence we conclude that by adding an active damping element, we can greatly enhance the ride comfort and vehicle stability in all kinds of poor road conditions. For any future study on the subject, emphasis must be given to designing a self-tuning PID controller or exploring other controlling methods. Secondly the results achieved in this paper with the help of simulation may be verified using experiments.

References

1. Khot, S.M., Patil, S., Bhaye, N.A.: Simulation study of MR damper for bump road profile. In: International Conference on Nascent Technologies in the Engineering Field (ICNTE) (2017)
2. Appleyard, M., Wellstead, P.E.: Active suspensions: some background. In: IEEE Proceeding on Control Theory Applications, vol. 142, no. 2, March 1995
3. Sun, J., Yang, Q.: Compare and analysis of passive and active suspensions under random road excitation. In: IEEE International Conference on Automation and Logistics, Shenyang, China, pp. 1577–1580, August 2009
4. Sun, J., Sun, Y.: Comparative study on control strategy of active suspension system. In: 3rd International Conference on Measuring Technology and Mechatronics Automation, pp. 729–732. IEEE Computer Society (2011)

5. Kuber, C.: Modelling simulation and control of an active suspension system. Int. J. Mech. Eng. Technol. (IJMET) **5**(11), 66–75 (2014)
6. Pei, Q., Na, J., Huang, Y., Wu, X.: Adaptive estimation and control of MR damper for semi-active suspension systems. In: Proceedings of the 35th Chinese Control Conference, China, 27–29 July 2016
7. Jonasson, M., Roos, F.: Design and evaluation of an active electromechanical wheel suspension system. Mechatronics **18**(4), 218–230 (2008)
8. Nekoui, M.A., Hadavi, P.: Optimal control of an active suspension system. In: 14th International Power Electronics and Motion Control Conference, EPE-PEMC 2010 (2010)
9. Khemliche, M., Dif, I., Latreche, S., Bouamama, B.O.: Modelling and analysis of an active suspension 1/4 of vehicle with bond graph. In: 1st International Symposium on Control, Communications and Signal Processing (ISCCSP 2004), pp. 811–814 (2004)
10. Aldair, A.A., Wang, W.J.: Design an intelligent controller for full vehicle nonlinear active suspension systems. Int. J. Smart Sens. Intell. Syst. **4**(2), 224–243 (2011)
11. Sun, S., Tang, X., Li, W., Du, H.: Advanced vehicle suspension with variable stiffness and damping MR damper. In: 2017 IEEE International Conference on Mechatronics (ICM), pp 444–448 (2017)
12. Rao, K.D.: Modelling, simulation and control of semi active suspension system for auto mobiles under MATLAB simulink using PID controller. In: Third International Conference on Advances in Control and Optimization of Dynamical Systems (IFAC), India, March 2014
13. Çakan, A., Botsali, F.M., Tınkır, M.: Modelling and controller comparison for quarter car suspension system by using PID and Type-1 fuzzy logic. Appl. Mech. Mater. **598**, 524–528 (2014)
14. Sam, Y.M., Osman, H.S.O., Ghani, M.R.A.: A class of proportional-integral sliding mode control with application to active suspension system. Syst. Control Lett. **51**, 217–223 (2004)
15. Ahmed, A.S., Ali, A.S., Ghazaly, N.M., Jaber, G.T.: PID controller of active suspension system for a quarter car model. Int. J. Adv. Eng. Technol. **8**(6), 899–909 (2015)
16. Al-Mutar, W.H., Abdalla, T.Y.: Quarter car active suspension system control using PID controller tuned by PSO. Iraq J. Electr. Electron. Eng. **11**(2), 151–158 (2015)
17. Rajeswari, K., Uma, M.: PID Controller for enhancing ride comfort of vehicle suspension system. IJCTA **8**(5), 2441–2450 (2015)
18. Hu, G., Liu, Q., Ding, R., Li, G.: Vibration control of semi-active suspension system with magneto rheological damper based on hyperbolic tangent model. Adv. Mech. Eng. **9**(5), 1–15 (2017)
19. Agharkakli, A., Sabet, G.S., Barouz, A.: Simulation and analysis of passive and active suspension system using quarter car model for different road profile. Int. J. Eng. Trends Technol. **3**(5), 636–644 (2012)
20. Hashemipour, S.H., Rezaei lasboei, M., Khaliji, M.: A study of the performance of the PID controller and nonlinear controllers in vehicle suspension systems considering practical constraints. Res. J. Recent Sci. **3**, 86–95 (2014)

Performance Evaluation of Jacobi Iterative Solution for Sparse Linear Equation System on Multicore and Manycore Architectures

Samiah Alzahrani[1], Mohammad Rafi Ikbal[2(✉)], Rashid Mehmood[3],
Mahmoud Fayez[2], and Iyad Katib[1]

[1] Faulty of Information Technology, King Abdul Aziz University,
Jeddah, Saudi Arabia
salzahrani0683@stu.kau.edu.sa, iakatib@kau.edu.sa
[2] Fujitsu Technology Solutions, Jeddah, Saudi Arabia
{mohammad.rafi,mahmoud.fayez}@ts.fujitsu.com
[3] High Performance Computing Center, King Abdulaziz University,
Jeddah, Saudi Arabia
RMehmood@kau.edu.sa

Abstract. One of the common and pressing challenges in solving real-world problems in various domains, such as in smart cities, involves solving large sparse systems of linear equations. Jacobi iterative method is used to solve such systems in case if they are diagonally dominant. This research focuses on the parallel implementation of the Jacobi method to solve large systems of diagonally dominant linear equations on conventional CPUs and Intel Xeon Phi coprocessor. The performance is reported on the two architectures with a comparison in terms of the execution times.

Keywords: Jacobi iterative method · Sparse linear equation systems
Intel MIC · Intel Xeon Phi

1 Introduction

Many applications in the field of Mathematics and Sciences involve solving linear equation systems. For instance, Markov modelling of smart city applications and systems give rise to very large linear equation systems, a problem referred to as the curse of dimensionality, see, for instance, [1–5]. There are many types of linear equation systems, which can be represented and solved using various methods. One category of such system of linear equations is Diagonally Dominant System of Linear Equations (DDSLE). DDSLEs are represented in the form Ax = B where A is a square matrix formed with coefficients in a system of linear equations. A system of equations is said to be diagonally dominant if n[th] coefficient of nth equation is higher than sum of all other absolute coefficients irrespective of the sign it might have. For example, if we have n linear equations with n unknowns. Then first coefficient of first equation should be larger than the sum of other coefficients and the second coefficient of second equation should be larger than sum of other coefficients and so on. It should be noted

© ICST Institute for Computer Sciences, Social Informatics and Telecommunications Engineering 2018
R. Mehmood et al. (Eds.): SCITA 2017, LNICST 224, pp. 296–305, 2018.
https://doi.org/10.1007/978-3-319-94180-6_28

that we only consider absolute value of the coefficient; the sign carried by the coefficient either positive or negative is ignored. Besides being diagonally dominant, these systems also tend to be sparse. Since they are sparse in nature, only very less proportionate of the values carry a value, rest of the values is zero.

In this paper, we have implemented Compressed Sparse Row (CSR) method for storing values of matrix during computation. This not only reduces the memory footprint of the application but improves performance of the application since iterations does not include zero-valued elements.

The objective of this research is to evaluate the performance of Intel many Integrated Core (MIC) Architecture, the Intel Xeon Phi co-processor, in solving large diagonally dominant system of linear equations. We are comparing the performance of the code on traditional Intel Xeon CPUs with Intel Xeon Phi co-processors.

2 Background

With the advent of technology in almost all domains, many applications depend on mathematical equations to solve variety of problems. These applications range from financial and trading software, navigation control systems, healthcare systems, astronomical systems, military applications, etc. For these to work efficiently and timely manner, solving mathematical equations in least possible time is crucial.

The Jacobi iterative method will be used to solve large diagonally dominant sparse matrices. Since these systems are sparse in nature, we have implemented compressed sparse row format to process the matrices. Since CSRs use comparatively smaller memory to store the sparse matrix as well as benefit performance of the application by eliminating iterations involved in processing zero-value based elements of the matrix. Jacobi's algorithm is implemented using OpenMP takes advantage of shared-memory systems to launch multiple threads, which run in parallel. Using OpenMP has another benefit; it runs on Intel MIC Architecture seamlessly. This enables us to execute the same code on Intel CPU and Intel Xeon Phi co-processor without any modification to the actual code except directives to run the code on Intel MIC architecture.

2.1 System of Linear Equations

System of linear equations is collection of equations with same solution or same set of values for its variables. We are using matrices to represent these equations and these matrices are diagonally dominant.

Following equation denotes a system of n linear equations of the form $Ax = d$

$$A = \begin{bmatrix} a_{11} & a_{12} & \cdots & a_{1n} \\ a_{21} & a_{22} & \cdots & a_{2n} \\ \vdots & \vdots & \ddots & \vdots \\ a_{n1} & a_{n2} & \cdots & a_{nn} \end{bmatrix} \quad x = \begin{bmatrix} x_1 \\ x_2 \\ \vdots \\ x_n \end{bmatrix} \quad d = \begin{bmatrix} d_1 \\ d_2 \\ \vdots \\ d_n \end{bmatrix} \tag{1}$$

Matrix A is diagonally dominant if it satisfies following equation. The location of the element in the matrix is represented as values of i and j.

$$|a_{ii}| \geq \sum_{i \neq j} |a_{ij}| \tag{2}$$

2.2 Sparse Matrix

Sparse matrices have a higher proportion of zero-valued elements compared to non-zero elements. Since compute applications allocate same amount of memory for all the elements in an array irrespective of the value, this increases memory footprint of the application [6, 7]. There are many methods to overcome this problem and use the system memory efficiently, one such format is coordinate format (COO) [8]. But COO is not efficient in practice. We have implemented Compressed Sparse Row (CSR) format to store and retrieve matrices efficiently. This format uses one array to store values of the matrix whose value is non-zero and two arrays as look up table using, which we can retrieve, position of any element in the original sparse matrix. Several other formats to store sparse matrices exist, see [9, 10], and the references therein.

Since we are using CSR format to store the values of the matrix, we have changed the iteration method to process only non-zero values of the matrix. This reduces execution time of the application as the system does not process zero-valued elements, which resulted in reduction in complexity of the algorithm to Eq. (4).

Complexity of traditional algorithm is as follows, where n is dimension of square matrix

$$O = \left(n^2\right)$$

Complexity of algorithm using CSR format. M is number of non-zero elements in a matrix where $M \ll n^2$ since the matrices are sparse

$$O = (M)$$

2.3 Jacobi Method and JOR Iterative Methods

Jacobi method is one of the prominently used methods to solve diagonally dominant linear equation. This is one of stationary iterative method to solve set of linear equations. This method is of the form $x^{(k)} = Fx^{(k-1)} + c$, in this equation both F and c do not depend on k where $x^{(k)}$ is an approximate value tending towards the solution of the linear equations. These equations are in the form $Ax = b$ where A is a square matrix and x, b $\in R^n$. Computations performed by Jacobi's equation can be described in the following equation where M is the iteration count.

$$x_i^{(M)} = a_{ii}^{-1}\left(d_i - \sum_{i \neq j} a_{ij} x_j^{(m-1)}\right) \tag{3}$$

In the above equation, I and j represents row and column index of an element in the matrix and a denotes the element itself. $x_i^{(M)}$ and $x_j^{(M-1)}$ represents the ith coefficient of iteration numbered M and M − 1 respectively. Following is matrix notation of the above given equation.

$$x^{(M)} = \frac{1}{D}\left[(U + L)x^{(M-1)} + b\right] \tag{4}$$

Where D, L and U are partitions of square matrix A into its diagonal, upper triangular part and lower triangular part respectively.

There are many possible cases where Jacobi method does not converge, in such cases an under-relaxation parameter is introduced. This parameter can also be used as a catalyst to improve the convergence rate of Jacobi method. Using under-relaxation in Jacobi method is known as Jacobi over relaxation (JOR). Which can be represented in Eq. (5)

$$x_i^{(M)} = \alpha \widehat{x}_i^{(M)} + (1 - \alpha)x_i^{(M-1)} \tag{5}$$

In the above equation $\widehat{x}$ denotes one Jacobi iteration as show in Eq. (3) and $0 < \alpha < 2$ is the relaxation parameter. i varies from 0 to n where n is number of rows in square matrix A. if $\alpha < 1$ then the method is known as under-relaxed method and if α is >1 then it is over-relaxed method. If $\alpha = 1$ then it would be called Jacobi method without relaxation. Both Jacobi and JOR equations exhibit very slow convergence rate as discussed in [10]. In Jacobi and JOR methods old approximation of the vector is a dependency in calculating new approximation, hence these iterative methods exhibit embarrassingly parallel behavior.

2.4 Intel Xeon Phi Coprocessor (Intel MIC)

Many Integrated Core (MIC) architecture is PCIe-based coprocessors which is added to traditional hardware to enhance the performance of the system. These coprocessors add an additional 60+ usable cores with each core supporting 4-way simultaneous multithreading to existing system. The MIC coprocessor are based on x86 ISA with 64-bit and 512-bit wide SIMD vector instructions and registers. These cores have similar architecture as traditional Intel Xeon processor which enables standard programming language techniques such as OpenMP to be used on the accelerator card.

2.5 Programming Model

Though Intel Xeon Phi has similar architecture as traditional Intel Xeon processors, it's programming model is little different since it is connected to the host system through the PCIe bus. These devices are designed such that applications can leverage full potential of vector processors, memory bandwidth and cache. Through existing parallel programming APIs like OpenMP and MPI are supported in Intel MIC architecture, application developer should restructure the code such that it run on Intel MIC efficiently. Intel MIC supports three programming modes.

Native Mode. To enable this mode, dedicated network must be configured on Intel Xeon Phi coprocessor with dedicated IP address and host name. Once network is configured, users can login or execute code directly on Intel MIC like any other Unix system since Intel Xeon Phi runs embedded Linux operating system. Since this environment is like any other Unix environment, users can execute their application directly by copying it to coprocessor or from a shared storage.

Offload Execution Mode. In this mode, the program initially starts executing on the host processor and then offloads the tasks to the MIC to execute a block of instructions. The process running on the host controls the exchange of data between host and device. While MIC is executing part of the program, host may or may not participate to work in parallel. Figure 1 show an overview of offload mode.

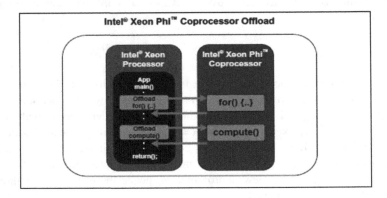

Fig. 1. Offload execution mode of Intel Xeon Phi

Symmetric Execution Mode. In this mode, the application processes execute on host and device. This may involve multiple hosts and device combinations. In modern application, the communication between processes takes place thorough Message Passing Interface (MPI). This mode is combination of traditional MPI programming model and Native mode execution of Intel MIC coprocessors since this model treats MIC as a node in a heterogeneous cluster.

3 Literature Review

Sparse matrix-vector multiplication (SpMV) is used in wide range of applications like signal processing, engineering, electronic circuit design, military, etc. Optimizing performance of applications solving sparse matrix-vector multiplication was topic of interest to various research communities and individuals.

In [11], they have implemented an extensive evaluation of SpMV kernel for both serial and parallel versions on diverse modern architectures. They have proposed number of optimization guidelines based on their study.

In [12], the authors have investigated optimization techniques to improve memory efficiency in SpMVs. Based on their study, they suggested to use register level optimization techniques if the size of the matrix is small. For larger matrices, which do not fit into registers available in the system, cache level optimization is recommended.

Vuduc [13] shows that the major challenge in developing highly optimized implementations of SpMV is selecting storage models and algorithm that take advantage of the properties of the matrix is unknown until execution. As per their observations, conventional implementations of SpMV can use only 10% or less CPU peak machine performance on cache-based superscalar architectures. While their implementations of SpMV, tuned using a methodology based on the empirical search, can, by contrast, reach up to 31% of peak machine speed and can be up to 4 times faster.

Design and implementation of SpMV on several important chip multiprocessor systems (CMP) is discussed in [14]. Since there are many available designs of CMP, selecting a design best suitable for solving SpMV along with selecting algorithms based on SpMV type was the challenge. Substantially, their results show that matrix and platform reliant on the tuning of SpMV for multicore.

A new strategy for improving the performance of SpMV is suggested in [15]. This solution involves using a loop transformation know as unroll-and-jam. Using this method improves performance by 11% which is a factor of 2.3. however; this approach is suitable only for sparse matrices that have dimensions of small number of predictable lengths.

One of the widely method used for SpMV application optimization is Blocking. There are two methods of Blocking, the first method exploits memory allocation at several levels like register [15, 16], L1 and L2 cache [12, 17] and storage buffers [17]. In second method indexing of elements is optimized to remove overhead which enhances memory bandwidth utilization [16, 18].

Intel Math Kernel Library (MKL) was used to optimize implementations of SpMV in paper [19]. As per their experiments, they could achieve 80% performance improvement with dense matrices. However; performance of sparse matrices was variable and the results out performed CPU in most cases.

In [20] they describe the factors that limit the SpMV performance Intel MIC architecture. The three factors are: low SIMD efficiency because of sparsity, the overhead caused by unstructured memory access and ununiform load balance caused due to uneven matrix dimensions. To overcome these problems, a new matrix format with name ELLPACK Sparse Block (ESB) was designed. This new matrix format was implemented on Knights Corner (KNC) which is latest generation of Intel Xeon Phi coprocessor, which has wider SIMD and other advanced features. To solve load imbalance problem, the authors proposed three load balancers.

The [21] improve the ELLPACK format to produce sliced ELLPACK with the use of SIMD vectorization on General Purpose Graphics Processing Units (GPGPUs). The SELL-C-σ (sliced ELLPACK) show its appropriateness on different hardware platforms. The authors aimed to find a format to process unified sparse matrix data efficiently on traditional CPUs. There are lot of improvement areas to achieve higher performance, these methods need to be explored.

Implementation of Compressed Sparse Row 5 (CSR5) to solve sparse matrices is discussed in [6]. The results of the experiments conclude that the performance improvement is average.

Fourth-order Runge-kitta method was implemented to solve sparse matrices in [22]. They used CSR format to store matrices and Intel MKL routes to solve the equations. They were able to achieve good performance improvement on CPU and Intel MIC

The work in [22, 23] aims to shorten the computation time for the transition matrices that arising from Markovian models of complicated systems on Intel Xeon Phi. They used CSR format as used in work [24], and HYB format is similar as in work [20]. Their method takes advantage of the thread-level parallelism and vectorization for the SpMV implementation. The numerical experiments result of CTMCs executed on Intel Xeon Phi coprocessors using offload mode show that HYB format delivers higher performance rate than data stored in CSR format.

4   Research Design and Methodology

First step in the experiment was to parallelize Jacobi algorithm. We have implemented serial version of the algorithm and tested the functionality, then we have parallelized the row operations such that each row operation will be processed by a separate thread on a processor such that n rowed matrix will spawn n processes. Once we have made sure that the results of serial version and parallel version is consistent, we have implemented Compressed Row Format (CSR) to store and retrieve sparse matrices and eliminated iterations which involve zero-valued elements of the matrix. These modifications add two advantages to the program. First advantage is that there is reduction in memory foot print of the application and performance increase in memory access as mentioned in [20]. The number of thread spawned is now decreased to M where M is number of elements in a sparse matrix whose value is not zero and $M < N^2$ where N is dimension of the matrix since the matrix is sparse in nature.

We have conducted our experiment on E5-2695v2 (Ivy Bridge) dual socket server with 12 cores on each socket with 2.4 GHz frequency. Each server has 96 GB of physical memory. The coprocessor used is Intel Xeon Phi 5110P. This coprocessor has 60 usable CPU cores operating at 1.05 GHz frequency and 8 GB memory.

We have executed multiple iterations of the program using OpenMP on traditional CPUs and using Offload model on Intel MIC and the results are plotted for comparison.

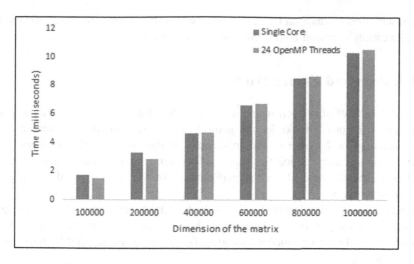

Fig. 2. Performance of single CPU *vs* 24 OpenMP threads

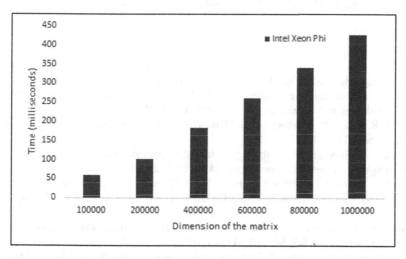

Fig. 3. Performance on Intel Xeon Phi coprocessor (Intel MIC)

5 Results

We have executed multiple iterations of the application with different matrix starting from 100000 to 1000000 and the results are plotted in Figs. 2 and 3. As seen in the Figs. 2 and 3, performance of the application on 24 CPUs using OpenMP does not show considerable performance over performance on single CPU. We have plotted a separate graph for the performance of Jacobi method on Intel Xeon Phi coprocessor since the performance of the application on Intel MIC architecture is very poor on comparison with performance on CPU. We believe that this is because of initialization and communication overhead compared to small workload.

6   Conclusions and Future Work

Based on the results of our experiments, we believe that Intel MIC architecture is not suitable platform for problem like Jacobi method to solve diagonally dominant sparse matrices. This may be because of the sparseness of the system which reduces the computations significantly. Since the workload is very small, communication and initialization overhead overshadows the performance of the application delivering a poor performance overall.

Our future work is to implement Jacobi method on dense matrices and evaluate the performance on heterogeneous architectures. We will also investigate further our implementation of the Jacobi method to identify the performance bottlenecks and improve the speedup.

Acknowledgements. The experiments reported in this paper were performed on the Aziz supercomputer at King Abdul Aziz University, Jeddah, Saudi Arabia.

References

1. Altowaijri, S., Mehmood, R., Williams, J.: A quantitative model of grid systems performance in healthcare organisations. In: 2010 International Conference on Intelligent Systems, Modelling and Simulation, pp. 431–436. IEEE (2010)
2. Mehmood, R., Lu, J.A.: Computational Markovian analysis of large systems. J. Manuf. Technol. Manag. **22**, 804–817 (2011)
3. Mehmood, R., Alturki, R., Zeadally, S.: Multimedia applications over metropolitan area networks (MANs). J. Netw. Comput. Appl. **34**, 1518–1529 (2011)
4. Mehmood, R., Meriton, R., Graham, G., Hennelly, P., Kumar, M.: Exploring the influence of big data on city transport operations: a Markovian approach. Int. J. Oper. Prod. Manag. **37**, 75–104 (2017)
5. Mehmood, R., Graham, G.: Big data logistics: a health-care transport capacity sharing model. Procedia Comput. Sci. **64**, 1107–1114 (2015)
6. Liu, W., Vinter, B.: CSR5: An Efficient Storage Format for Cross-Platform Sparse Matrix-Vector Multiplication (2015)
7. Pissanetzky, S.: Sparse Matrix Technology electronic edition
8. Saad, Y.: Iterative Methods for Sparse Linear Systems. Society for Industrial and Applied Mathematics, Philadelphia (2003)
9. Mehmood, R.: Serial disk-based analysis of large stochastic models. In: Baier, C., Haverkort, B.R., Hermanns, H., Katoen, J.-P., Siegle, M. (eds.) Validation of Stochastic Systems. LNCS, vol. 2925, pp. 230–255. Springer, Heidelberg (2004). https://doi.org/10.1007/978-3-540-24611-4_7
10. Mehmood, R., Crowcroft, J.: Parallel iterative solution method for large sparse linear equation systems. Technical report Number UCAM-CL-TR-650, Computer Laboratory, University of Cambridge, Cambridge, UK (2005)

11. Goumas, G., Kourtis, K., Anastopoulos, N., Karakasis, V., Koziris, N.: Performance evaluation of the sparse matrix-vector multiplication on modern architectures. J. Supercomput. **50**, 36–77 (2009)
12. Im, E.-J., Yelick, K., Vuduc, R.: Sparsity: optimization framework for sparse matrix kernels. Int. J. High Perform. Comput. Appl. **18**, 135–158 (2004)
13. Vuduc, R.W.: Automatic performance tuning of sparse matrix kernels (2003). https://dl.acm.org/citation.cfm?id=1023242
14. Williams, S., Oliker, L., Vuduc, R., Shalf, J., Yelick, K., Demmel, J.: Optimization of sparse matrix-vector multiplication on emerging multicore platforms. Parallel Comput. **35**, 178–194 (2009)
15. Mellor-Crummey, J., Garvin, J.: Optimizing sparse matrix-vector product computations using unroll and jam. Int. J. High Perform. Comput. Appl. **18**, 225–236 (2004)
16. Pinar, A., Heath, M.T.: Improving performance of sparse matrix-vector multiplication. In: Proceedings of the 1999 ACM/IEEE conference on Supercomputing (CDROM) - Supercomputing 1999, p. 30–es. ACM Press, New York (1999)
17. Nishtala, R., Vuduc, R., Demmel, J.W., Yelick, K.A.: When cache blocking of sparse matrix vector multiply works and why. Appl. Algebra Eng. Commun. Comput. **18**, 297–311 (2007)
18. Vuduc, R.W., Moon, H.-J.: Fast sparse matrix-vector multiplication by exploiting variable block structure. In: Yang, L.T., Rana, O.F., Di Martino, B., Dongarra, J. (eds.) HPCC 2005. LNCS, vol. 3726, pp. 807–816. Springer, Heidelberg (2005). https://doi.org/10.1007/11557654_91
19. Deshmukh, O., Negrut, D.: Characterization of Intel Xeon Phi for linear algebra workloads (2014)
20. Liu, X., Smelyanskiy, M., Chow, E., Dubey, P.: Efficient sparse matrix-vector multiplication on x86-based many-core processors. In: Proceedings of the 27th international ACM conference on International conference on supercomputing - ICS 2013, p. 273. ACM Press, New York (2013)
21. Kreutzer, M., Hager, G., Wellein, G., Fehske, H., Bishop, A.R.: A unified sparse matrix data format for efficient general sparse matrix-vector multiplication on modern processors with wide simd units. SIAM J. Sci. Comput. **36**, C401–C423 (2014)
22. Bylina, B., Potiopa, J.: Explicit fourth-order Runge-Kutta method on Intel Xeon Phi coprocessor. Int. J. Parallel Program. **45**, 1073–1090 (2017)
23. Bylina, B., Potiopa, J.: Data structures for Markov chain transition matrices on Intel Xeon Phi. In: 2016 Federated Conference on Computer Science and Information Systems (2016)
24. Saule, E., Kaya, K., Çatalyürek, Ü.V.: Performance evaluation of sparse matrix multiplication kernels on Intel Xeon Phi. Presented at the 2014 (2014)

Parallel Sparse Matrix Vector Multiplication on Intel MIC: Performance Analysis

Hana Alyahya[1(✉)], Rashid Mehmood[2], and Iyad Katib[1]

[1] Computer Science Department, Faculty of Computing
and Information Technology, King Abdulaziz University,
Jeddah 21589, Kingdom of Saudi Arabia
Hana.alyahya@gmail.com, iakatib@kau.edu.sa
[2] High-Performance Computing Center, King Abdulaziz University,
Jeddah, Kingdom of Saudi Arabia
RMehmood@kau.edu.sa

Abstract. Numerous important scientific and engineering applications rely on and are hindered by, the intensive computational and storage requirements of sparse matrix-vector multiplication (SpMV) operation. SpMV also forms an important part of many (stationary and non-stationary) iterative methods for solving linear equation systems. Its performance is affected by factors including the storage format used to store the sparse matrix, the specific computational algorithm and its implementation. While SpMV performance has been studied extensively on conventional CPU architectures, research on its performance on emerging architectures, such as Intel Many Integrated Core (MIC) Architecture, is still in its infancy. In this paper, we provide a performance analysis of the parallel implementation of SpMV on the first-generation of Intel Xeon Phi Coprocessor, Intel MIC, named Knights Corner (KNC). We use the offload programming model to offload the SpMV computations to MIC using OpenMP. We measure the performance in terms of the execution time, offloading time and memory usage. We achieve speedups of up to 11.63x on execution times and 3.62x on offloading times using up to 240 threads compared to the sequential implementation. The memory usage varies depending on the size of the sparse matrix and the number of non-zero elements in the matrix.

Keywords: SpMV · Intel Many Integrated Core Architecture (MIC)
KNC · OpenMP · CSR · Xeon Phi

1 Introduction

Numerous important scientific, engineering and smart city applications require computations of sparse matrix-vector multiplication (SpMV) [1–5]. The SpMV operation is also an important part of many iterative solvers of linear equation systems, both stationary (e.g. Jacobi method) and non-stationary (e.g., Conjugate Gradient (CG)) [6]. The performance of SpMV is affected by factors including the storage format used to store the sparse matrix, the specific computation algorithm and its implementation. SpMV is considered a bottleneck due to its intensive computational and storage needs. Sparse matrices that arise from real life problems typically are large but consist of a

© ICST Institute for Computer Sciences, Social Informatics and Telecommunications Engineering 2018
R. Mehmood et al. (Eds.): SCITA 2017, LNICST 224, pp. 306–322, 2018.
https://doi.org/10.1007/978-3-319-94180-6_29

relatively small number of nonzero elements. Efficient storage formats are required to store only the nonzero elements such that the use of memory is minimized while providing flexible and fast access to the matrix nonzero elements. Many sparse storage formats have been proposed over the years, well-known of these include, among others, the Coordinate format (COO), Compressed Sparse Row (CSR) format, Modified Sparse Row (MSR), Modified MTBDD format, and the Diagonal format [7–9].

The design of the current systems brings new challenges and opportunities. Compared to systems over the last years, today's systems show that while the number of cores increases the performance get better [10]. The multicore, many-core and storage capabilities allow developers to optimize their algorithms and benefit from those technologies. Many Integrated Core (MIC) architecture is a highly parallel engine and efficient processor architecture that achieve high performance through utilization of large of number of cores like vector register and high bandwidth on package memory. Intel Knights Corner (KNC) is the name of the first generation based on MIC architecture. The second generation of Intel Xeon Phi will be based on Intel Knights Landing (KNL) [11] chip and it will be available as stand-alone processor in addition to coprocessor.

In this paper, we provide a performance analysis of parallel implementation of SpMV on the first-generation of Intel Xeon Phi Coprocessor named Knights Corner (KNC). We used the offload programming model to offload the SpMV to MIC. OpenMP directive constructs was used for parallelization. The well-known Compressed Row Storage (CSR) format was chosen to store the sparse matrix efficiently. To measure the performance, we have calculated the execution time, offloading time and memory usage. The experimental results show that the performance of the parallel implementation achieved up to 11.63x performance gain on execution time and 3.62x on offloading time compared to the sequential implementation. The memory usage varies depending on the size of the sparse matrix and the number of non-zero elements in the matrix.

The rest of the paper is organized as follows: In Sect. 2, background on the SpMV computation and Intel MIC architecture is presented. Section 3 reviews the literature related to parallel implementation of SpMV. Section 4 explains the methodology used in this paper. Section 5 discusses the results and gives performance analysis of the SpMV. Section 6 concludes the paper.

2   Background

2.1   Sparse Matrix Vector Multiplication (SpMV)

The sparse matrix vector multiplication kernel is shown in Eq. (1) where A is a square sparse matrix N × N, x and y are vectors of length N. The matrix A is multiplied by vector x and added to vector y

$$y = y + Ax \tag{1}$$

Due to the irregular pattern of the non-zero values in the sparse matrix A, the SpMV considered to be one of the most time-consuming kernel. As result, the performance of the SpMV is poor. The compressed row storage format CSR is one of the solution to efficiently store the sparse matrices and reduce the memory overhead. CSR store the sparse matrices as follow: it has three arrays, val[nnz] array of size nnz where nnz is the number of non-zero elements in matrix A. val[nnz] array is used to store the value of non-zero elements. Col_in[nnz] is an array of size nnz and it stores the column indices of non-zeros. Row_ptr[n + 1] is an array of size n + 1 and it stores non-zeros in each row [8].

2.2 Intel Many Integrated Core Architecture (MIC)

The Intel Many Integrated Core Architecture is an architecture developed by Intel company. The key feature of this architecture is that in one chip, there are many intel® processor cores. Another advantage of this architecture is that it supports many programming languages such as the standard C, Fortran, and C++. The flexibility of compiling and running the code in any of Intel® Xeon® processors is also an important feature. In addition, it supports the most widely used parallel programming models such as OpenMP and MPI [12]. The Intel products that based on this architecture are more likely used in the high-performance computing applications as well as in supercomputers [13].

Intel Xeon Phi coprocessor is based on Intel MIC architecture. It supports up to 61 small x86 cores that works together. It has 8 memory controllers and support up to 16 GDDR channels. It has a transfer speed of 5.5GT/s in theory. Intel Xeon Phi has two level of cache memory. The instruction level cache with size of 32 KB and the data cache with size of 32 KB [14]. Figure 1 shows an overview of Intel MIC architecture.

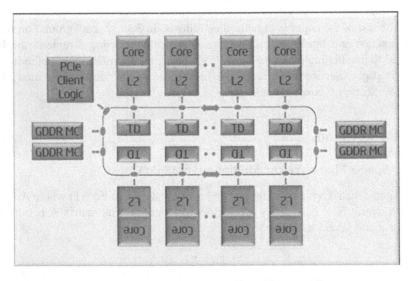

Fig. 1. Overview of Intel MIC architecture [6]

Xeon Phi has two execution modes: offload execution and native (coprocessor) execution [15]. In the offload mode, the host send part of the code to xeon phi and the output data is sent back from the coprocessor to xeon. Whereas, in the native mode, the code is run natively in the coprocessor. Figures 2 and 3 shows the two modes.

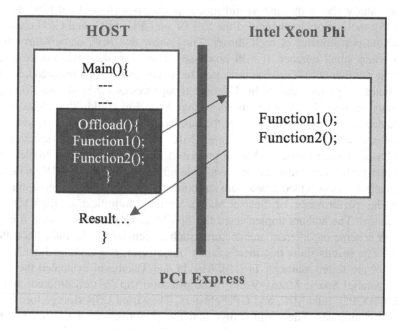

Fig. 2. Offloading mode in Xeon Phi

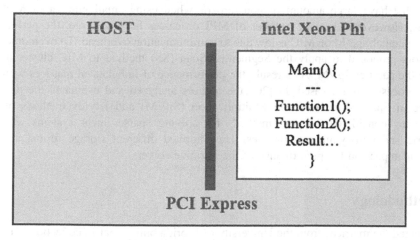

Fig. 3. Native mode in Xeon Phi

3 Related Work

Numerous studies have been done in the SpMV computation as it is used in many scientific and engineering applications. Ye et al. [9] report an implementation of SpMV computations on Intel MIC architecture using OpenMP, MPI, and hybrid MPI/OpenMP models. Their study shows that the hybrid model performs well on Intel MIC architecture. In [15], the authors implemented the SpMV on CPU, MIC, and GPU clusters and evaluate the performance of each cluster. They show that MIC outperform other accelerators using small number of MPI processes. However, the performance goes down when the number of MPI process increases due to communication overhead. Saule et al. [16] studies the performance of Intel Xeon Phi coprocessor for SpMV and focuses on the memory bandwidth. Their results show that Xeon Phi couldn't reach its peak performance due to the memory latency not the bandwidth. Xing et al. [17] presented a parallel implementation of SpMV on Intel MIC architecture using specialized ELLPACK-based storage format and three proposed load balancer. Their implementation has better performance than the best available implementation of SpMV on GPU.

In [18], the authors designed a new data structure for general sparse matrix storage to improve the performance of Sparse Matrix-Vector Multiplication (SpVM) on modern hardware. The authors implemented the SpVM using standard storage format CSR and their scheme on different architectures such as general CPUs, Intel Xeon Phi and GPGPU. The results show that their scheme outperforms the CSR on Intel Xeon Phi on most of the tested matrices. In [19], Maeda and Takahashi evaluated the performance of parallel Sparse Matrix-Vector Multiplication (SpVM) on different architectures such as CPU, Intel MIC, and GPU clusters. They used CSR storage format to store the sparse matrices. The result shows that the performance of parallel SpVM using CPU cluster in comparison to single process is increased by 42.57. In some matrices the performance is low due to load imbalance and communication overheads. The performance of parallel SpVM on accelerators is higher than on CPU cluster in the matrices that have large amount of non-zero or when using small number of MPI processes. However, when the number of MPI processes become large, the performance of parallel SpVM on MIC is low due to communication overhead. To overcome, the authors proposed to apply the Segmented Scan (SS) method to MIC cluster to improve the parallel SpVM. As a result, the performance of imbalanced matrices with 64 MPI processes is increased. In [20], the authors analyzed and evaluated the performance of Sparse Matrix Vector Multiplication (SpVM) and Krylov methods on GPUs. They considered different methods for solving sparse linear systems with symmetric and non-symmetric matrices. They applied different storage format and show their impact on the performance of the iterative solvers.

4 Methodology

We collected the matrices from the University of Florida online matrix collection [21]. We collected square matrices only and ignore other matrices. The SpMV is based on the off-diagonal matrices only because we are implementing the Jacobi iterative method for future work. The sparse matrices are form different application domains such as optimization problem, directed graph, undirected random graph, circuit simulation problem, undirected graph, directed weighted graph, undirected multigraph, computational fluid dynamics problems, structural problem, and electromagnetics problem. Table 1 shows the application and their abbreviation. For simplicity, we will use abbreviation in the remaining parts of the paper. The details of the matrices are given in Table 2. We mention the dimension, the non-zero elements, the non-zero elements per row, the non-zero elements off diagonal, and the application domain. Figures 4, 5, 6, and 7 plots sparsity structure of some matrices from the collection.

Table 1. Applications name and their abbreviation

Application name	Abbreviation
Optimization problem	OP
Directed graph	DG
Undirected random graph	URG
Circuit simulation problem	CSP
Undirected graph	UG
Directed weighted graph	DWG
Undirected multigraph	UMG
Computational fluid dynamics problem	CFDP
Structural problem	SP
Electromagnetics problem	EMP
Model reduction problem	MRP

Table 2. Sparse matrices properties

Name	Size	nnz	nnz/row	Off diagonal nnz	Application
nlpkkt240	28.0 M	401.2 M	14.33	373.2 M	OP
arabic-2005	22.7 M	640.0 M	28.14	420.8 M	DG
rgg_n_2_24_s0	16.8 M	132.6 M	7.90	88.4 M	URG
circuit5 M	16.8 M	50.3 M	10.71	33.6 M	CSP
delaunay_n24	16.8 M	50.3 M	3.00	33.6 M	UG
nlpkkt200	16.2 M	232.2 M	14.30	216.0 M	OP
wb-edu	9.8 M	57.2 M	5.81	38.0 M	DG
nlpkkt160	8.3 M	118.9 M	14.25	110.6 M	OP
indochina-2004	7.4 M	194.1 M	26.18	127.7 M	DG
ljournal-2008	5.4 M	79.0 M	14.73	51.9 M	DG
cage15	5.2 M	99.2 M	19.24	94.0 M	DWG
soc-LiveJournal1	4.8 M	69.0 M	14.23	45.7 M	DG
channel-500x100x100-b050	4.8 M	42.7 M	8.89	28.5 M	UG
kron_g500-logn21	2.1 M	91.0 M	43.41	14.1 M	UMG
HV15R	2.0 M	283.1 M	140.33	281.1 M	CFDP
wikipedia-20051105	1.6 M	19.8 M	12.08	13.2 M	DG

(*continued*)

Table 2. (*continued*)

Name	Size	nnz	nnz/row	Off diagonal nnz	Application
G3_circuit	1.6 M	4.6 M	2.92	3.0 M	CSP
Flan_1565	1.6 M	59.5 M	38.01	57.9 M	SP
af_shell10	1.5 M	27.1 M	17.96	25.6 M	SP
cage14	1.5 M	27.1 M	18.02	25.6 M	DWG
Hook_1498	1.5 M	31.2 M	20.83	29.7 M	SP
StocF-1465	1.5 M	11.2 M	7.67	9.8 M	CFDP
Geo_1438	1.4 M	32.3 M	22.46	29.7 M	SP
Serena	1.4 M	33.0 M	23.69	31.6 M	SP
in-2004	1.4 M	16.9 M	12.23	11.0 M	DG
atmosmodd	1.3 M	8.8 M	6.94	7.5 M	CFDP
hollywood-2009	1.1 M	57.5 M	50.46	38.0 M	UG
dielFilterV3real	1.1 M	45.2 M	40.99	44.1 M	EMP
bone010	986.7 K	36.3 M	36.82	35.3 M	MRP
ldoor	952.2 K	23.7 M	24.93	22.8 M	SP
audikw_1	943.7 K	39.3 M	41.64	38.4 M	SP
RM07R	381.7 K	37.5 M	98.16	37.1 M	CFDP

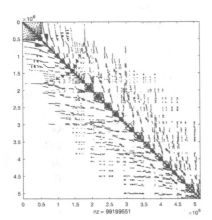

Fig. 4. Sparsity of matrix Cage15

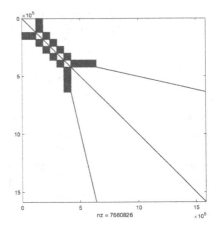

Fig. 5. Sparsity of matrix G3_circuit

We have a total of 32 sparse matrices all of them are in the Matrix Market format. We convert them to CSR and apply parallel SpMV computation. The parallelization process works as follow: the instruction is divided among the threads. Each thread will do the calculation and bring the results back. This process continue until the loop is finished. The number of threads used are 1, 4, 16, 32, 64, 128, and 240. Figure 8 shows the workflow.

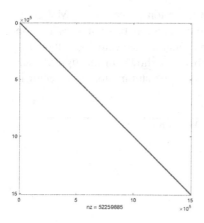

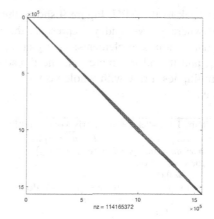

Fig. 6. Sparsity of matrix af_shell10   **Fig. 7.** Sparsity of matrix Flan_1565

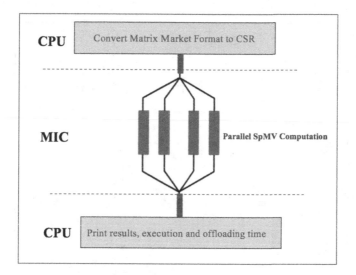

Fig. 8. Workflow

Algorithm 1 shows the pseudocode of the parallel SpMV. In line 2, an OpenMP pragma is added to the outer loop so, each thread will do the computation separately until they reach the end of the loop. The outer loop will begin with zero until it reaches the size of Matrix A which is n in this case. The inner loop will start from the first row that contains non-zero elements and end at last row that contains non-zero. Line 6 shows the main operation. Each row will be multiplied by the values of vector x and then will be added to vector y. When the outer loop finishes the result will be returned and sent back to the CPU. Figure 9 shows the parallelization process of SpMV computation where y_1, y_2, and y_n represents the y vector, colored boxes represents the sparse matrix non-zero elements, x_1, x_2, and x_n represents the x vector, and thread $_0$, thread $_1$, and thread $_{th\_n}$ represents the thread number. As shown in the figure, each thread multiplies a row with whole vector x. At the end, the summation of y vector is performed.

Algorithm 1 Parallel Sparse Matrix Vector Multiplication With CSR, y=y+Ax

---
1: **procedure** SPMV-CSR($val, x, n, row\_ptr, col\_in$)
2:     #pragma omp parallel for private(j)
3:     **for** $i = 0 : n$ **do**
4:         $y = 0.0$
5:         **for** $j = row\_ptr[i] : row\_ptr[i + 1]$ **do**
6:             $y+ = val[j] * x[col\_in[j]]$
7:         **end for**
8:     **end for**
9: **end procedure**

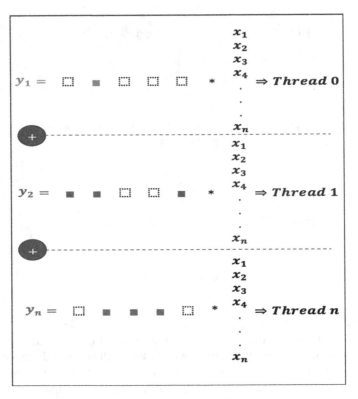

Fig. 9. Parallelization of SpMV

5   Results and Analysis

5.1   Environmental Setup

For experiments, we use Aziz supercomputer which is a high-performance computer located in King Abdul-Aziz University, Jeddah. It is one of the top 500 supercomputers in the world and one of the top 10 supercomputers in Kingdom of Saudi Arabia [22]. Table 3 shows the specification of tools used in the experiments.

Table 3. Specification of tools used

	Tools/Library	Version
OS	Linux	2.6.32-358.23.2.el6.x86_64
OpenMP	OpenMP	17.0.2
C Compiler	Intel C Compiler (icc)	17.0.2

5.2   Experimental Results

To implement the parallel SpMV efficiently on Intel MIC architecture we have followed three steps. Firstly, we read the sparse matrix in CSR format since the downloaded matrices are in the Matrix Market (MM) format. This is done using the CPU as it is having large memory compared to MIC. Secondly, when the matrix and vector is ready, we offloaded the part of the code that has the SpMV computation to MIC. After the SpMV offloaded to MIC, we use OpenMP pragmas to parallelize the "for" loops. Finally, the results are sent from the coprocessor to the host and the host will print the results and the execution time. We calculate the execution time and offloading time using different number of threads 1, 4, 8, 16, 32, 64, 128, and 240. In addition, we calculate amount of memory used by each matrix. Note that the execution time is the time taken to execute the SpMV computation and offloading time is the time taken to offload the SpMV computation to MIC and that includes the execution time. For simplicity, we divided the matrices into four groups according to their sizes, Groups 1, 2, 3, and 4, each group have eight matrices. The details of these matrices have been given earlier in Sect. 4.

Figures 10, 11, 12, and 13 show the execution time against the number of threads for Groups 1, 2, 3, and 4, respectively. It can be clearly seen in Fig. 10 that using 240 threads gives the best execution time among others. On average, the execution time of parallel implementation with 240 threads is 4.59x faster than the serial one. Group No.2 has exactly the same behavior as the first one except the last three matrices. The best execution time can be found in 16 threads for matrix named kron_g500-logn21 and 128 threads for matrices HV15R and wikipedia-20051105. Group No.3 and 4 are different, the execution time varies from one matrix to another but still the parallel execution is better than the serial one.

Figures 14, 15, 16, and 17 show the offloading time against the number of threads to group 1, 2, 3, and 4. For offloading time, all four groups have the same behavior of execution time. The best offloading time in Fig. 14 is when using 240 threads. The

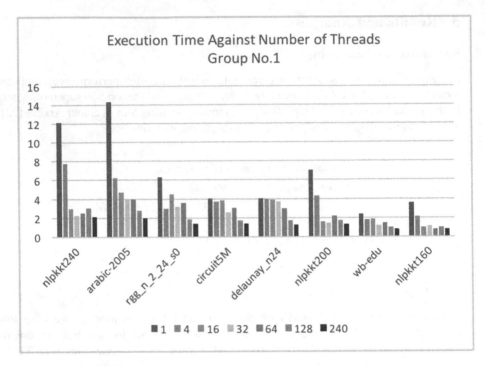

Fig. 10. Execution time against number of threads Group No. 1

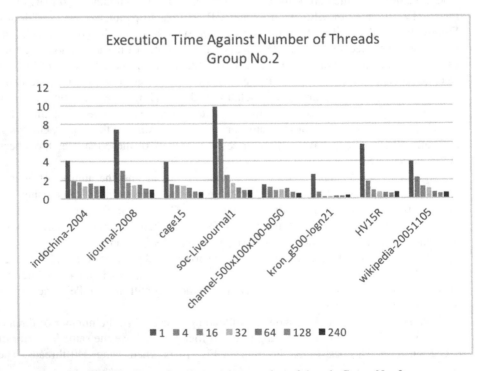

Fig. 11. Execution time against number of threads Group No. 2

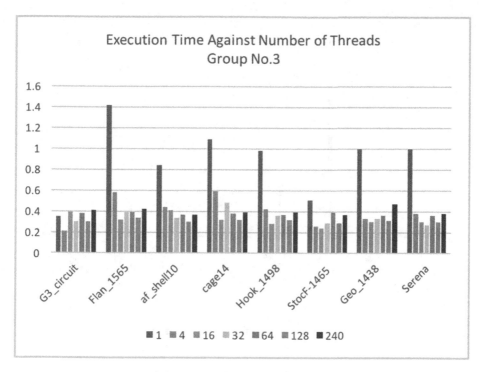

Fig. 12. Execution time against number of threads Group No. 3

second group is the same except the las three matrices which has best offloading time when using 16 and 128 threads. Although, the offloading time in Group No. 3 and 4 varies from one matrix to the another, the parallel implementation still better than serial one.

Finally, Fig. 18 shows the memory usage against the number of off diagonal non-zeros. It can be clearly seen that the off diagonal non-zero has a strong effect in the memory. The larger the off diagonal non-zeros are the larger memory is needed. However, that doesn't apply to some matrices which may be affected by other factors rather than the off diagonal non-zeros.

To summarize, the execution time of the parallel implementation is 4.89x faster than the sequential implementation. The offloading time of the parallel implementation is 1.65x faster than the sequential one. The memory usage depends on the off diagonal non-zeros and some other factors.

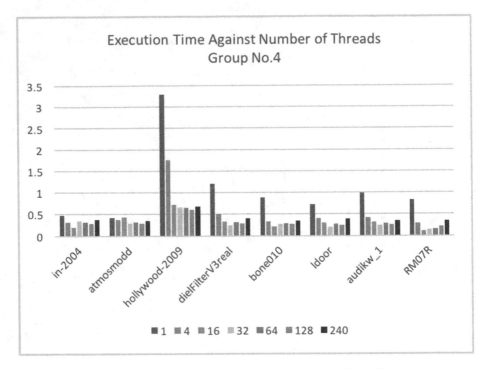

Fig. 13. Execution time against number of threads Group No. 4

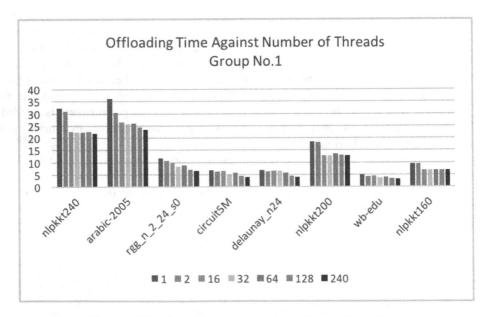

Fig. 14. Offloading time against number of threads Group No. 1

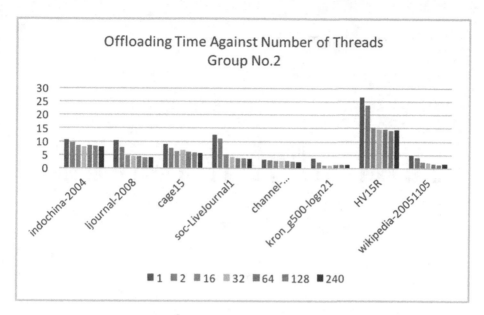

Fig. 15. Offloading time against number of threads Group No. 2

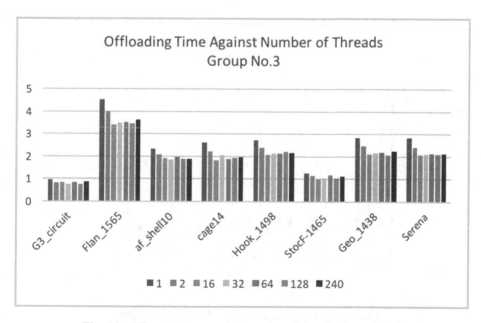

Fig. 16. Offloading time against number of threads Group No. 3

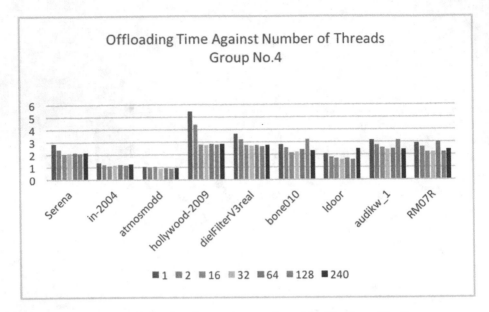

Fig. 17. Offloading time against number of threads Group No. 4

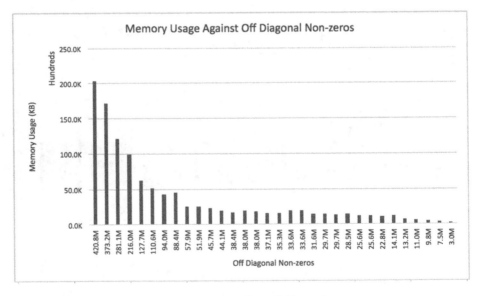

Fig. 18. Memory usage against off diagonal non-zeros

6   Conclusion

In this paper, we presented a parallel implementation of SpMV computation using Intel MIC architecture. The standard storage format CSR used to store the sparse matrices. To measure the performance, we use execution time, offloading time, and memory usage. The performance of the parallel SpMV achieved up to 11.63x on the Intel Xeon Phi coprocessor. In addition, the offloading time was improved by up to 3.62 times with parallel implementation. The memory usage varies depending on the off diagonal non-zero elements but in most cases the larger is the number of non-zeros the larger memory is needed.

Acknowledgments. The experiments reported in this paper were performed on the Aziz supercomputer at King AbdulAziz University, Jeddah, Saudi Arabia.

References

1. Mehmood, R., Lu, J.A.: Computational Markovian analysis of large systems. J. Manuf. Technol. Manag. **22**, 804–817 (2011)
2. Mehmood, R., Alturki, R., Zeadally, S.: Multimedia applications over metropolitan area networks (MANs). J. Netw. Comput. Appl. **34**, 1518–1529 (2011)
3. Mehmood, R., Meriton, R., Graham, G., Hennelly, P., Kumar, M.: Exploring the influence of big data on city transport operations: a Markovian approach. Int. J. Oper. Prod. Manag. **37**, 75–104 (2016)
4. Altowaijri, S., Mehmood, R., Williams, J.: A quantitative model of grid systems performance in healthcare organisations. In: ISMS 2010 - UKSim/AMSS 1st International Conference on Intelligent Systems, Modelling and Simulation, pp. 431–436 (2010)
5. Mehmood, R., Graham, G.: Big data logistics: a health-care transport capacity sharing model. Procedia Comput. Sci. **64**, 1107–1114 (2015)
6. Mehmood, R.: Disk-Based Techniques for Efficient Solution of Large Markov Chains (2004)
7. Banu, S.J.: Performance Analysis on Parallel Sparse Matrix Vector Multiplication Micro-Benchmark Using Dynamic Instrumentation Pintool, pp. 129–136 (2013)
8. Mehmood, R., Crowcroft, J.: Parallel iterative solution method for large sparse linear equation systems. Technical report Number UCAM-CL-TR-650, Computer Laboratory, University of Cambridge, Cambridge, UK (2005)
9. Mehmood, R.: Serial disk-based analysis of large stochastic models. In: Baier, C., Haverkort, Boudewijn R., Hermanns, H., Katoen, J.-P., Siegle, M. (eds.) Validation of Stochastic Systems. LNCS, vol. 2925, pp. 230–255. Springer, Heidelberg (2004). https://doi.org/10.1007/978-3-540-24611-4_7
10. Giles, M.B., Reguly, I.: Trends in high-performance computing for engineering calculations. Philos. Trans. R. Soc. A. **372**, 20130319 (2014)
11. Sodani, A., Gramunt, R., Corbal, J., Kim, H.S., Vinod, K., Chinthamani, S., Hutsell, S., Agarwal, R., Liu, Y.C.: Knights landing: second-generation Intel Xeon Phi product. IEEE Micro **36**, 34–46 (2016)
12. Cramer, T., Schmidl, D., Klemm, M., Mey, D.: OpenMP Programming on Intel Xeon Phi Coprocessors: An Early Performance Comparison. Marc@Rwth, pp. 38–44 (2012)
13. Intel® Many Integrated Core Architecture - Advanced

14. Wang, E., Zhang, Q., Shen, B., Zhang, G., Lu, X., Wu, Q., Wang, Y.: High-Performance Computing on the Intel® Xeon Phi™. Springer, Cham (2014). https://doi.org/10.1007/978-3-319-06486-4

15. Maeda, H., Takahashi, D.: Performance evaluation of sparse matrix-vector multiplication using GPU/MIC cluster. In: 2015 Third International Symposium on Computing and Networking, pp. 396–399 (2015)

16. Saule, E., Kaya, K., Atalyürek, U.V.Ç.: Performance Evaluation of Sparse Matrix Multiplication Kernels on Intel Xeon Phi (2013)

17. Liu, X., Smelyanskiy, M., Chow, E., Dubey, P.: Efficient sparse matrix-vector multiplication on x86-based many-core processors. In: Proceedings of 27th International ACM Conference on Supercomputing ICS 2013, p. 273 (2013)

18. Kreutzer, M., Hager, G., Wellein, G.: A unified sparse matrix data format for modern processors with wide SIMD units. SIAM J. Sci. Comput. 36, 1–25 (2013). https://arxiv.org/abs/1307.6209v1

19. Maeda, H., Takahashi, D.: Parallel sparse matrix-vector multiplication using accelerators. In: Gervasi, O., et al. (eds.) ICCSA 2016. LNCS, vol. 9787, pp. 3–18. Springer, Cham (2016). https://doi.org/10.1007/978-3-319-42108-7_1

20. Ahamed, A.-K.C., Magoules, F.: Iterative methods for sparse linear systems on graphics processing unit. In: 2012 IEEE 14th International Conference on High Performance Computing and Communication 2012 and IEEE 9th International Conference on Embedded Software Systems, pp. 836–842 (2012)

21. Search the University Florida Matrix Collection. http://yifanhu.net/GALLERY/GRAPHS/search.html

22. About Aziz. http://hpc.kau.edu.sa/Pages-About-Aziz-en2.aspx

Parallel Shortest Path Graph Computations of United States Road Network Data on Apache Spark

Yasir Arfat[1(✉)], Rashid Mehmood[2], and Aiiad Albeshri[1]

[1] Department of Computer Science, FCIT, King Abdulaziz University,
Jeddah 21589, Saudi Arabia
yasirarfat081@gmail.com, aaalbeshri@kau.edu.sa
[2] High Performance Computing Center, King Abdulaziz University,
Jeddah 21589, Saudi Arabia
RMehmood@kau.edu.sa

Abstract. Big data is being generated from various sources such as Internet of Things (IoT) and social media. Big data cannot be processed by traditional tools and technologies due to their properties, volume, velocity, veracity, and variety. Graphs are becoming increasingly popular to model real-world problems; the problems are typically large and, hence, give rise to large graphs, which could be analysed and solved using big data technologies. This paper explores the performance of single source shortest path graph computations using the Apache Spark big data platform. We use the United States road network data, modelled as graphs, and calculate shortest paths between vertices. The experiments are performed on the Aziz supercomputer (a Top500 machine). We solve problems of varying graph sizes, i.e. various states of the US, and analyse Spark's parallelization behavior. As expected, the speedup is dependent on both the size of the data and the number of parallel nodes.

Keywords: Big data · Apache spark · Apache hadoop · Graph analytics
Apache GraphX · Shortest paths · Road networks

1 Introduction

Graphs are becoming increasingly popular to model real-world problems [1]. Graph analytics play an important role in information discovery and problem solving. A graph can be any real-life application that can be used to find a relation, routing, and a path. Graphs have many applications such as image analysis [2], social network analysis [3, 4], smart cities [5, 6], scientific and high performance computing [7–9], transportation systems [10], Web analyses [11], and biological analyses [12]. In these applications, a large amount of data is being generated every second, known as big data. Big Data refers to the emerging technologies that are designed to extract value from data having four Vs characteristics; volume, variety, velocity and veracity [13, 14]. Volume defines the generation and collection of the vast amount of data. Variety defines the type of the data stored or generated. Types include structured, semi-structured and unstructured data. Velocity describes the timeline related to the generation and processing of big data.

© ICST Institute for Computer Sciences, Social Informatics and Telecommunications Engineering 2018
R. Mehmood et al. (Eds.): SCITA 2017, LNICST 224, pp. 323–336, 2018.
https://doi.org/10.1007/978-3-319-94180-6_30

Veracity refers to the challenges related to the lack of uncertainty in data. Big Data V's and Graphs have a close relationship. For example, volume could represent the number of edges and nodes, and velocity could be considered as the graph's streaming edges. A graph could be uncertain (veracity) and has the variety characteristics because data sources could vary.

The processing of graphs in a distributed environment is a great challenge due to the size of the graph. Typically, a large graph is partitioned for processing. A graph can be partitioned to balance the load on the various machine in a cluster. These partitions are processed in a parallel distributed environment. For the computation of the graph data on the distributed platform, there is a need for scalability and efficiency. These are the two key elements to achieve the good performance. We also need to move our data closer to computation to minimize the overhead of data transfer among the nodes in the cluster. Load balancing and data locality plays a major role in achieving this purpose. It can utilize the whole resource of the system during processing. Moreover, big data is so huge that cannot be able to process by traditional tools and technologies. There are many platforms for graph processing, but these platforms have many issues. Parallel computation of large graphs is a common problem. Therefore, in this scenario parallel distributed platforms are suitable for processing large graphs. In this work, we have used the Graphx [15] for parallel distributed graph processing which is an attractive framework for the graph processing.

In this work, we explore the performance of single source shortest path graph computations using the Apache Spark big data platform. We use the United States road network data, modelled as graphs, and calculate shortest paths between vertices. The experiments are performed on the Aziz supercomputer (a Top500 machine). We solve problems of varying graph sizes, i.e. various states of the US, and analyse Spark's parallelization behaviour. As expected, the speedup is dependent on both the size of the data and the number of parallel nodes.

The rest of the paper is organized as follows. Section 2 gives background material and literature review. Section 3 discusses design and methodology. Section 4 analyses the result. The conclusions and future directions are given in Sect. 5.

2   Background Material and Literature Review

Graph computation has great importance for analysis in various applications. In this section, we explored the state of the art work that already has been done for the graph analysis.

Apache Spark [16] is an open source tool for processing the large data set. It is also next generation of big data applications and alternate for Hadoop. To overcome the issues like disk I/O and performance improvement of Hadoop they introduced the spark. It has several features like memory computation that make it unique. It provides facility like cashing the data in memory. Spark supports the several programming languages, i.e., Python, Java, and Scala. Graphx [15] is an open source platform for the processing graph data. It has various characteristics such as flexibility, speed, parallel graph computation, extends the spark RDD. Hadoop [17] is an open source software to process the big data. It has several characteristics scalability, reliability, fault tolerance, high availability, local processing & storage, distributed and parallel computing faster and cost effective. Hadoop as many components but most important components are MapReduce and HDFS.

Kajdanowicz et al. [18] analyzed three parallel large graph processing approaches such as Bulk Synchronous Parallel (BSP) MapReduce and map-side join. These strategies implemented for the calculation of single source shortest path (SSSP) and relational influence propagation (RIP) of graph nodes for collective classification. They find out that iterative graph processing performs well as compared to MapReduce using the BSP. Liu et al. [19] have described graph partitioning is a major issue for parallel large graph processing. These challenges are a replication of vertices, unbalanced partitioning, and communication between partitions. To solve these problems, they proposed a new graph partitioning framework for the parallel processing of a large graph. The primary goal of this framework was to minimize the bandwidth, balance the load and memory. It has three greedy graph partitioning algorithms. They run theses algorithms using different dataset and find out these algorithms can solve the issue of graph partitioning based on the specification and needs. Wang et al. [20] presented a new approach for maximal clique and k-plex enumeration. It finds the dense subgraph using the binary graph partitioning. It divides the graph in such a way that enables each partition of a graph to process it parallel. It was implanted using the MapReduce. The presented approach has smaller search space and more parallelizable. Braun et al. [21] proposed a technique for the analysis social network using a knowledge based system. The main goal of this approach was mine the interests of the social network represent as graphs. It analyses the relationship between directed graphs and captures the mutual friends using the undirected graph. To analyse the performance of the chosen approach, they have used the Facebook and Twitter dataset.

Laboshin et al. [22] have presented a framework based on the MapReduce for the analysis of web traffic. The primary objective of using this framework was to scale the storage and computing resources for the extensive network. Liu et al. [23] have presented a clustering algorithm for the distributed density peaks to overcome the issue in distance based algorithms. It also calculates the distance between all pairs of vertices. Using this algorithm, the computational cost will be decreased. This algorithm is based on the Apache GraphX [15]. Aridhi et al. [24] analysed various big graph mining frameworks. The primary focus was on the pattern mining that consists of the discovering useful and exciting information from the large graph using mining algorithms. They did detailed analysis on the various mining approaches for the big graphs. Drosou et al. [25] presented a new framework called enhanced Graph Analytical Platform (GAP). It uses the top down approach for the mining the large volume of data. It gives strength many other key features such as HR clustering. It works efficiently for the big data acquiring useful insights. Zhao et al. [26] analysed of different graph processing platforms. They compared these platforms regarding data parallel and graph parallel. For the computation of graph and resource utilization graph platforms works well as compared to data parallel. On the other hand, they find out that regarding size, data parallel graph platforms are superior in performance.

Mohan et al. [27] did a comparison on the parallel graph processing big data platforms. They compared features and performance of these platforms. Pollard et al. [28] presented a new approach for the analysis of scalability and performance of the parallel graph processing platforms. They analysed the power consumption and performance of the most commonly used algorithm (BFS, SSSP and Page Rank) on the graph processing packages (Graph-Mat, Graph500 Graph Benchmark Suite, and PowerGraph) using different datasets. Suma et al. [29] have also done an important on smarter societies for logistics and planning. They evaluated the proposed approach using parallel distributed framework. Miller et al. [30] presented the graph analytics for query processing to find the shortest path for specific patterns. They introduced the algorithms which show that vertex centric and graph centric algorithms are easily parallelizable. They also argue that MapReduce is not effective for the computation of iterative algorithms. Chakaravarthy et al. [31] have presented a new algorithm that was originated from Delta-stepping and Bellman-Ford algorithms. The main goal of this algorithms was to classify the edges, reducing the inner node traffic and optimization of direction. They have used the SSSP for unweighted graph find out the paths among all other nodes as destination.

Yinglong et al. [32] have described that big data analytics are important to discover for such entities that can easily represent in the form of a graph. It is the primary challenge for the processing of computation of graph-based patterns. They proposed a new system that allows the user to organize the data for the architecture of parallel computing. It also consists of visualization, graph storage, and analytics. They also analyze the data locality regarding graph processing and its effects on the performance of cache memory on a processor. Zhang et al. [33] proposed a new algorithm for the fast graph search that it transforms the complex graphs into vectorial representations based on the prototype in the database. After this, it also accelerates the query efficiency in the Euclidean space by employing locality sensitive hashing. They evaluated their approach against the real datasets, which achieves the high performance in accuracy and efficiency.

Shao et al. [34] have proposed a new approach partitioning aware graph computation engine (PAGE). The benefit of this method is that it controls the online graph partitioning statistics of under lying results of a graph. Second, it monitors the parallel processing resources and enhances the computation resources. Third, it was also designed to support the various graph partitioning qualities. For evaluation of chosen schemes, they showed that it performs well under various partitioning approaches with different qualities. Chen et al. [35] have proposed a new framework of graph partitioning to enhance the performance of the network for graph partitioning itself, storage of partitioned graph and vertex oriented processing of graph. They have developed all these optimizations for the cloud network environments. They also have used the two models such as partition sketch and machine graph. The basic purpose of using these two graphs was to capture the features of graph partitioning process and network performance. Zeng et al. [36] have proposed new parallel multi-level stepwise partitioning algorithm. They divided this algorithm into two phases; one is an aggregate phase and second is partition phase. In aggregate phase, it uses the multilevel weighted label propagation for aggregation of the large graph into the small graph. But in a second phase: It has the K-way balance-partitioning performs on the weighted based on the stepwise mining RatioCut method. It reduces the RatioCut step by step. In each step, sets of vertices are extracted by reducing the part of RatioCut, and these vertices are removed from the graph. In this, they have obtained the k-way balanced partitioning by this algorithm. In experiments, they have made the comparison with various other existing partitioning approaches using the dataset of a graph.

Lee et al. [37] have introduced vertex block (VBs) partitioner. It is a distributed model for the data partitioner for the large-scale graphs in the cloud. It has three features. First, It has the vertex bock (VBs), and it also extends the extended vertex block (EVBs) as building blocks for the semantic large-scale graphs. Second, vertex block partitioner uses vertex block grouping algorithm to place the high correlation in the graph into the same partition. Third, the VB partitioner speed up the parallel processing of graph pattern queries by minimizing the inter-partition query processing. In results, they showed that proposed approach has higher query latency and scalability over large-scale graphs. Xu et al. [38] have proposed a log based dynamic graph partitioning method. This method uses the recodes and reuses the historical statistical information to refine the partitioning result. It can be used as middleware and deployed to many existing parallel graph-processing systems. It also uses the historical partitioning results for the creation of a hyper graph, and it also uses a new hyper graph streaming strategy to generate the better stream graph partitioning result. Moreover, it also dynamically partitions the huge graph and also uses the system to optimize the graph partitioning to enhance the performance. Yang et al. [39] proposed a new approach called self-evolving distributed graph management environment (sedge). It reduces the communication during the processing of the graph query on the multiple machines. It also has two level of partitioning such as primary partition and dynamic secondary partitioning. These two types of partitions can adapt any kind of real environment. Results show that it enhances the distributed graph processing on the commodity clusters.

3 Design and Methodology

In this section, we discuss the design methodology of our work. We have used three big data tools Apache Hadoop [17], Apache Spark [16] and Apache Graphx [15]. We also setup an Apache Spark cluster. The Hadoop HDFS is used for input and output storage. We process the data using Apache Graphx on Spark cluster and store the output in HDFS. We have also used the Apache Spark's data locality and load balancing techniques. Data locality is of great importance while processing Spark jobs. Computing the jobs and data together have significant effects on performance processing. If the data and code are not together, to improve the job performance we have to move them together. Usually, the data size is greater than the code. Hence it is easy to move the code in serialized form than data in the form of chunks. Spark has inbuilt scheduler for achieving data locality. Data locality is all about how to place the data close to each other to process faster. There are various types [40] of data locality in the spark. These are Process Local, Node Local, No Pref, Rack local, and any. Spark prefers to schedule all tasks at the best locality level, but this is not always possible. On the other hand, to balance the load among all nodes in the cluster, there are two types [41] of partitioning scheme in Apache GraphX. These are vertex-cut and edges-cut. However, GraphX only uses vertex-cut scheme for graph partitioning. The vertex-cut scheme has different types partition strategy, but in our work, we have used the "2D Edge Partitioning" technique.

In Algorithm 1, we have developed a new approach for the computing the SSSP using load balancing and maintaining data locality. In our technique, first, we set the data locality either as the process level, node level or rack level. If any node needs the task or data from another node, it will check the data initially in its process and then check the node. Before requesting from the other node, it will wait for 3 s. If data or task is not available on the node then it will check within the rack, similarly again it will wait for 3 s.

For the Load balancing, we applied graph based partitioning scheme called the 2D edges partitioning which equally partitioning the graph and distributes among all the nodes in the cluster. Next step, we input the edges list and nodes list. It will be map into edges RDDs and vertices RDDs, from these two RDDs we shall draw a graph. After this, we shall input the source vertex to find the shortest path between all other vertices from given vertex. Next step we shall apply Dijkstra algorithm to find shortest paths. In the end, we shall print all the shortest path determined by the Dijkstra algorithm with their total distance.

Algorithm 1: Single Source Shortest Path (SSSP) using GraphX

Input: List of vertices, List of edges, source vertex
Output: list of shortest paths
  1: **Function main** (vertices, edges)
  2:         Locality (local execution, true)
  3:         Locality (locality wait for process, 3S)
  4:         Locality (locality wait for node, 3S)
  5:         locality (locality wait for rack, 3S)
  6:         Nodes List ← path for the input vertices file.
  7:         Edges List ← path for the input vertices file.
  8:         Vertices ← map nodes List
  9:         Edges ← map Edges List
 10:         Graph ← create graph from vertices and edges
 11:         Graph Partition ← partition graph by partitioning strategy edge partitioning2D
 12:         Finding the shortest distance formula from using shortest path algorithm
 13:         Source Vertex: ← Vertex
 14:         Computed Dijkstra Algorithms
 15:         Prints the shortest paths

3.1   The Road Network Dataset

In this section, we shall present the description of the dataset that we have for the performance analysis of graph computations. We have used the DIMACS [42] dataset. This dataset has whole USA road network in the form of graph data. We took the entire USA and Five states of the USA, District of Columbia (DC), Rhode Island (RI), Colorado (CO), Florida (FL), California (CA). The graph data that we have chosen is undirected it has the billions of edges and vertices. Following Table 1. shows the no of edges and vertices in different states and the complete USA.

Table 1. USA road network dataset

Name of road network	Vertices	Edges	Type
District of Columbia (DC)	9559	14909	Undirected
Rhode Island (RI)	53658	69213	Undirected
Colorado (CO)	435,666	1,057,066	Undirected
Florida (FL)	1,070,376	2,712,798	Undirected
California (CA)	1,890,815	4,657,742	Undirected
USA (whole country)	23,947,347	58,333,344	Undirected

We also have visualized road network dataset using Gephi [43]. We have only visualized the DC and RI state data set as shown in Figs. 1 and 2 respectively. We could not visualize the other states data due to the large size which cannot be handled

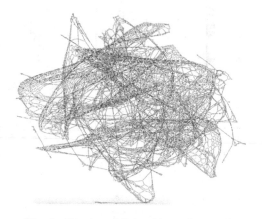

Fig. 1. District of Columbia road network

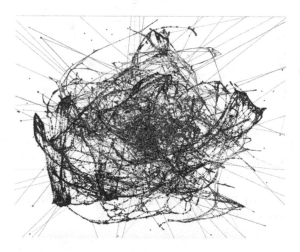

Fig. 2. Rhodes Island road network

on a single PC. We have only visualized two states to perceive the structure of road network datasets.

We have plotted the degree distribution and the histogram of vertex degrees of different states and full USA road network dataset. The primary purpose of this plot was to see the nature of dataset that we are using in the research. In Fig. 3(i), it shows the DC road network dataset visualization and degree of distribution. However, has four thousand vertices with degree 3, and Fig. 3(ii) forty-nine thousand vertices have the degree 6 in FL. In CO road network dataset Fig. 3(iii) shows more no of vertices with degree 6 and over thirteen thousand vertices have degree 4. On the other hand, in Fig. 3(iv) whole USA road network dataset majority of vertices has degree 6.

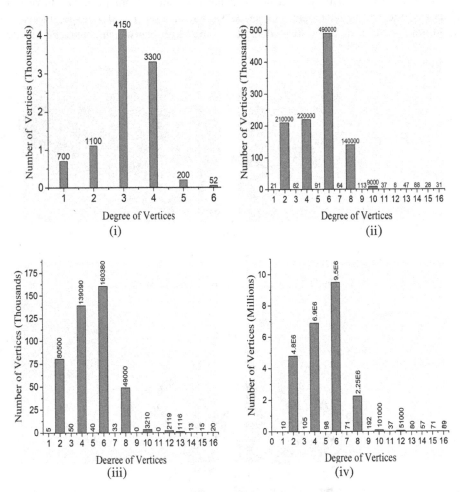

Fig. 3. Visualization of (i) District of Columbia road network (ii) Florida road network (iii) Colorado road network (iv) Whole USA road network

3.2   Experimental Setup

For experimental setup, we have built the spark cluster setup using the Aziz super-computer. In this configuration, we have used the different Aziz nodes, as it varies for the same dataset for 1, 2, 4, 8 and 16 Aziz nodes. We have used Apache Hadoop HDFS to store input and output data where as for the processing of the data we used the Apache spark. Rest of software and hardware configuration is given below in Table 2.

Table 2. Configuration environment

The node type	Master	Slave
Software and Hardware environment	Linux centOS, JDK 1.7, Processor 2.4 GHz, Apache Spark 2.0.2, GraphX, 24 cores, Apache Hadoop HDFS	Linux centOS, JDK 1.7, Processor 2.4 GHz, 24 cores, Apache Spark 2.0.1, GraphX Apache Hadoop HDFS
Memory	94 G	94 G per slave
Quantity	1	Different slave as 1, 2, 4, 8 and 16

4   Results and Analysis

We implemented the parallel and sequential code on the spark cluster using the Aziz supercomputer. The difference between the results for the sequential version and for a single node is that the single node provides a parallel Spark execution of the shortest path algorithm using multiple cores. We have run the code sequentially on the Aziz supercomputer for all different USA states DC, RI, CO, FL, CA and the whole USA. We found that sequentially on Apache Spark it takes 4.07 s for DC road network and 5.05 s for RI road network. In CO road network it took 7.54 s, whereas 17.76 s taken by FAL road network. In CA road network, it takes 37.92 s. These are all timing has been shown in Fig. 4, which we run sequentially on Apache Spark. On the other hand, we also run the whole USA road network sequentially that took 476.33 s for the processing as shown in Fig. 5.

Similarly, we run the data for the 1, 2, 4, 8 and 16 Aziz nodes using the Apache Spark cluster parallel using and note down the timing of each as shown in Fig. 4. For 1 Aziz node, it took 2.70,2.90, 6.67, 10.77 and 24.62 s for the processing of DC, RI, CO, FL and CA states road network dataset respectively. Using 2 Aziz nodes, it also takes 2.42, 2.49, 4.70, 9.04 and 21.90 s for the processing of DC, RI, CO, FL and CA states road network dataset using our approach respectively. Using our technique, the running of 4 Aziz nodes, a processing time of different states as follows: 2.39, 2.41, 4.01, 8.89 and 19.49 s for DC, RI, CO, FL, and CA road network. For 8 Aziz nodes, it takes 2.30, 2.34, 3.90, 8.48 and 18.89 s for DC, RI, CO, FL, and CA road network. Again, we double the Aziz nodes up to 16, run the code using our developed approach it takes 2.22, 2.28, 3.62, 7.99 and 16.18 s for DC, RI, CO, FL, and CA road network. In this case, we can compare our results with 8 Aziz nodes, but there is not much speed up due to a small dataset and transfer time. We also run the whole USA road network dataset using our approach as we found that on 1, 2, 4, 8, 16 Aziz nodes it takes 155.63,

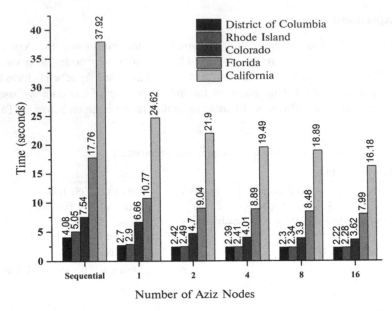

Fig. 4. Performance comparison of different Aziz nodes using states of USA road network dataset.

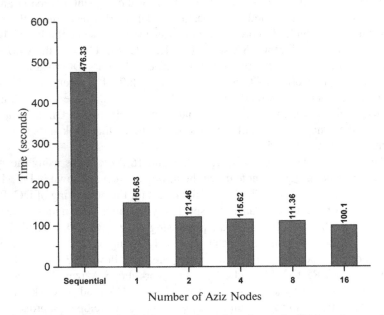

Fig. 5. Performance comparison of different Aziz nodes using entire USA road network dataset.

121.46, 115.62, 111.36, and 100.10 s for processing of data parallel on Apache Spark as shown in Fig. 5.

We have executed our code for a different number of USA states, as well as the whole USA road network dataset. We have achieved a good speed up as given in Figs. 4 and 5. In Fig. 4, there is a comparison of different USA states road network dataset, each state has different size of the dataset. Smaller data affects the scale of parallelism that can be achieved. Moreover, it is computationally expensive. However, when we move from a small data set (i.e., DC to CA) to a higher size of dataset get more speed up and consumes less time using different Aziz nodes. However, there is also increase in the execution time when we shall use the more nodes in the cluster, and our data is small. It happens due to the transfer of data among the nodes in the cluster. Therefore, we can only get the parallelism with certain no of nodes, or we have to see that how many numbers of nodes are needed to process the particular dataset to achieve good speedup.

5 Conclusion and Future Work

Graph analytics plays an important role in discovering and understanding the useful information. Graphs also have many applications such smart cities, social media, biological networks, etc. these applications have a significant amount data that cannot be processed on the traditional tools and technologies. So, parallel distributed platforms are suitable for the processing of large size of data.

In this work, we processed parallel distributed graph based SSSP using GraphX and Apache Spark cluster on Aziz. We applied the load balancing and data locality based approach to compute the SSSP. We have used the DIMACS road network dataset for a research experiment. This dataset contains different states of road network dataset and whole USA road network. We found that our approach takes less time for the execution and increase the speedup. However, we also find out that if data is small, there is speed up but not much. On the other hand, it is observed that if the data is significant, we can achieve high performance. However, there are certain constraints such as reduction in speed when the number of nodes in a cluster increase. We obtain speed up and high performance at a particular number of nodes. For future work, we shall apply this approach our health care transport application for computation of SSSP.

Acknowledgments. The authors acknowledge with thanks the technical and financial support from the Deanship of Scientific Research (DSR) at the King Abdulaziz University (KAU), Jeddah, Saudi Arabia, under the grant number G-661-611-38. The experiments reported in this paper were performed on the Aziz supercomputer at King Abdulaziz University.

References

1. Lu, Y., Cheng, J., Yan, D., Wu, H.: Large-scale distributed graph computing systems. Proc. VLDB Endow. **8**, 281–292 (2014)
2. Sanfeliu, A., Alquézar, R., Andrade, J., Climent, J., Serratosa, F., Vergés, J.: Graph-based representations and techniques for image processing and image analysis. Pattern Recognit. **35**, 639–650 (2002)
3. Ding, Y., Yan, S., Zhang, Y.B., Dai, W., Dong, L.: Predicting the attributes of social network users using a graph-based machine learning method. Comput. Commun. **73**, 3–11 (2016)
4. Khan, A., Uddin, S., Srinivasan, U.: Adapting graph theory and social network measures on healthcare data. In: Proceedings of the Australasian Computer Science Week Multiconference on - ACSW 2016, pp. 1–7. ACM Press, New York (2016)
5. Mehmood, R., Graham, G.: Big data logistics: a health-care transport capacity sharing model. Procedia Comput. Sci. **64**, 1107–1114 (2015)
6. Mehmood, R., Meriton, R., Graham, G., Hennelly, P., Kumar, M.: Exploring the influence of big data on city transport operations: a Markovian approach. Int. J. Oper. Prod. Manag. (2016). Forthcoming
7. Hendrickson, B., Kolda, T.G.: Graph partitioning models for parallel computing. Parallel Comput. **26**, 1519–1534 (2000)
8. Mehmood, R., Crowcroft, J.: Parallel iterative solution method for large sparse linear equation systems. Comput. Lab. Univ. (2005)
9. Kwiatkowska, M., Parker, D., Zhang, Y., Mehmood, R.: Dual-processor parallelisation of symbolic probabilistic model checking. In: DeGroot, D., Harrison, P. (eds.) Proceedings - IEEE Computer Society's Annual International Symposium on Modeling, Analysis, and Simulation of Computer and Telecommunications Systems, MASCOTS, pp. 123–130. IEEE, Volendam (2004)
10. Alazawi, Z., Abdljabar, M.B., Altowaijri, S., Vegni, A.M., Mehmood, R.: ICDMS: an intelligent cloud based disaster management system for vehicular networks. In: Vinel, A., Mehmood, R., Berbineau, M., Garcia, C.R., Huang, C.-M., Chilamkurti, N. (eds.) Nets4Cars/Nets4Trains 2012. LNCS, vol. 7266, pp. 40–56. Springer, Heidelberg (2012). https://doi.org/10.1007/978-3-642-29667-3_4
11. Junghanns, M., Petermann, A., Neumann, M., Rahm, E.: Management and analysis of big graph data: current systems and open challenges. In: Zomaya, A., Sakr, S. (eds.) Handbook of Big Data Technologies, pp. 457–505. Springer International Publishing, Cham (2017). https://doi.org/10.1007/978-3-319-49340-4_14
12. Oh, S., Ha, J., Lee, K., Oh, S.: DegoViz: an interactive visualization tool for a differentially expressed genes heatmap and gene ontology graph. Appl. Sci. **7**, 543 (2017)
13. Mehmood, R., Faisal, M.A., Altowaijri, S.: Future networked healthcare systems: a review and case study. In: Big Data: Concepts, Methodologies, Tools, and Applications, pp. 2429–2457. IGI Global (2016)
14. Arfat, Y., Aqib, M., Mehmood, R., Albeshri, A., Katib, I., Albogami, N., Alzahrani, A.: Enabling smarter societies through mobile big data fogs and clouds. Procedia Comput. Sci. **109**, 1128–1133 (2017)
15. GraphX | Apache Spark
16. Apache Spark: Apache Spark™ - Lightning-Fast Cluster Computing
17. Welcome to Apache™ Hadoop®! - index.pdf. https://hadoop.apache.org/index.pdf
18. Kajdanowicz, T., Kazienko, P., Indyk, W.: Parallel processing of large graphs. Futur. Gener. Comput. Syst. **32**, 324–337 (2014)

19. Liu, X., Zhou, Y., Guan, X., Sun, X.: A feasible graph partition framework for random walks implemented by parallel computing in big graph. In: Chinese Control Conference, CCC 2015, pp. 4986–4991, September 2015
20. Wang, Z., Chen, Q., Hou, B., Suo, B., Li, Z., Pan, W., Ives, Z.G.: Parallelizing maximal clique and k-plex enumeration over graph data. J. Parallel Distrib. Comput. **106**, 79–91 (2017)
21. Braun, P., Cuzzocrea, A., Leung, C.K., Pazdor, A.G.M., Tran, K.: Knowledge Discovery from Social Graph Data. Procedia Comput. Sci. **96**, 682–691 (2016)
22. Laboshin, L.U., Lukashin, A.A., Zaborovsky, V.S.: The big data approach to collecting and analyzing traffic data in large scale networks. Procedia Comput. Sci. **103**, 536–542 (2017)
23. Liu, R., Li, X., Du, L., Zhi, S., Wei, M.: Parallel implementation of density peaks clustering algorithm based on spark. Procedia Comput. Sci. **107**, 442–447 (2017)
24. Aridhi, S., Mephu Nguifo, E.: Big graph mining: frameworks and techniques. Big Data Res. **6**, 1–10 (2016)
25. Drosou, A., Kalamaras, I., Papadopoulos, S., Tzovaras, D.: An enhanced Graph Analytics Platform (GAP) providing insight in Big Network Data. J. Innov. Digit. Ecosyst. **3**, 83–97 (2016)
26. Zhao, Y., Yoshigoe, K., Xie, M., Zhou, S., Seker, R., Bian, J.: Evaluation and analysis of distributed graph-parallel processing frameworks. J. Cyber Secur. Mobil. **3**, 289–316 (2014)
27. Mohan, A., Remya, R.: A review on large scale graph processing using big data based parallel programming models. Int. J. Intell. Syst. Appl. **9**, 49–57 (2017)
28. Pollard, S., Norris, B.: A Comparison of Parallel Graph Processing Benchmarks (2017)
29. Suma, S., Mehmood, R., Albugami, N., Katib, I., Albeshri, A.: Enabling next generation logistics and planning for smarter societies. Procedia Comput. Sci. **109**, 1122–1127 (2017)
30. Miller, J.A., Ramaswamy, L., Kochut, K.J., Fard, A.: Research directions for big data graph analytics. In: Proceedings of the 2015 IEEE International Congress on Big Data, BigData Congress 2015, pp. 785–794 (2015)
31. Chakaravarthy, V.T., Checconi, F., Petrini, F., Sabharwal, Y.: Scalable single source shortest path algorithms for massively parallel systems. In: Proceedings of the 28th International Parallel and Distributed Processing Symposium, IPDPS, pp. 889–901 (2014)
32. Xia, Y., Tanase, I.G., Nai, L., Tan, W., Liu, Y., Crawford, J., Lin, C.: Explore efficient data organization for large scale graph analytics and storage. In: Proceedings of the 2014 IEEE BigData Conference, pp. 942–951 (2014)
33. Zhang, B., Liu, X., Lang, B.: Fast Graph Similarity Search via Locality Sensitive Hashing. In: Ho, Y.-S., Sang, J., Ro, Y.M., Kim, J., Wu, F. (eds.) PCM 2015. LNCS, vol. 9314, pp. 623–633. Springer, Cham (2015). https://doi.org/10.1007/978-3-319-24075-6_60
34. Shao, Y., Cui, B., Ma, L.: PAGE: A partition aware engine for parallel graph computation. IEEE Trans. Knowl. Data Eng. **27**, 518–530 (2015)
35. Chen, R., Yang, M., Weng, X., Choi, B., He, B., Li, X.: Improving large graph processing on partitioned graphs in the cloud. In: Proceedings of the Third ACM Symposium on Cloud Computing, SoCC 2012, pp. 1–13 (2012)
36. Zeng, Z., Wu, B., Wang, H.: A parallel graph partitioning algorithm to speed up the large-scale distributed graph mining. In: Proceedings of the 1st International Workshop on Big Data, Streams and Heterogeneous Source Mining: Algorithms, Systems, Programming Models and Applications - BigMine 2012, pp. 61–68 (2012)
37. Lee, K., Liu, L.: Efficient data partitioning model for heterogeneous graphs in the cloud. In: Proceedings of the International Conference on High Performance Computing, Networking, Storage and Analysis, pp. 1–12 (2013)
38. Xu, N., Chen, L., Cui, B.: LogGP: a log-based dynamic graph partitioning method. Proc. VLDB Endow. **7**, 1917–1928 (2014)

39. Yang, S., Yan, X., Zong, B., Khan, A.: Towards effective partition management for large graphs. In: Proceedings of the 2012 International Conference on Management Data - SIGMOD 2012, pp. 517–528 (2012)
40. Spark Data Locality Documentation. https://spark.apache.org/docs/latest/tuning.html#data-locality
41. GraphX Partitioning Scheme Documentation. https://spark.apache.org/docs/latest/graphx-programming-guide.html#optimized-representation
42. DIMACS Implementation Challenge. http://www.dis.uniroma1.it/challenge9/download.shtml
43. Gephi - The Open Graph Viz Platform. https://gephi.org/

A Safety IoT-Based System
for a Closed Environment

El-Hadi Khoumeri[✉], Rabea Cheggou,
Mohamed El-Amine Bekhouche, and Sofiane Oubraham

LTI Laboratory, Ecole Nationale Superieure de Technologie,
Dergana, Algiers, Algeria
{elhadi.khoumeri, rabea.cheggou, m_bekhouche,
s_oubraham}@enst.dz

Abstract. Nowadays, the storage of large volumes of data became possible and affordable. In the same way, the computing power of microprocessors has multiplied tenfold, and digital cameras became extremely efficient at an increasingly low cost. With the generalization of the use of digital images, motion analysis in video sequences has proved to be an indispensable tool for various applications such as video surveillance, medical imaging, robotics etc. The security of people and property is a complex issue. Monitoring an environment to better prevent the danger and act accordingly in real time has led us to carry out research in this direction. We present a system for monitoring, authenticating and counting people in a public space. The basis of our application relies on cameras and motion sensor, all centralized in a single interface.

Keywords: Safety · Security · Counting people · Raspberry pi
PIR sensor · Fire detection

1 Introduction

Estimating the flow of people in real time can be very useful information for several applications such as security management or people. Thus, due to the advancement of image processing algorithms and computer technology, video cameras are used extensively in recent years to track and count people. The management of security and surveillance requires considerable attention in the Smart Cities, errors must be very limited. Fires, thefts or intrusions are undesirable events that could lead to a great loss of social wealth and human life. To avoid these losses, various alarm systems have been developed by the industry such as smoke detectors, temperature sensors, intelligent surveillance cameras, and this with the development of technologies at affordable prices. Among the new technologies is the Internet of Things (IoT), which consists of connecting all devices to the Internet in order to communicate with each other. The integration of this technology will create practical and effective means in the area of surveillance and security.

The system proposed in this document includes the use of affordable instruments based on the Raspberry Pi card, including a camera module, a motion sensor and an ultrasonic sensor. Three main functions are performed. Firstly, individuals and vehicles

© ICST Institute for Computer Sciences, Social Informatics and Telecommunications Engineering 2018
R. Mehmood et al. (Eds.): SCITA 2017, LNICST 224, pp. 337–352, 2018.
https://doi.org/10.1007/978-3-319-94180-6_31

flow control, into the entrance of a building or a public institution using a facial recognition and read the license plate. Secondly, the camera is designed to detect fire, it is linked to an alarm system to alert user. Thirdly, detection of movement and intrusion in the building. A web page has been developed to manage the building entrance (real-time information on vehicles and individuals, database manipulation, history of the inputs and output). The design and the implementation of a facial recognition, license plate identification, people counting and fire detection algorithms are based on image processing. The use of the OpenCV and Python is largely in line with our solution with a high level of reliability.

1.1   Internet of Things (IoT)

The Internet of Things was first introduced in 1999, the IoT is an essential part of modern embedded systems which describes a network of physical objects connected to the Internet in order to communicate and share data between them. The purpose of the IoT is to make use of these large amounts of data to make the systems more efficient and automated. There are several examples of IoT solutions to various problems, such as the use of light beams and IR sensors to analyze the occupancy level of a home and to adjust the airflow of the ventilation system, using video streams and location data to better count the number of people in an area [1].

IoT systems often have to deal with large quantities of sensors and data. It is important that a system be able to develop its performance in order to manage an increased workload, such as more users, multiple sensors and actuators, or additional functionality. The architecture of the IoT systems can be described as being divided into three distinct layers (sensor, network, and application layer). The sensor layer includes sensors, the network layer processes data from sensors and the application layer that represents applications such as smart home. Lee and Kim [2] also point out other aspects that must be taken into account when designing IoT systems. It is important that the communication between the devices works correctly regardless of the scale of the area of application.

1.2   Related Works

Surveillance and security research generally proposes a unique solution for each module. Our solution offers a global solution with several modules in one application. In [3] a novel filters which is unified to detect either the vehicle license or the vehicles from the digital camera imaging sensors of urban surveillance systems in the smart cities. Another example [4] an intelligent system for facial recognition. In [5] they describe the development of visualisation application software used to control operational and technical functions in the Smart Home system or Smart Home care system via the wireless control system. In these articles [6–8] a system with different means of communication is proposed for the smart home. Al-Audah et al. proposed a system that uses the Lab-VIEW software based on a camera vision [9]. Another system called ALPR (Automatic License Plate Recognition) is developed for the detection and recognition of vehicle license plates [10]. A real-time system based on FPGA that provides an optimal solution for facial recognition is presented in [11]. In [12] they propose a specific face recognition system designed around ARM9 platform. Premal and Vinsley presented a mobile camera for real-time detection of forest fires [13].

Several studies have been conducted on how to count people. Today, there are lot of methods to accomplish this task. The researchers have previously shown that, when several sensors are combined, greater accuracy can be achieved either with cameras or with other optical sensors of persons [14]. In [15] they have set up a network counting sensors inside a building in order to determine the occupancy levels of the room and use the data to control a ventilation system, by increasing the air flow if occupancy of the levels by persons increased. One of the main issue with computer vision systems is the need to separate objects of interest from the remaining pixels. Several proposed counting systems, like the ones described in [14–16], use two cameras to help with this process, a method also known as stereovision. Another common procedure is to use background subtraction, as seen for example in [17]. Using this method, the acquired images are subtracted to a previously saved background of the same capture scene and the resulting image contains the pixels of newer objects which might be people.

2 Methodology

The solution proposed in our project, security and surveillance with Raspberry Pi consists of different systems: facial recognition, vehicle license plate recognition, fire detection with access control and people counting.

2.1 Hardware Design

The proposed solution is based on a real-time processing video sequences, which requires the use of a powerful tool to ensure constraints (speed and real time). We choose the Raspberry Pi 2 card that meets our needs. It is a small single-board computer that was originally developed for computer science education and has since become popularised by digital hobbyists and makers of Internet of Things (IoT) devices. Raspberry P is about the size of a credit card; it has a 64-bit quad-core ARMv8 processor and uses a Raspbian Linux distribution as operating system (OS) (Fig. 1).

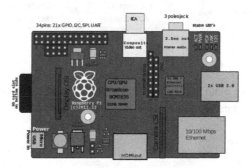

Fig. 1. The raspberry Pi 2 components.

The Raspberry Pi is contained a single circuit board and features ports for: HDMI, USB 2.0, composite video, analog audio, power, internet, and SD card. All sensors used in this project shows in the Fig. 2.

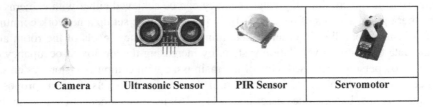

| Camera | Ultrasonic Sensor | PIR Sensor | Servomotor |

Fig. 2. The hardware used

2.1.1 Facial Recognition

Lot of algorithms for extracting face characteristics are proposed in the OpenCV library, such as the LBP (Local binary patterns), Eigenface and Fisherface algorithms. We chose the LBP algorithm [18] as a solution in our project. The facial recognition process can be divided into three main phase's shows below (Fig. 3):

Fig. 3. Facial recognition process.

2.1.2 License Plate Identification

The developed algorithm consists in three primary steps: Step 1: Finding the license plate, Step 2: Segmenting each of the individual characters from the license plate. And Step 3: Identifying and recognizing each of the characters. The following diagram in Fig. 4 shows the different phases of recognition [19].

Fig. 4. Plate identification process.

The detection of the plate is the most important and difficult phase, it determines the rapidity and the robustness of the system. Steps represented in Fig. 5.

Fig. 5. Block diagram of Plate identification Module.

The detected characters require an optical character recognition (OCR) system to identify the vehicle's license plate, steps shows in. OCR is a technology that automatically recognizes characters using an optical mechanism. There are several OCR algorithms that are open source and written in deferent languages (C++, Python, or Java). We choose the "Tesseract" algorithm because of its extensibility and flexibility, that makes the recognition operation simple and reliable [20] (Fig. 6).

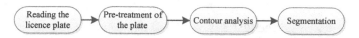

Fig. 6. Block diagram of Plate identification process

2.1.3 Fire Detection

Fire detection is performed in several ways, for example, by using temperature, humidity and smoke analysis. However, these techniques are not reliable because they cannot provide other information such as the location of the fire, the size of the fire, and these techniques can lead to false alarms. There are many types of color schemes such as RGB, CMYK, YCbCr, YUV, HSL, HSV. However, each of the color spaces has their advantages and disadvantages. Before you can detect a fire with a camera, you must know the specific properties of a fire that distinguish it from the other objects that the camera sees. The YCbCr color space is used here because of its ability to effectively distinguish luminance information from other color models [21]. The diagram in Fig. 7 shows the diagram of the proposed algorithm.

Fig. 7. Fire detection process.

2.1.4 People Counting and Tracking

Features of an image containing objects to be detected are extracted uses a method called BLOB (Binary Large Object) analysis. This method is used so as to identify the objects/regions called BLOBs using pixel connectivity and further more parameters like area, centroid, and number of BLOBs available in the test image. Preprocessing of the input test image is done prior to the BLOB analysis like thresholding to get a binary image. BLOB analysis is one of the fundamental techniques and it consist a set of related (connected) pixels in a binary image. In image processing a BLOB is described as area (region) of connected pixels. Our goal is to design a system capable of counting the number of people entering or leaving an area in a video sequence. The general scheme of the design of our system is represented by the following diagram Fig. 8:

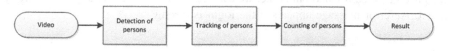

Fig. 8. People counting system

3 Proposed Model

The proposed design of our system is presented in details, then we discuss the results of the tests in order to evaluate the functioning and the reliability of system. Our target is to design a system that meets the proposed solution, the general diagram of the prototype design of our system, is presented in Fig. 9.

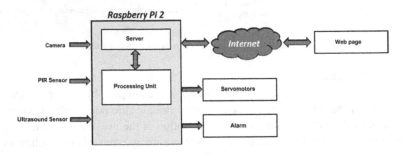

Fig. 9. Architecture of proposed solution.

The Raspberry Pi is the master device of our system, equipped with a camera that presents the video acquisition device and interfaced directly with the Raspberry Pi module via a USB interface, a PIR sensor that is connected directly with the Raspberry Pi ports. The PIR is able to detect movement. The ultrasound sensor is dedicated to managing the camera, acts as a presence detector, so it activates the shot as soon as it detects the presence of a vehicle or person. The processing of the data acquired by the input devices is carried out by the Raspberry Pi, which is responsible to make the decision to actuate the actuator, and then trigger an alarm, and to record the data. For the detection of people pedestrians go into a well determined field, the video stream is captured with a camera placed at height with head view, this video is separated into several frames (images), and one image by 30 ms, each image is processed separately so that people can be detected. For tracking people in video sequences, people will be tracked in the video sequences by memorizing their coordinates and their movements (incoming or outgoing). Thus, in the step of counting people, we will count the number of people who have entered and who are out.

The Webpage developed with PHP, JavaScript and HTML. Figure 10 shows the login page. First, every user must identify himself by entering the password and username.

After logged on, the user will be redirected to the display webpage as shown in Fig. 11. This webpage allows displaying in real time all functionalities cited before. It is also used to stream video online i.e. we can see the live streaming anywhere through internet. An error message appears if the login is wrong

Fig. 10. Login page

Fig. 11. Home page

4   Algorithms

4.1   Facial Recognition

The flowchart in Fig. 12 presents the different phases of the facial recognition system, which are learning and recognition. The learning module is designed for the purpose of creating or adding faces of new person to the database. First the user must enter an identifier, and then the video acquisition begins. If the camera detects a face, a calculation of the detected face biometrics is performed using the LBP (Local binary patterns) algorithm. When the acquisition is done, the biometrics characteristics are stored in a database. The recognition phase is necessary to verify the existence of the biometrics characteristics of an individual in database. First the ultrasonic sensor detects the presence of the person, then the video acquisition starts and the face detection begin. When a face is detected the LBP model starts calculating different face characteristic. The resulting calculation will be compared with the database to find a similarity.

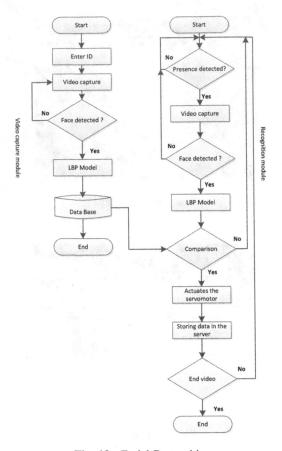

Fig. 12. Facial Recognition

If the authentication is done (the face is known in the database), the Raspberry Pi card actuates the servomotor for opening the door. All the information about every operation is stored on the server and it is accessible via the web page.

4.2 License Plate Identification System

The Fig. 13 shows the flowchart of the license plate identification system. When the ultrasonic sensor detects a vehicle, the camera is triggered by initiating the detection of the license plate. A portal can be opened by controlling a servomotor if the license plate number is authenticated

4.3 Fire Detection System

The fire detection system is shown in Fig. 14, first the camera begins to capture the video in order to do the processing on the Raspberry Pi card, using the fire detection algorithm. If the fire is detected, the alarm will warn the user.

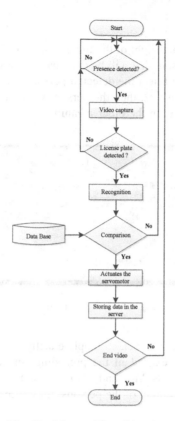

Fig. 13. License Plate Detection

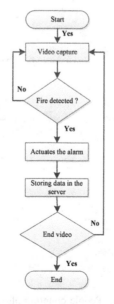

Fig. 14. Fire Detection

4.4 People Counting

For this part we take H as the height of the image and L as the width (see Fig. 15). For each contour we have a person, that will be detected, we have the center of gravity Cg (Cx, Cy) of this contour. To select the detected person entering or leaving, proceed as follows: if Cy is greater than H/2, then the person will exit, nevertheless if it is lower than the person will enter i.e. in the other meaning.

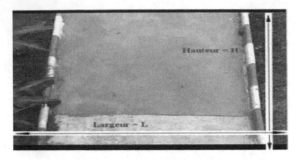

Fig. 15. Image dimension

So that we can count the number of people exactly, after each disappearance of a contour which had already existed in the preceding image, the Cg coordinates are compared with two thresholds Min and Max, these two thresholds determine the accuracy of the input or the output of the persons, if cy is lower than the threshold Min

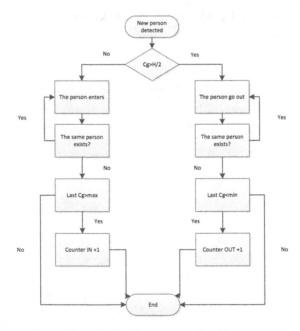

Fig. 16. People counting algorithm

then the person is out, otherwise if cy is above the threshold Max so the person is entered. The algorithm of people counting shows in Fig. 16.

Our prototype is illustrated in Fig. 17. Beforehand, all the identification data of the individuals and vehicles must be saved in the data base via the registration page.

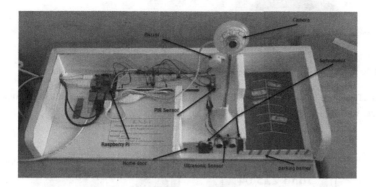

Fig. 17. System design

5 Experimental Results

5.1 Facial Recognition Test

To be able to recognise new face, the system takes 20 photos for the same person and save them in a data base. This person is associated with an identifier previously defined in the database (Fig. 18).

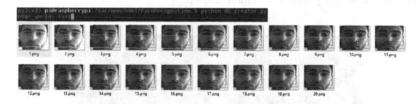

Fig. 18. Creation of the database for facial recognition

Now the system can identify the person, it displays on the screen the identifier and the index of confidence (Fig. 19). This index is calculated by the LBP model. More than the confidence value is minimal, and then recognition is better.

When an unidentified person is detected, the unknown message is displayed on the screen and the door will not open.

Fig. 19. Door opening with Facial recognition

5.2 Plate License Recognition Test

The raspberry Pi waits for an input from the ultrasonic sensor to activate the camera. The image will be displayed on the webpage as shown in Fig. 20.

Fig. 20. Reading license plates

The barrier will be lifted if the license plate is recognised like demonstrated in Fig. 21. Otherwise the portal will remain closed.

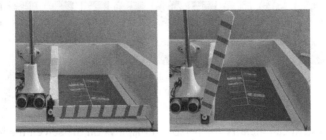

Fig. 21. The opening of the portal when the plate is recognized

5.3 Fire Detection Test

The fire alarm warms the user by sending a sound alarm and submitting a message alert (Fig. 22).

Fig. 22. Fire detection

5.4 Motion Detection Test

Motion detection involves the presence of an intruder in the field of view of the PIR sensor. A sound alarm alerts the user and a message is sent by Raspberry Pi is displayed on the webpage (Fig. 23).

Fig. 23. The screenshot of the message sent by Raspberry Pi

5.5 Tracking and Counting People

To test our system of tracking and counting we placed the camera at the entrance of a building, the background of the plan shows in Fig. 24.

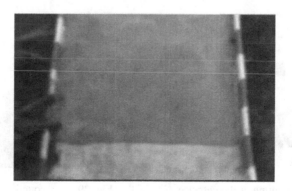

Fig. 24. The detected background

The following figure (Fig. 25) shows the principle of detection of movement while keeping their center of gravity.

When the person overtakes the yellow virtual line (out) the counter increases by +1 (Fig. 26).

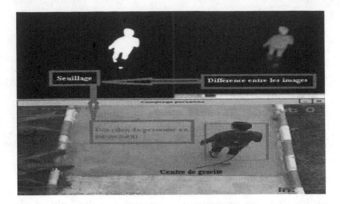

Fig. 25. Detection of a person going out

Fig. 26. Increase the out counter

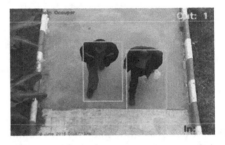

Fig. 27. Detection of two incoming persons and IN = 2

Fig. 28. Car counting at the entrance

Fig. 29. Car counting at the exit

Figure 27 shows when two people enter at the same time and increase the entrance counter +2. The results of the surveillance camera from the parking entrance for car counting gives us the following results (Figs. 28 and 29):

6   Conclusion

In this paper, a design of an advanced security and safety system for Smart Cities has been presented. It reduces the human interactions, by using Internet of Things (IoT). It is absolutely an affordable system that can be used in various areas like supermarket, street, parking, official building, school, etc. This system is dedicated to be used in Smart Cities bringing together three modules in one package. Our system offers a new platform that brings together several solutions in one. The platform can support other sensors like earthquake, carbon dioxide and radiation.

References

1. Stenbrunn, A., Lindquist, T.: Hosting a building management system on a smart network camera. Bachelor Thesis, Malmo University School of Technology, June 2015
2. Tang, N.C., Lin, Y.Y., Weng, M.F.: Cross camera knowledge transfer for multiview people counting. IEEE Trans. Image Process. **24**(1), 80–93 (2015)
3. Hu, L., Ni, Q.: IoT-driven automated object detection algorithm for urban surveillance systems in smart cities. IEEE Internet Things J. **5**(2), 747–754 (2017)
4. Aslan, E.S., Özdemir, Ö.F., Hacıoğlu, A., İnce, G.: Smart pass automation system. In: 24th Signal Processing and Communication Application Conference (SIU), Zonguldak, Turkey (2016)
5. Vanus, J., Kucera, P., Martinek, R., Koziorek, J.: Development and testing of a visualization application software, implemented with wireless control system in smart home care. Human-centric Comput. Inf. Sci. **4**(1), 1–19 (2014)
6. Li, M., Lin, H.-J.: Design and implementation of smart home control systems based on wireless sensor networks and power line communications. IEEE Trans. Ind. Electron. **62**(7), 4430–4442 (2015)
7. Zuo, F., De With, P.H.: Real-time embedded face recognition for smart home. IEEE Trans. Consumer Electron. **51**(1), 183–190 (2005)
8. Kumar, S.: Ubiquitous smart home system using android application, arXiv preprint arXiv: 1402.2114 (2014)
9. Al-Audah, Y.K., Al-Juraifani, A.K., Deriche, M.A.: A real-time license plate recognition system for Saudi Arabia using LabVIEW. In: 2012 3rd International Conference on Image Processing Theory, Tools and Applications (IPTA), Istanbul, pp. 160–164 (2012)
10. Saleem, N., Muazzam, H., Tahir, H.M., Farooq, U.: Automatic license plate recognition using extracted features. In: 2016 4th International Symposium on Computational and Business Intelligence (ISCBI), Olten, pp. 221–225 (2016)
11. Matai, J., Irturk, A., Kastner, R.: Design and implementation of an FPGA-based real-time face recognition system. In: 2011 IEEE 19th Annual International Symposium on Field-Programmable Custom Computing Machines, Salt Lake City, UT, pp. 97–100 (2011)
12. Ru, F., Peng, X., Hou, L., Wang, J., Geng, S., Song, C.: The design of face recognition system based on ARM9 embedded platform. In: 2015 IEEE 11th International Conference on ASIC (ASICON), Chengdu, pp. 1–4 (2015)
13. Premal, C.E., Vinsley, S.S.: Image processing based forest fire detection using YCbCr colour model. In: 2014 International Conference on Circuits, Power and Computing Technologies [ICCPCT-2014], Nagercoil, pp. 1229–1237 (2014)

14. Soumaya, F.T.: Développement d'un système de reconnaissance faciale à base de la méthode LBP pour le contrôle d'accès. École National Supérieure de Technologie (ENST), Alger, chapitre 2, pp. 19–25 (2016)

15. Hutchins, J., Ihler, A., Smyth, P.: Modeling count data from multiple sensors. In: IEEE 2nd International Workshop on Computational Advances in Multi Sensor Adaptive Processing (2007)

16. Kuutti, J., Saarikko, P., Sepponen, R.E.: Real time building zone occupancy detection and activity visualizing a visitor counting sensor network. Aalto University, Department of Electrical Engineering and Automation, Finland (2015)

17. Kim, B., Lee, G.-G., Yoon, J.-Y., Kim, J.-J., Kim, W.-Y.: A method of counting pedestrians in crowded scenes. In: Huang, D.-S., Wunsch, D.C., Levine, D.S., Jo, K.-H. (eds.) ICIC 2008. LNCS (LNAI), vol. 5227, pp. 1117–1126. Springer, Heidelberg (2008). https://doi.org/10.1007/978-3-540-85984-0_134

18. Kong, D., Gray, D.: A viewpoint invariant approach for crowd counting. In: 18th International Conference Pattern Recognition, vol. 1, pp. 1187–1190 (2006)

19. Chaari, A.: Nouvelle approche d'identification dans les bases de données biométriques basée sur une classification non supervisée. Modélisation et simulation, Université d'Evry-Val d'Essonne, Français (2009)

20. Mithe, R., Indalkar, S., Divekar, N.: Optical character recognition. Int. J. Recent Technol. Eng. (IJRTE) 2(1), 72–75 (2013)

21. binti Zaidi, N.I., binti Lokman, N.A.A., bin Daud, M.R., Achmad, H., Chia, K.A.: Fire recognition using RGB And YCBCR color space. ARPN J. Eng. Appl. Sci. 10(21) (2015)

IoT-Based Implementation and Mobility-Driven Management of the Smart and Energy Efficient Home Appliance Ecosystem

Aakash Ahmad[✉], Ahmed B. Altamimi,
and Mohammad T. Alshammari

College of Computer Science and Engineering,
University of Ha'il, Ha'il, Saudi Arabia
{a.abbasi, altamimi.a, md.alshammari}@uoh.edu.sa

Abstract. The Internet of Things (IoTs) have emerged as a disruptive technology and an enabling platform to ensure a connected world that offers improved life style, enhanced services, and socio-economic opportunities. Smart city systems can exploit the IoT platform to offer innovative solutions that transform conventional cities and societies into knowledge and technology-driven metropoles. Smart and energy efficient buildings and homes are central to the success of the smart city infrastructure.

Objectives: The proposed project aims to exploit the IoT infrastructure for deploying interconnected home appliances (eco-system implementation) that are manipulated through portable and context-aware mobile devices (eco-system management). The objectives of this project are to synergize the academic research and industrial development to (i) implement the home appliance eco-system that communicates with devices and humans, and (ii) transforms conventional homes into energy efficient smart homes.

Keywords: Internet of Things · Mobile Cloud Computing · Smart homes
Software engineering

1 Research Motivation and Solution Framework

Internet of Things (IoT) have become an enabling platform to interconnect humans, systems, services, devices and things to ensure a connected world to offer improved life style, enhanced urban services, work practices and interactions [1]. A study on the recent state of the IoT has highlighted that approximately 25 billion devices will be connected to the Internet of Things by 2020[1]. Smart city systems rely on the IoT platform to offer improved and digitized urban services such as smart health, transportation management, and energy efficient building and homes. Smart homes and buildings are the fundamental units for the implementation and operations of smart city

---

[1] D. Evans. The Internet of Things How the Next Evolution of the Internet Is Changing Everything, 2011. http://www.iotsworldcongress.com/documents/4643185/3e968a44-2d12-4b73-9691-17ec508f f67b.

© ICST Institute for Computer Sciences, Social Informatics and Telecommunications Engineering 2018
R. Mehmood et al. (Eds.): SCITA 2017, LNICST 224, pp. 353–356, 2018.
https://doi.org/10.1007/978-3-319-94180-6_32

systems. To date, some critical issues such as automation, security, self-adaptation and context awareness needs to be resolved to implement the IoT-driven smart cities and smart homes effectively and efficiently. The primary challenge is:

'how to exploit the IoT platform to develop self-adaptive and context-aware smart homes that increase energy efficiency while decreasing operational costs'

The challenge highlights that in order to exploit IoT platform for building smart homes, (i) a trade-off between energy efficiency and operational costs needs to be maintained, and (ii) the system must be self-adaptive and context-aware.

Solution Overview - In order to address the challenge(s) above, i.e.; to support energy efficient smart homes, an overview of the proposed solution is illustrated in Fig. 1. Specifically, to implement a smart home we propose an ecosystem of the interconnected home appliances that operate dynamically and enable energy efficiency. For example, the ambient lighting in the home adapts itself based on the dynamic contextual information such as energy consumption, time of the day, or events in the surrounding. Moreover, based on the contextual information such as time or movements in the surroundings can trigger the surveillance, temperature control or background lights. The home appliance ecosystem needs to be monitored, analyzed and managed dynamically with human decision support is needed to deploy and customize an efficient and economic system.

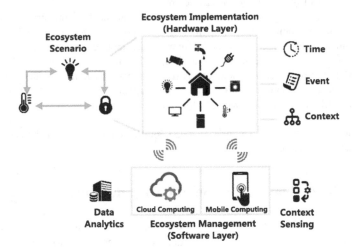

Fig. 1. Overview of home appliance ecosystem to support energy efficient smart homes

The home appliance ecosystem needs to be implemented and managed as:

– *Implementation of the home appliance eco-system* is mainly the hardware level functionality. To implement the system, home appliances and devices needs to be equipped with sensors that sense the contextual information (time, event, energy consumption) and enable the communication among the home appliances. For example, when the surveillance system detects an unusual movement at a specific time of the day such information must be communicated with the security system and lighting control.

- *Management of the home appliance eco-system* is primarily concerned with the software defined logic to manage and manipulate the appliance ecosystem. We utilize the Mobile Cloud Computing (MCC) that represents the state-of-the-art mobile computing technology to develop systems that are portable, context-aware yet resource sufficient [1]. The mobile computing layer consists of the context-aware and mobility-driven interface that empowers its user to interact with the ecosystem and manipulate it. The cloud computing layers supports all the processing and storage of the appliance ecosystem to support analytics and human decision support to manage and conserve the energy.

2   Contributions and Outcomes

We highlight the primary contributions of the proposed solution as:

- *Unification of mobile and cloud computing technologies* that supports the context-awareness and mobility of a mobile device with elasticity and analytics of cloud servers to manage home appliances and their eco-system in smart home context.
- *Applying the system engineering approach* to seamlessly integrate the hardware devices (for eco-system implementation) and software resources (for eco-system management). The integrated system enables the communication between devices and humans, and transforms a conventional home into an energy efficient smart home.

Industry Academic Collaboration: The project can foster academic-industrial collaboration - with our industrial partner[2] - to research innovative embedded systems (electrical and software) that leads to industrial scale development of commercialized product(s) to support smart buildings and homes. The collaboration can benefit the development of IoT-driven solutions that go beyond smart homes and address socio-economic challenges (e.g.; traffic management, disaster recovery) in the context of smart cities or digital societies.

Novelty Beyond State-of-the-Art: The research state-of-the-art primarily focuses on the security and energy efficiency of the smart homes based on cloud [2] and fog computing [3]. Our proposed solution aims to leverage MCC as state-of-the-art mobile computing technology [1, 4] to not only incorporate context-awareness but also support analytics and decision support to manage energy efficient smart homes.

---

[2] MicroMerger (Pvt.) Ltd. is an IT Engineering company based in United Kingdom and Pakistan. www.micromerger.com/.

References

1. Fernand, N., Loke, S.W., Rahayu, W.: Mobile cloud computing: a survey. Future Gener. Comput. Syst. (FGCS) **29**, 84–106 (2013)
2. Saravanan, T., Nagarajan, R., Kumar, R., Prakash, V., Rajkumar, R.: IoT based smart home design for power and security management. Asian J. Appl. Sci. Technol. (AJAST) **1**(2), 260–264 (2017)
3. Bansal, M., Chana, I., Clarke, S.: Enablement of IoT based context-aware smart home with fog computing. J. Cases Inf. Technol. (JCIT) **19**(4), 19–33 (2017)
4. Ahmad, A., Altamimi, A., Alreshidi, A.: Towards establishing a catalogue of patterns for architecting mobile cloud software. In: 9th International Conference on Software Engineering and Application (SEAS) (2017)

Land Suitability Assessment for the Potential Location of Transit Oriented Development (TOD)

Herika Muhamad Taki[1(✉)], Mohamed Mahmoud H. Maatouk[1],
Emad Mohammed Qurnfulah[1], and Satria Antoni[2]

[1] Department of Urban and Regional Planning, FED,
King Abdulaziz University, Jeddah 21589, Saudi Arabia
htaki0001@stu.kau.edu.sa,
{mmaatouk,mqurnfulah}@kau.edu.sa
[2] Department of Marine Geology, FMS, King Abdulaziz University,
Jeddah 21589, Saudi Arabia
satria.scientist@yahoo.com

Abstract. Jakarta Metropolitan Region is Indonesia's largest metropolitan region with various urban transportation problems such as traffic jam, and pollution. Some efforts to remedy these problems have been carried out, but unfortunately, they have not been able to solve the problem thoroughly. To overcome these problems, it requires not only provision of network systems but also the adoption of innovative concepts through the application of integration between land use and transportation. One solution concept offered is the concept of Transit Oriented Development (TOD). The method of this study was using land suitability assessment based on Geographical Information System (GIS) to select the significant area for potential TOD. The criteria used were based on the opinions of experts through Analytical Hierarchy Process (AHP) technique. The results showed that some potential area for TOD are particularly concentrated in the middle of the Jakarta Metropolitan Region (JMR) and its surrounding areas. This indicates that there is a potential for the development of TOD-based transit areas in the region in order to encourage the use of public transport based commuter trains.

Keywords: Jakarta Metropolitan Region (JMR)
Transit Oriented Development (TOD) · Geographic Information System (GIS)
Spatial statistical analysis

1 Introduction

The objective of this study was to develop a method of land suitability assessment using AHP technique by integrating various assessment criteria from experts [1]. The second objective was to apply this method in the context of GIS by conducting case studies in the metropolitan area of Jakarta [3]. It helped identify the most potential location for Transit Oriented Development (TOD). TOD is a concept to incorporate various functional activities in the area around the transit station [2].

© ICST Institute for Computer Sciences, Social Informatics and Telecommunications Engineering 2018
R. Mehmood et al. (Eds.): SCITA 2017, LNICST 224, pp. 357–359, 2018.
https://doi.org/10.1007/978-3-319-94180-6_33

2 Methods

2.1 Land Suitability Assessment

Land suitability assessment using the Eq. 1

$$Si = \sum_{i=1}^{n} (WiXRi) \tag{1}$$

Where, Wi = the result of multiplication of all related weights, Ri = the standard assessment of each pixel on the map, n = the number of criteria under element.

2.2 Spatial Autocorrelation Analysis for Identifying Existence of Spatial Clusters

The moran's index (I) is a spatial autocorrelation measurement (Eq. 2):

$$I = \frac{n \sum_{i=1}^{n} \sum_{j=1}^{n} w_{ij}(x_j - \bar{x})(x_j - \bar{x})}{\sum_{i=1}^{n} w_i(x_i - \bar{x})^2} \tag{2}$$

Where, n is the number of cases. x is the mean of the variable. Wij is a weight indexing location of i relative to j.

2.3 Hot Spot and Outlier Analysis for Mapping Spatial Clusters

Hot spot analysis using *Getis-Ord Gi** is formulated as Eq. 3 below:

$$G_i^* = \frac{\sum_{j=1}^{n} w_{ij}(d)x_j}{\sum_{j=1}^{n} x_j} \tag{3}$$

Where, Wij is a spatial weight and (d) is the spatial object, while xj is the attribute value for feature j in distance d.

3 Results and Discussion

3.1 Land Suitability Distribution

The result of land suitability analysis was the highly suitable class (S1) only has 2.3% of the study area Table 1. Otherwise, permanently not suitable class (N2) has the biggest percentage (36,4%)

Table 1. The distribution of potential TOD based on percentage and area

Suitable rating	Class	Percentage (%)	Area (ha)
Highly suitable	S1	2.3	174.69302
Moderately suitable	S2	9	682.65415
Marginally suitable	S3	28.1	2135.25561
Currently not suitable	N1	24.3	1847.69085
Permanently not suitable	N2	36.4	2769.68325
Total		100	7609.97688

3.2 Cluster Using Anselin Local Moran's I and Hot Spot Using Getis-Ord Gi*

The results in Figs. 1 and 2 show that the potential location for TOD, is located in the center area of the cluster and hot spots (strongly red color with high value).

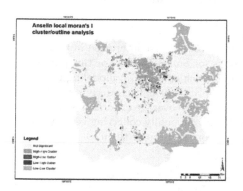 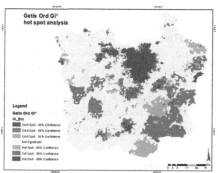

Fig. 1. Cluster map (Color figure online)   **Fig. 2.** Hot spot map (Color figure online)

4 Conclusion

There was a spatial pattern of potential TOD index in the study area, where the area with high TOD tends to concentrate in the middle of JMR, while the area with low TOD tends to spread in the whole area. The middle of JMR means the capital of Jakarta along with Tangerang City, Depok City, and Bogor City.

References

1. Bunruamkaew, K., Murayam, Y.: Site suitability evaluation for ecotourism using GIS & AHP: a case study of Surat Thani Province Thailand. Procedia Soc. Behav. Sci. **21**, 269–278 (2011)
2. Taki, H.M., et al.: Planning TOD with land use and transport integration: a review. J. Geosci. Eng. Environ. Technol. **2**(1), 84 (2017)
3. Taki, H.M., et al.: Re-Assessing TOD index in Jakarta Metropolitan Region (JMR). J. Appl. GEOSPATIAL Inf. **1**(1), 26–35 (2017)

Towards a Model-Based Testing Framework for the Security of Internet of Things for Smart City Applications

Moez Krichen[1,2]([✉]), Omar Cheikhrouhou[3,4], Mariam Lahami[2],
Roobaea Alroobaea[3], and Afef Jmal Maâlej[2]

[1] Faculty of CSIT, Al-Baha University, Al Baha, Saudi Arabia
moez.krichen@redcad.org
[2] ReDCAD Laboratory, University of Sfax, Sfax, Tunisia
{mariam.lahami,afef.jmal}@redcad.org
[3] College of CIT, Taif University, Taif, Saudi Arabia
{o.cheikhrouhou,r.robai}@tu.edu.sa
[4] ISIMA, University of Monastir, Monastir, Tunisia

Abstract. This is a work in progress in which we are interested in testing security aspects of Internet of Things for Smart Cities. For this purpose we follow a Model-Based approach which consists in: modeling the system under investigation with an appropriate formalism; deriving test suites from the obtained model; applying some coverage criteria to select suitable tests; executing the obtained tests; and finally collecting verdicts and analyzing them in order to detect errors and repair them.

Keywords: Internet of Things · Smart cities · Security models
Generation · Coverage · Test · Security · Verdicts

1 Introduction

Internet of Things (IoT) is a promising technology that permits to connect every-day things or objects to the Internet by giving them the capabilities to sense the environment and interact with other objects and/or human beings through the Internet.

This evolving technology has promoted a new generation of innovative and valuable services. Today's cities are getting smarter by deploying intelligent systems for traffic control, water management, energy management, public transport, street lighting, etc. thanks to these services. Nevertheless, these services can easily be compromised and attacked by malicious parties in the absence of proper mechanism for providing adequate security.

Recent studies have shown that the attackers are using smart home appliances to launch serious attacks such as infiltrating to the network or sending malicious email or launching malicious actions such as Distributed Denial of Service (DDoS) attack. Therefore, security solutions need to be proposed, set up and tested to mitigate these identified attacks.

© ICST Institute for Computer Sciences, Social Informatics and Telecommunications Engineering 2018
R. Mehmood et al. (Eds.): SCITA 2017, LNICST 224, pp. 360–365, 2018.
https://doi.org/10.1007/978-3-319-94180-6_34

In this work, we aim to adopt a Model-Based Security Testing (MBST) app-roach to check the security of IoT applications in the context of smart cities. The MBST approach consists in specifying the desired IoT application in an abstract manner using an adequate formal specification language and then deriving test-suites from this specification to find security vulnerabilities in the application under test in a systematic manner.

The work introduced here is a piece of a broader approach dealing with the security of IoT applications for smart cities and consisting of the following steps:

- Identify and assess the threats and the attacks in smart cities IoT applications.
- Design and develop security mechanisms for standard protocols at the appli-cation and the network layer.
- Evaluate the performance and the correctness of the proposed security pro-tocols using simulation and implementation on real devices.

The rest of this paper is organized as follows. Section 2 introduces some preliminaries about IoT and smart cities. Section 3 discusses main threats and challenges related to these two fields. Section 4 presents our approach. Section 5 reports on related research efforts dealing with IoT security testing. Finally Sect. 6 concludes the paper.

2   Preliminaries

2.1   Internet of Objects

Recent advances in communication and sensing devices make our everyday objects smarter. This smartness is resulted from the capability of objects to sense the environment, to process the captured (sensed) data and to communi-cate it to users either directly or through Internet. The integration of these smart objects to the Internet infrastructure is promoting a new generation of innova-tive and valuable services for people. These services include home automation, traffic control, public transportation, smart water metering, waste and energy management, etc. When integrated in a city context, they make citizens' live better and so form the modern smart city.

2.2   Smart Cities

In October 2015, ITU-T's Focus Group on Smart Sustainable Cities (FG-SSC) agreed on the following definition of a smart sustainable city: "A Smart Sustain-able City (SSC) is an innovative city that uses information and communication technologies (ICTs) and other means to improve quality of life, efficiency of urban operation and services, and competitiveness, while ensuring that it meets the needs of present and future generations with respect to economic, social and environmental aspects".

3   Threats and Challenges

3.1   Threats

Indeed, connecting our everyday "things" to the public Internet opens these objects to several kinds of attacks. Taking the example of a traffic control system. If the hackers could insert fake messages to these traffic control system devices, they can make traffic perturbations and bottlenecks. Another example related to home automation, if attackers gain access to smart devices such as lamps, doors, etc., it could manipulate doors and steal the house properties. The main security threats in the IoT are summarized and they can be summarized as follows: 1. Cloning of smart things by untrusted manufacturers; 2. Malicious substitution of smart things during installation; 3. Firmware replacement attack; 4. Extraction of security parameters since smart things may be physically unprotected; 5. Eavesdropping attack if the communication channel is not adequately protected; 6. Man-in-the-middle attack during key exchange; 7. Routing attacks; 8. Denial-of-service attacks; and 9. Privacy threats.

3.2   Challenges

Due to its specific characteristic, new issues are raised in the area of IoT:

- Data collection trust: If the huge collected data is not trusted (e.g., due to the damage or malicious input of some sensors), the IoT service quality will be greatly influenced and hard to be accepted by users.
- User privacy: In order to have intelligent context-aware services, users have to share their personal data or privacy such as location, contacts, etc. Providing intelligent context-aware services and at the same time preserving user privacy are two conflicting objectives that induce a big challenge in the IoT.
- Resource Limitation: Most of IoT devices are limited in terms of CPU, memory capacity and battery supply. This renders the application of the conventional Internet security solutions not appropriate.
- Inherent complexity of IoT: the fact that multiple heterogeneous entities located in different contexts can exchange information with each other, further complicates the design and the deployment of efficient, inter-operable and scalable security mechanisms.

4   Proposed Approach

In this section, we define a workflow that covers the different steps of a classical model based testing process, namely: Model Specification, test generation, test selection, test execution and evaluation activities as depicted in Fig. 1.

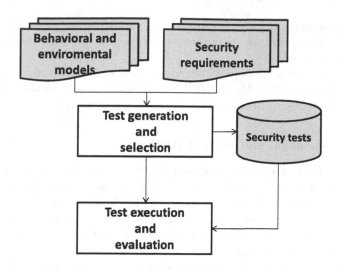

Fig. 1. Model based security testing process.

4.1 Modelling Issues

We use *timed automata* [2] with deadlines [4] to model the applications under test and the security aspects of interest. A timed automaton over the set of actions Act is a tuple $A = (Q, q_0, X, \mathsf{Act}, e)$, where: Q is a finite set of *locations*; $q_0 \in Q$ is the initial location; X is a finite set of *clocks*; e is a finite set of *edges*. Each edge is a tuple (q, q', ψ, r, d, a), where: $q, q' \in Q$ are the source and destination locations; ψ is the *guard*, a conjunction of constraints of the form $x \# c$, where $x \in X$, c is an integer constant and $\# \in \{<, \leq, =, \geq, >\}$; $r \subseteq X$ is a set of clocks to *reset* to zero; $d \in \{\mathsf{lazy, delayable, eager}\}$ is the *deadline*; $a \in \mathsf{Act}$ is the action.

4.2 Test Generation and Selection

The used test generation technique is based on model checking. The main idea is to formulate the test generation problem as a reachability problem that can be solved with the model checker tool UPPAAL [3]. However, instead of using model annotations and reachability properties to express coverage criteria, the observer language is used.

In this direction, we reuse the finding of Hessel et al. [7] by exploiting its extension of UPPAAL namely UPPAAL CO√ER[1]. This tool takes as inputs a model, an observer and a configuration file. The model is specified as a network of timed automata (.xml) that comprises a SUT part and an environment part. The observer (.obs) expresses the coverage criterion that guides the model exploration during test case generation. The configuration file (.cfg) describes mainly the interactions between the system part and the environment part in terms of

---

[1] http://user.it.uu.se/~hessel/CoVer/index.php

input/output signals. It may also specify the variables that should be passed as parameters in these signals. As output, it produces a test suite containing a set of timed traces (.xml).

Our test generation module is built upon these well-elaborated tools. The key idea here is to use UPPAAL CO√ER and its generic and formal specification language for coverage criteria to generate tests for security purposes.

4.3   Test Execution and Verdict Analysis

For the execution of the obtained security tests, we aim to use a standard-based test execution platform, called TTCN-3 test system for Runtime Testing (TT4RT), developed in a previous work [9]. To do so, security tests should be mapped to the TTCN-3 notation since our platform supports only this test language. Then, test components are dynamically created and assigned to execution nodes in a distributed manner.

Each test component is responsible for (1) stimulating the SUT with input values, (2) comparing the obtained output data with the expected results (also called oracle) and (3) generating the final verdict. The latter can be pass, fail or inconclusive. A pass verdict is obtained when the observed results are valid with respect to the expected ones. A fail verdict is obtained when at least one of the observed results is invalid with respect to the expected one. Finally, an inconclusive verdict is obtained when neither a pass or a fail verdict can be given. After computing for each executed test case its single verdict, the proposed platform deduces the global verdict.

5   Related Work

In this section we give a very brief overview on contributions form the literature and from our previous work related to Model-Based Security Testing (MBST) for IoT Applications in Smart Cities.

Authors of [6] propose a good survey on more than one hundred publications on model-based security testing extracted from the most relevant digital libraries and classified according to specific criteria. Even though this survey reports on a large number of articles about MBST it does not contain any reference to IoT applications or Smart Cities. Contrary to that the authors of [1] propose a model-based approach to test IoT platforms (with tests provided as services) but they do not deal with security aspects at all.

In this work we aim to combine these two directions namely: Model-Based testing and Security Testing for IoT applications in Smart Cities. For that purpose we will take advantage of our previous findings [5,8–10] related to these fields. In [5] a survey about Secure Group Communication in Wireless Sensor Networks is proposed. We will extend the notions proposed in this survey to the case of IoT applications. We will also exploit our previous results about test techniques of dynamic distributed systems [8,9]. Finally we will adopt the same methodology as in [10] to combine security and load tests for IoT applications.

6   Conclusion

Our work is at its beginning and a lot of efforts are needed at all levels on both theoretical and experimental aspects. First we need to deal with modelling issues. In this respect we need to extend our modelling formalism and to identify the particular elements of IoT applications to model (using extended timed automata). Models must not be big in order to avoid test number explosion. For that purpose we need to keep an acceptable level of abstraction. As a second step we have to adapt our test generation and selection algorithms to take into account security requirements of the applications under test. The new algorithms must be validated theoretically and proved to be correct. In the same manner we need to upgrade our tools to implement the new obtained algorithms. Finally we need to validate our approach with concrete examples with realistic size.

References

1. Ahmad, A., Bouquet, F., Fourneret, E., Le Gall, F., Legeard, B.: Model-based testing as a service for IoT platforms. In: Margaria, T., Steffen, B. (eds.) ISoLA 2016, Part II. LNCS, vol. 9953, pp. 727–742. Springer, Cham (2016). https://doi.org/10.1007/978-3-319-47169-3_55
2. Alur, R., Dill, D.: A theory of timed automata. Theor. Comput. Sci. **126**, 183–235 (1994)
3. Behrmann, G., David, A., Larsen, K.G.: A tutorial on UPPAAL. In: Bernardo, M., Corradini, F. (eds.) SFM-RT 2004. LNCS, vol. 3185, pp. 200–236. Springer, Heidelberg (2004). https://doi.org/10.1007/978-3-540-30080-9_7
4. Bornot, S., Sifakis, J., Tripakis, S.: Modeling urgency in timed systems. In: de Roever, W.-P., Langmaack, H., Pnueli, A. (eds.) COMPOS 1997. LNCS, vol. 1536, pp. 103–129. Springer, Heidelberg (1998). https://doi.org/10.1007/3-540-49213-5_5
5. Cheikhrouhou, O.: Secure group communication in wireless sensor networks: a survey. J. Netw. Comput. Appl. **61**, 115–132 (2016)
6. Felderer, M., Zech, P., Breu, R., Büchler, M., Pretschnerr, A.: Model-based security testing: a taxonomy and systematic classification. Softw. Test. Verif. Reliab. **26**(2), 119–148 (2016)
7. Hessel, A., Larsen, K.G., Mikucionis, M., Nielsen, B., Pettersson, P., Skou, A.: Testing real-time systems using UPPAAL. In: Hierons, R.M., Bowen, J.P., Harman, M. (eds.) Formal Methods and Testing. LNCS, vol. 4949, pp. 77–117. Springer, Heidelberg (2008). https://doi.org/10.1007/978-3-540-78917-8_3
8. Krichen, M.: A formal framework for black-box conformance testing of distributed real-time systems. IJCCBS **3**(1/2), 26–43 (2012)
9. Lahami, M., Krichen, M., Jmaïel, M.: Safe and efficient runtime testing framework applied in dynamic and distributed systems. Sci. Comput. Program. (SCP) **122**(C), 1–28 (2016)
10. Jmal Maâlej, A., Krichen, M.: A model based approach to combine load and functional tests for service oriented architectures. In: Proceedings of the 10th Workshop on Verification and Evaluation of Computer and Communication System, VECoS 2016, Tunis, Tunisia, 6–7 October 2016, pp. 123–140 (2016)

Author Index

Printed in the United States
By Bookmasters